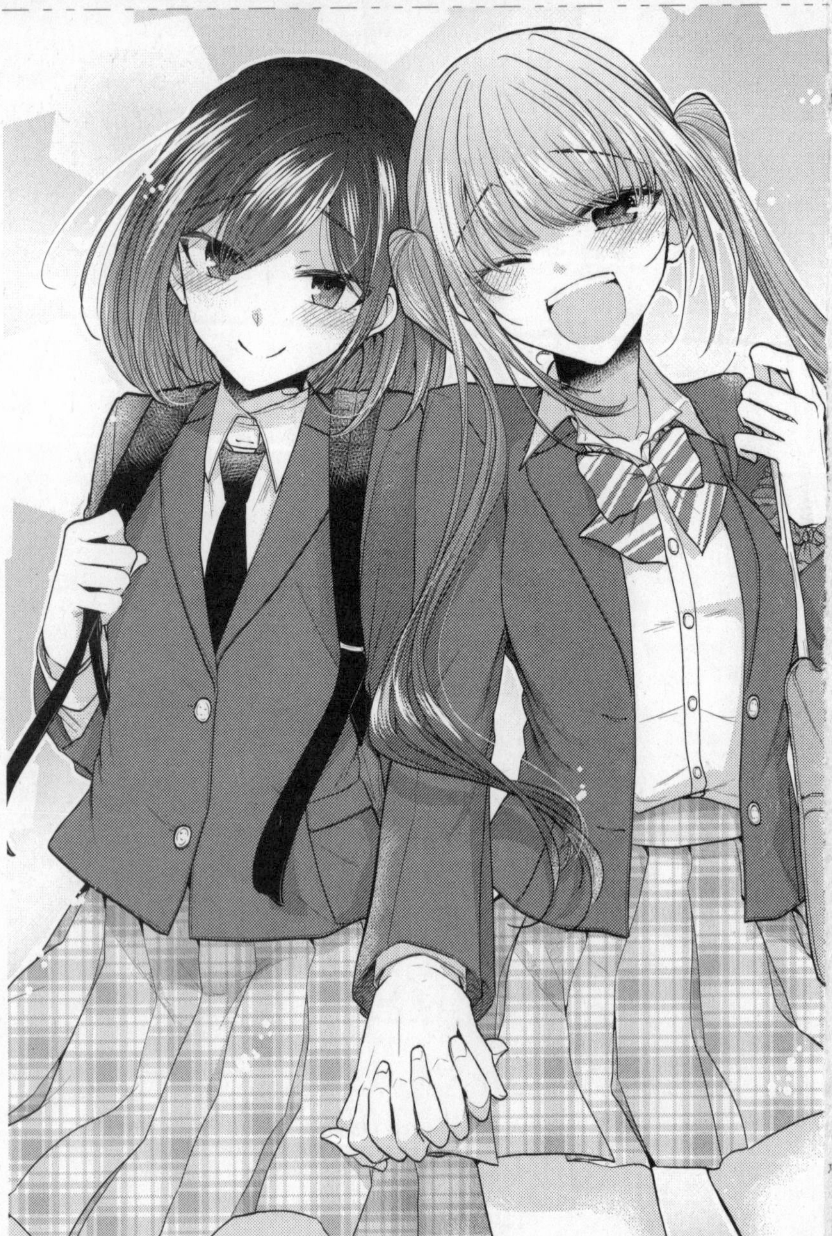

f a i l e d   p r i n c e s s e s   v o l u m e   s i x

contents

CHAPTER 32

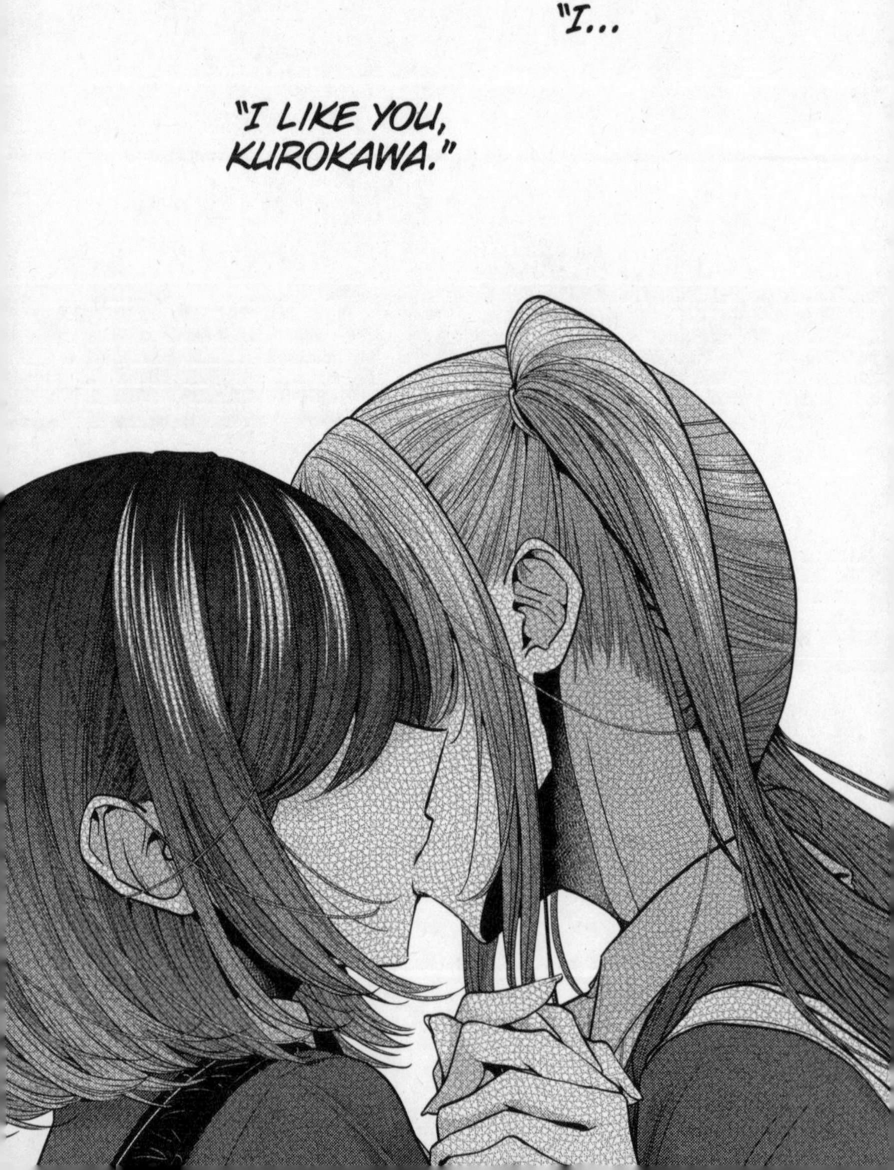
"I...
"I LIKE YOU, KUROKAWA."

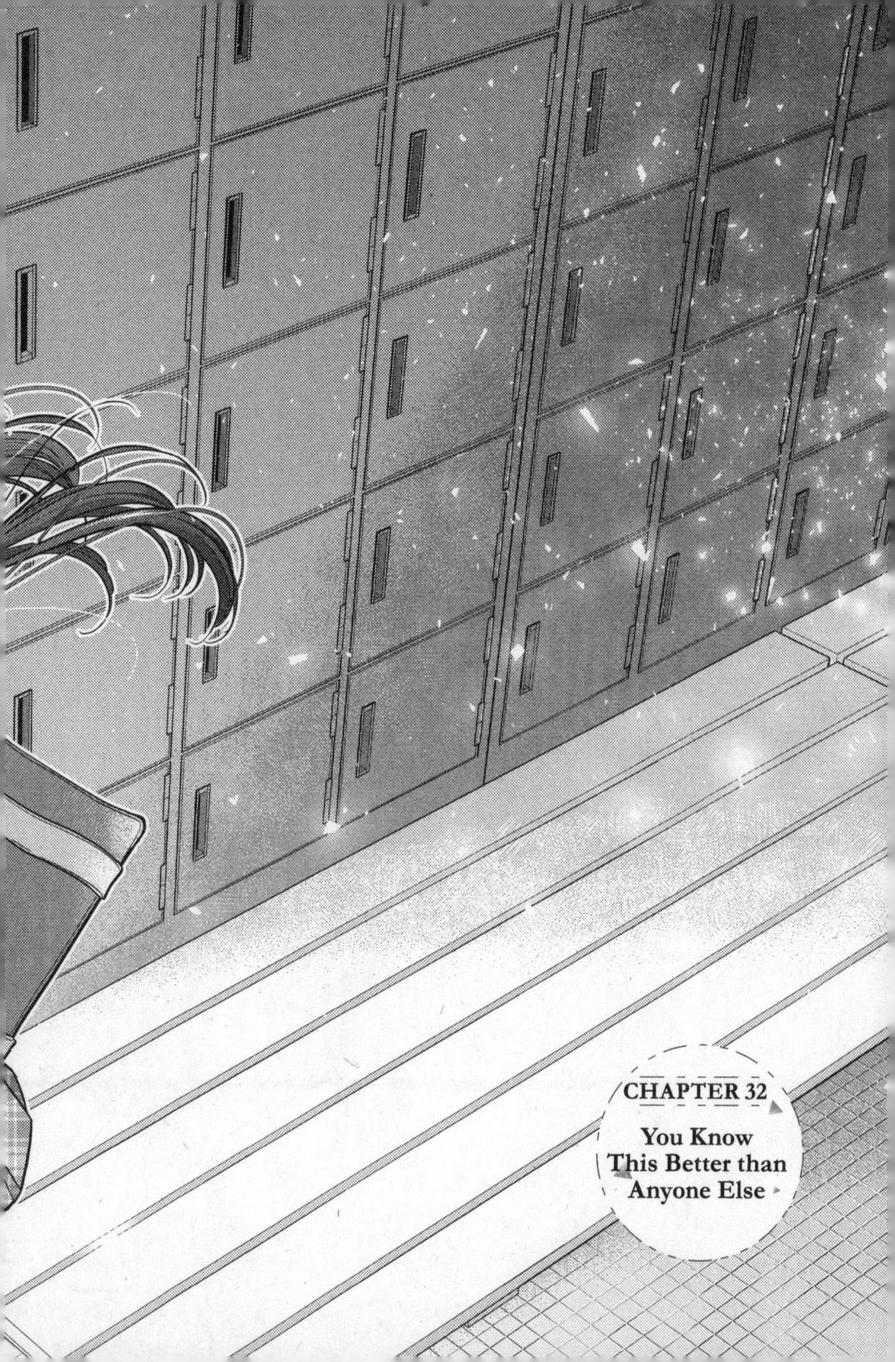
CHAPTER 32
You Know This Better than Anyone Else

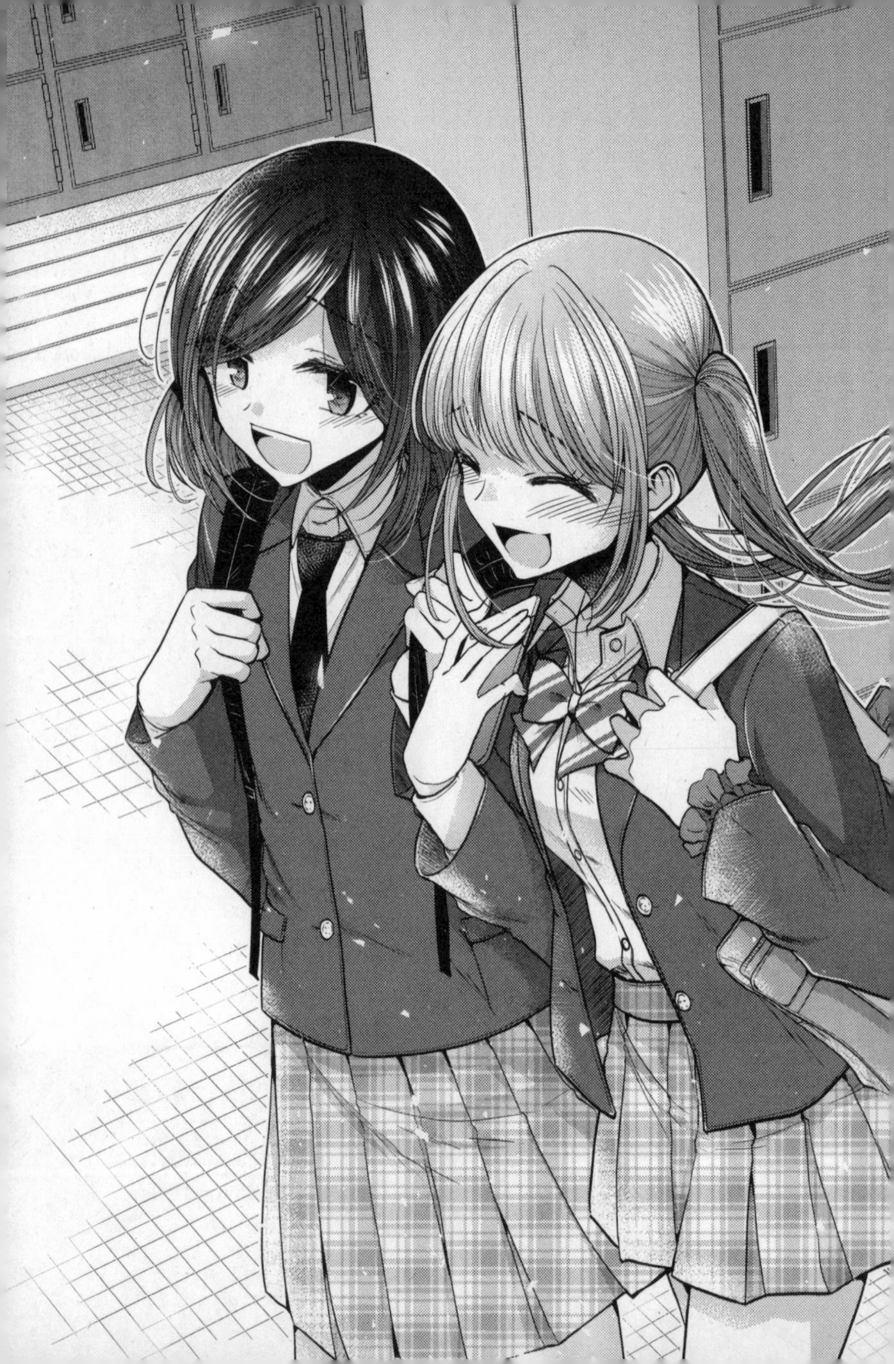

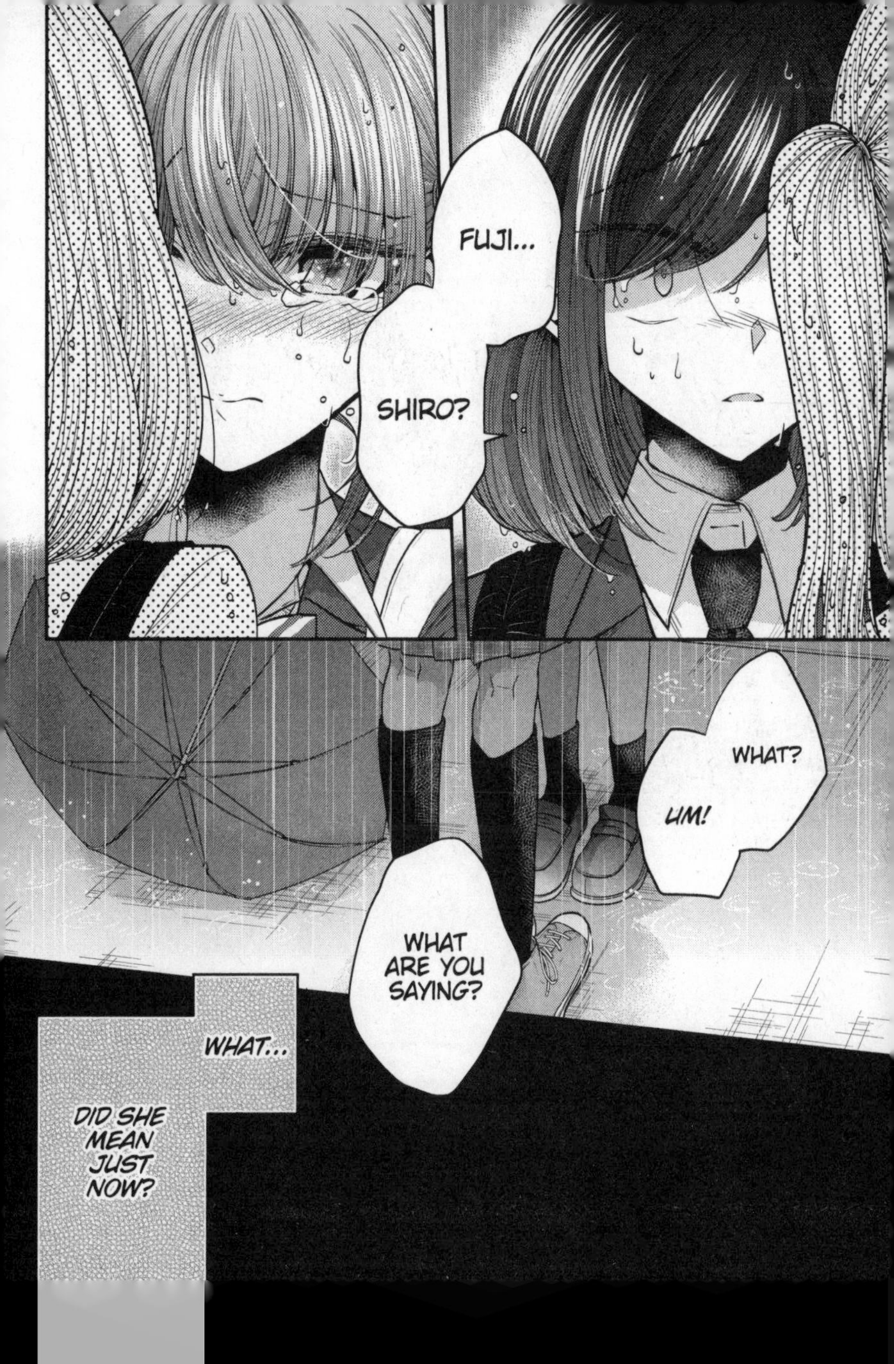
FUJI...
SHIRO?
WHAT?
UM!
WHAT ARE YOU SAYING?
WHAT...
DID SHE MEAN JUST NOW?

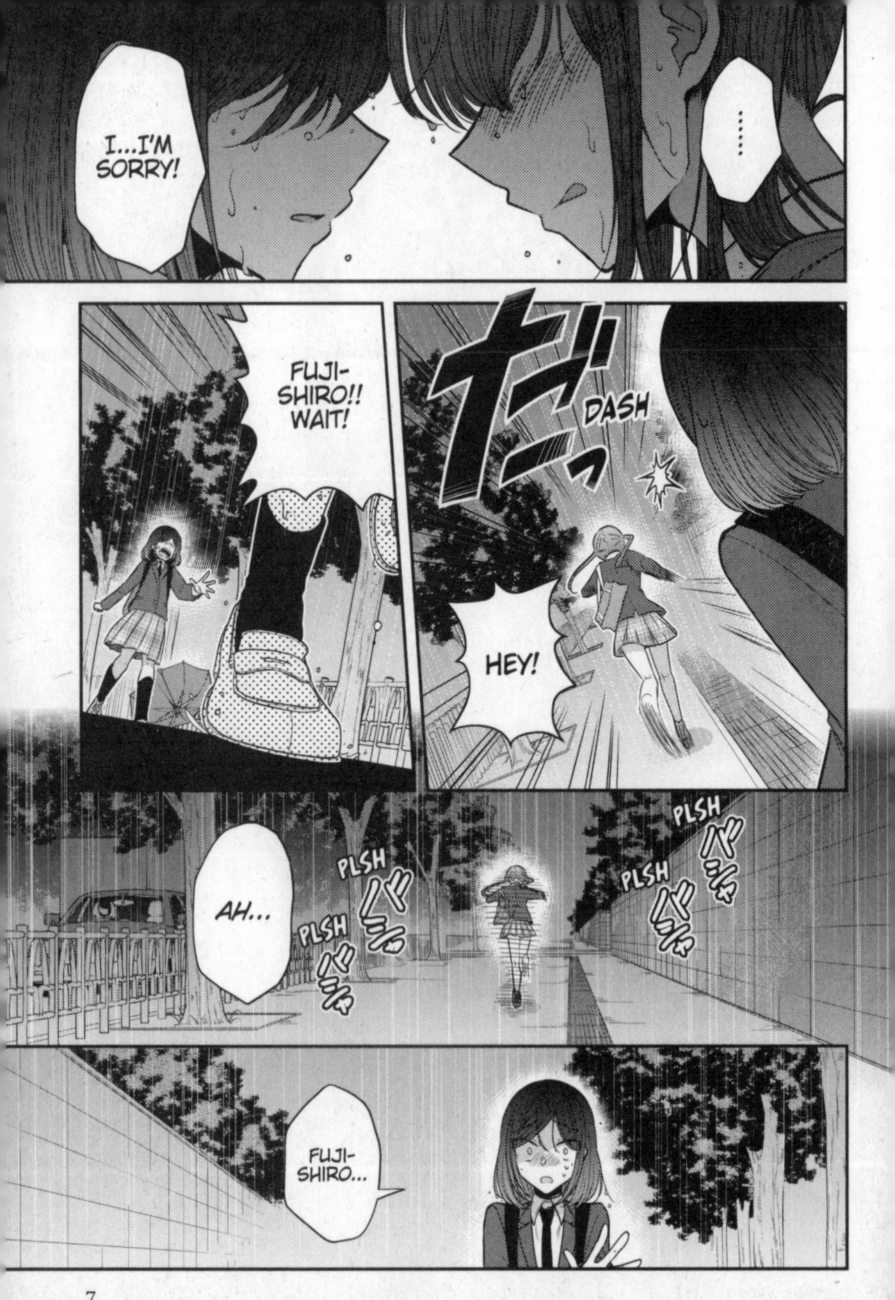
......
I...I'M SORRY!
DASH
HEY!
FUJI-SHIRO!! WAIT!
PLSH
PLSH
PLSH
AH...
PLSH
FUJI-SHIRO...

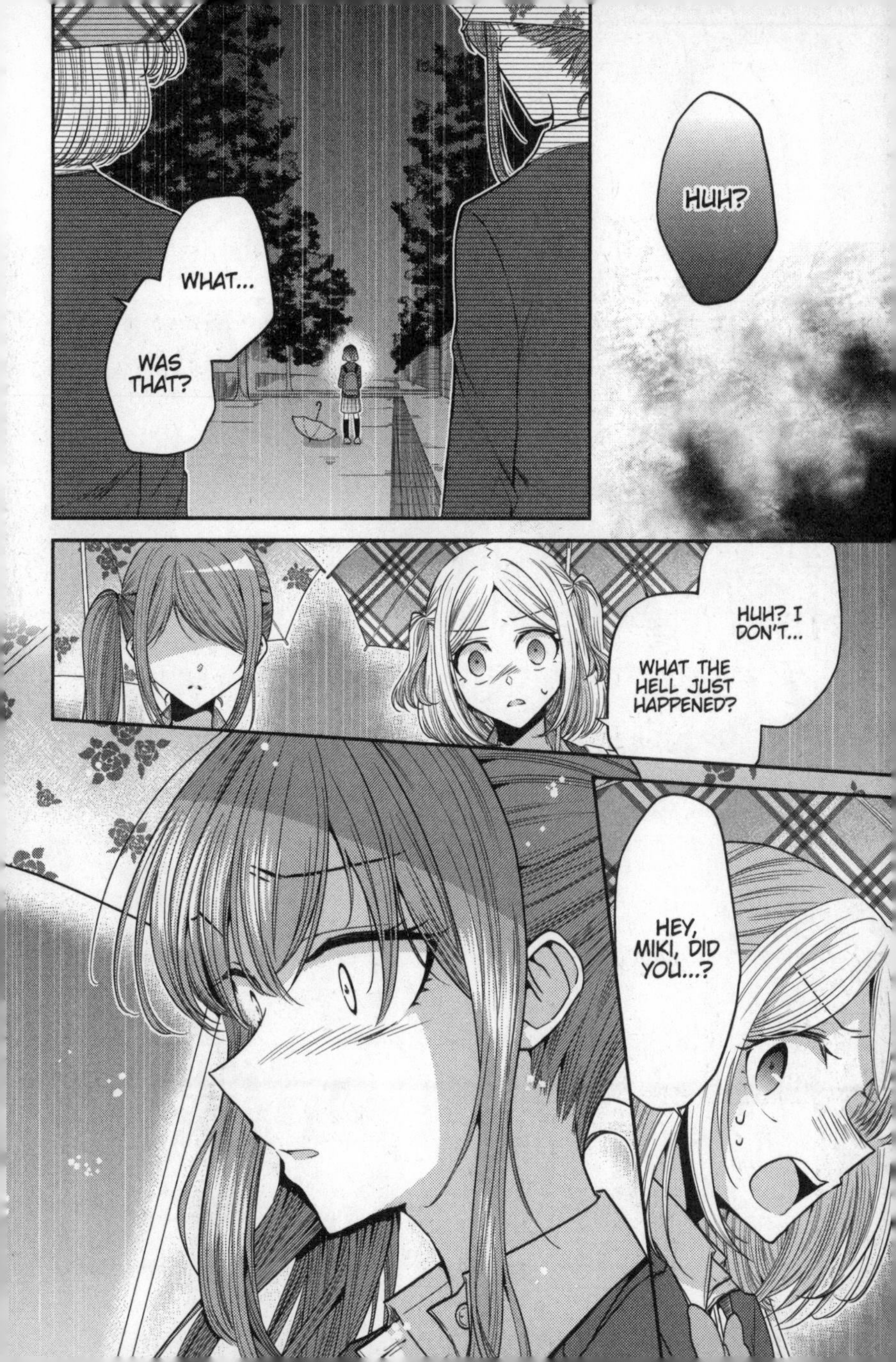
HUH?
WHAT... WAS THAT?
HUH? I DON'T... WHAT THE HELL JUST HAPPENED?
HEY, MIKI, DID YOU...?

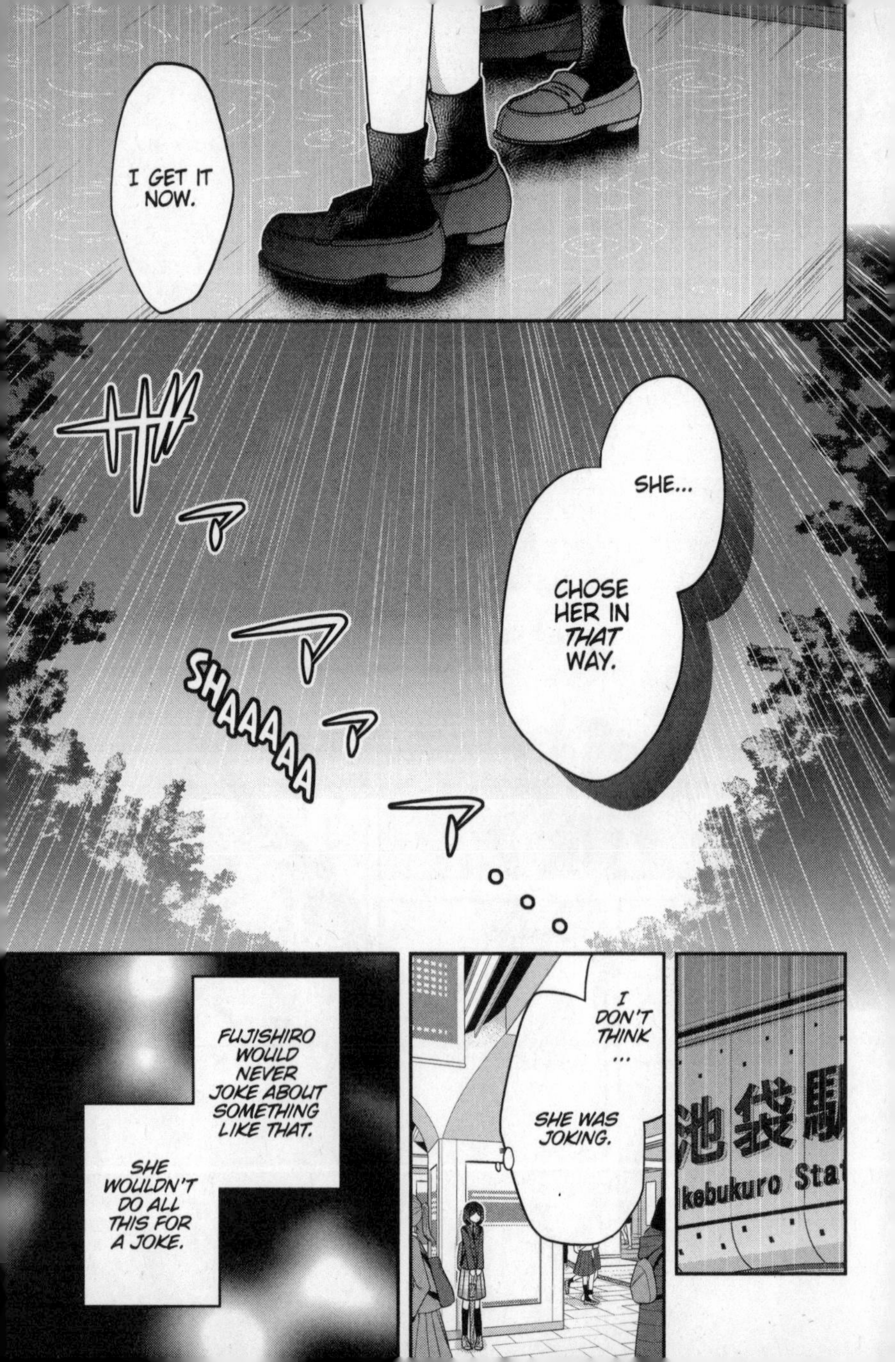
I GET IT NOW.
SHE...
CHOSE HER IN THAT WAY.
SHAAAAA
I DON'T THINK...
SHE WAS JOKING.
FUJISHIRO WOULD NEVER JOKE ABOUT SOMETHING LIKE THAT.
SHE WOULDN'T DO ALL THIS FOR A JOKE.

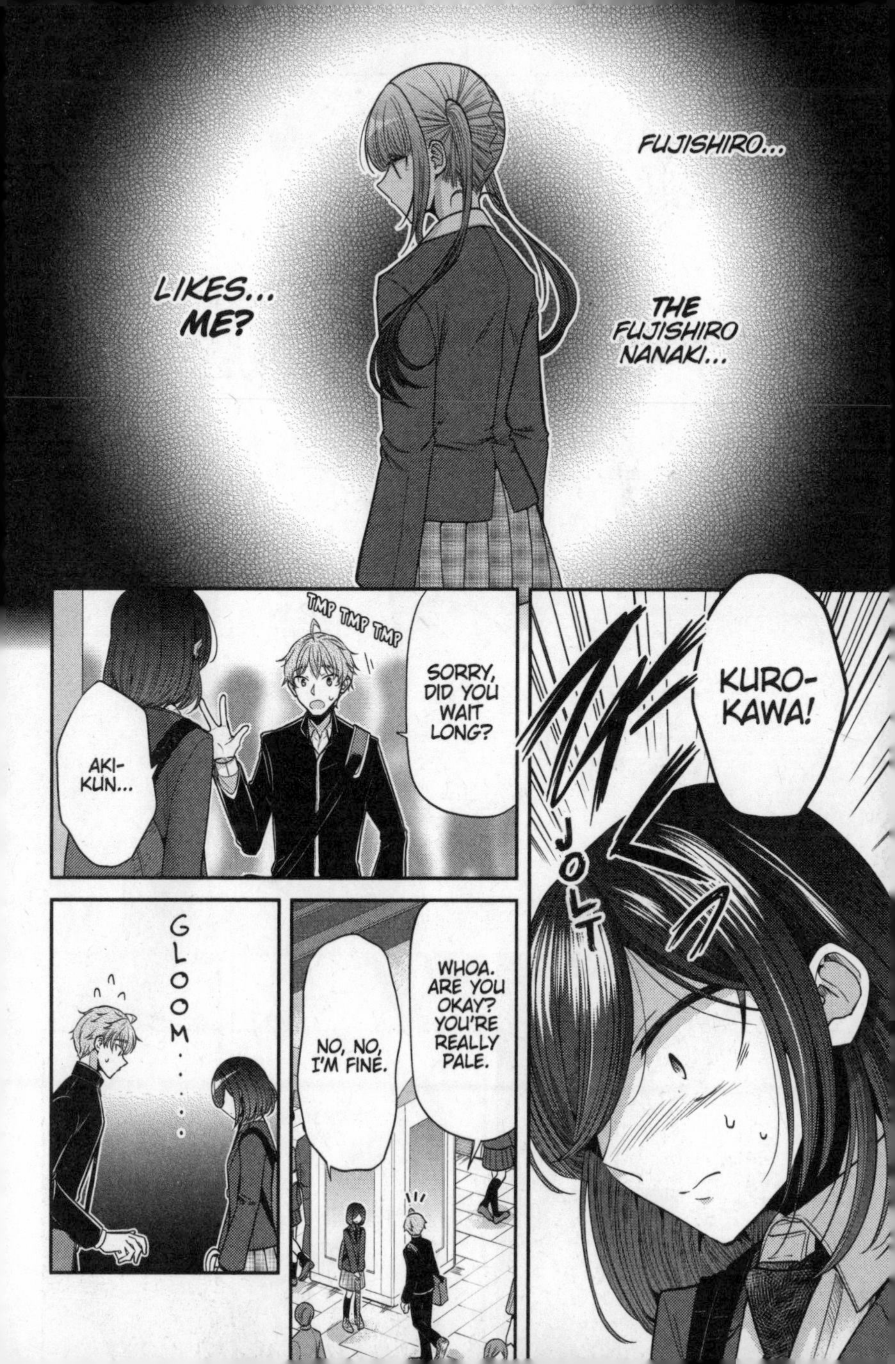
FUJISHIRO...
THE FUJISHIRO NANAKI...
LIKES... ME?
KURO-KAWA!
JOLT
TMP TMP TMP
SORRY, DID YOU WAIT LONG?
AKI-KUN...
WHOA. ARE YOU OKAY? YOU'RE REALLY PALE.
NO, NO, I'M FINE.
GLOOM......

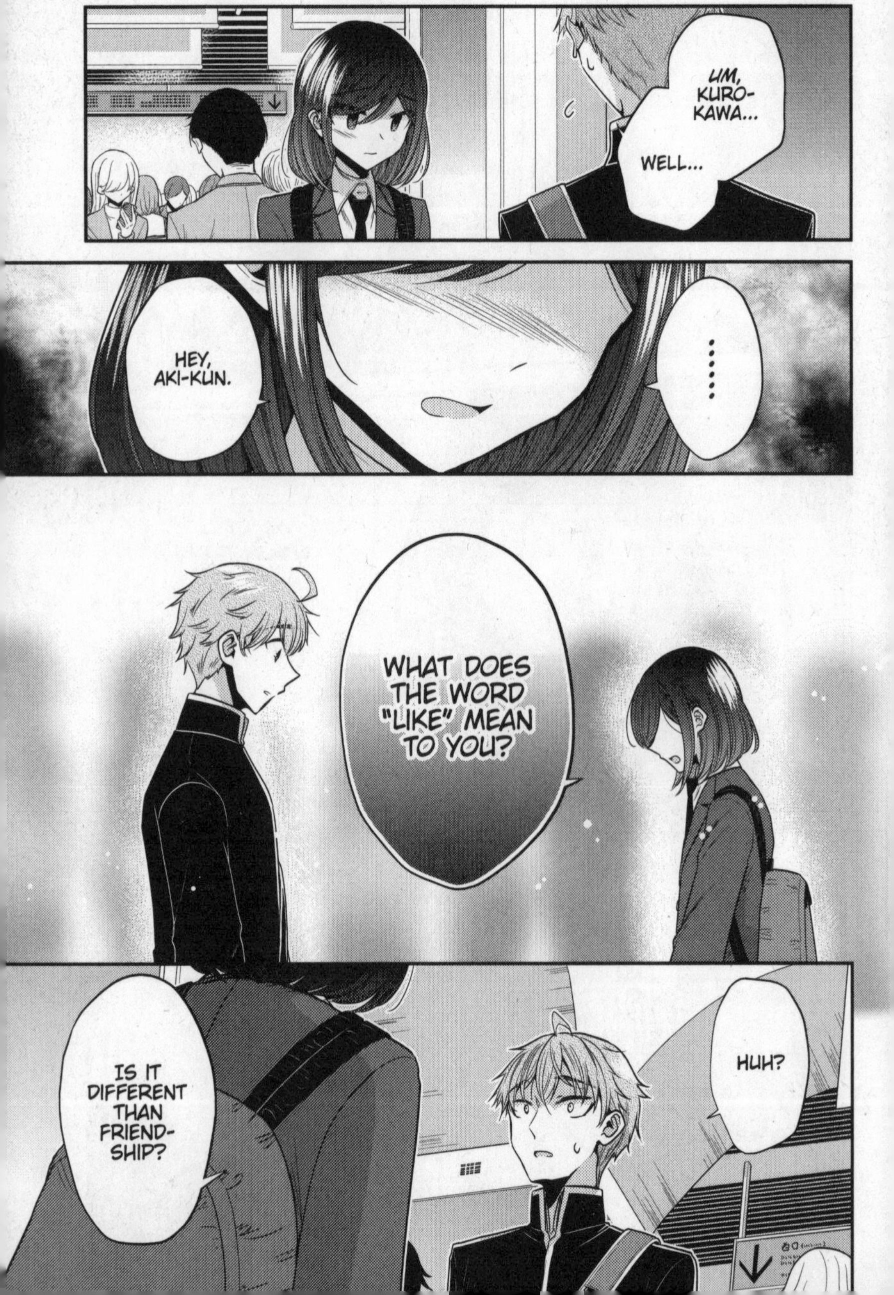
UM, KURO-KAWA...
WELL...
......
HEY, AKI-KUN.
WHAT DOES THE WORD "LIKE" MEAN TO YOU?
HUH?
IS IT DIFFERENT THAN FRIEND-SHIP?

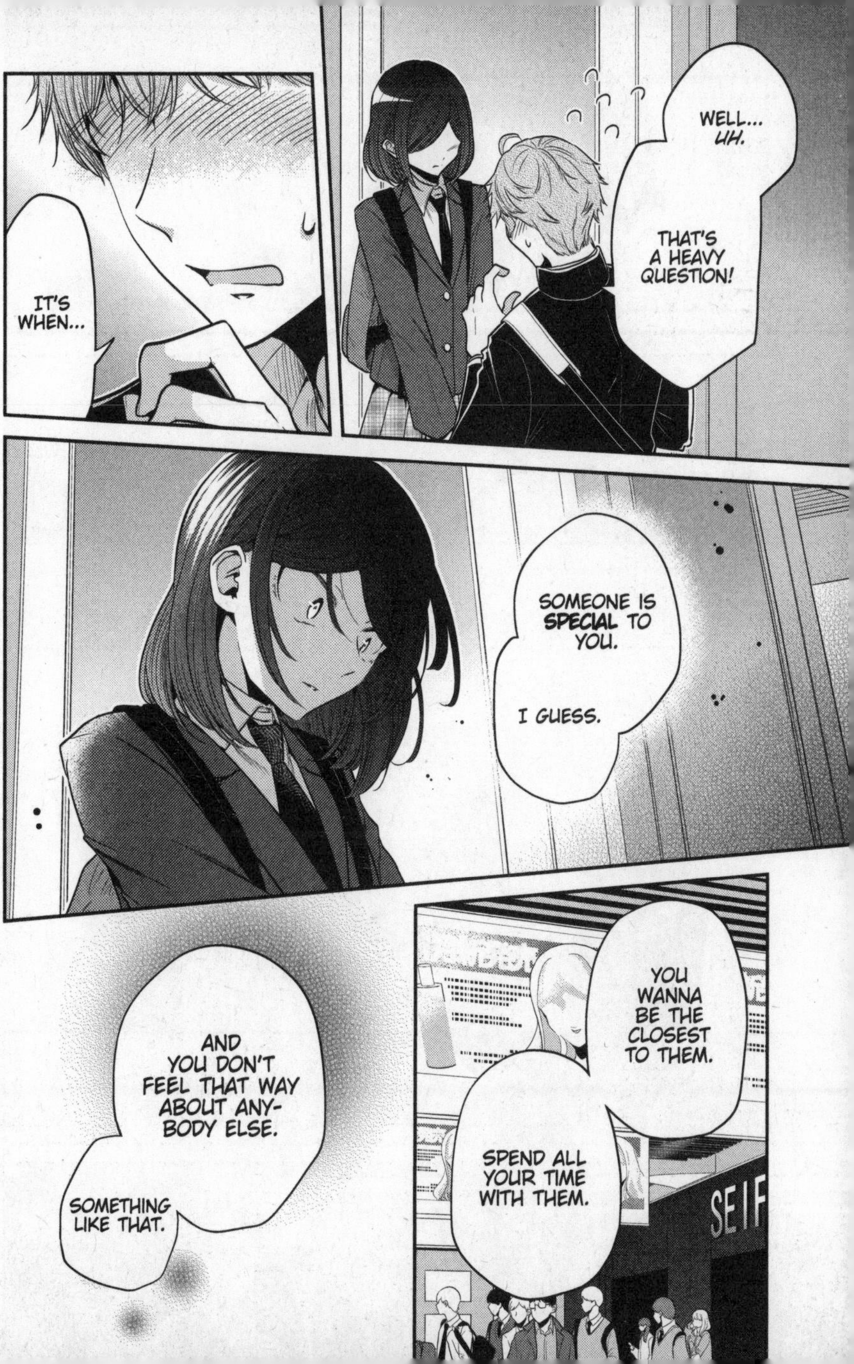
WELL... UH.
THAT'S A HEAVY QUESTION!
IT'S WHEN...
SOMEONE IS **SPECIAL** TO YOU.
I GUESS.
YOU WANNA BE THE CLOSEST TO THEM.
SPEND ALL YOUR TIME WITH THEM.
AND YOU DON'T FEEL THAT WAY ABOUT ANY-BODY ELSE.
SOMETHING LIKE THAT.

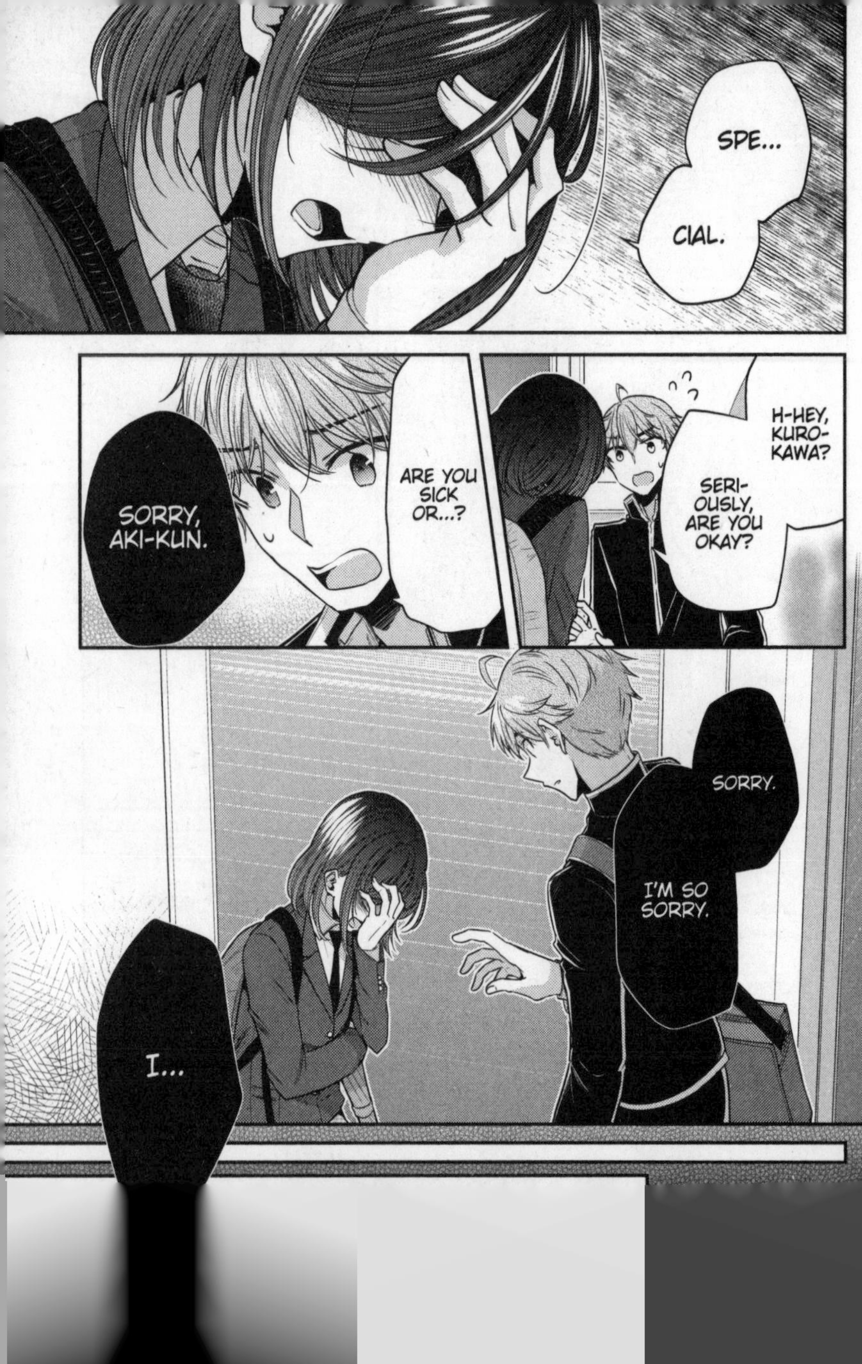
SPE...
CIAL.
H-HEY, KURO-KAWA?
SERI-OUSLY, ARE YOU OKAY?
ARE YOU SICK OR...?
SORRY, AKI-KUN.
SORRY.
I'M SO SORRY.
I...

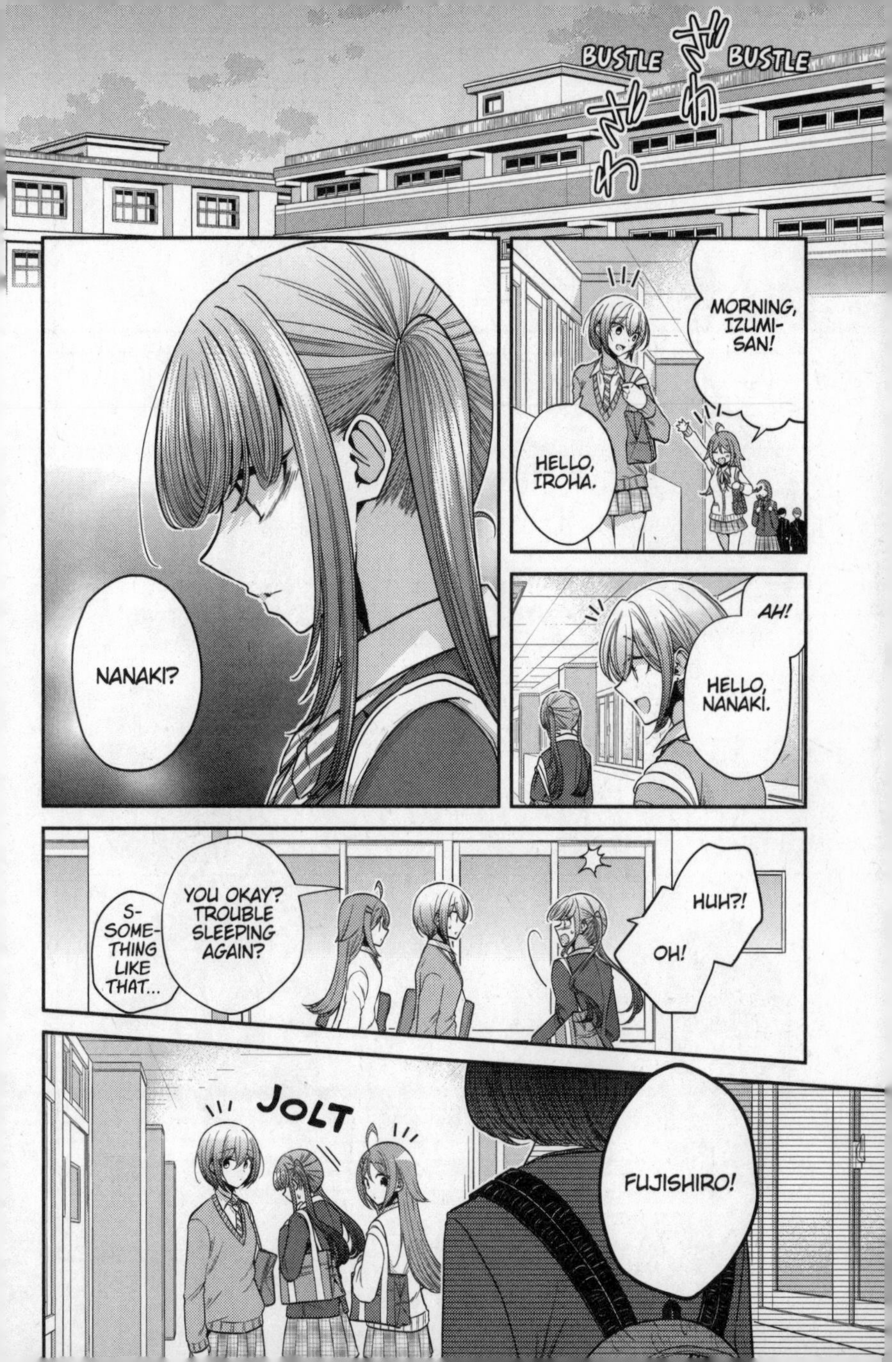
BUSTLE
ざわざわ
BUSTLE
MORNING, IZUMI-SAN!
HELLO, IROHA.
AH!
HELLO, NANAKI.
NANAKI?
HUH?!
OH!
YOU OKAY? TROUBLE SLEEPING AGAIN?
S-SOMETHING LIKE THAT...
FUJISHIRO!
JOLT

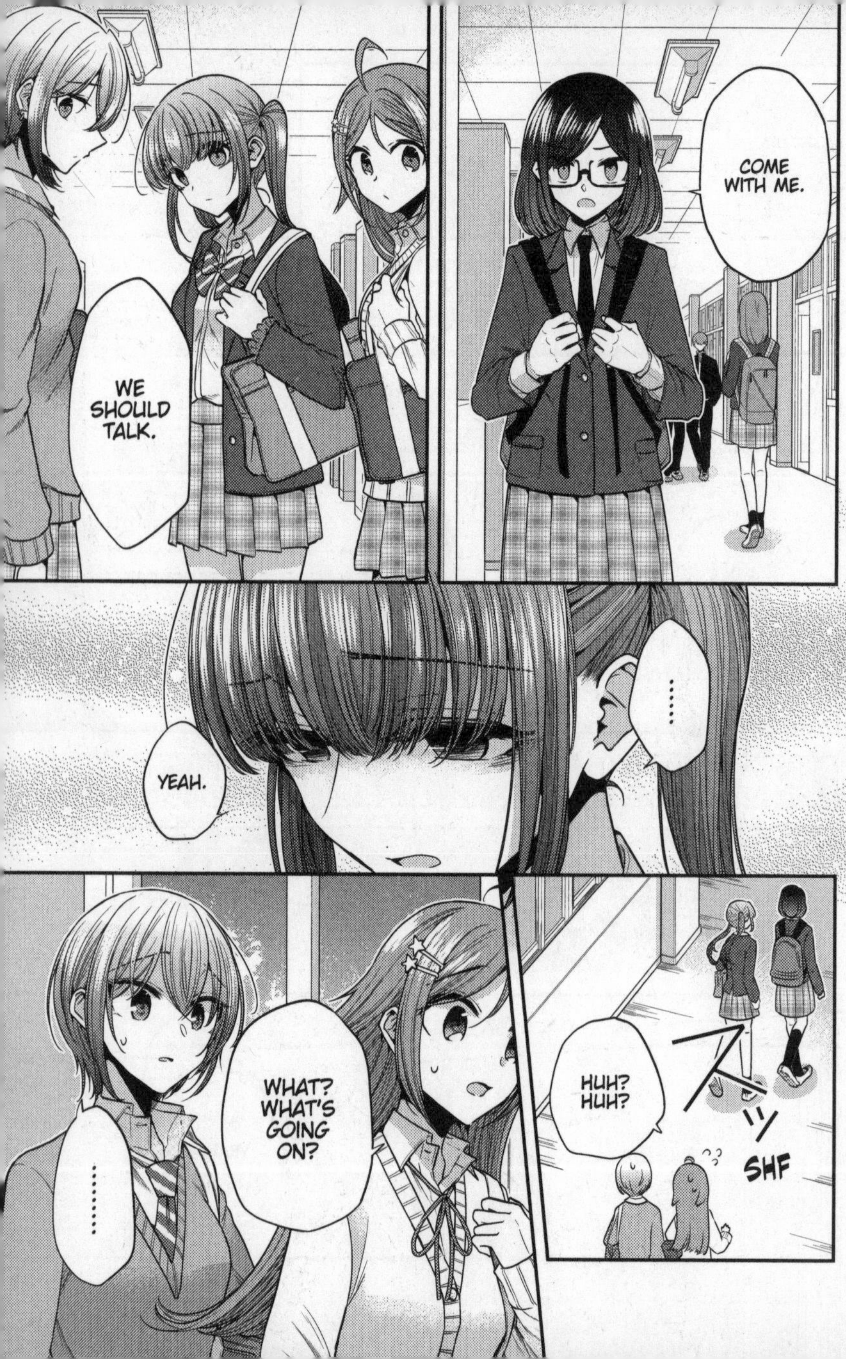
COME WITH ME.
WE SHOULD TALK.
......
YEAH.
HUH? HUH?
SHF
WHAT? WHAT'S GOING ON?
......

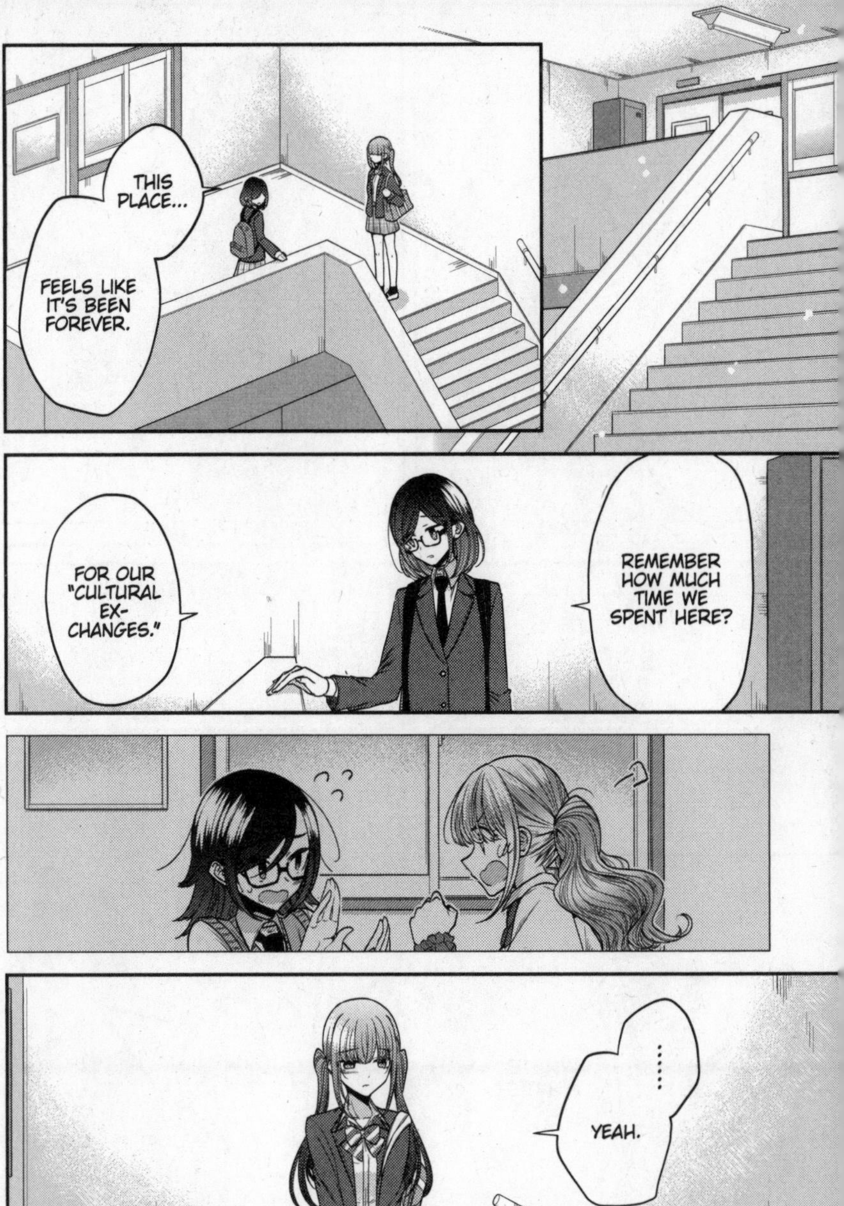
THIS PLACE...
FEELS LIKE IT'S BEEN FOREVER.
REMEMBER HOW MUCH TIME WE SPENT HERE?
FOR OUR "CULTURAL EX-CHANGES."
......
YEAH.

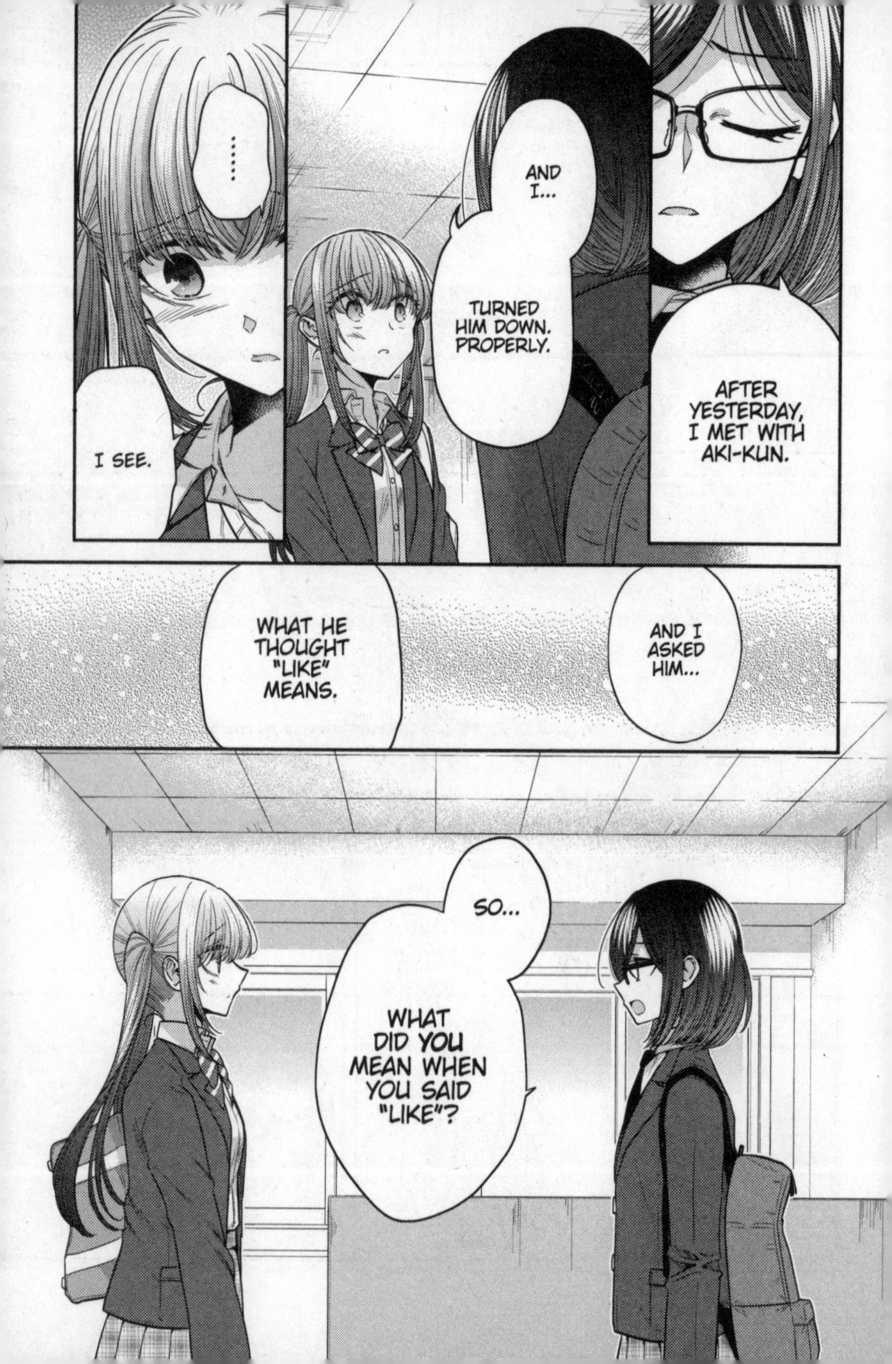
AFTER YESTERDAY, I MET WITH AKI-KUN.
AND I...
TURNED HIM DOWN. PROPERLY.
......
I SEE.
AND I ASKED HIM...
WHAT HE THOUGHT "LIKE" MEANS.
SO...
WHAT DID YOU MEAN WHEN YOU SAID "LIKE"?

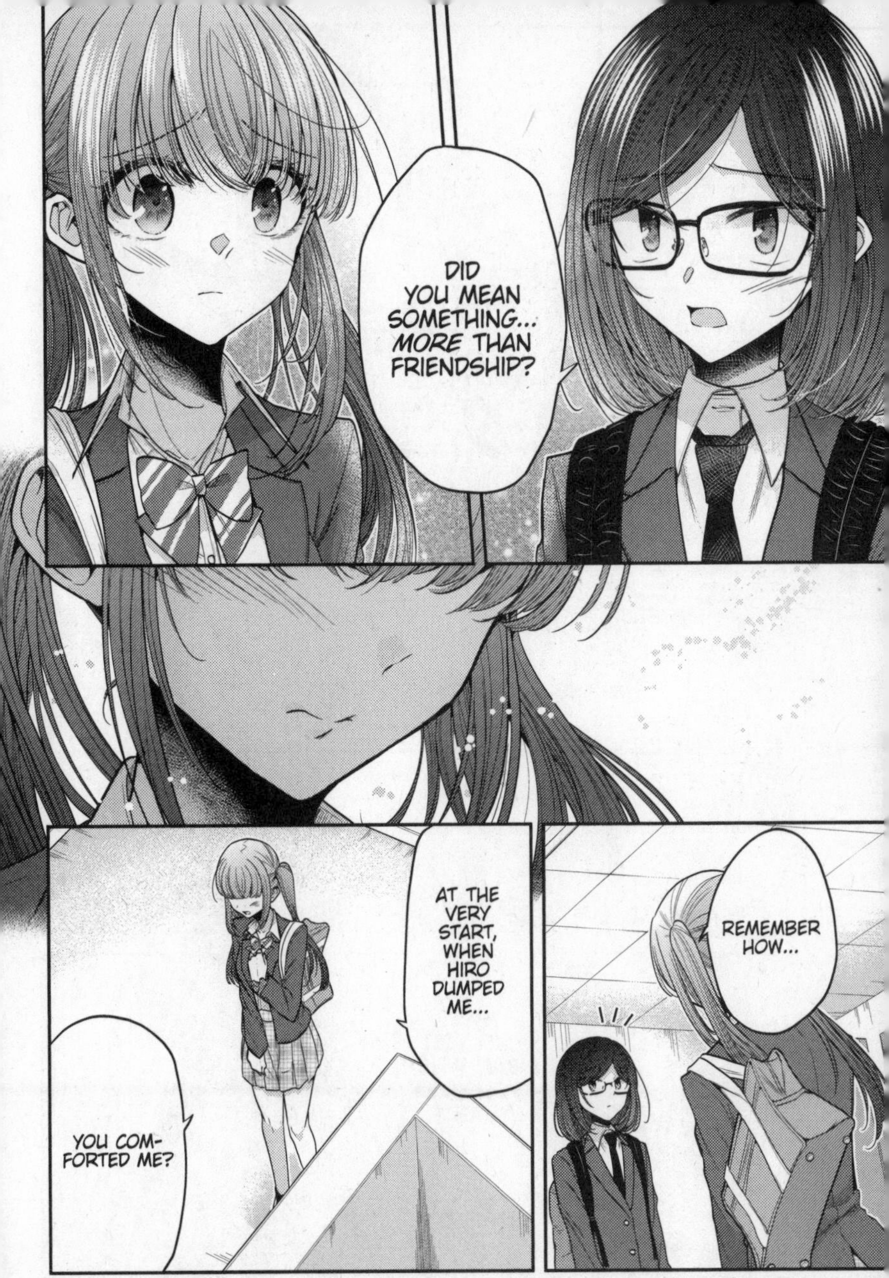
DID YOU MEAN SOMETHING... *MORE* THAN FRIENDSHIP?
REMEMBER HOW...
AT THE VERY START, WHEN HIRO DUMPED ME...
YOU COM-FORTED ME?

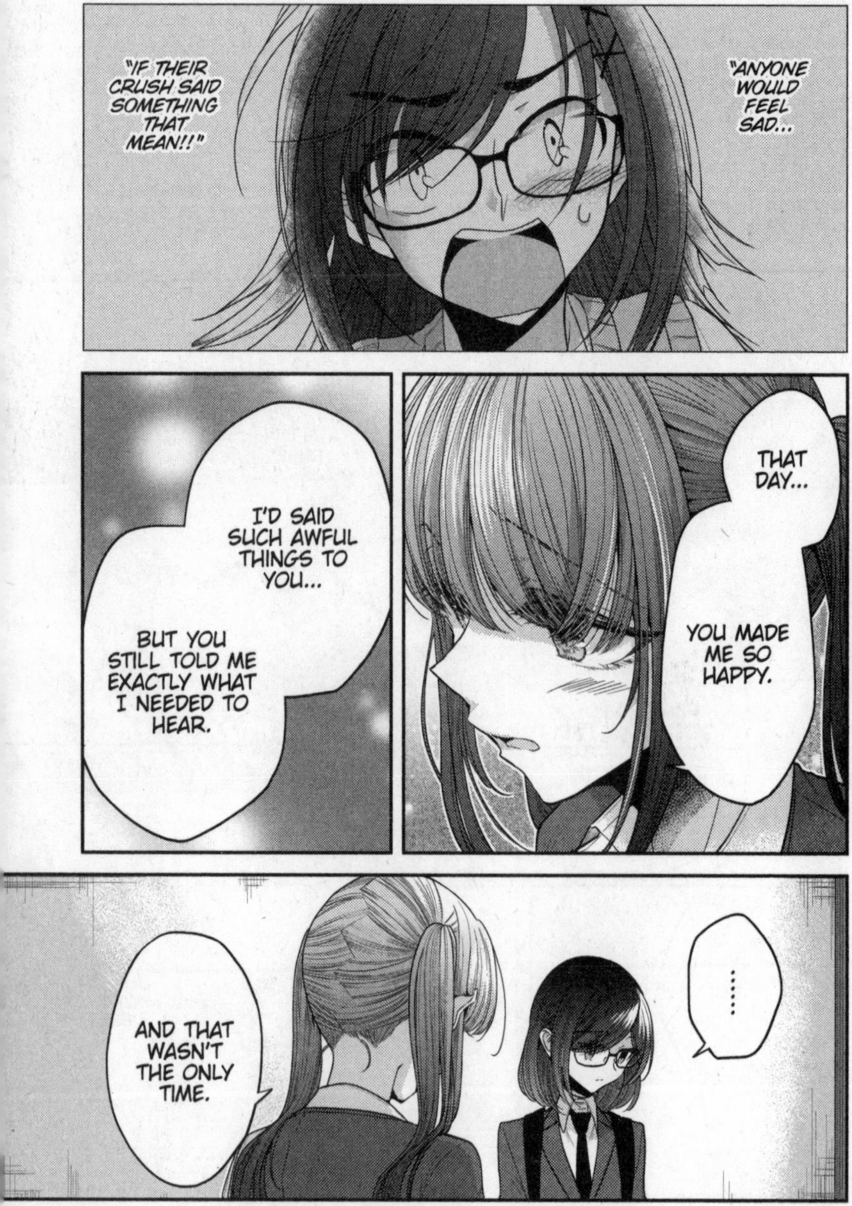
"ANYONE WOULD FEEL SAD...
"IF THEIR CRUSH SAID SOMETHING THAT MEAN!!"
THAT DAY...
YOU MADE ME SO HAPPY.
I'D SAID SUCH AWFUL THINGS TO YOU...
BUT YOU STILL TOLD ME EXACTLY WHAT I NEEDED TO HEAR.
......
AND THAT WASN'T THE ONLY TIME.

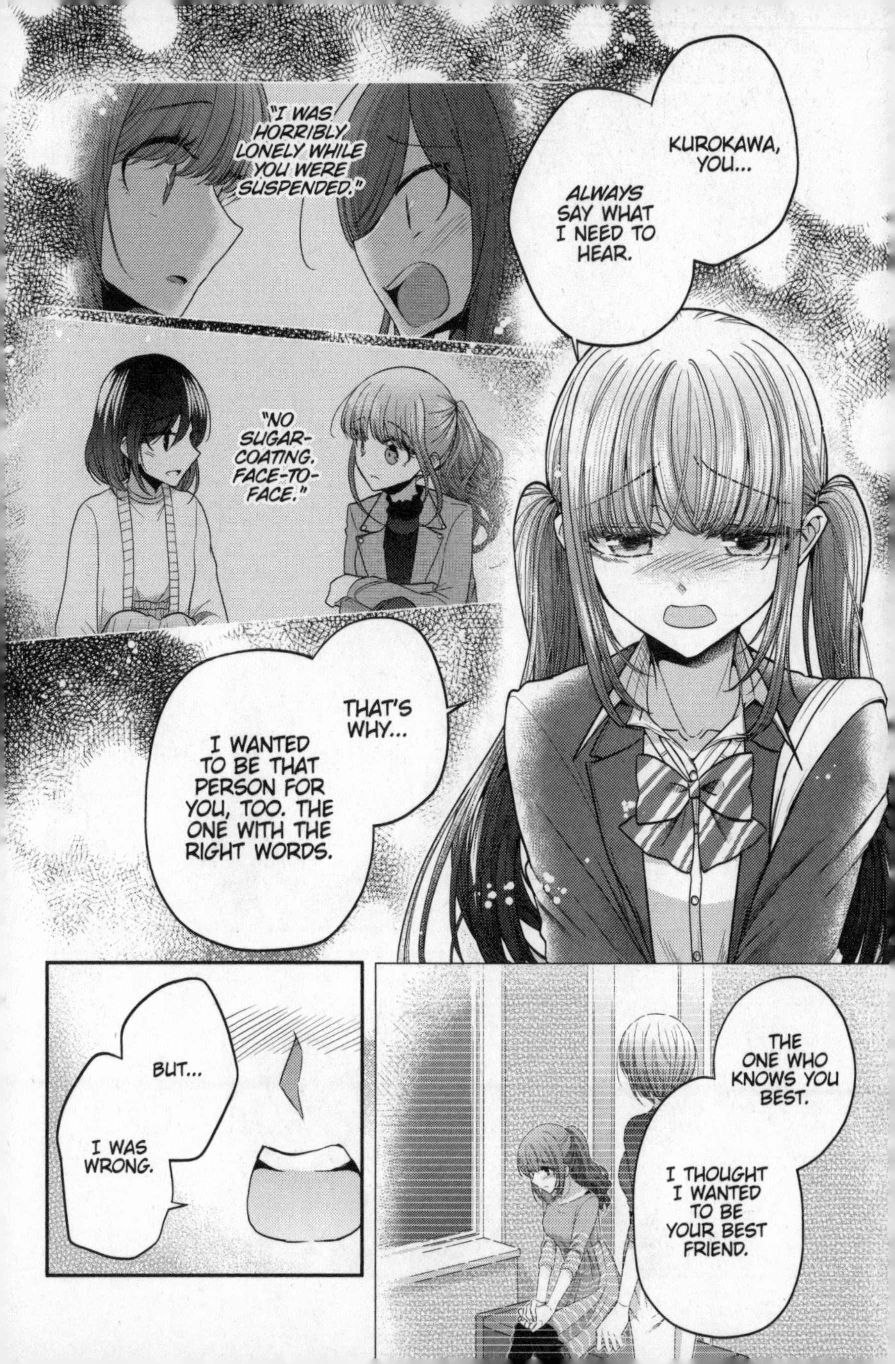
KUROKAWA, YOU...
ALWAYS SAY WHAT I NEED TO HEAR.
"I WAS HORRIBLY LONELY WHILE YOU WERE SUSPENDED."
"NO SUGAR-COATING. FACE-TO-FACE."
THAT'S WHY...
I WANTED TO BE THAT PERSON FOR YOU, TOO. THE ONE WITH THE RIGHT WORDS.
THE ONE WHO KNOWS YOU BEST.
I THOUGHT I WANTED TO BE YOUR BEST FRIEND.
BUT...
I WAS WRONG.

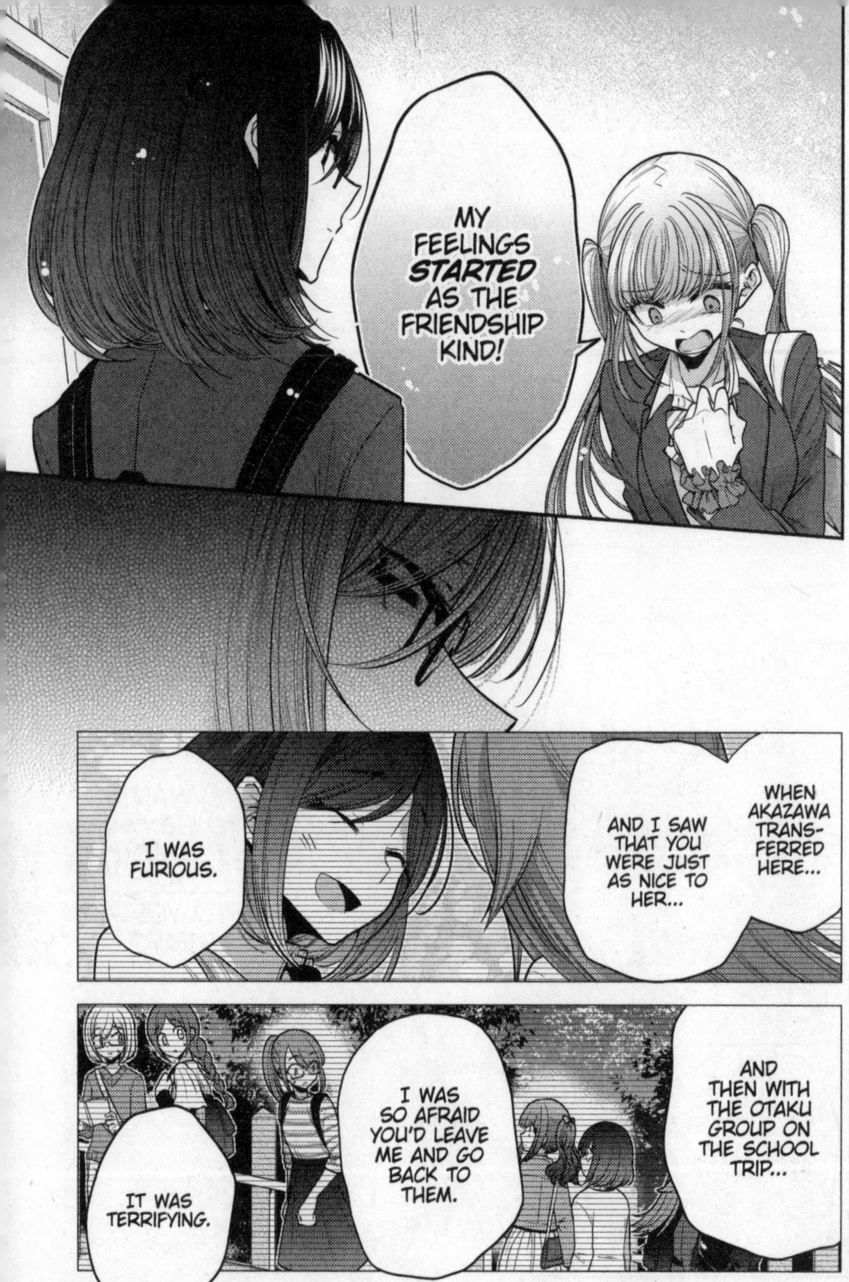
MY FEELINGS STARTED AS THE FRIENDSHIP KIND!
WHEN AKAZAWA TRANS-FERRED HERE...
AND I SAW THAT YOU WERE JUST AS NICE TO HER...
I WAS FURIOUS.
AND THEN WITH THE OTAKU GROUP ON THE SCHOOL TRIP...
I WAS SO AFRAID YOU'D LEAVE ME AND GO BACK TO THEM.
IT WAS TERRIFYING.

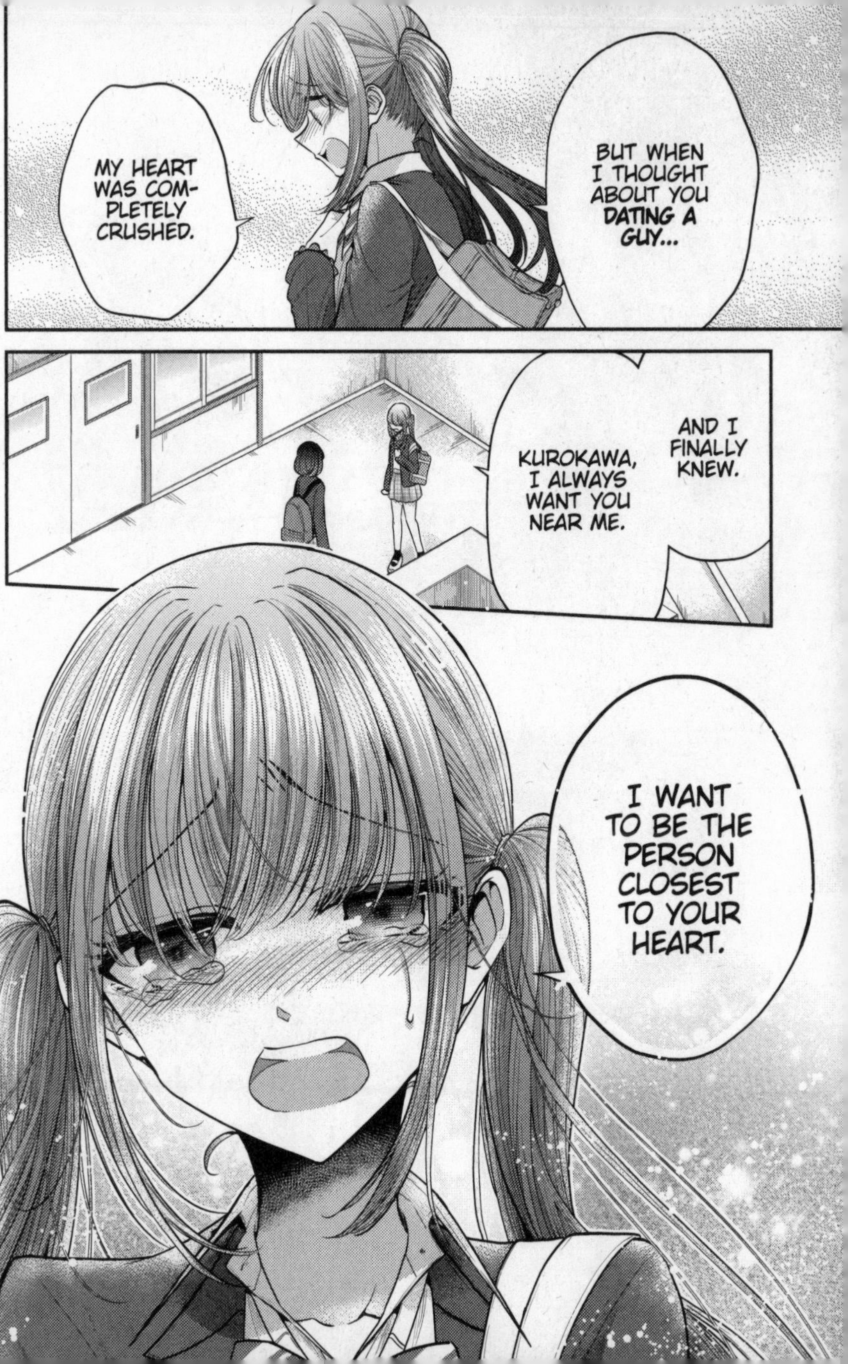
BUT WHEN I THOUGHT ABOUT YOU DATING A GUY...
MY HEART WAS COM-PLETELY CRUSHED.
AND I FINALLY KNEW.
KUROKAWA, I ALWAYS WANT YOU NEAR ME.
I WANT TO BE THE PERSON CLOSEST TO YOUR HEART.

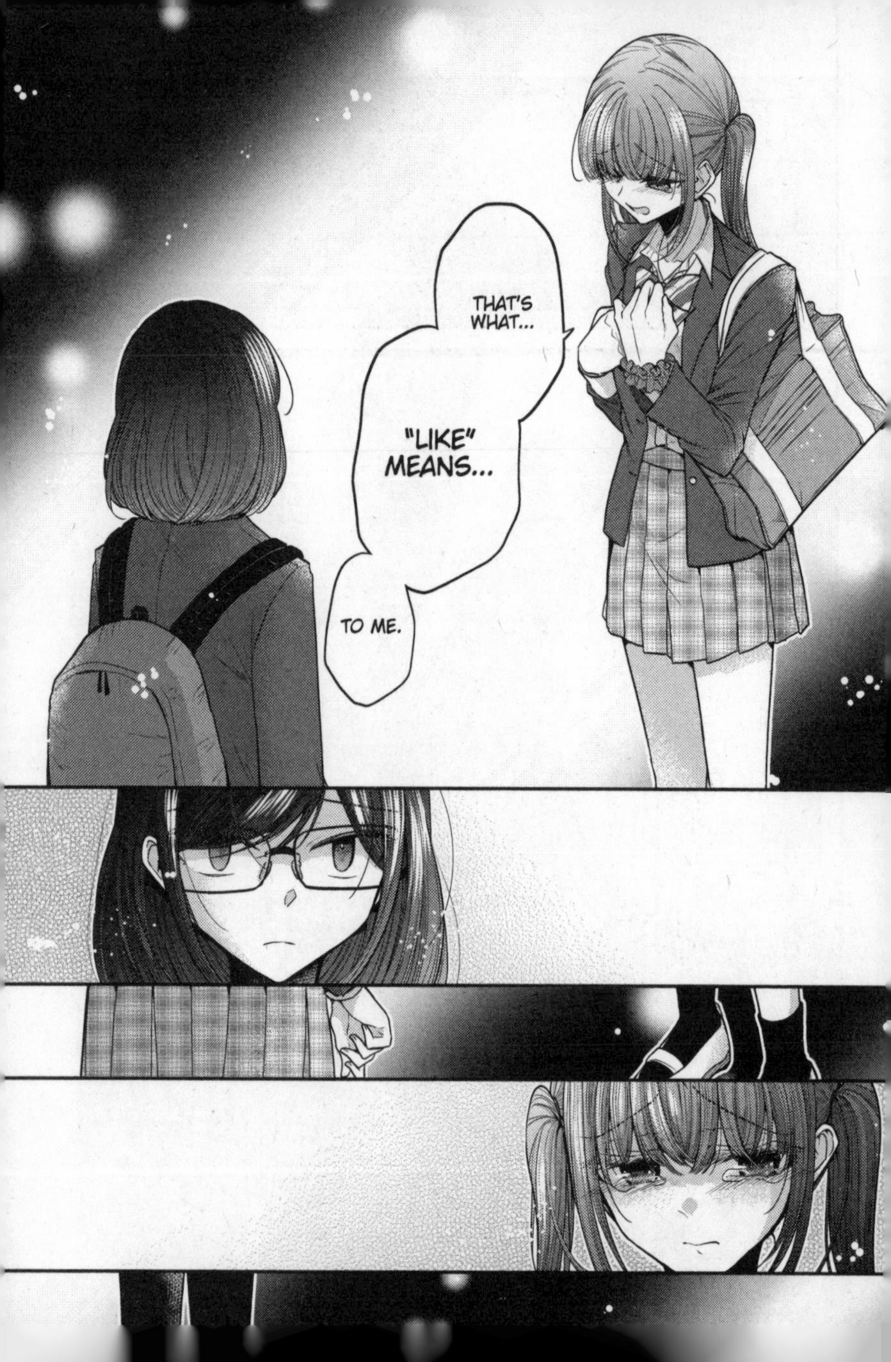
THAT'S WHAT...
"LIKE" MEANS...
TO ME.

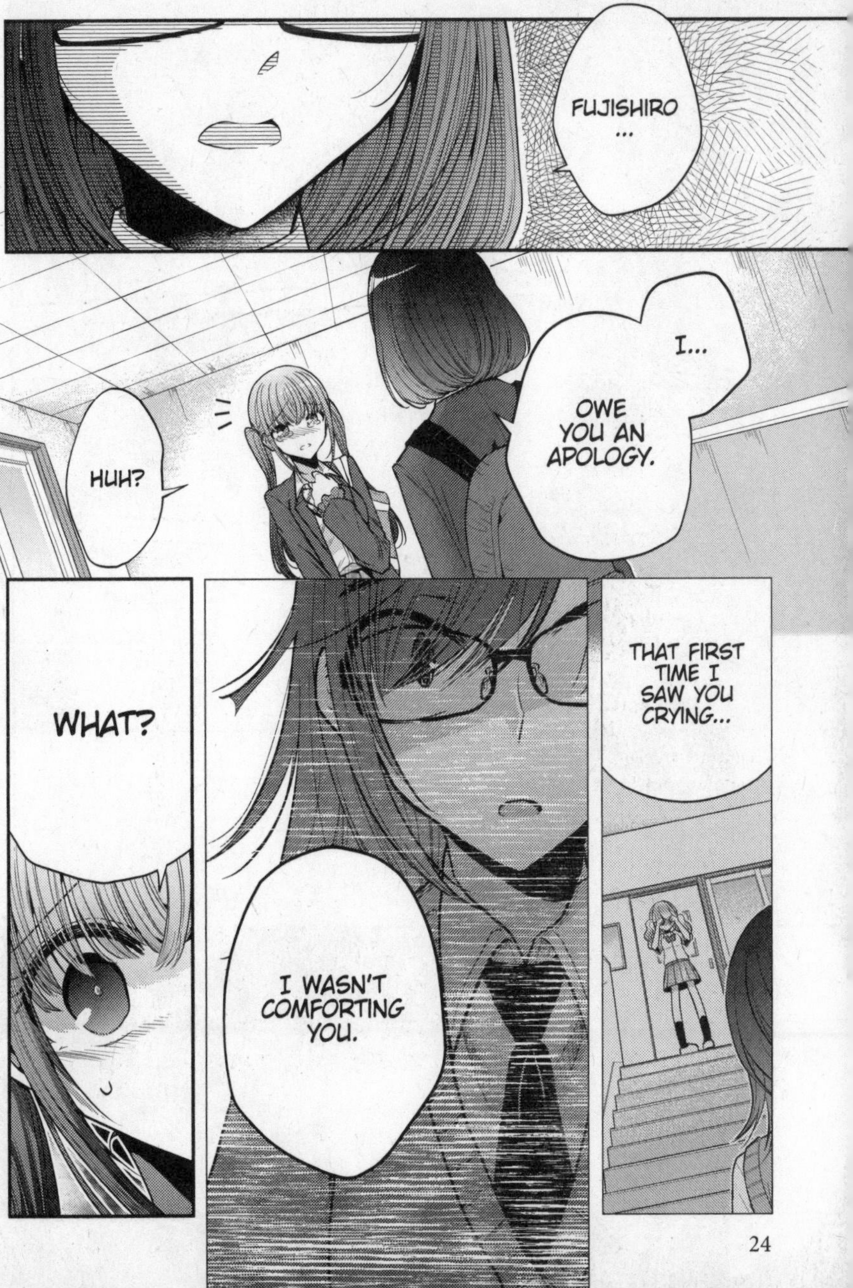
FUJISHIRO ...
I... OWE YOU AN APOLOGY.
HUH?
THAT FIRST TIME I SAW YOU CRYING...
I WASN'T COMFORTING YOU.
WHAT?

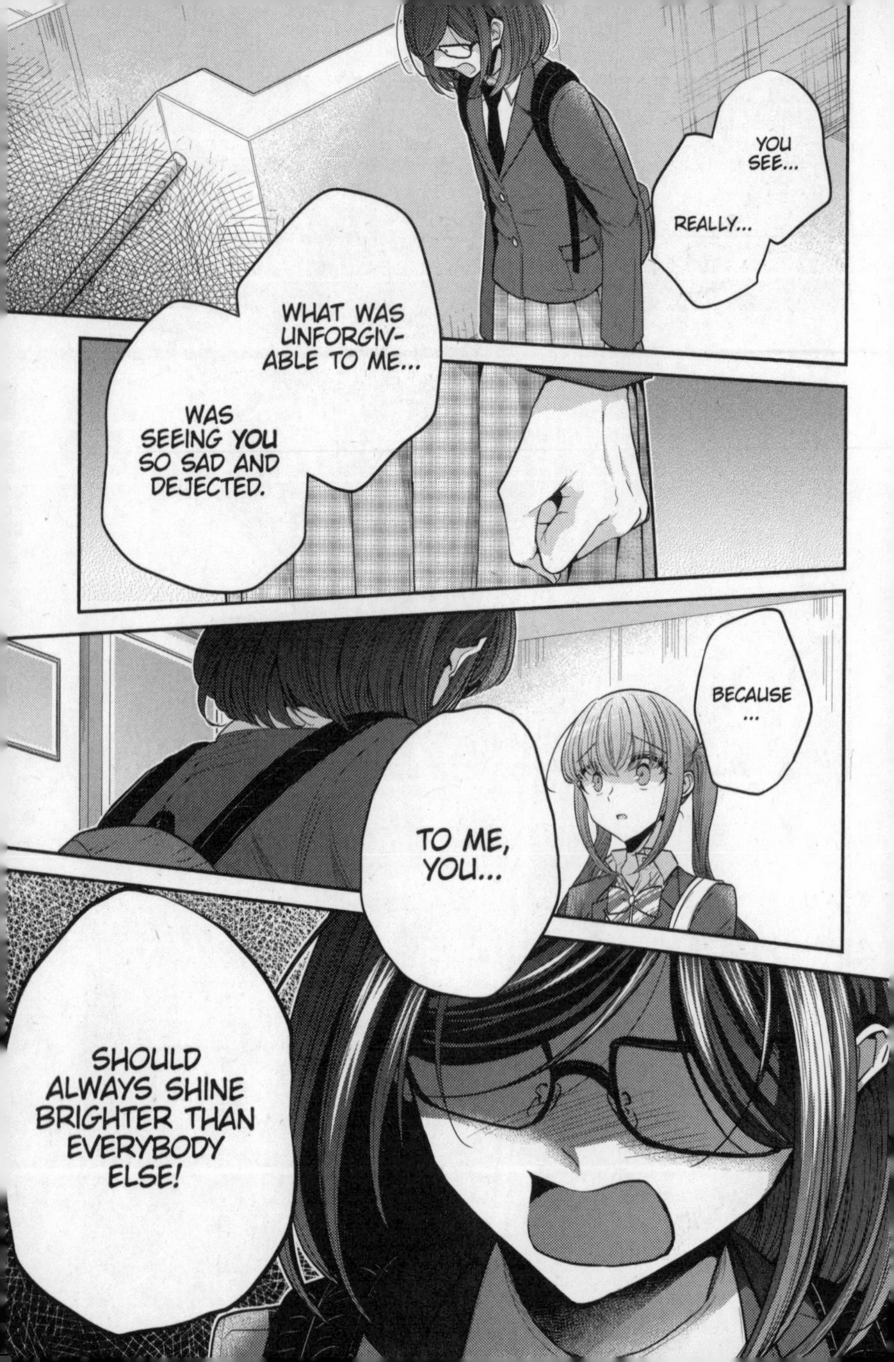
YOU SEE...
REALLY...
WHAT WAS UNFORGIV-ABLE TO ME...
WAS SEEING YOU SO SAD AND DEJECTED.
BECAUSE...
TO ME, YOU...
SHOULD ALWAYS SHINE BRIGHTER THAN EVERYBODY ELSE!

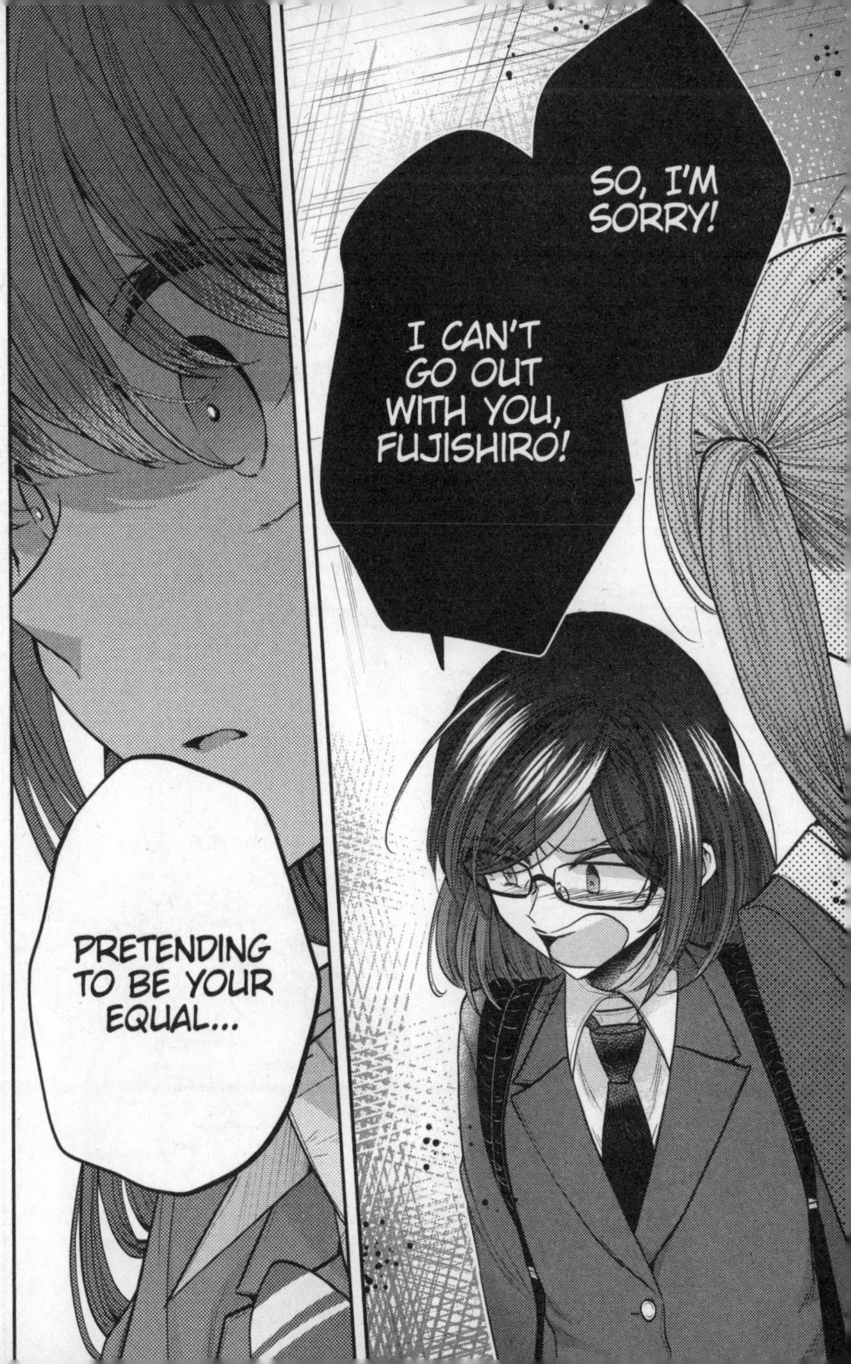
SO, I'M SORRY!
I CAN'T GO OUT WITH YOU, FUJISHIRO!
PRETENDING TO BE YOUR EQUAL...

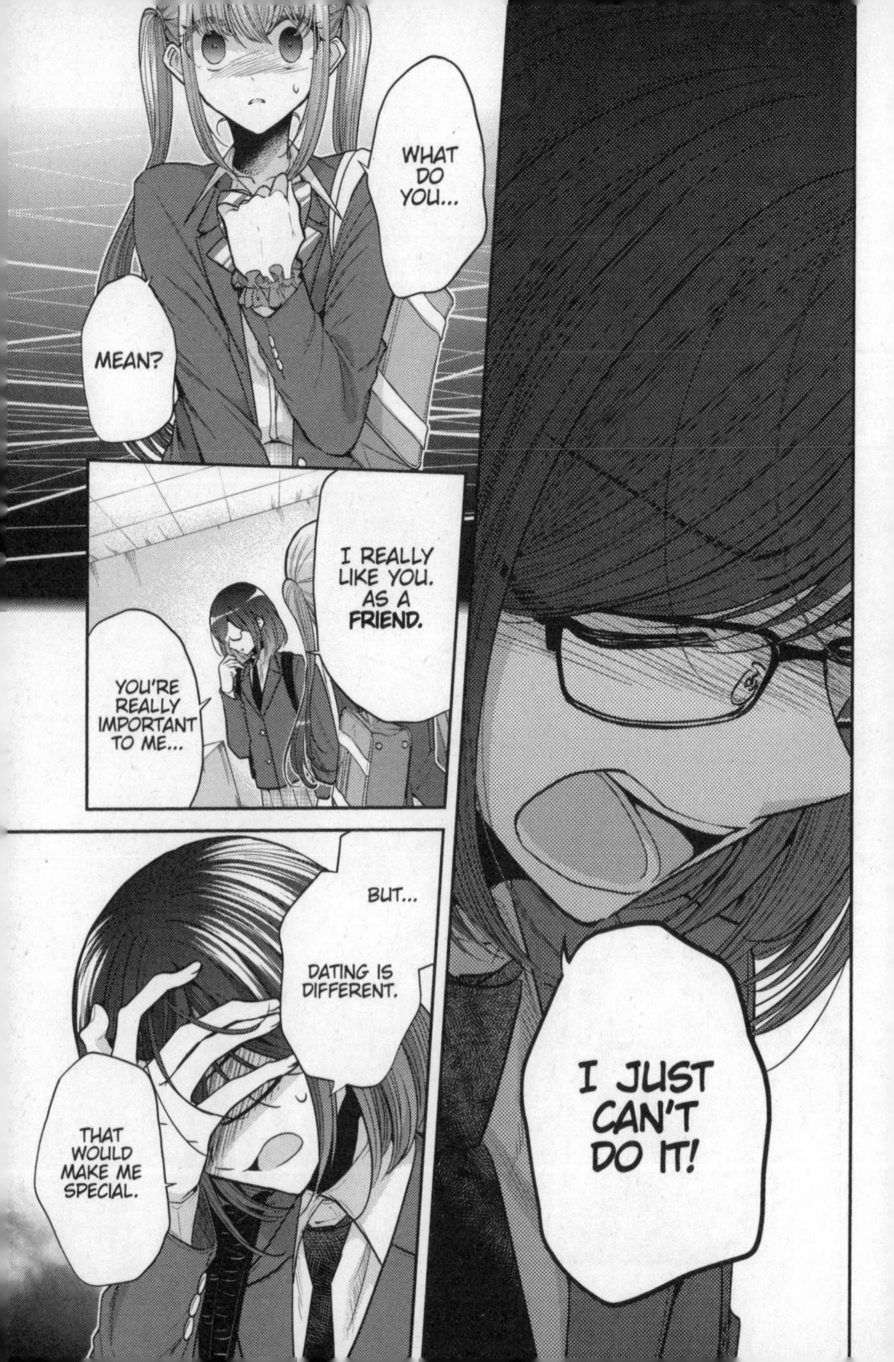
I JUST CAN'T DO IT!
WHAT DO YOU...
MEAN?
I REALLY LIKE YOU. AS A FRIEND.
YOU'RE REALLY IMPORTANT TO ME...
BUT...
DATING IS DIFFERENT.
THAT WOULD MAKE ME SPECIAL.

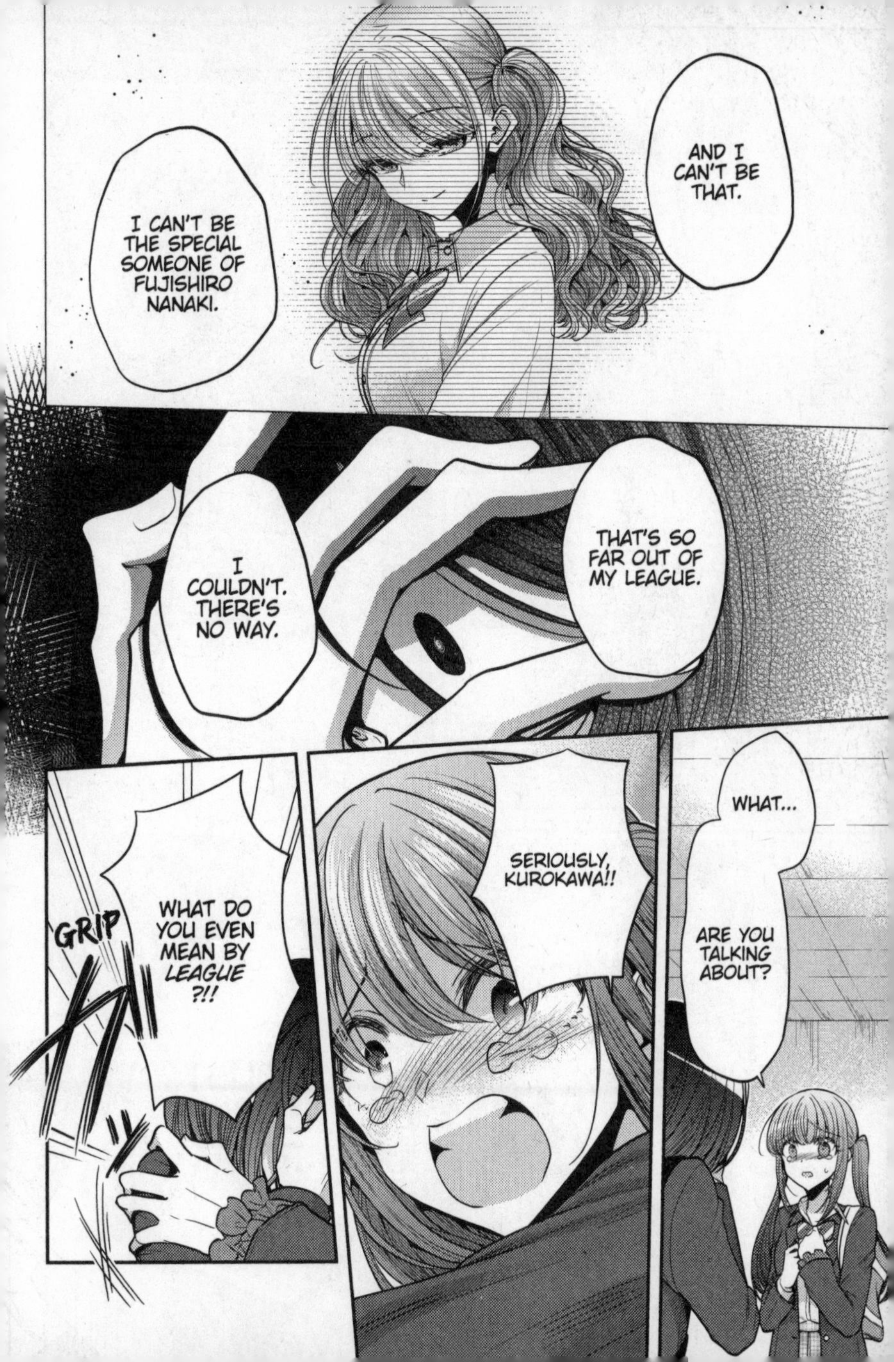
AND I CAN'T BE THAT.
I CAN'T BE THE SPECIAL SOMEONE OF FUJISHIRO NANAKI.
THAT'S SO FAR OUT OF MY LEAGUE.
I COULDN'T. THERE'S NO WAY.
WHAT...
ARE YOU TALKING ABOUT?
SERIOUSLY, KUROKAWA!!
WHAT DO YOU EVEN MEAN BY LEAGUE ?!!
GRIP

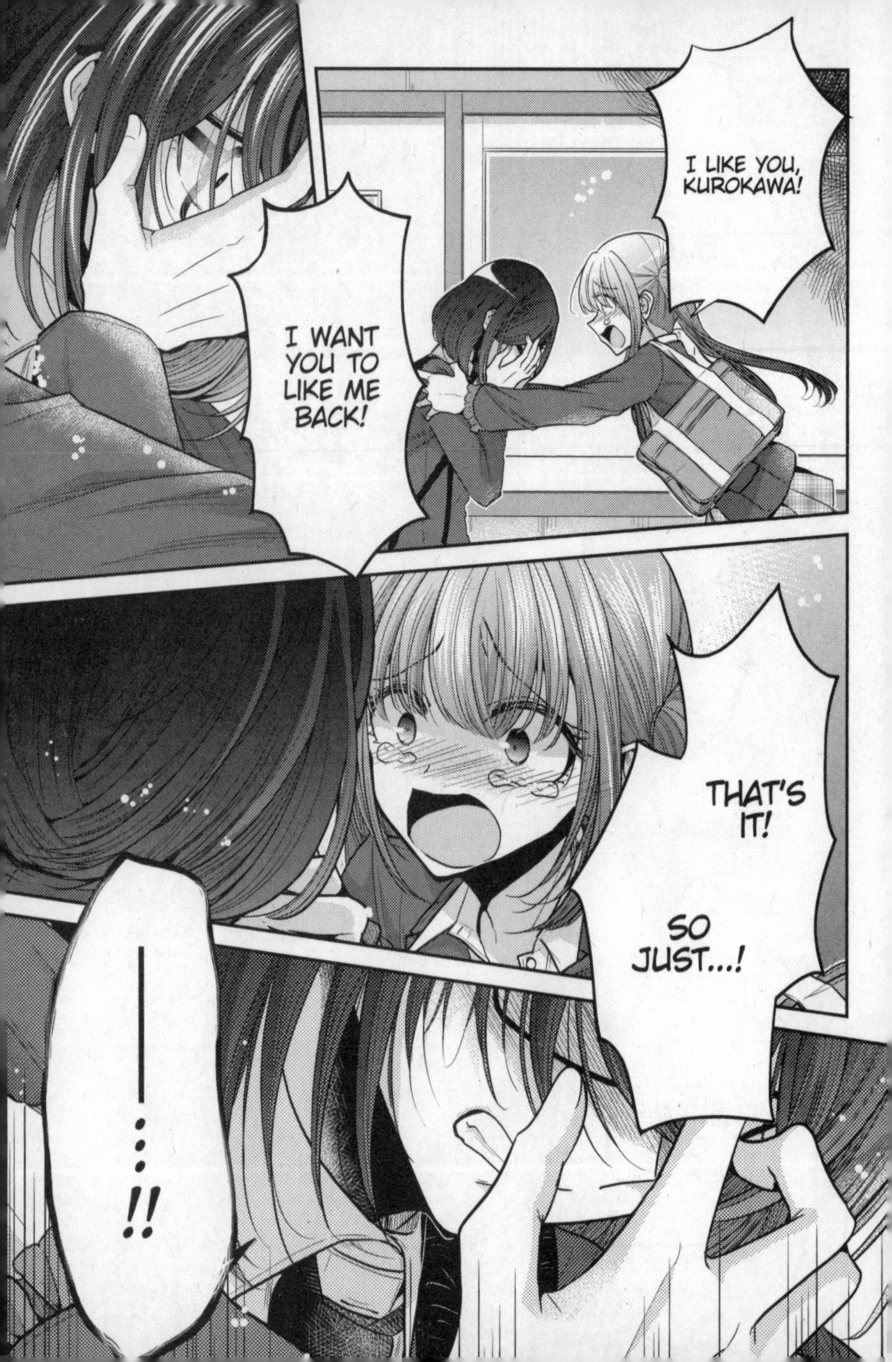
I LIKE YOU, KUROKAWA!
I WANT YOU TO LIKE ME BACK!
THAT'S IT!
SO JUST...!
——...!!

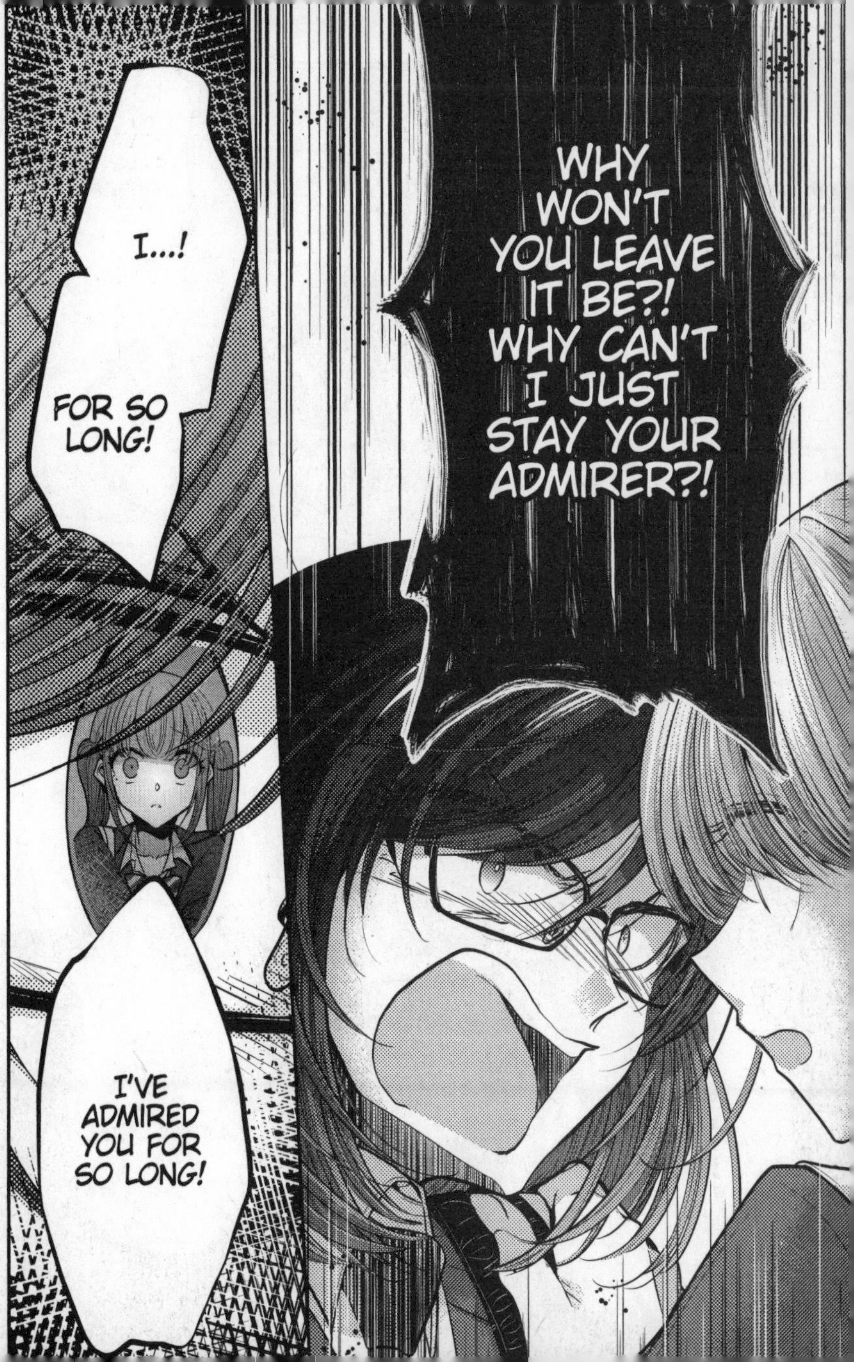
WHY WON'T YOU LEAVE IT BE?! WHY CAN'T I JUST STAY YOUR ADMIRER?!
I...!
FOR SO LONG!
I'VE ADMIRED YOU FOR SO LONG!

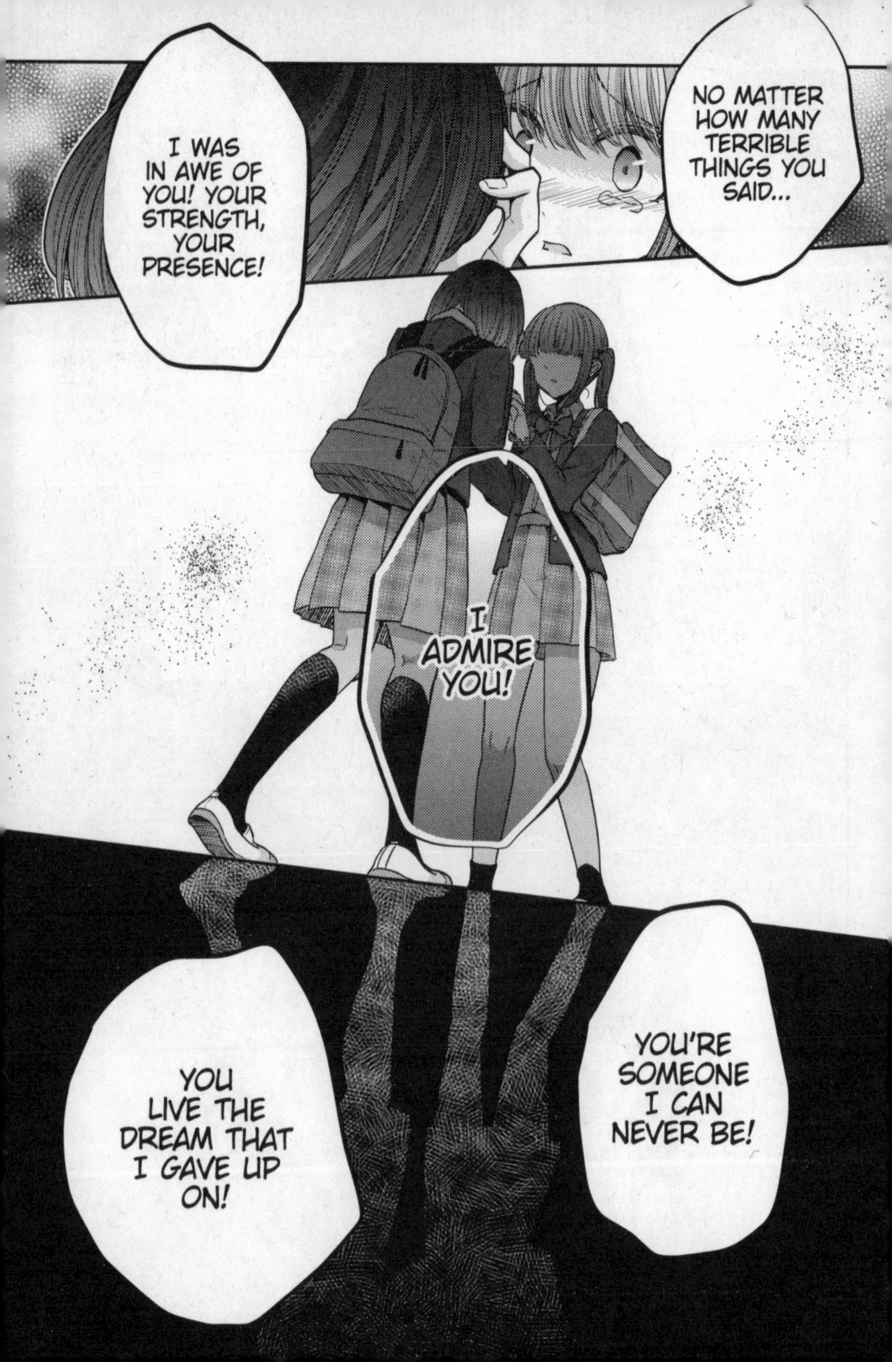
NO MATTER HOW MANY TERRIBLE THINGS YOU SAID...
I WAS IN AWE OF YOU! YOUR STRENGTH, YOUR PRESENCE!
I ADMIRE YOU!
YOU'RE SOMEONE I CAN NEVER BE!
YOU LIVE THE DREAM THAT I GAVE UP ON!

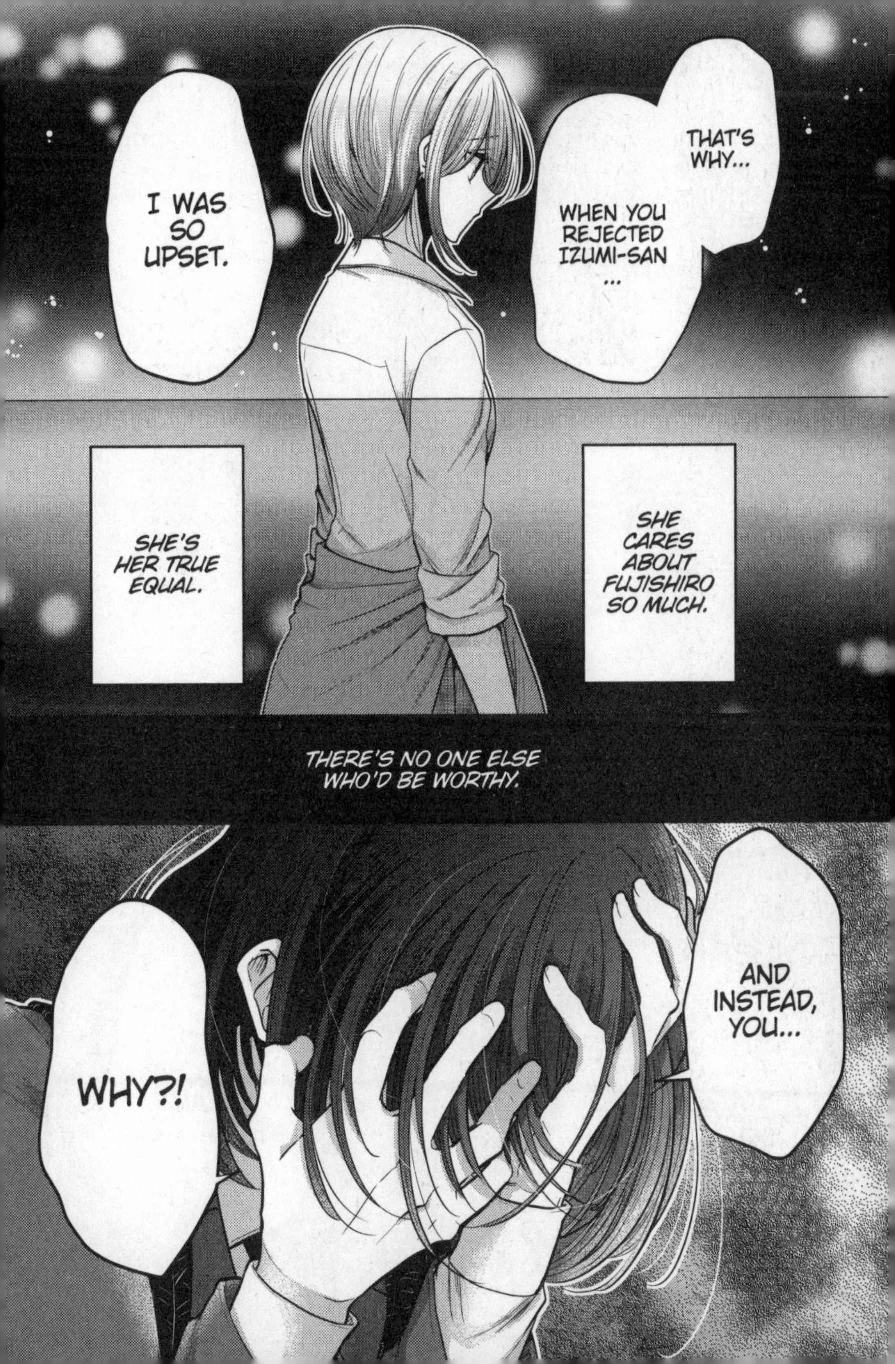
THAT'S WHY...
WHEN YOU REJECTED IZUMI-SAN ...
I WAS SO UPSET.
SHE CARES ABOUT FUJISHIRO SO MUCH.
SHE'S HER TRUE EQUAL.
THERE'S NO ONE ELSE WHO'D BE WORTHY.
AND INSTEAD, YOU...
WHY?!

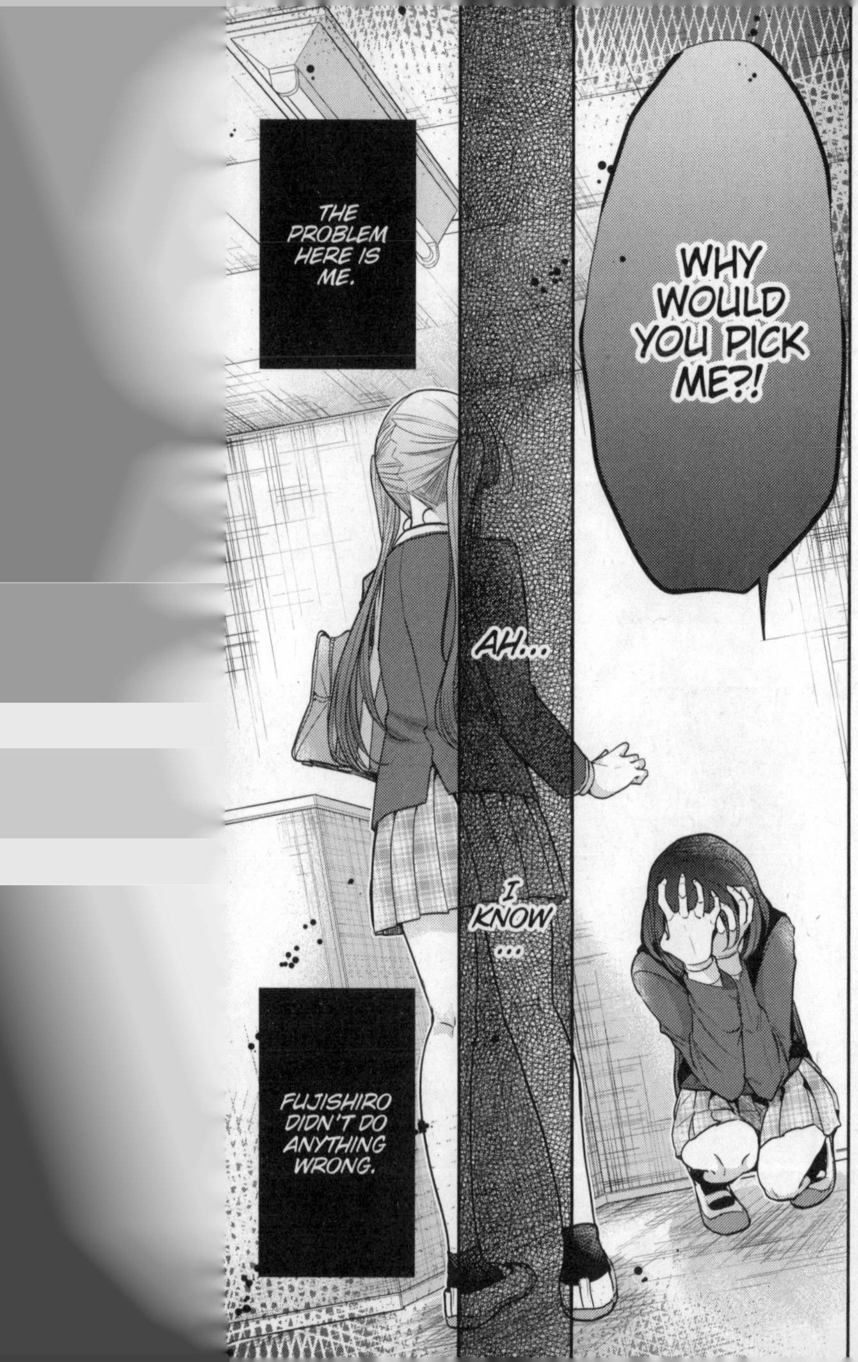
WHY WOULD YOU PICK ME?!
AH...
I KNOW...
THE PROBLEM HERE IS ME.
FUJISHIRO DIDN'T DO ANYTHING WRONG.

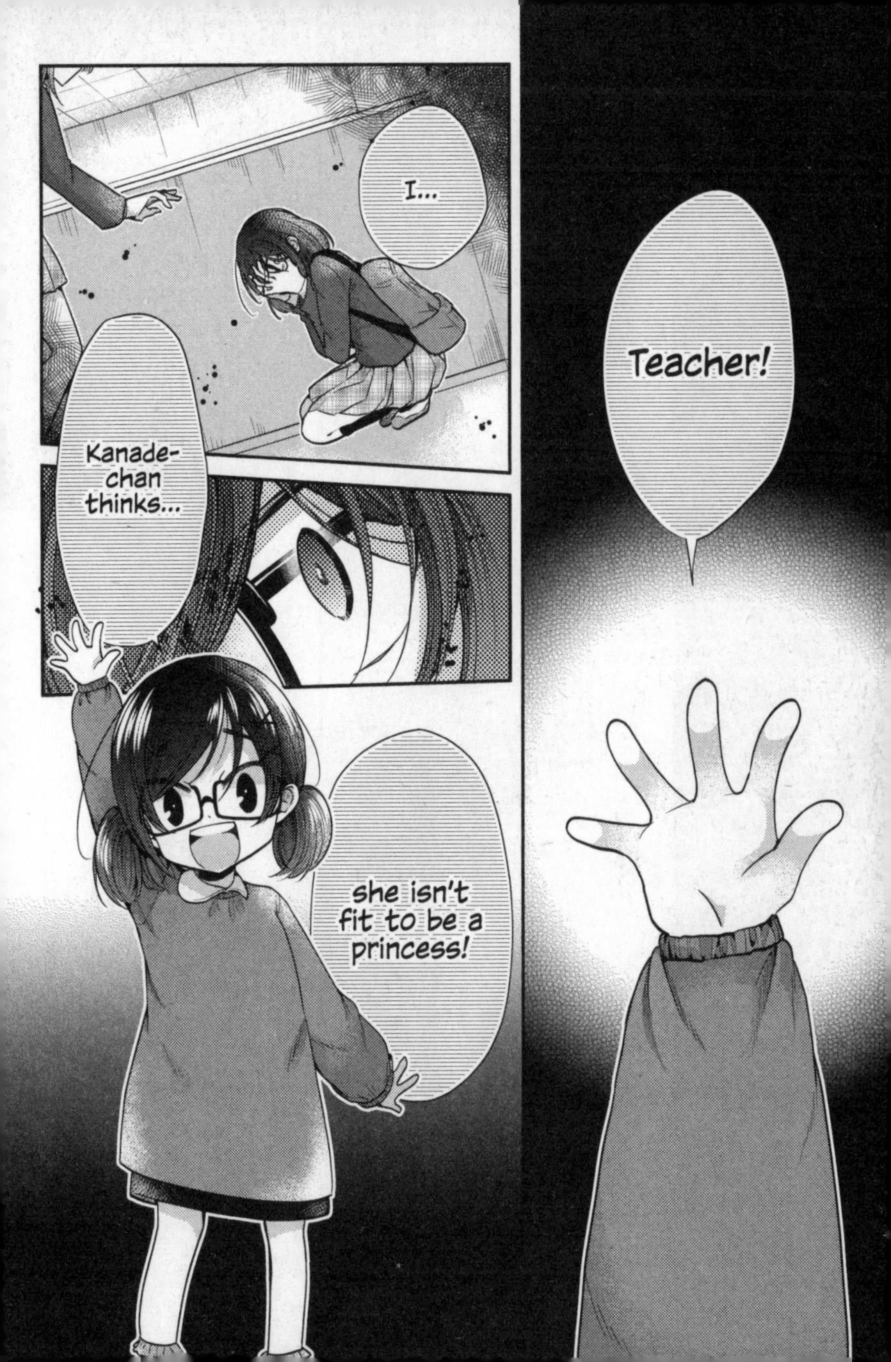
Teacher!
I...
Kanade-chan thinks...
she isn't fit to be a princess!

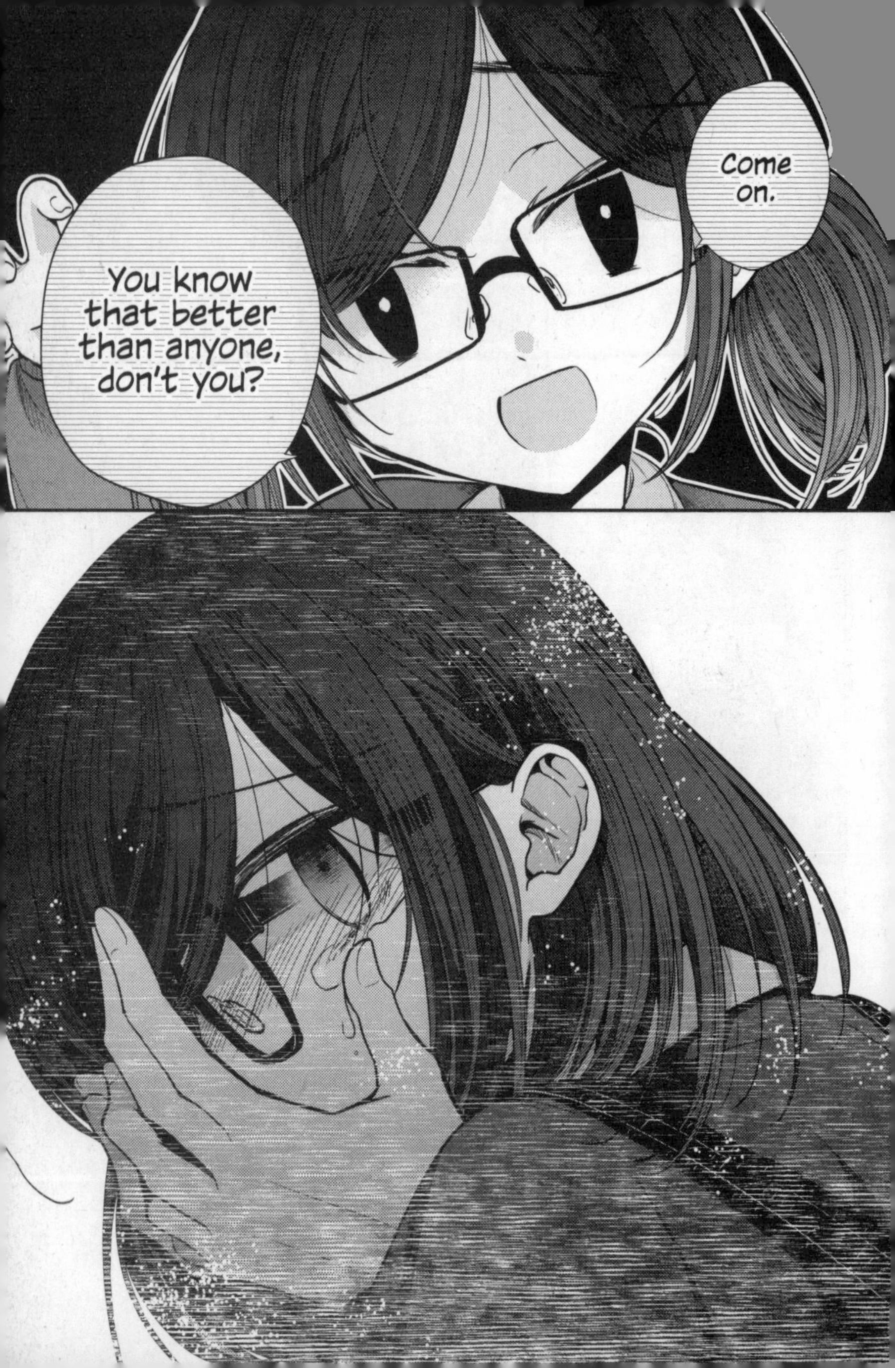
Come on.
You know that better than anyone, don't you?

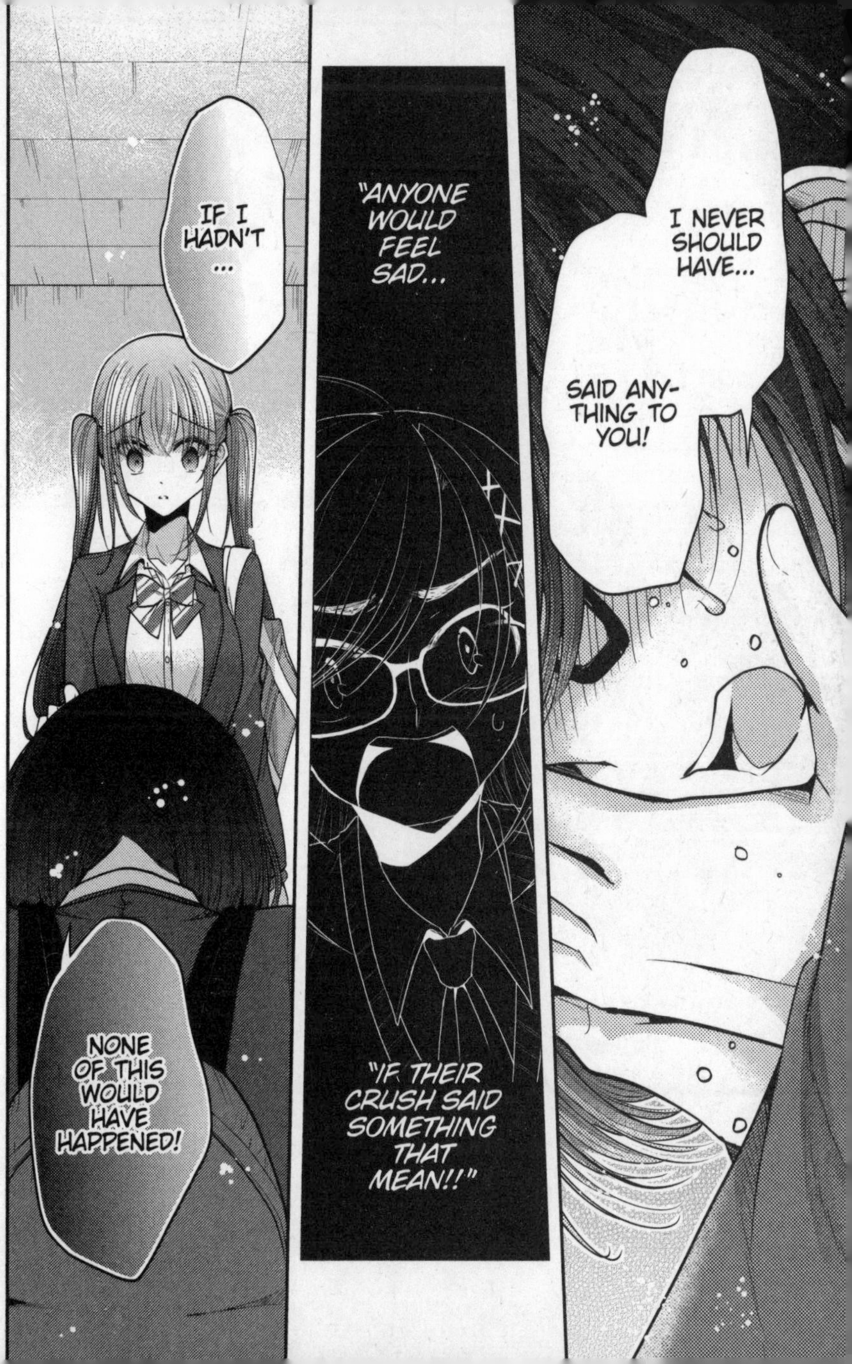
I NEVER SHOULD HAVE...
SAID ANY-THING TO YOU!
"ANYONE WOULD FEEL SAD...
"IF THEIR CRUSH SAID SOMETHING THAT MEAN!!"
IF I HADN'T ...
NONE OF THIS WOULD HAVE HAPPENED!

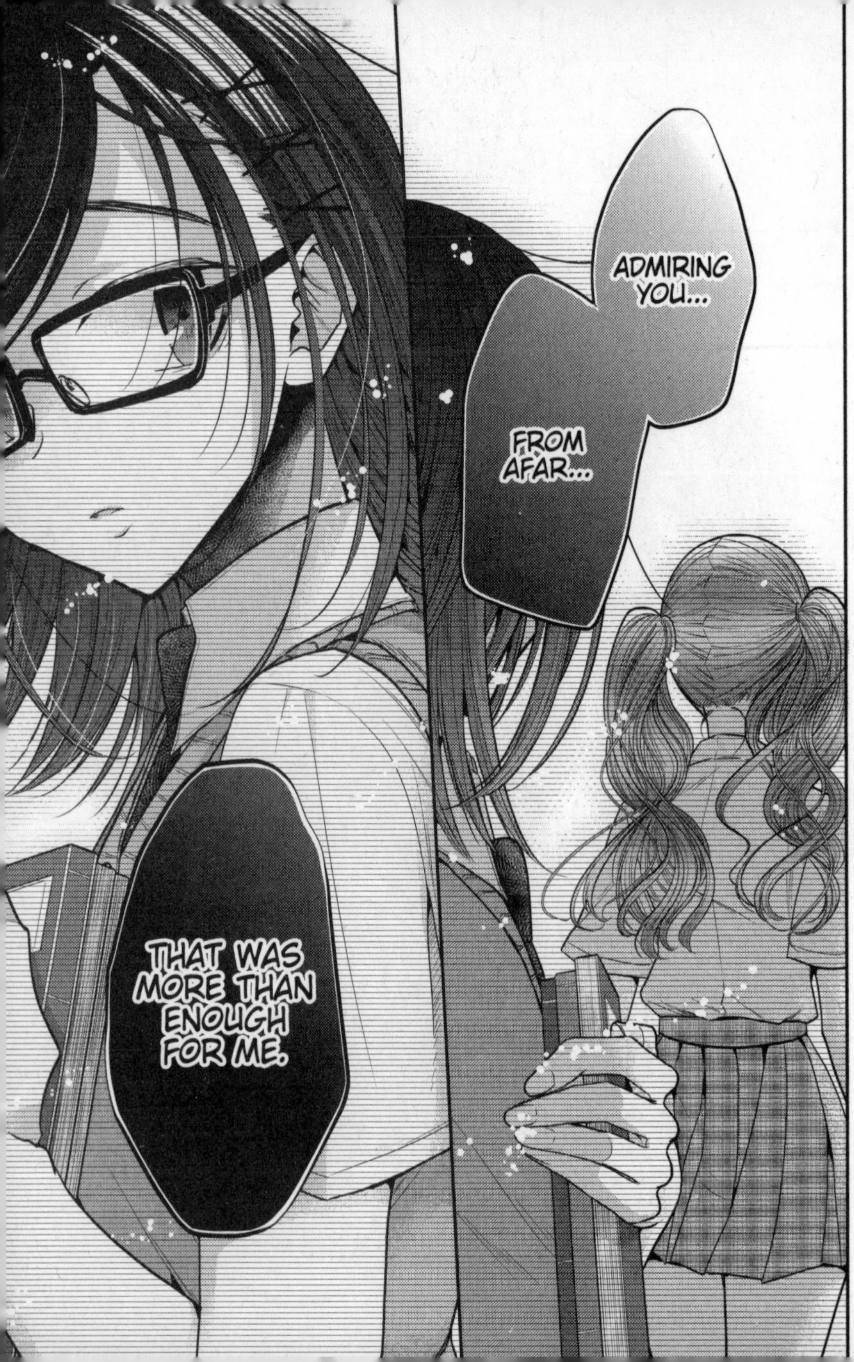
ADMIRING YOU...
FROM AFAR...
THAT WAS MORE THAN ENOUGH FOR ME.

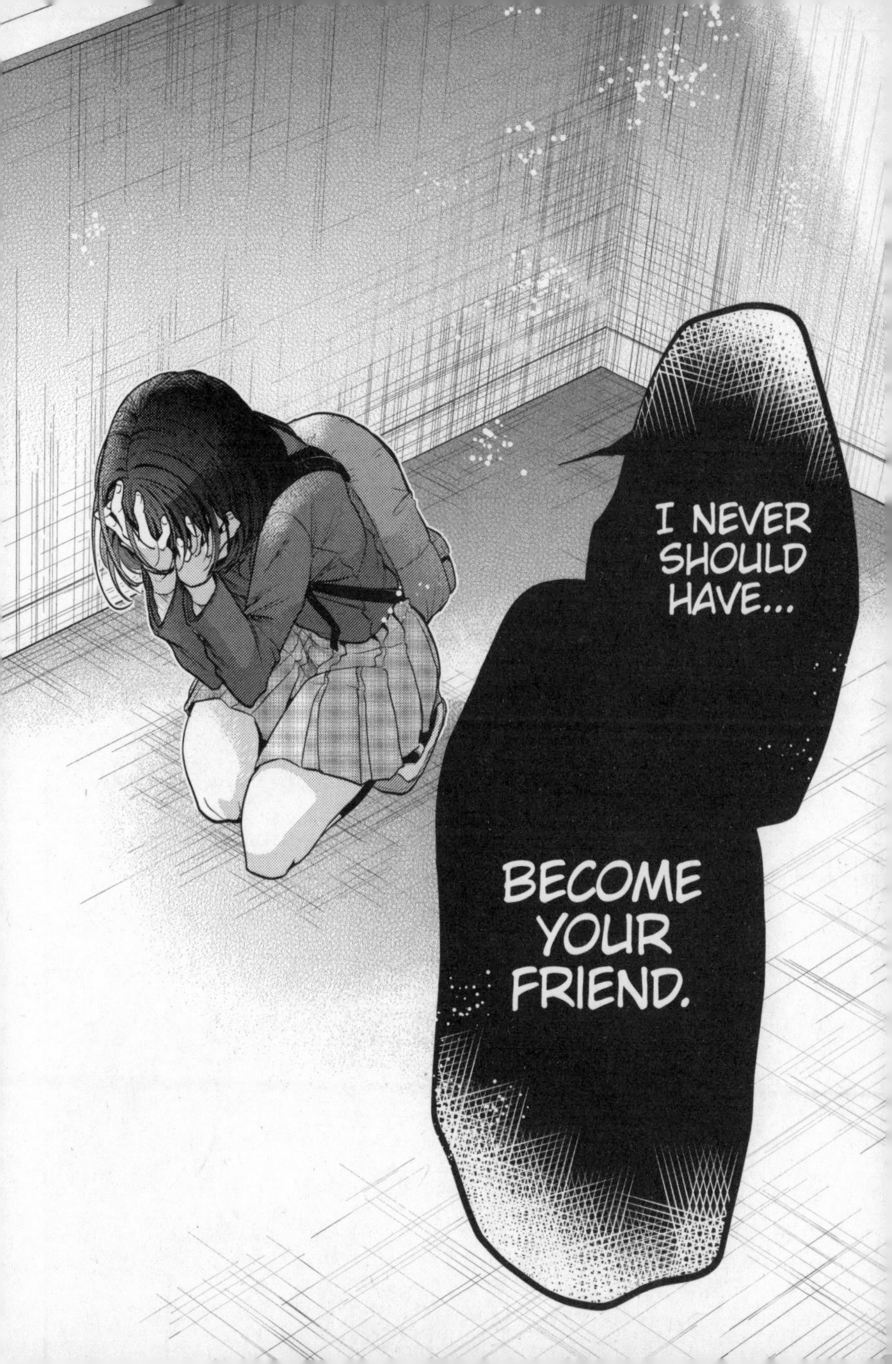
I NEVER SHOULD HAVE...
BECOME YOUR FRIEND.

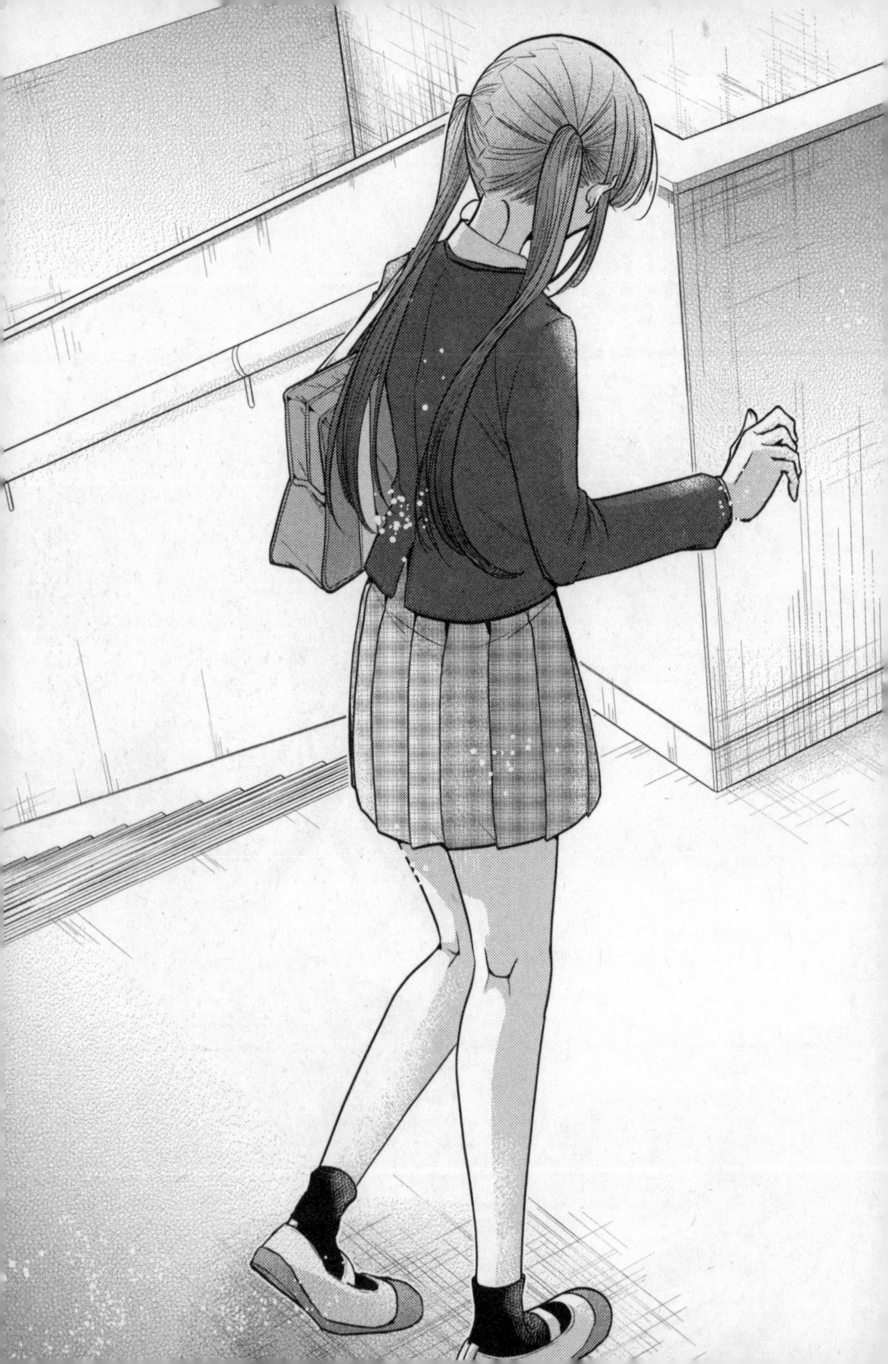

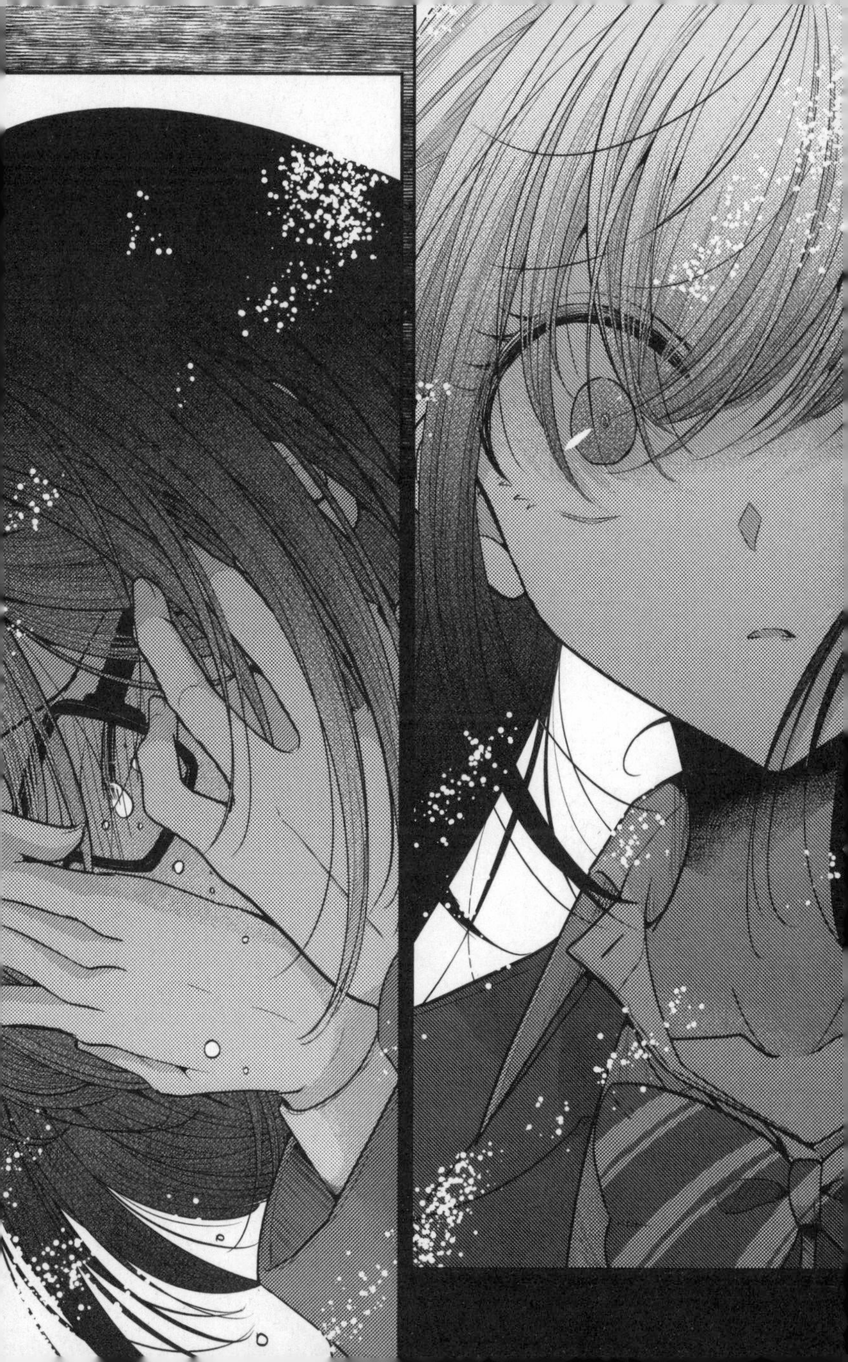

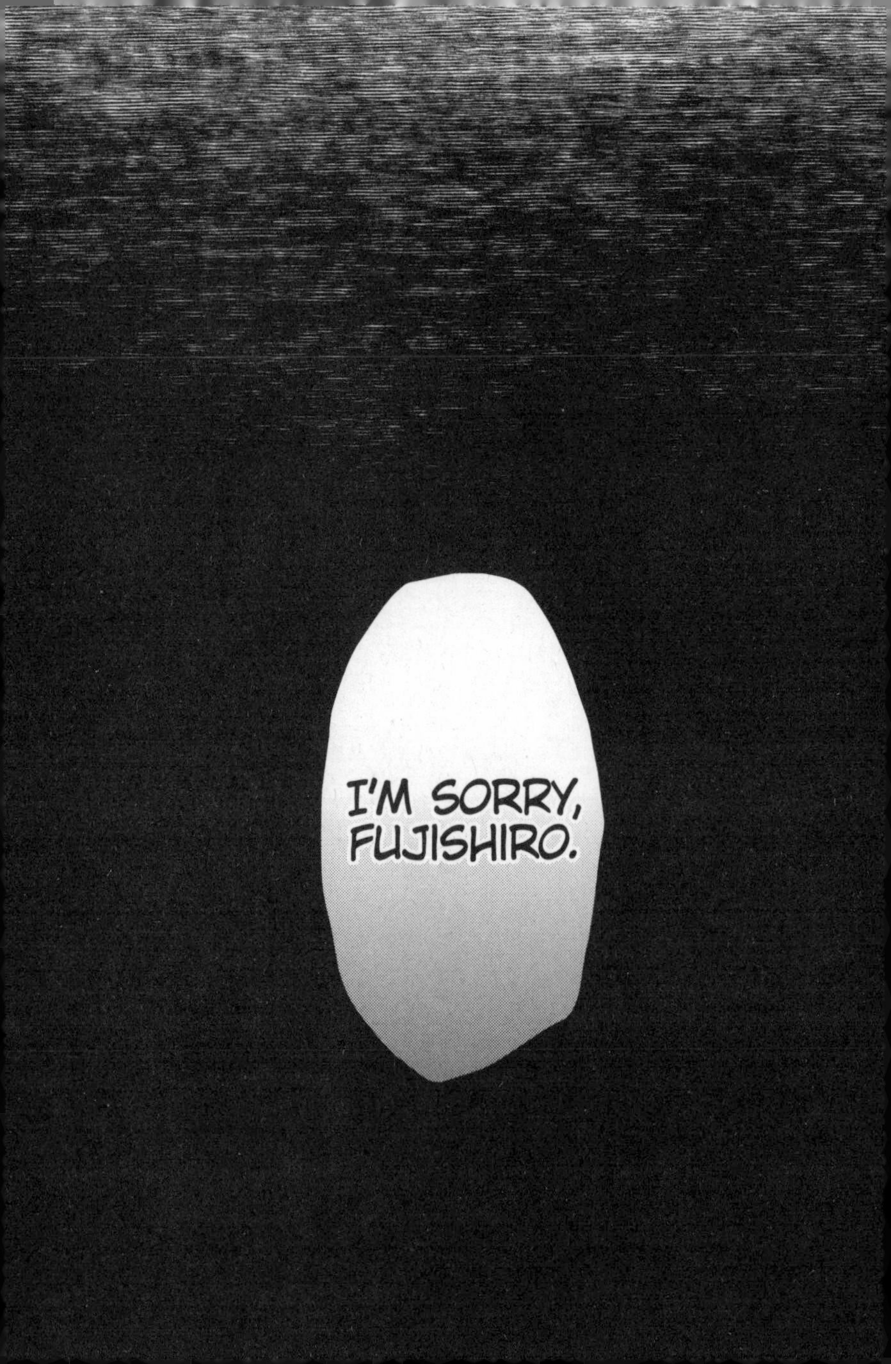
I'M SORRY, FUJISHIRO.

Failed Princesses

CHAPTER 33

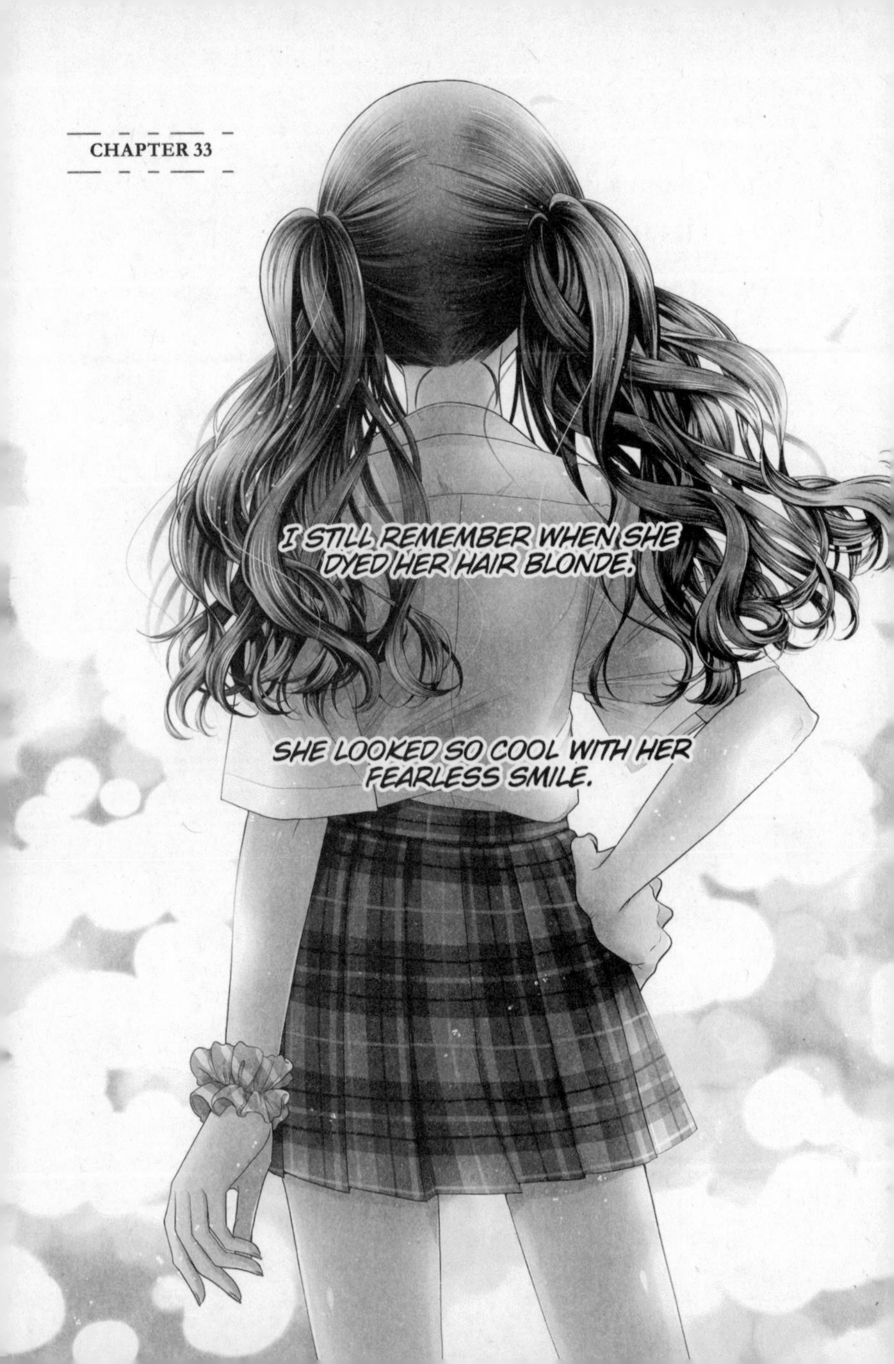
I STILL REMEMBER WHEN SHE DYED HER HAIR BLONDE.
SHE LOOKED SO COOL WITH HER FEARLESS SMILE.

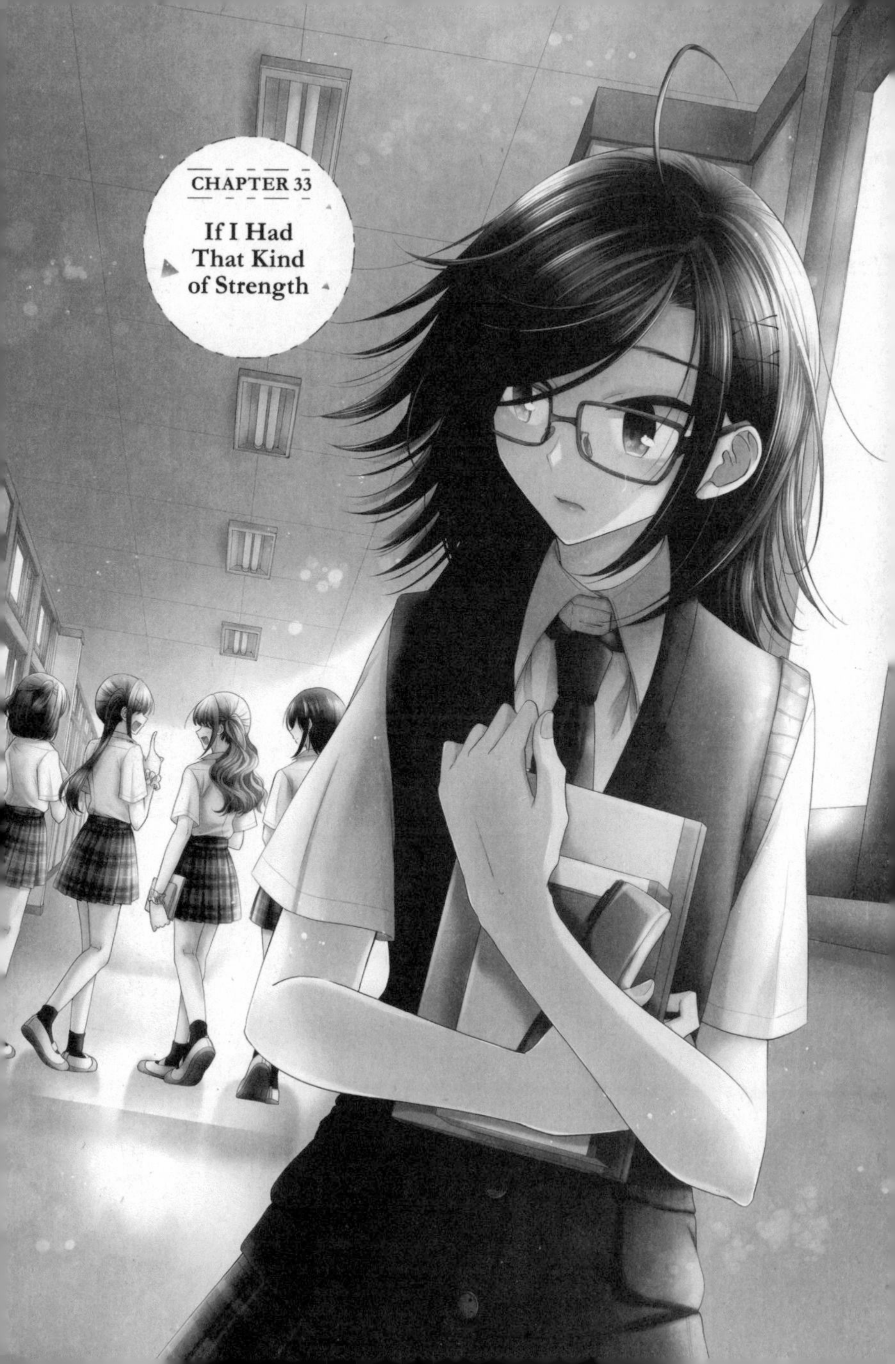
CHAPTER 33
If I Had That Kind of Strength

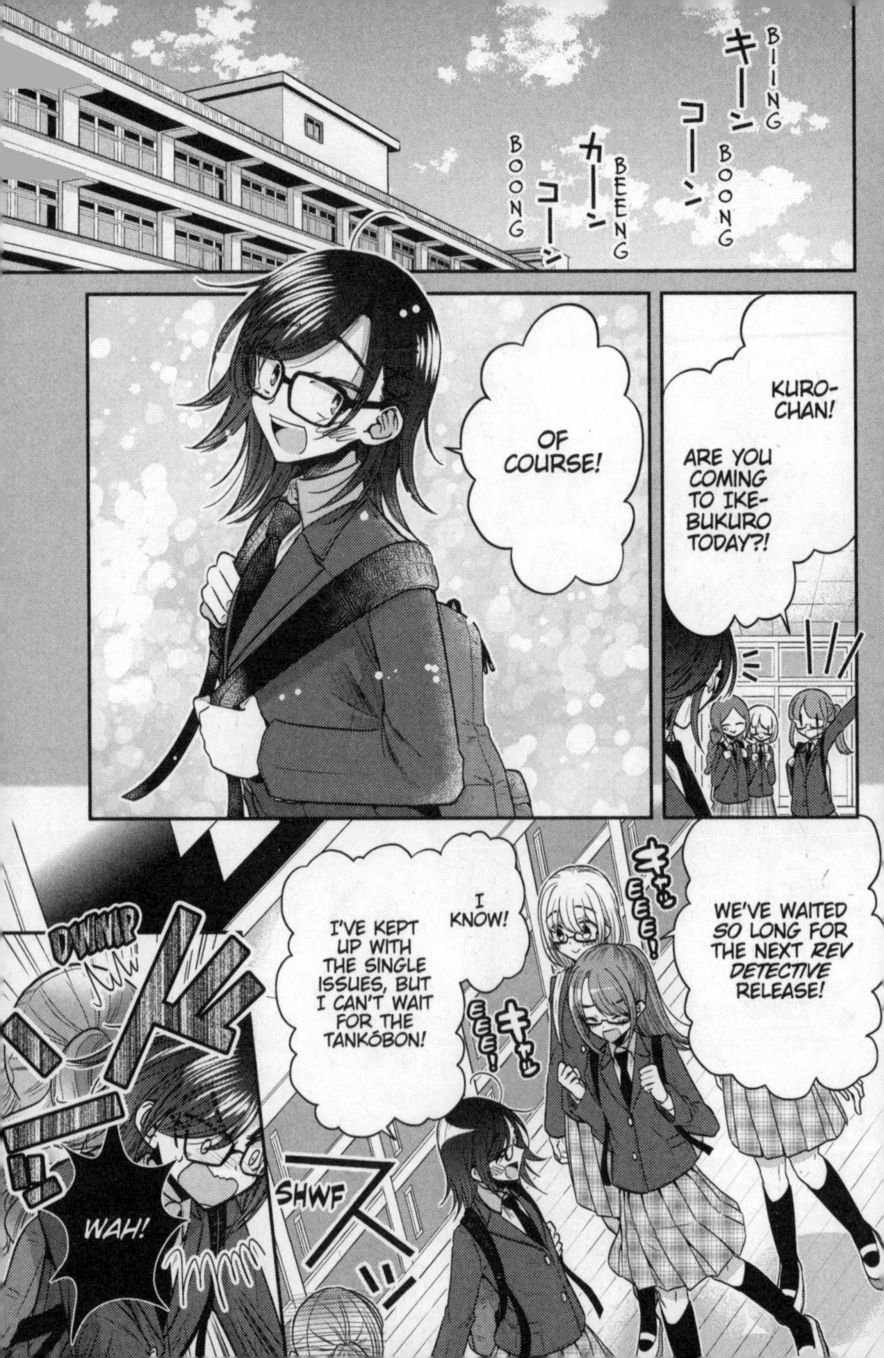
キーンコーン
BIING BOONG
カーンコーン
BEEENG BOONG
KURO-CHAN!
ARE YOU COMING TO IKE-BUKURO TODAY?!
OF COURSE!
WE'VE WAITED SO LONG FOR THE NEXT *REV DETECTIVE* RELEASE!
キャー
EEEE!
I KNOW!
I'VE KEPT UP WITH THE SINGLE ISSUES, BUT I CAN'T WAIT FOR THE TANKŌBON!
キャー
EEEE!
SHWF
DWNP
WAH!

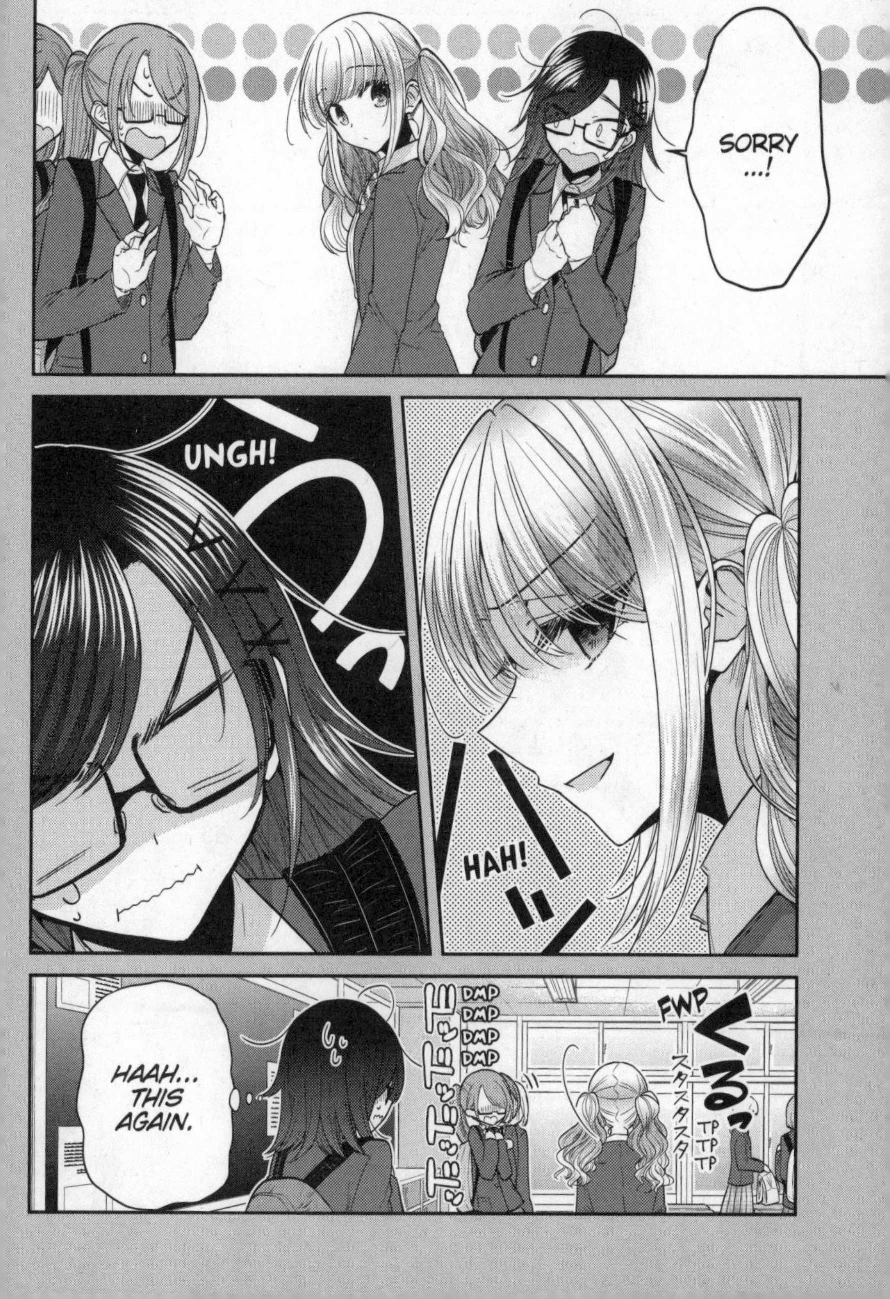
SORRY ...!
HAH!
UNGH!
FWP
くるっ
TP TP TP
スタスタ
DMP DMP DMP DMP
HAAH... THIS AGAIN.

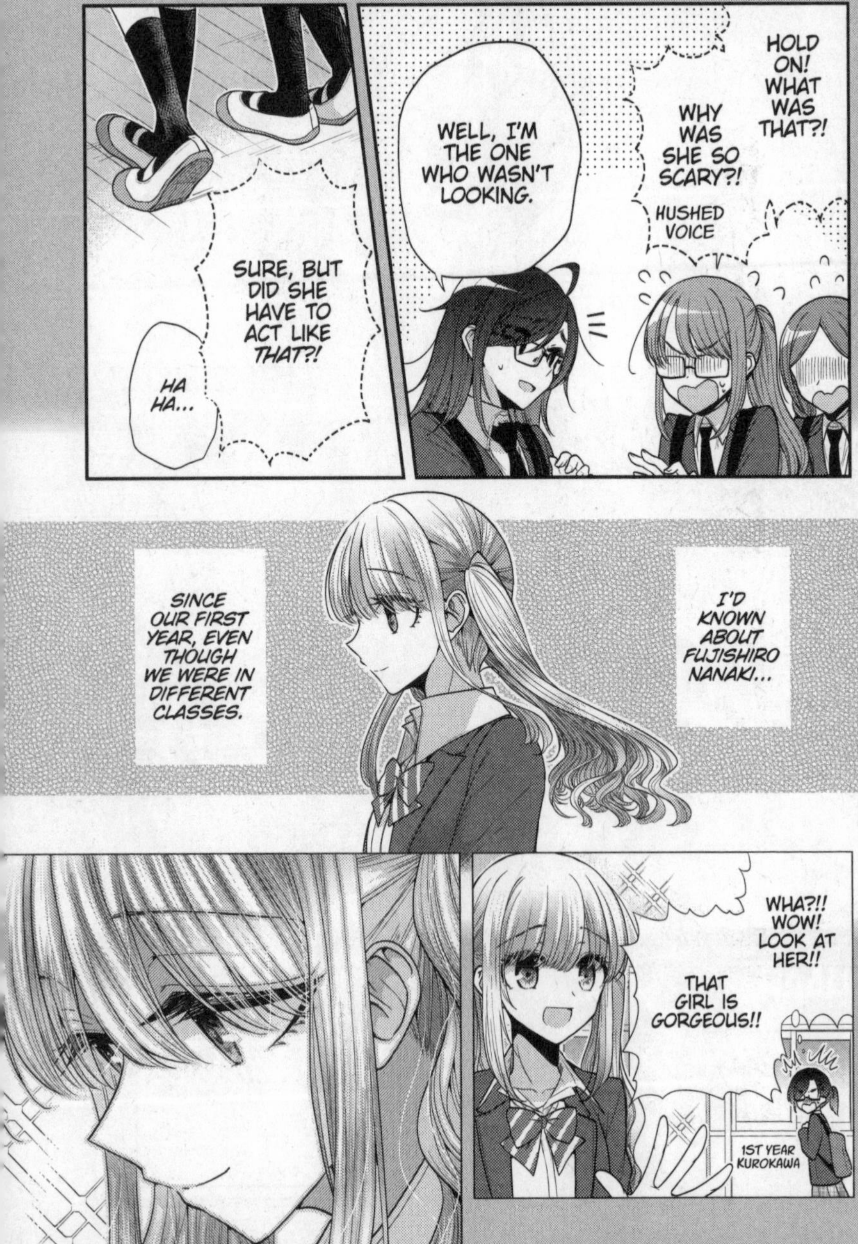
HOLD ON! WHAT WAS THAT?!
WHY WAS SHE SO SCARY?!
HUSHED VOICE
WELL, I'M THE ONE WHO WASN'T LOOKING.
SURE, BUT DID SHE HAVE TO ACT LIKE THAT?!
HA HA...
I'D KNOWN ABOUT FUJISHIRO NANAKI...
SINCE OUR FIRST YEAR, EVEN THOUGH WE WERE IN DIFFERENT CLASSES.
WHA?!! WOW! LOOK AT HER!!
THAT GIRL IS GORGEOUS!!
1ST YEAR KUROKAWA

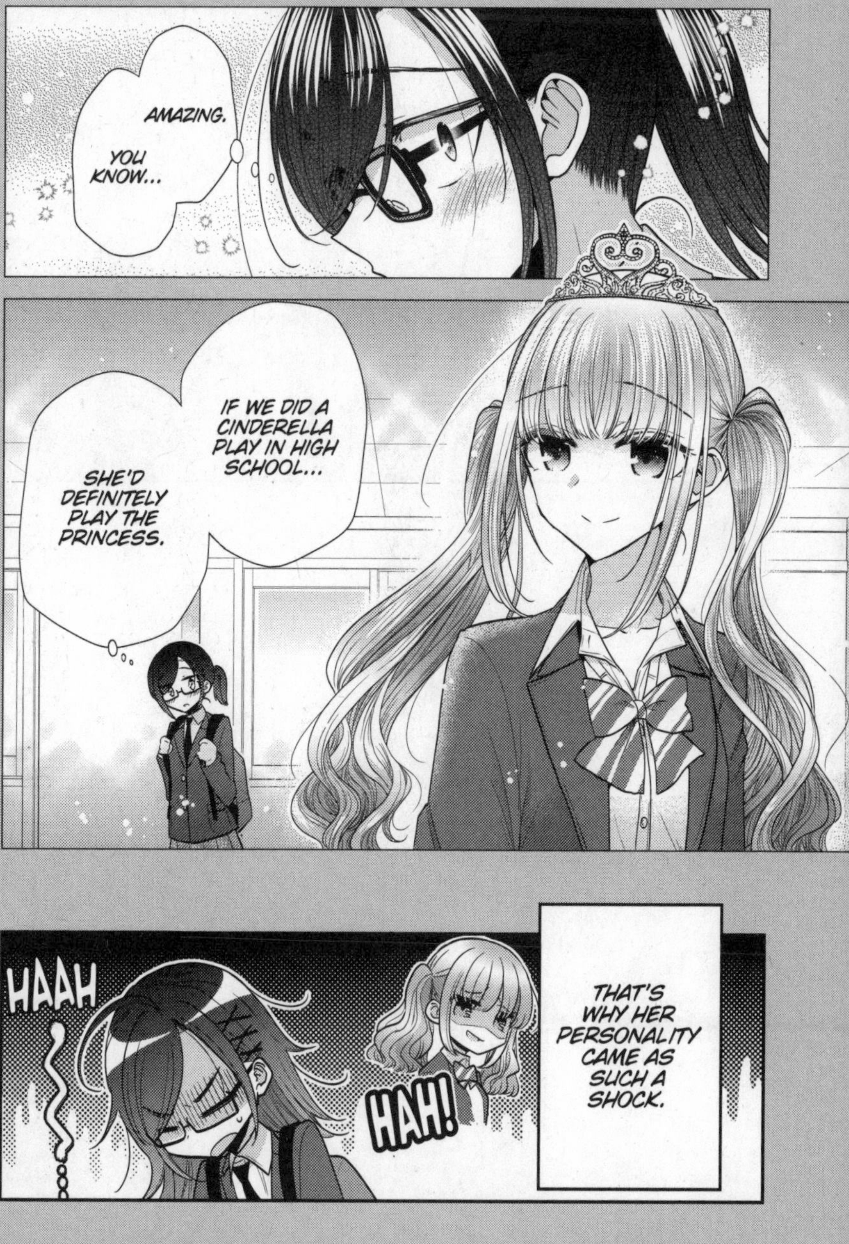

AMAZING.
YOU KNOW...
IF WE DID A CINDERELLA PLAY IN HIGH SCHOOL...
SHE'D DEFINITELY PLAY THE PRINCESS.
THAT'S WHY HER PERSONALITY CAME AS SUCH A SHOCK.
HAH!
HAAH

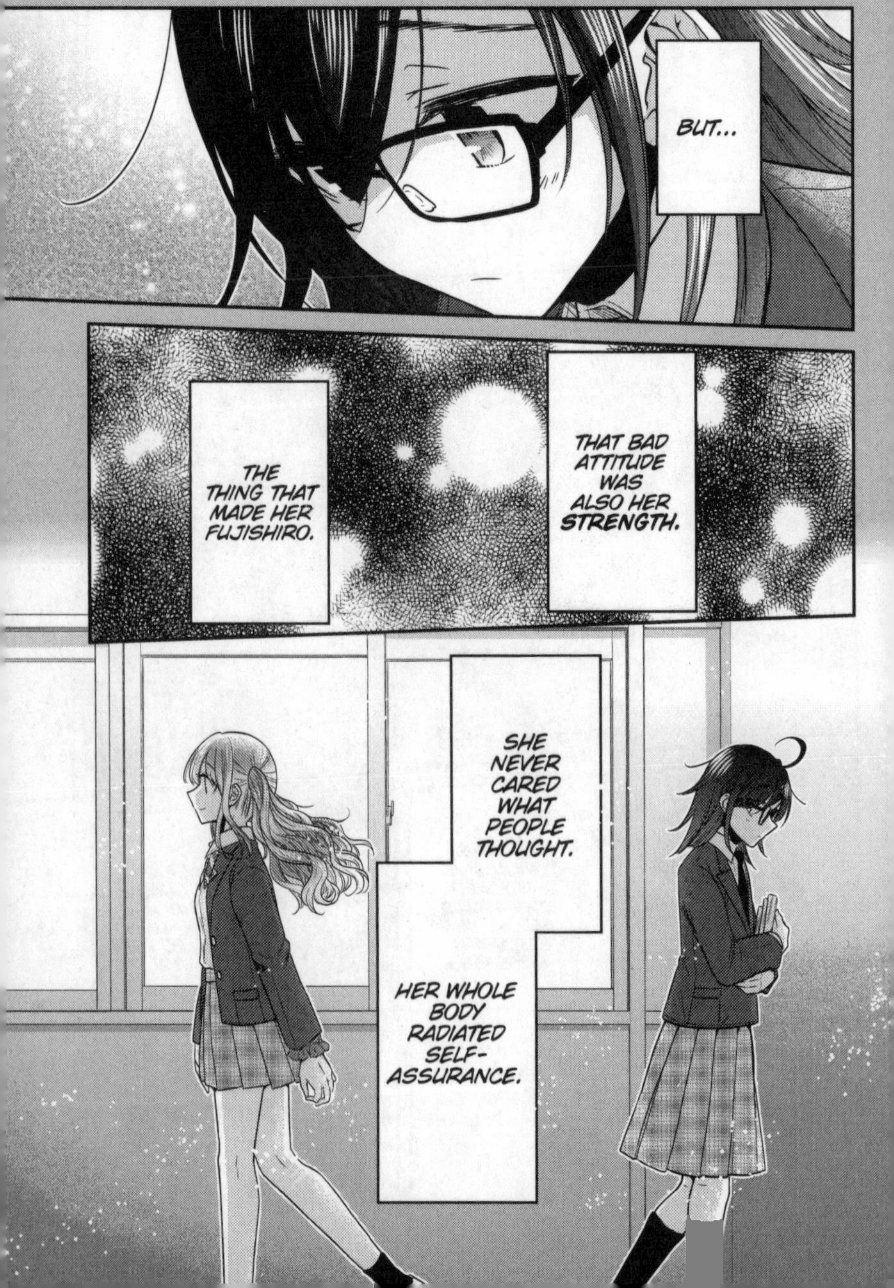
BUT...
THAT BAD ATTITUDE WAS ALSO HER STRENGTH.
THE THING THAT MADE HER FUJISHIRO.
SHE NEVER CARED WHAT PEOPLE THOUGHT.
HER WHOLE BODY RADIATED SELF-ASSURANCE.

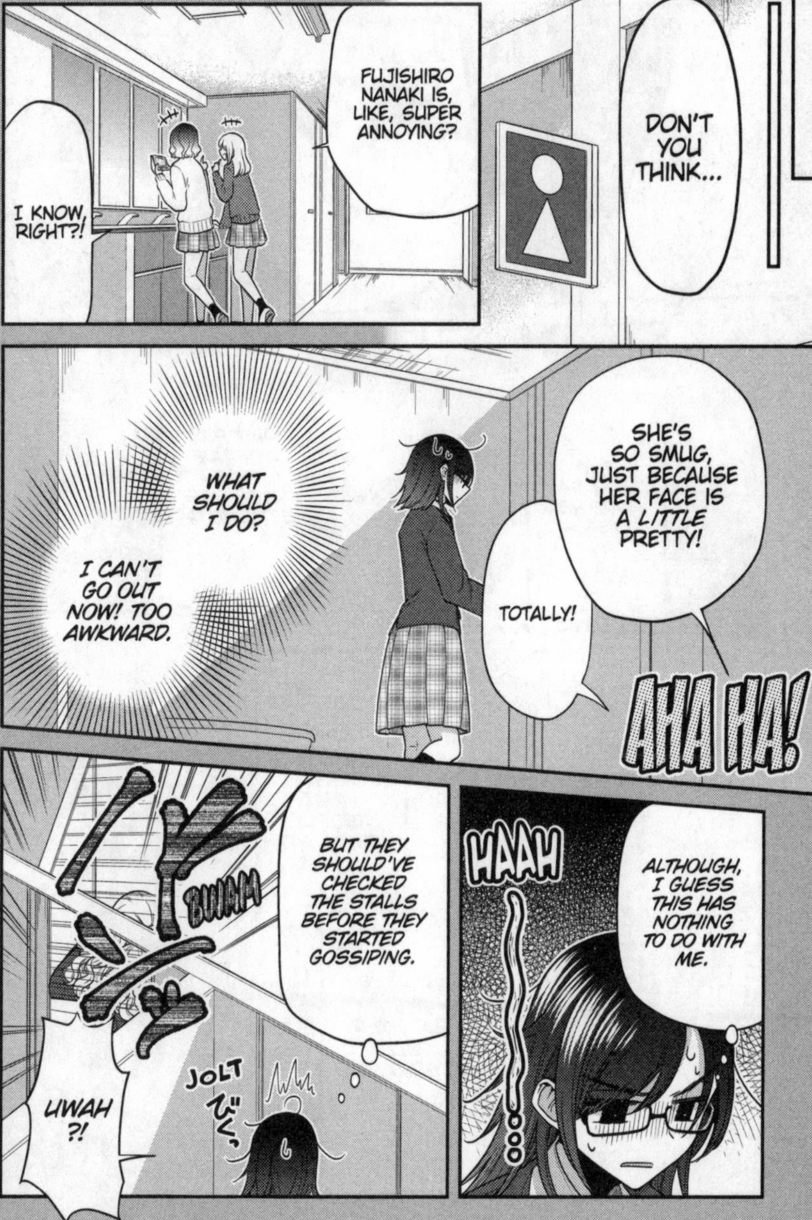
DON'T YOU THINK...
FUJISHIRO NANAKI IS, LIKE, SUPER ANNOYING?
I KNOW, RIGHT?!
SHE'S SO SMUG, JUST BECAUSE HER FACE IS A *LITTLE* PRETTY!
TOTALLY!
AHA HA!
WHAT SHOULD I DO?
I CAN'T GO OUT NOW! TOO AWKWARD.
HAAH
ALTHOUGH, I GUESS THIS HAS NOTHING TO DO WITH ME.
BUT THEY SHOULD'VE CHECKED THE STALLS BEFORE THEY STARTED GOSSIPING.
BWAM
UWAH ?!
JOLT

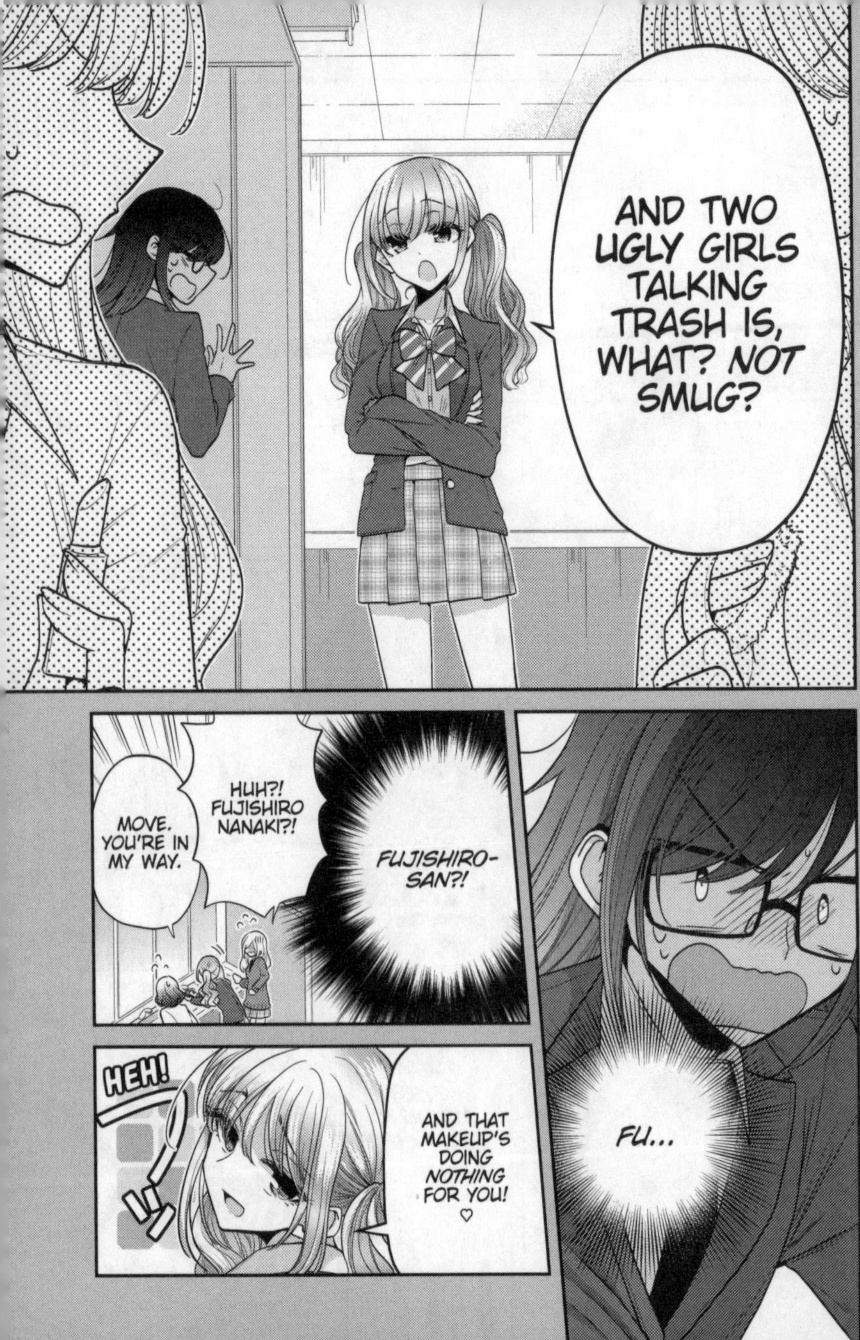
AND TWO UGLY GIRLS TALKING TRASH IS, WHAT? NOT SMUG?
FU...
FUJISHIRO-SAN?!
HUH?! FUJISHIRO NANAKI?!
MOVE. YOU'RE IN MY WAY.
AND THAT MAKEUP'S DOING NOTHING FOR YOU! ♡
HEH!

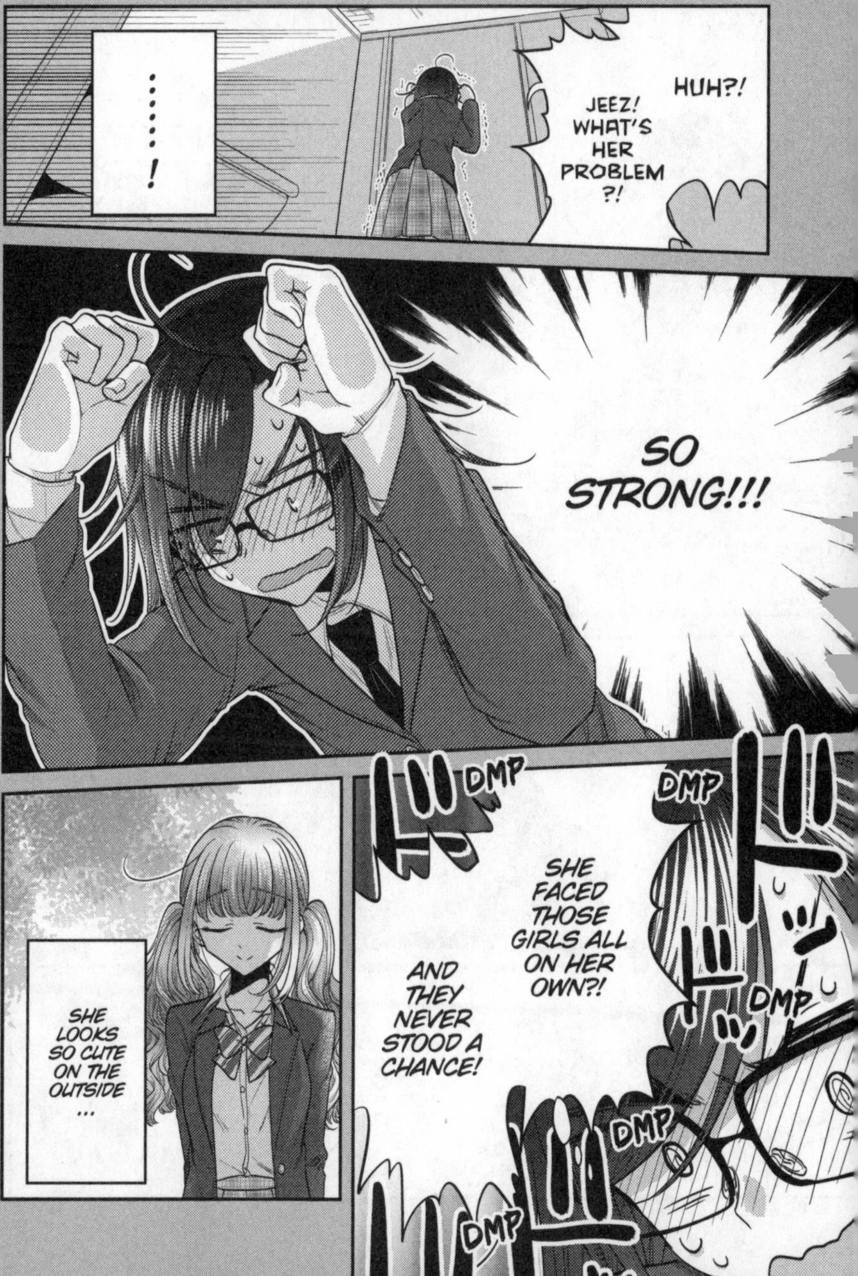
HUH?!
JEEZ! WHAT'S HER PROBLEM?!
......!
SO STRONG!!!
DMP
DMP
SHE FACED THOSE GIRLS ALL ON HER OWN?!
AND THEY NEVER STOOD A CHANCE!
DMP
DMP
DMP
SHE LOOKS SO CUTE ON THE OUTSIDE...

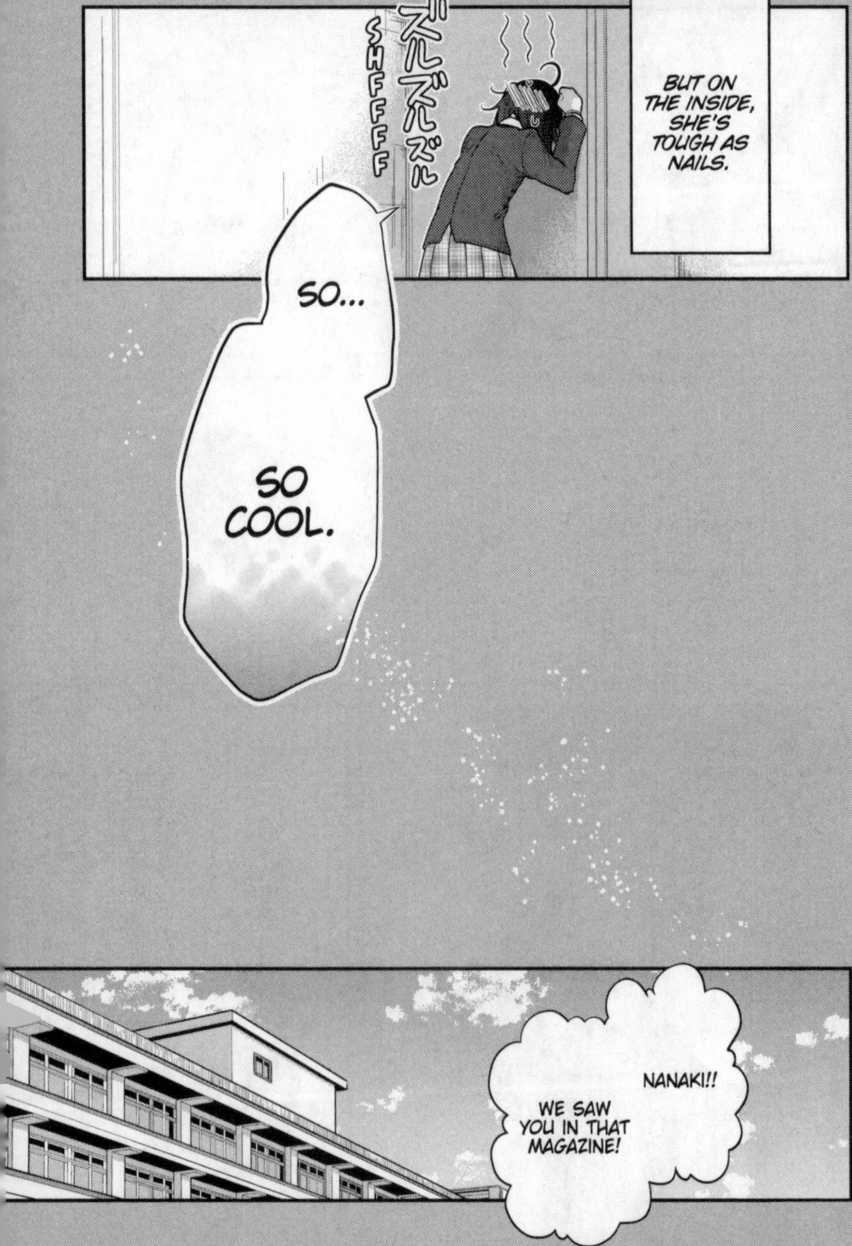
BUT ON THE INSIDE, SHE'S TOUGH AS NAILS.
ズルズルズル
SHFFFF
SO...
SO COOL.
NANAKI!!
WE SAW YOU IN THAT MAGAZINE!

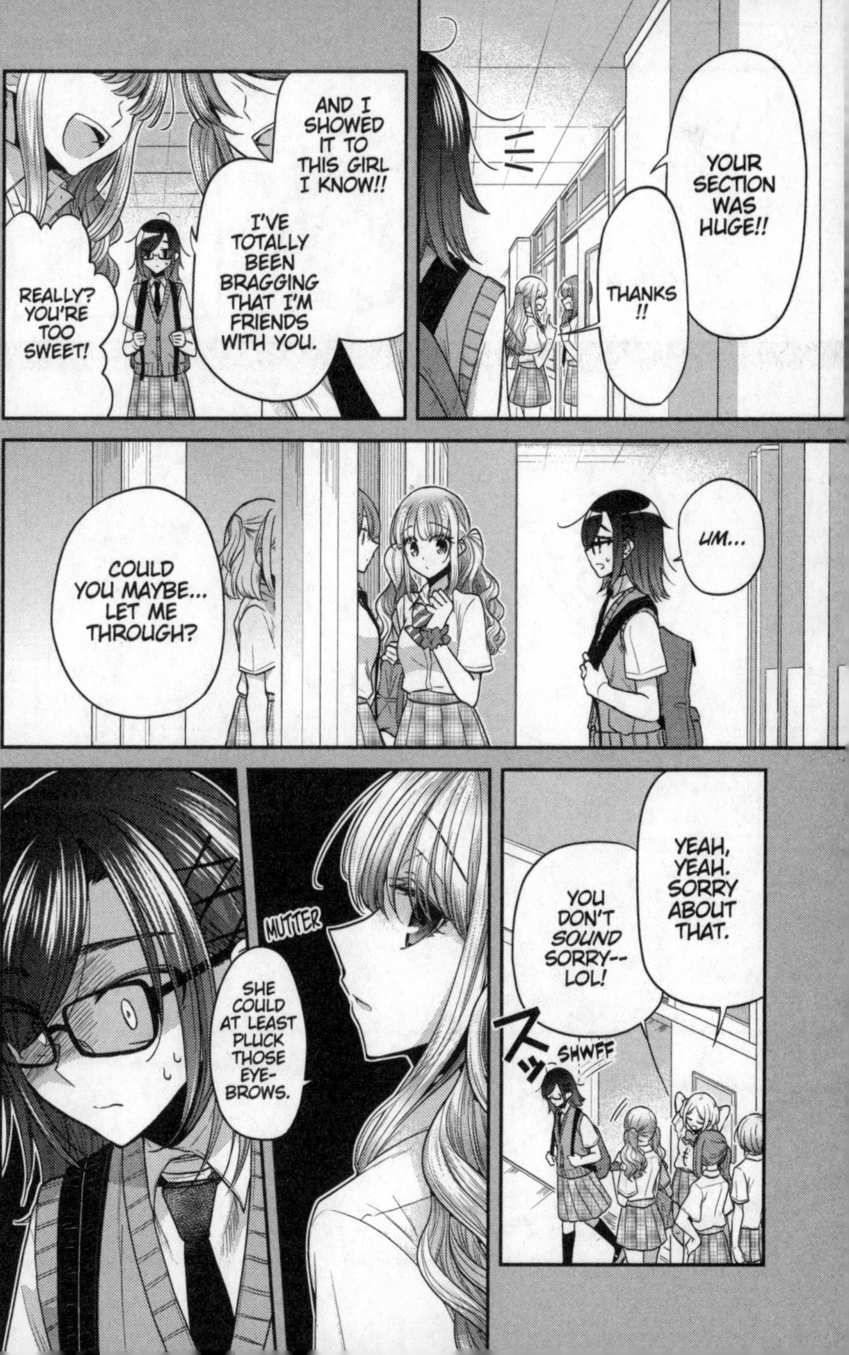

YOUR SECTION WAS HUGE!!
THANKS!!
AND I SHOWED IT TO THIS GIRL I KNOW!!
I'VE TOTALLY BEEN BRAGGING THAT I'M FRIENDS WITH YOU.
REALLY? YOU'RE TOO SWEET!
UM...
COULD YOU MAYBE... LET ME THROUGH?
YEAH, YEAH. SORRY ABOUT THAT.
YOU DON'T SOUND SORRY--LOL!
SHWFF
MUTTER
SHE COULD AT LEAST PLUCK THOSE EYE-BROWS.

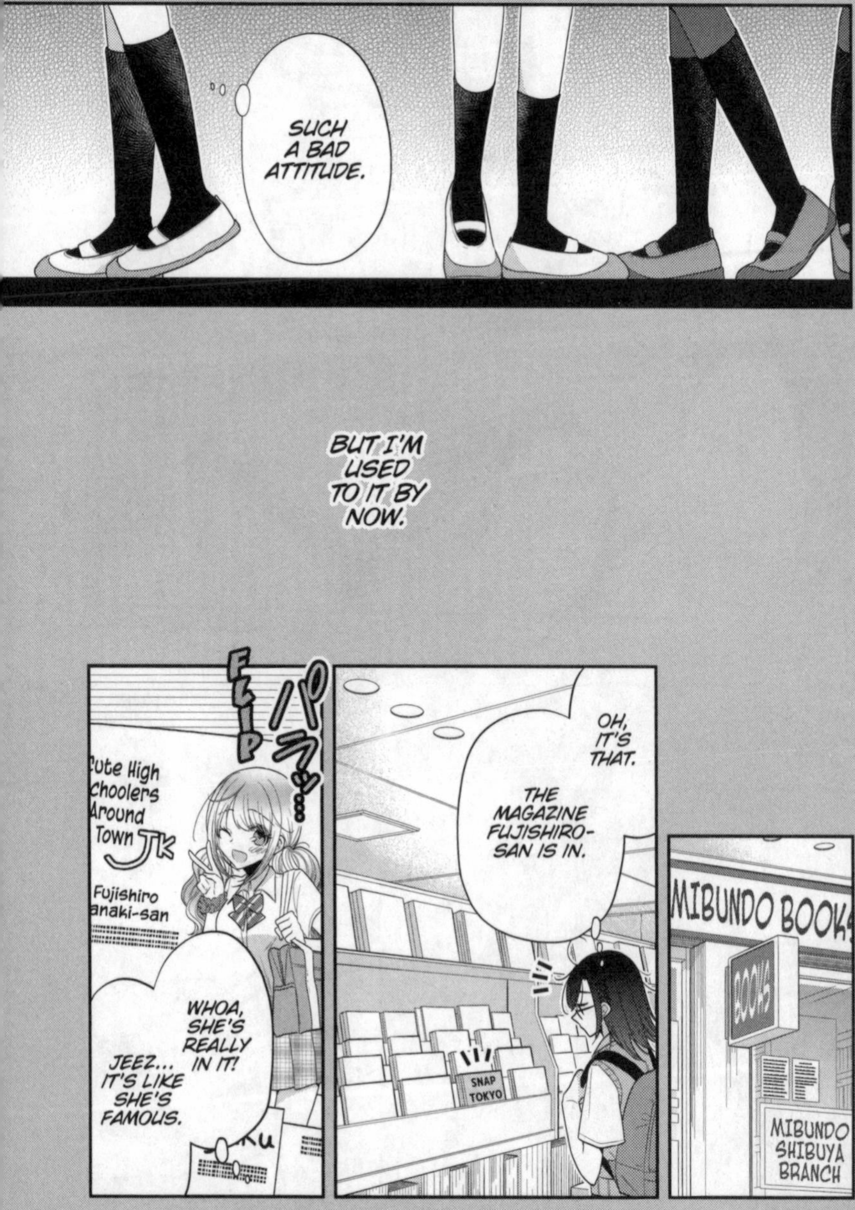
SUCH A BAD ATTITUDE.
BUT I'M USED TO IT BY NOW.
MIBUNDO BOOKS
BOOKS
MIBUNDO SHIBUYA BRANCH
OH, IT'S THAT.
THE MAGAZINE FUJISHIRO-SAN IS IN.
SNAP TOKYO
FLIP
ute High choolers Around Town JK
Fujishiro anaki-san
WHOA, SHE'S REALLY IN IT!
JEEZ... IT'S LIKE SHE'S FAMOUS.

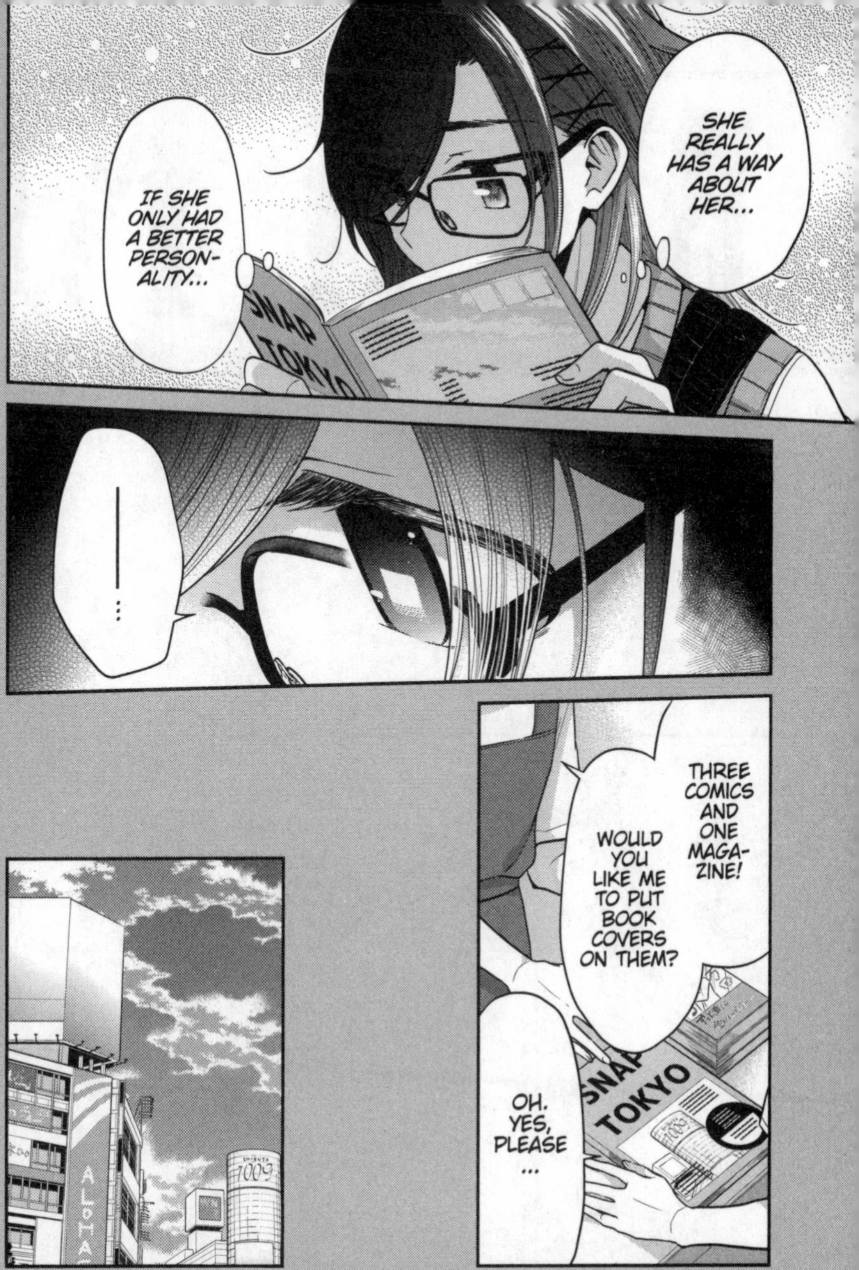
SHE REALLY HAS A WAY ABOUT HER...
IF SHE ONLY HAD A BETTER PERSON-ALITY...
SNAP TOKYO
―――...
THREE COMICS AND ONE MAGA-ZINE!
WOULD YOU LIKE ME TO PUT BOOK COVERS ON THEM?
OH. YES, PLEASE ...
SNAP TOKYO

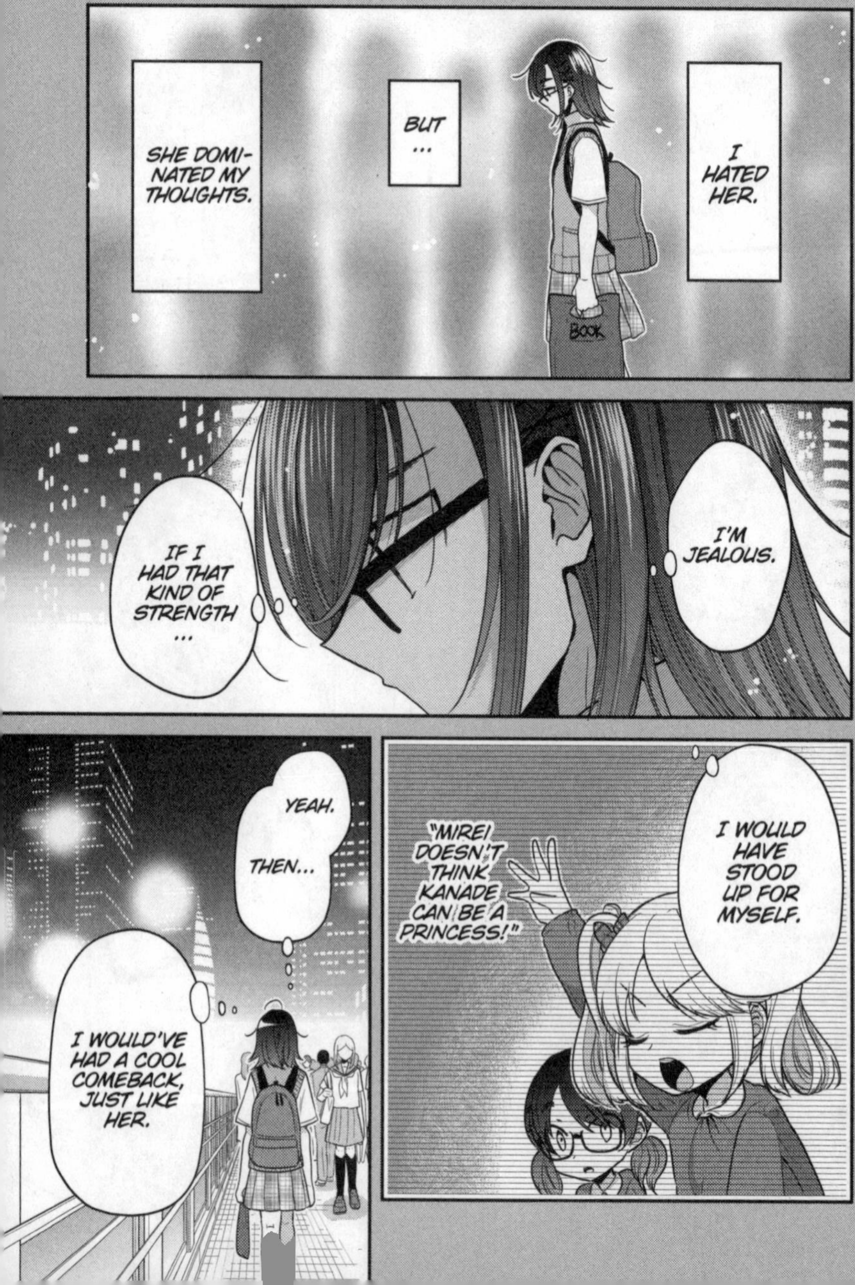
I HATED HER.
BUT ...
SHE DOMINATED MY THOUGHTS.
I'M JEALOUS.
IF I HAD THAT KIND OF STRENGTH ...
I WOULD HAVE STOOD UP FOR MYSELF.
"MIREI DOESN'T THINK KANADE CAN BE A PRINCESS!"
YEAH.
THEN...
I WOULD'VE HAD A COOL COMEBACK, JUST LIKE HER.

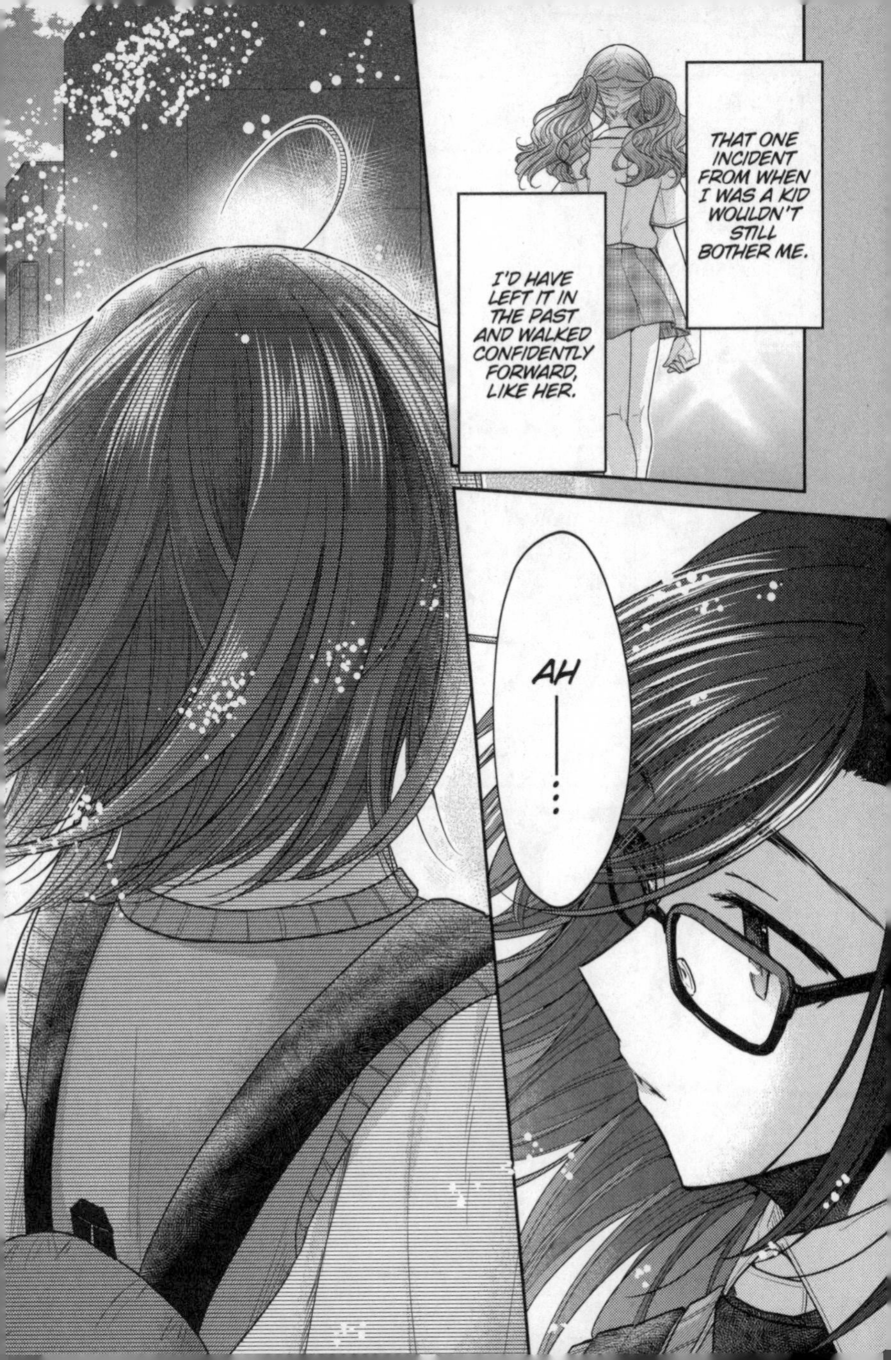
THAT ONE INCIDENT FROM WHEN I WAS A KID WOULDN'T STILL BOTHER ME.
I'D HAVE LEFT IT IN THE PAST AND WALKED CONFIDENTLY FORWARD, LIKE HER.
AH —...

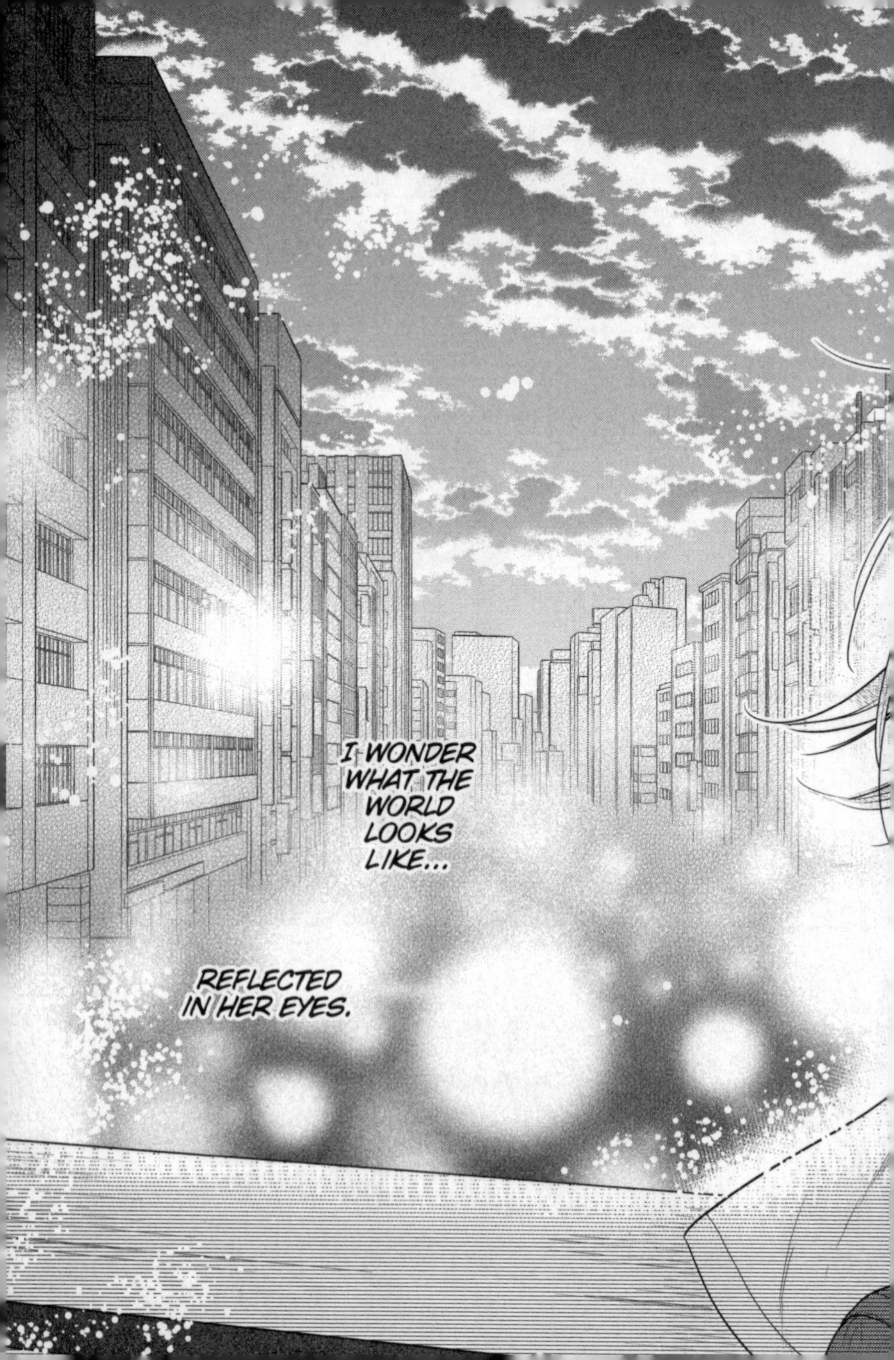
I WONDER WHAT THE WORLD LOOKS LIKE...
REFLECTED IN HER EYES.

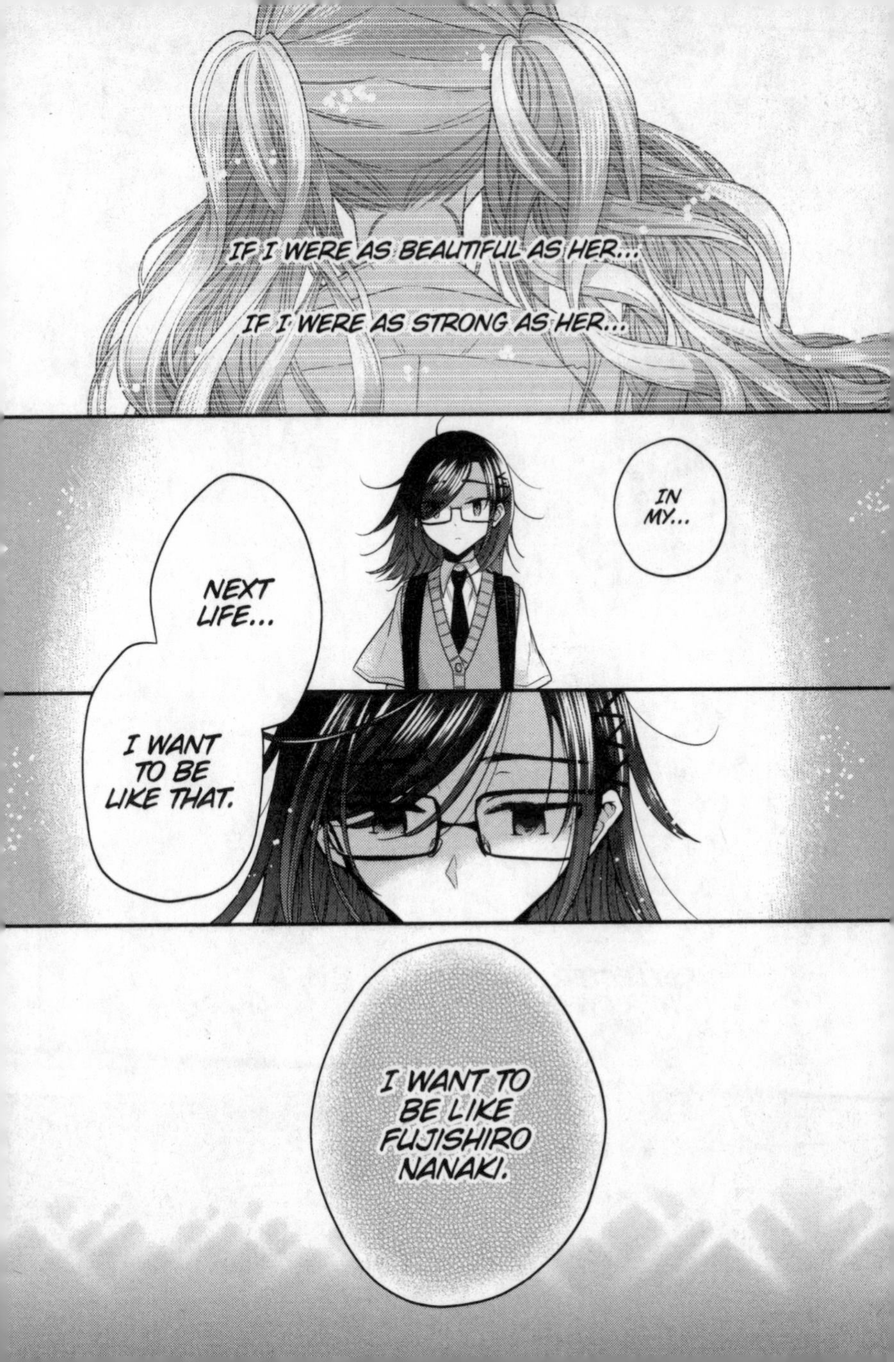
IF I WERE AS BEAUTIFUL AS HER...
IF I WERE AS STRONG AS HER...
IN MY...
NEXT LIFE...
I WANT TO BE LIKE THAT.
I WANT TO BE LIKE FUJISHIRO NANAKI.

Chapter 34

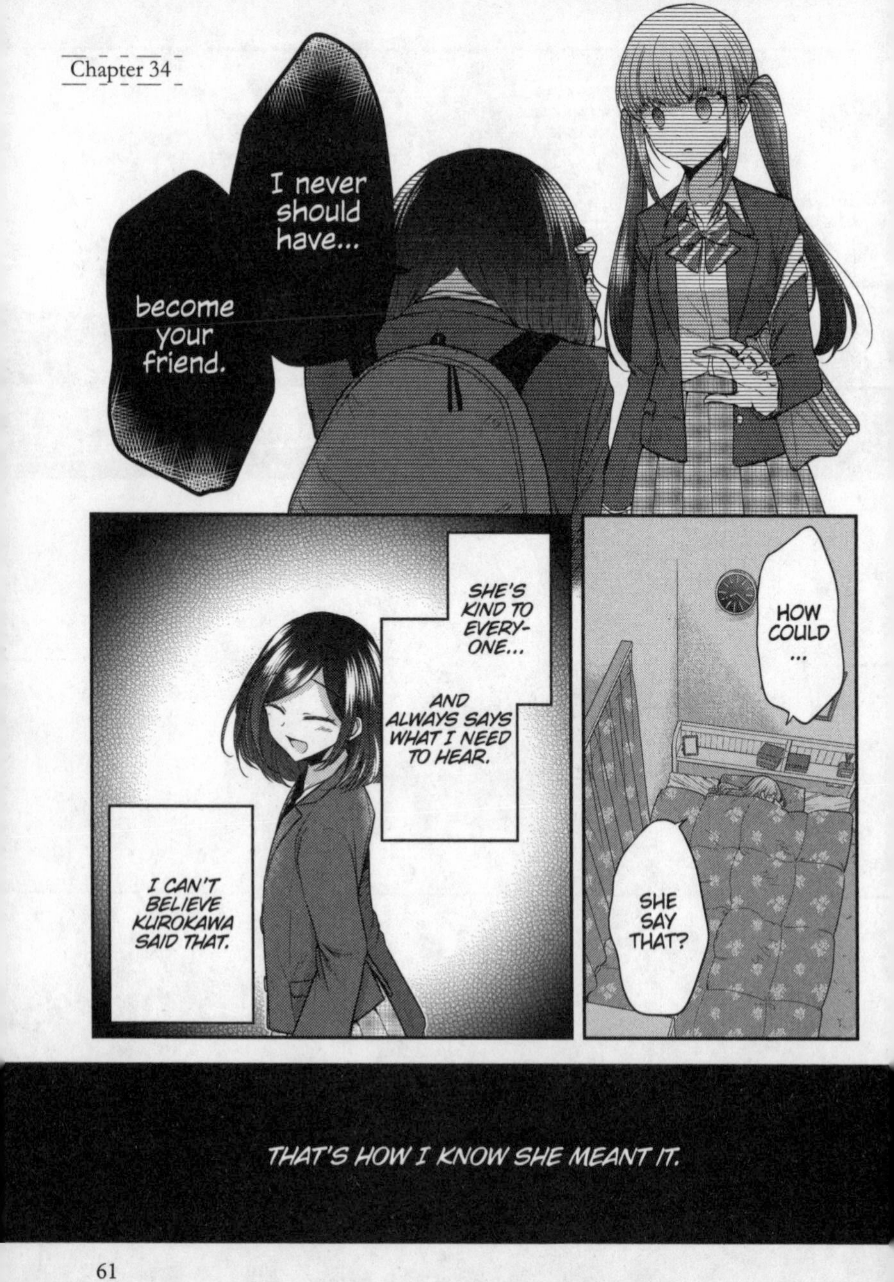
I never should have...
become your friend.
HOW COULD ...
SHE SAY THAT?
SHE'S KIND TO EVERY-ONE...
AND ALWAYS SAYS WHAT I NEED TO HEAR.
I CAN'T BELIEVE KUROKAWA SAID THAT.
THAT'S HOW I KNOW SHE MEANT IT.

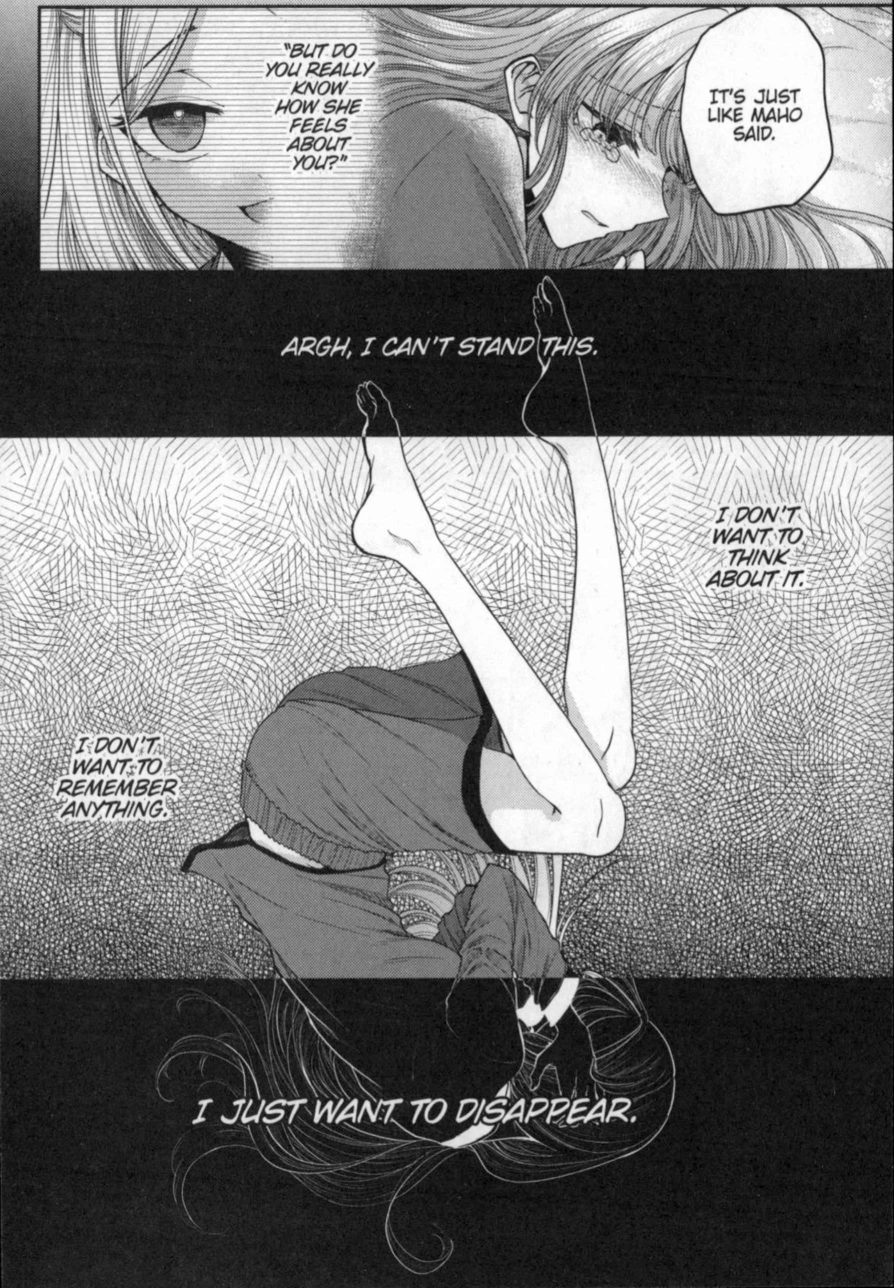
IT'S JUST LIKE MAHO SAID.
"BUT DO YOU REALLY KNOW HOW SHE FEELS ABOUT YOU?"
ARGH, I CAN'T STAND THIS.
I DON'T WANT TO THINK ABOUT IT.
I DON'T WANT TO REMEMBER ANYTHING.
I JUST WANT TO DISAPPEAR.

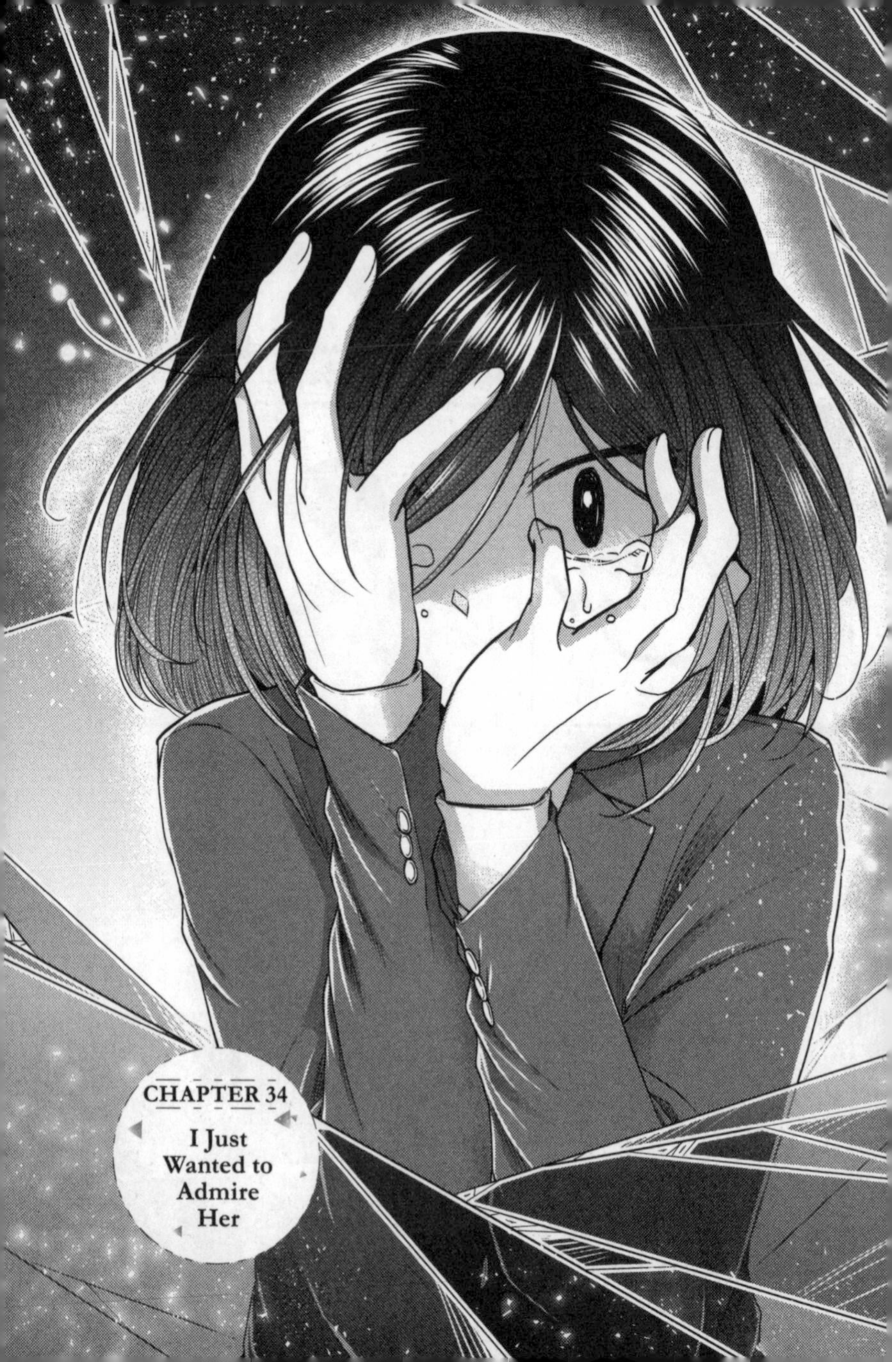
CHAPTER 34
I Just Wanted to Admire Her

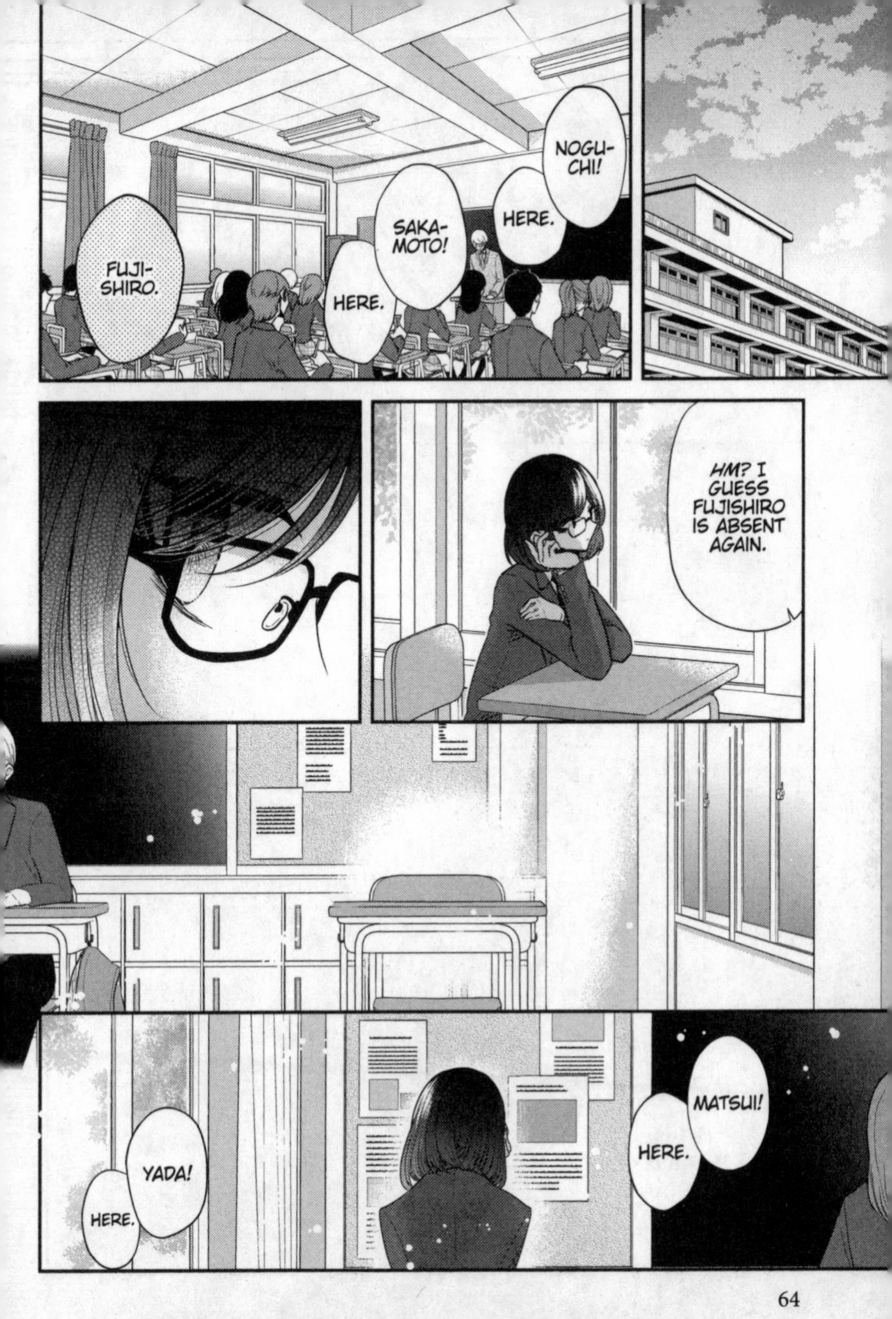
NOGU-CHI!
HERE.
SAKA-MOTO!
HERE.
FUJI-SHIRO.
HM? I GUESS FUJISHIRO IS ABSENT AGAIN.
MATSUI!
HERE.
YADA!
HERE.

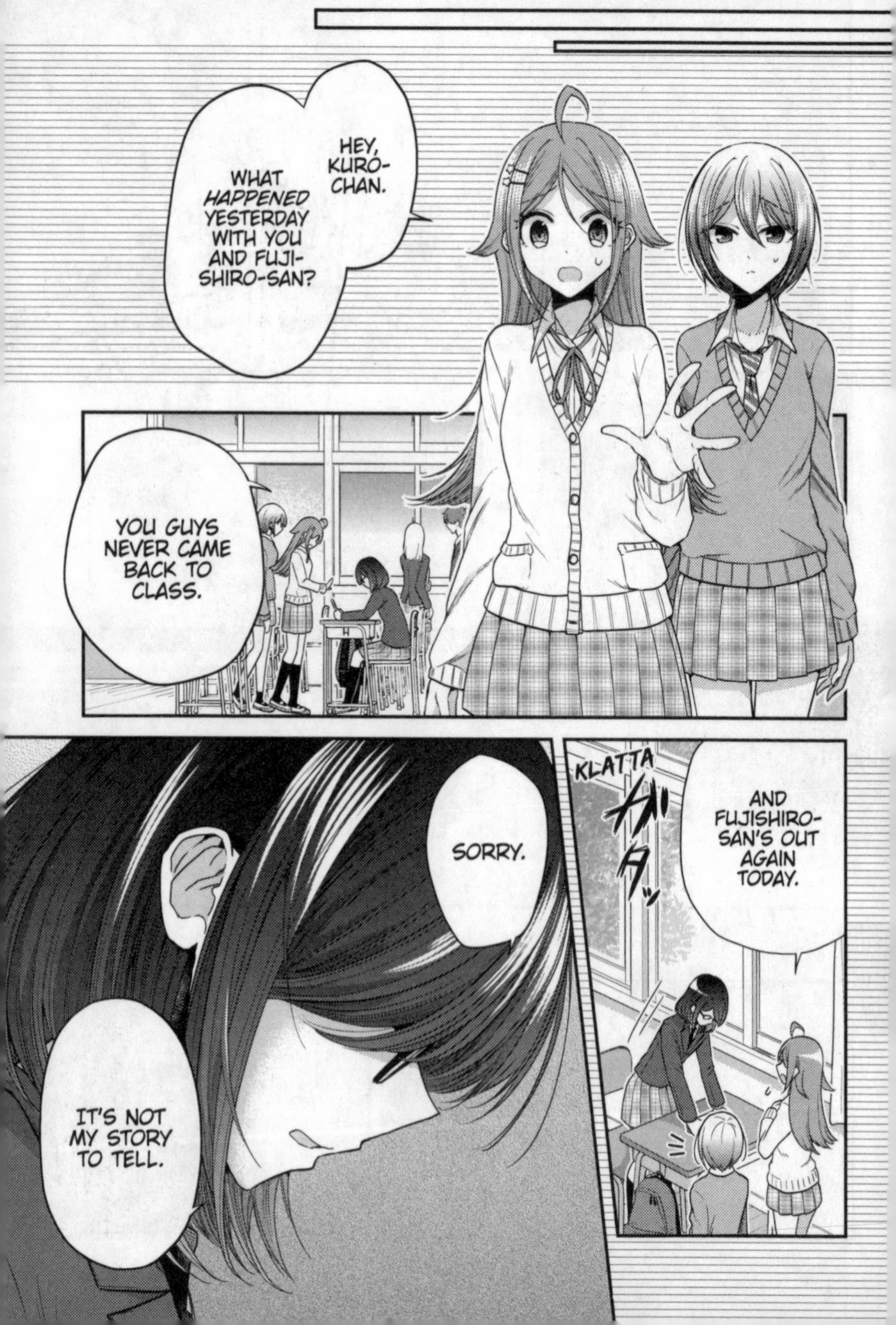
HEY, KURO-CHAN. WHAT HAPPENED YESTERDAY WITH YOU AND FUJI-SHIRO-SAN?
YOU GUYS NEVER CAME BACK TO CLASS.
KLATTA
AND FUJISHIRO-SAN'S OUT AGAIN TODAY.
SORRY.
IT'S NOT MY STORY TO TELL.

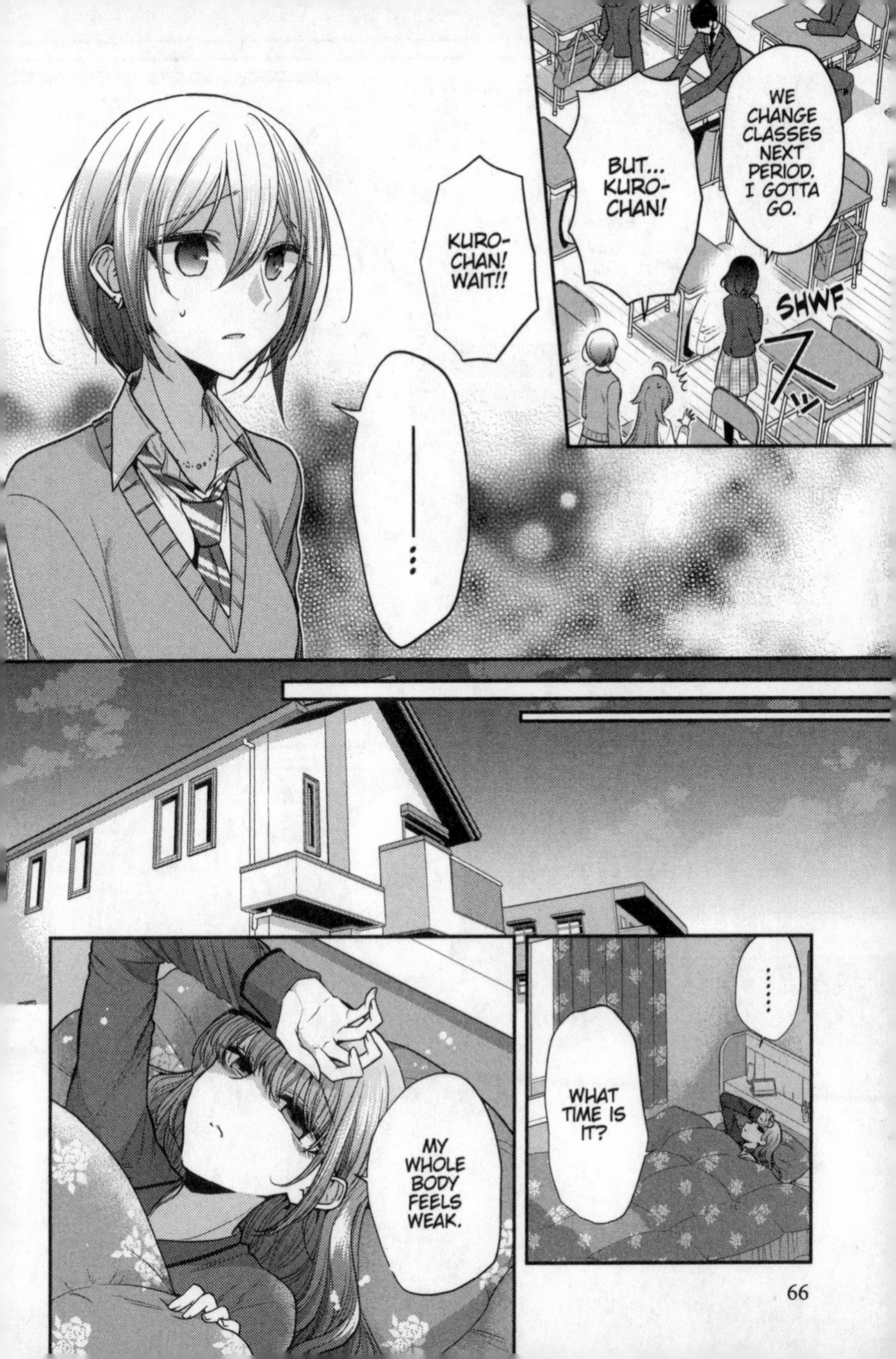
WE CHANGE CLASSES NEXT PERIOD. I GOTTA GO.
BUT... KURO-CHAN!
SHWF
KURO-CHAN! WAIT!!
—...
......
WHAT TIME IS IT?
MY WHOLE BODY FEELS WEAK.

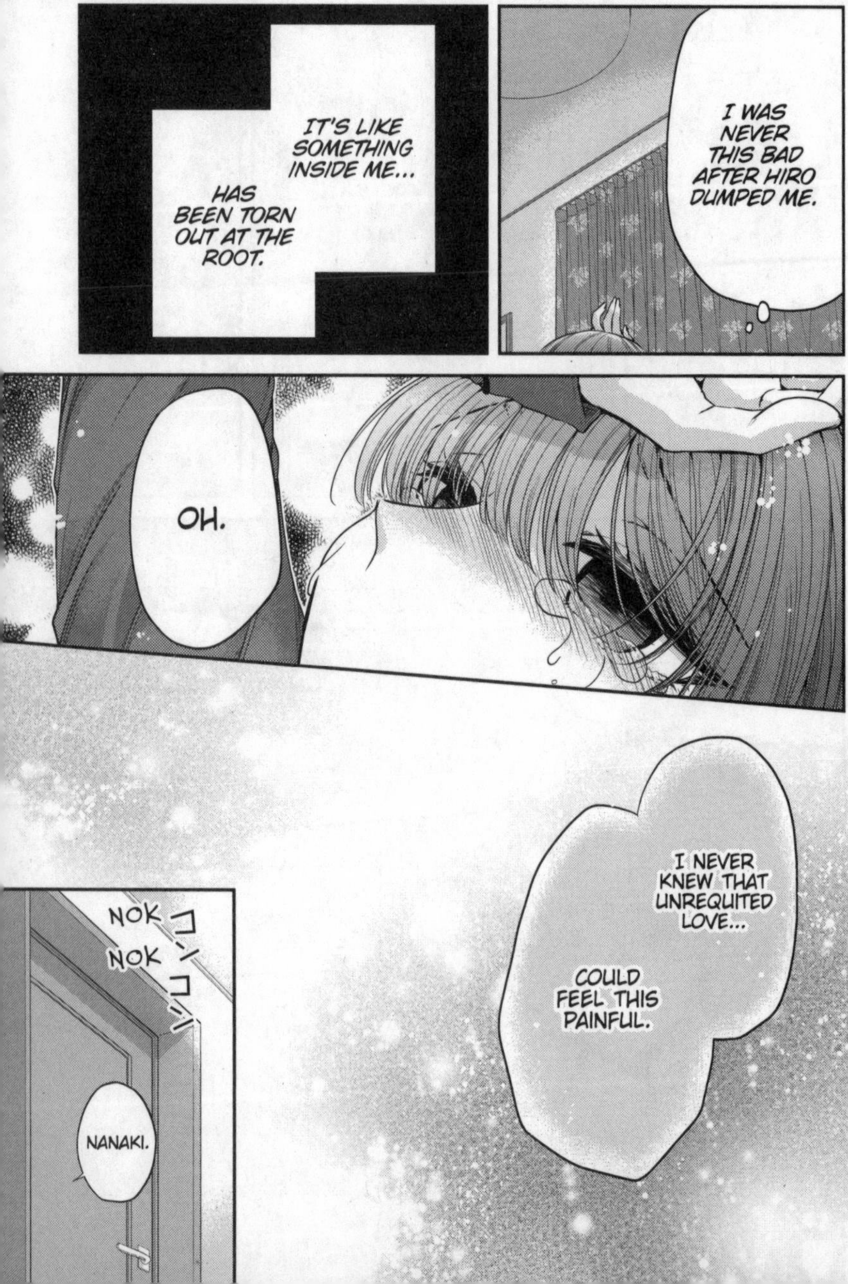
I WAS NEVER THIS BAD AFTER HIRO DUMPED ME.
IT'S LIKE SOMETHING INSIDE ME...
HAS BEEN TORN OUT AT THE ROOT.
OH.
I NEVER KNEW THAT UNREQUITED LOVE...
COULD FEEL THIS PAINFUL.
NOK NOK
NANAKI.

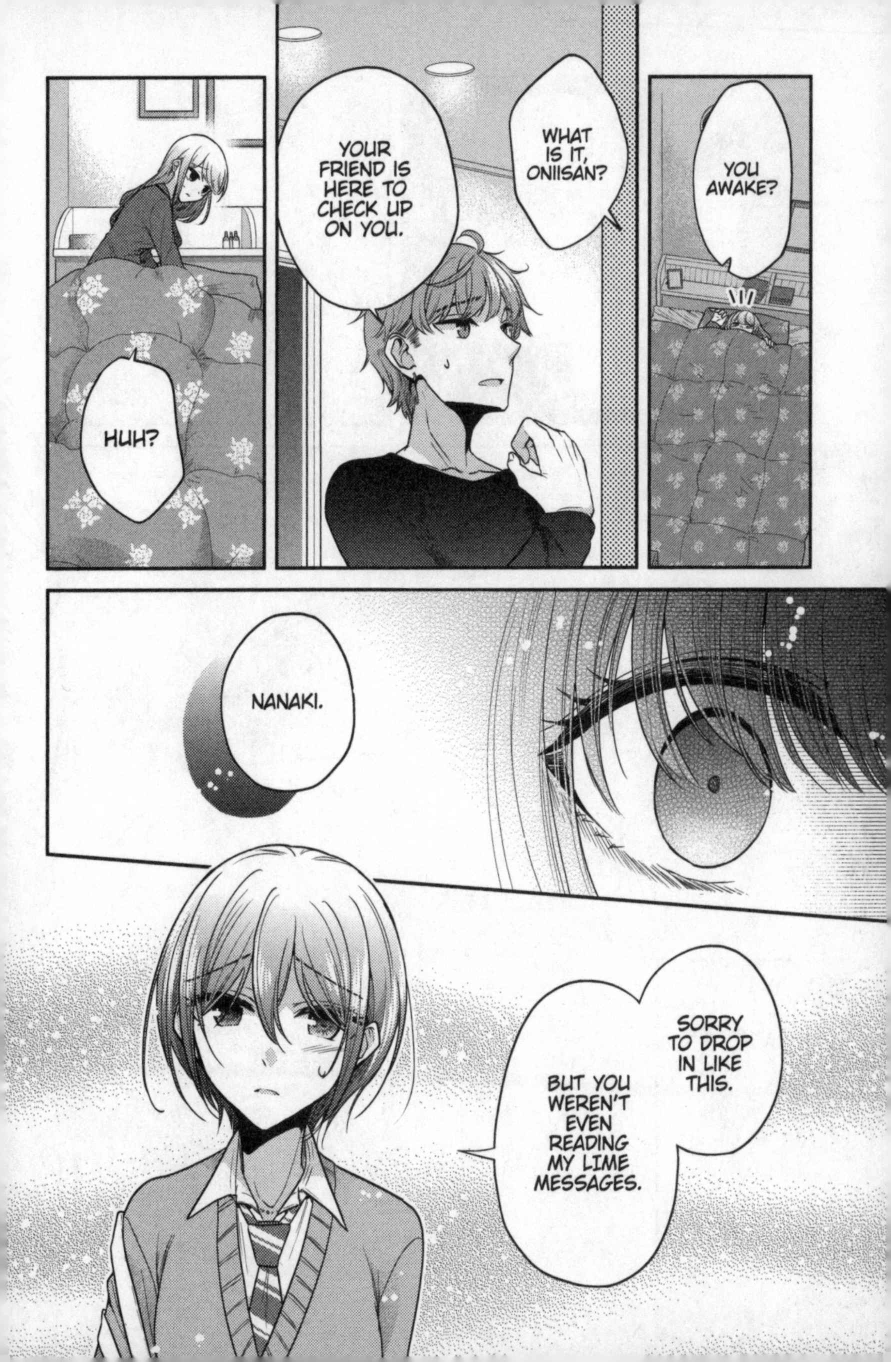
YOU AWAKE?
WHAT IS IT, ONIISAN?
YOUR FRIEND IS HERE TO CHECK UP ON YOU.
HUH?
NANAKI.
SORRY TO DROP IN LIKE THIS.
BUT YOU WEREN'T EVEN READING MY LIME MESSAGES.

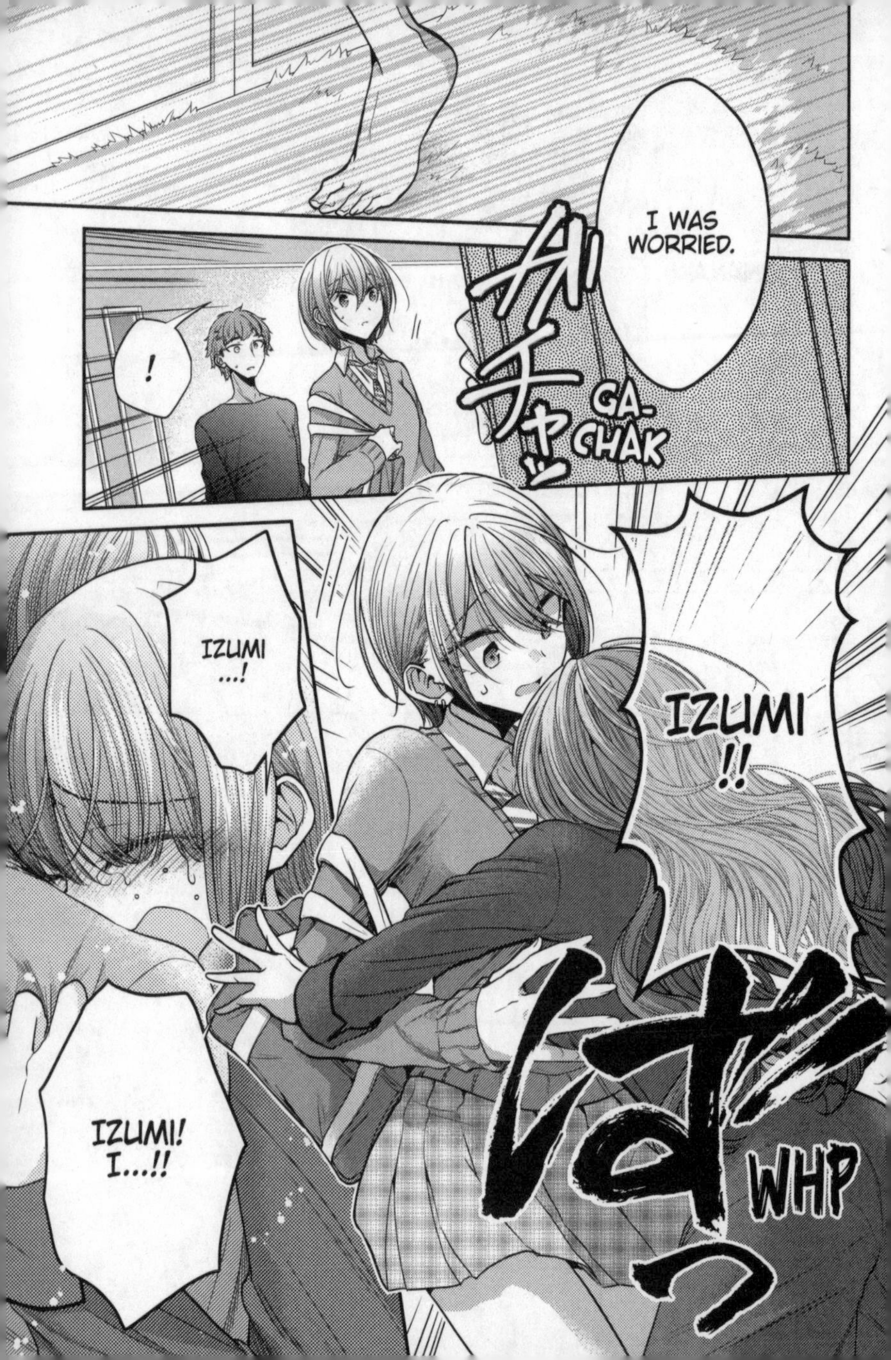
I WAS WORRIED.
ガチャッ
GA-CHAK
!
IZUMI !!
IZUMI ...!
ばっ
WHP
IZUMI! I...!!

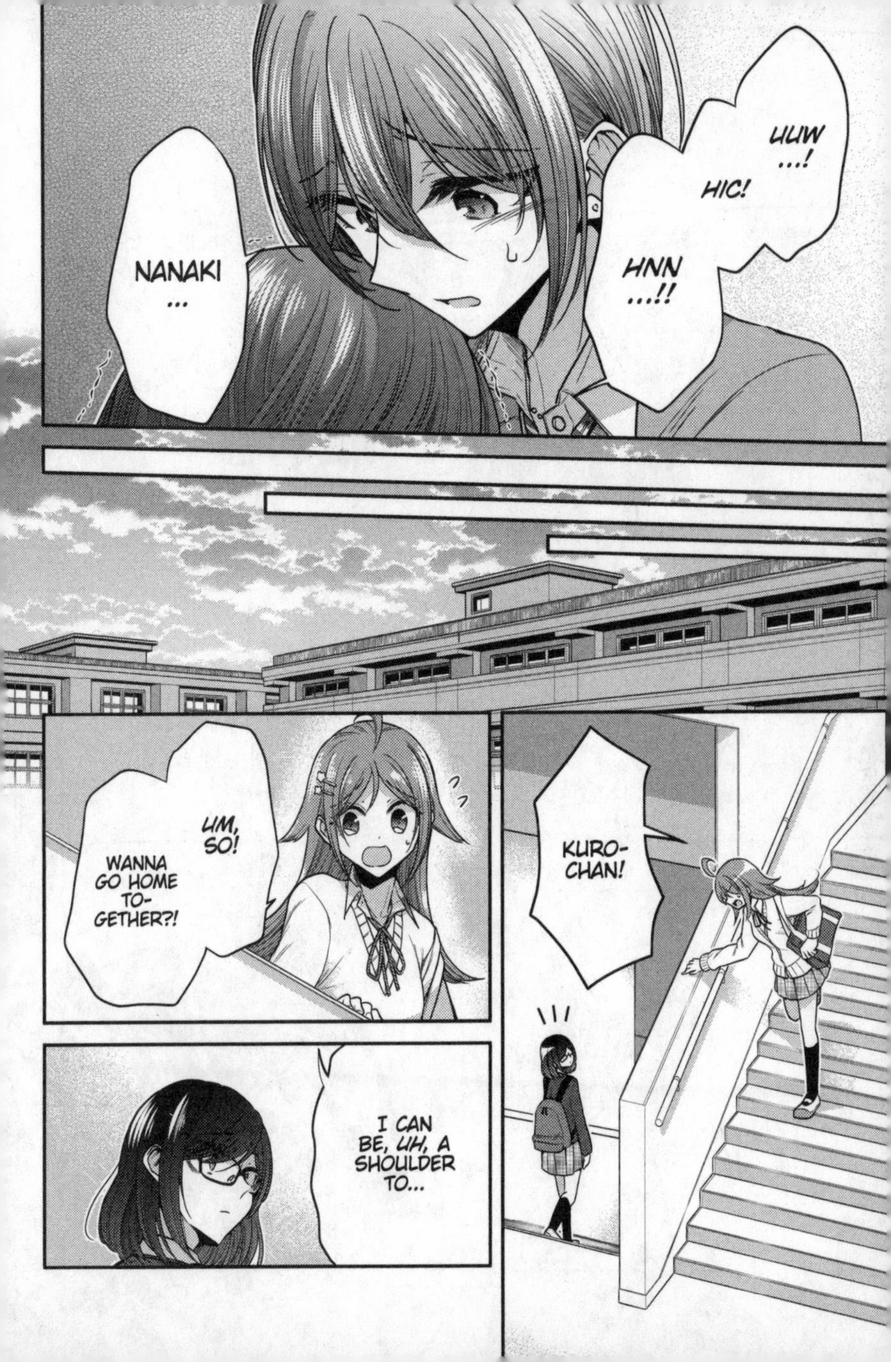
UUW ...!
HIC!
HNN ...!!
NANAKI ...
KURO-CHAN!
UM, SO!
WANNA GO HOME TO-GETHER?!
I CAN BE, UH, A SHOULDER TO...

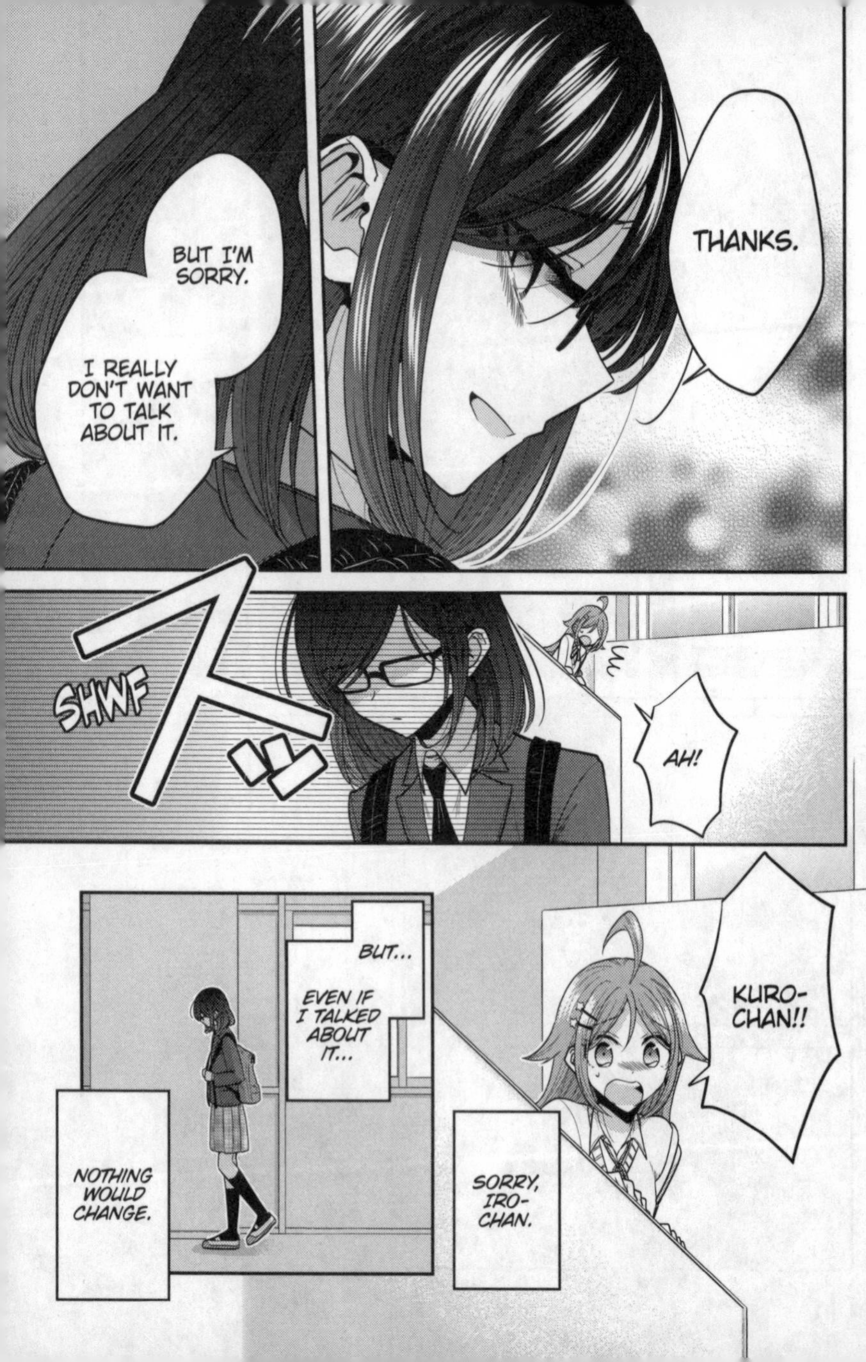
THANKS.
BUT I'M SORRY.
I REALLY DON'T WANT TO TALK ABOUT IT.
AH!
SHWF
KURO-CHAN!!
SORRY, IRO-CHAN.
BUT...
EVEN IF I TALKED ABOUT IT...
NOTHING WOULD CHANGE.

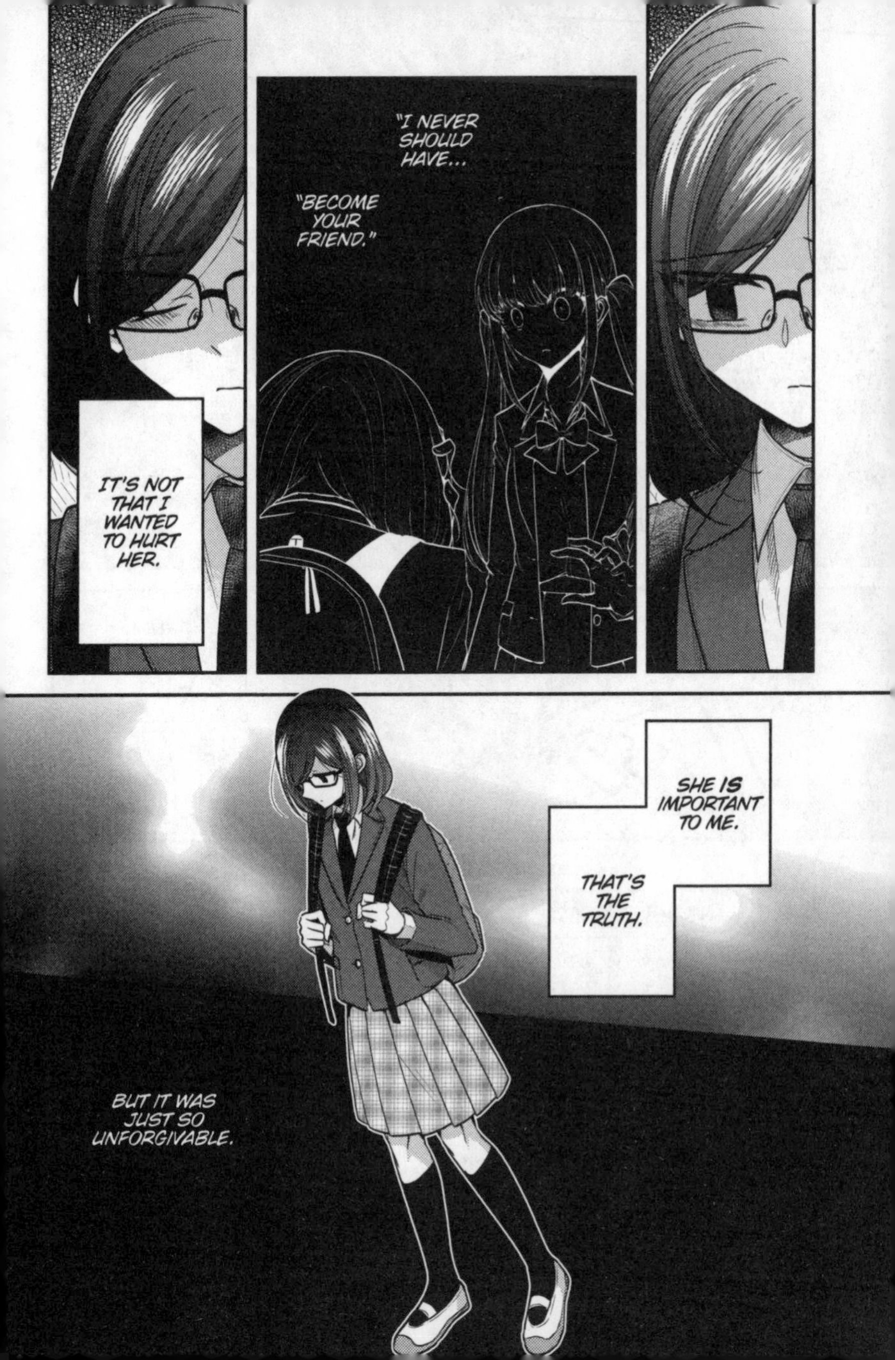
"I NEVER SHOULD HAVE...
"BECOME YOUR FRIEND."
IT'S NOT THAT I WANTED TO HURT HER.
SHE IS IMPORTANT TO ME.
THAT'S THE TRUTH.
BUT IT WAS JUST SO UNFORGIVABLE.

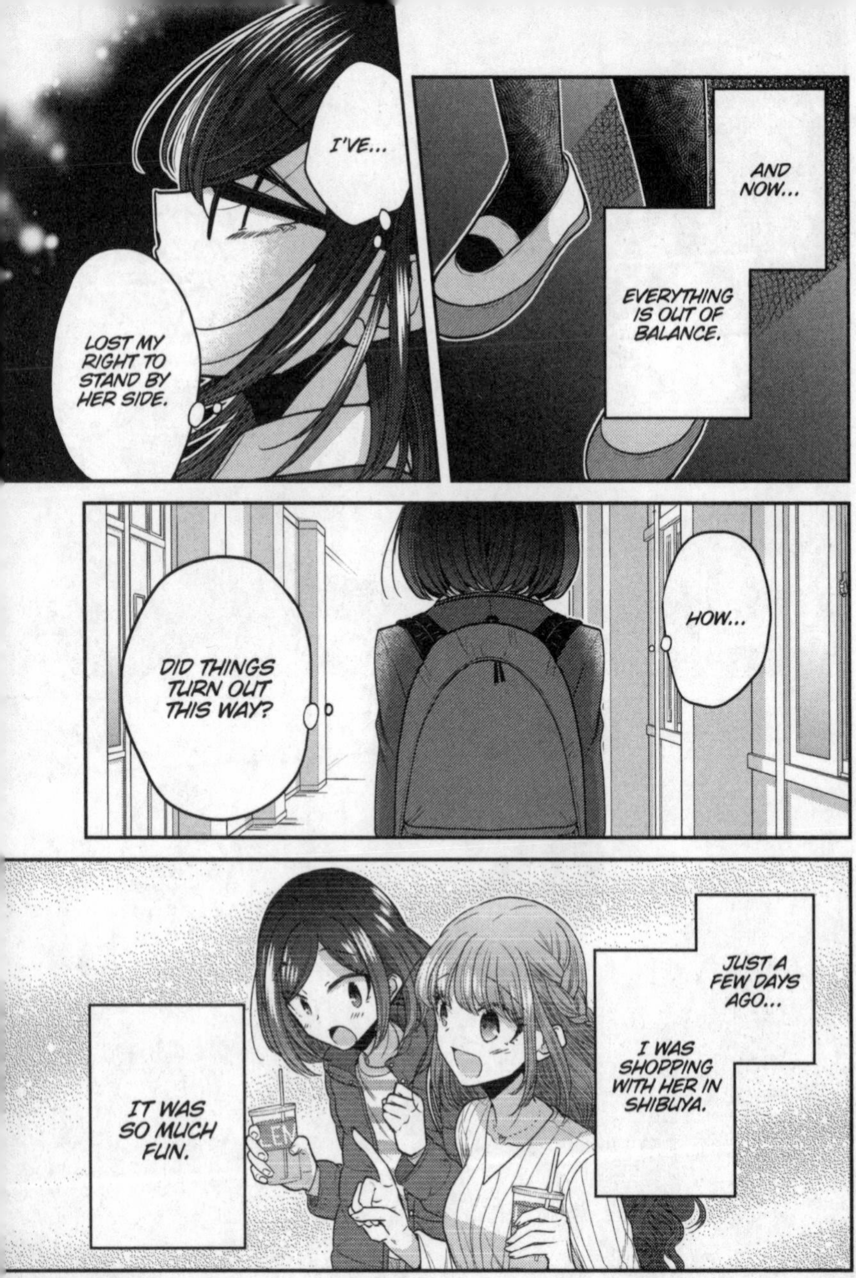
AND NOW...
EVERYTHING IS OUT OF BALANCE.
I'VE...
LOST MY RIGHT TO STAND BY HER SIDE.
HOW...
DID THINGS TURN OUT THIS WAY?
JUST A FEW DAYS AGO...
I WAS SHOPPING WITH HER IN SHIBUYA.
IT WAS SO MUCH FUN.

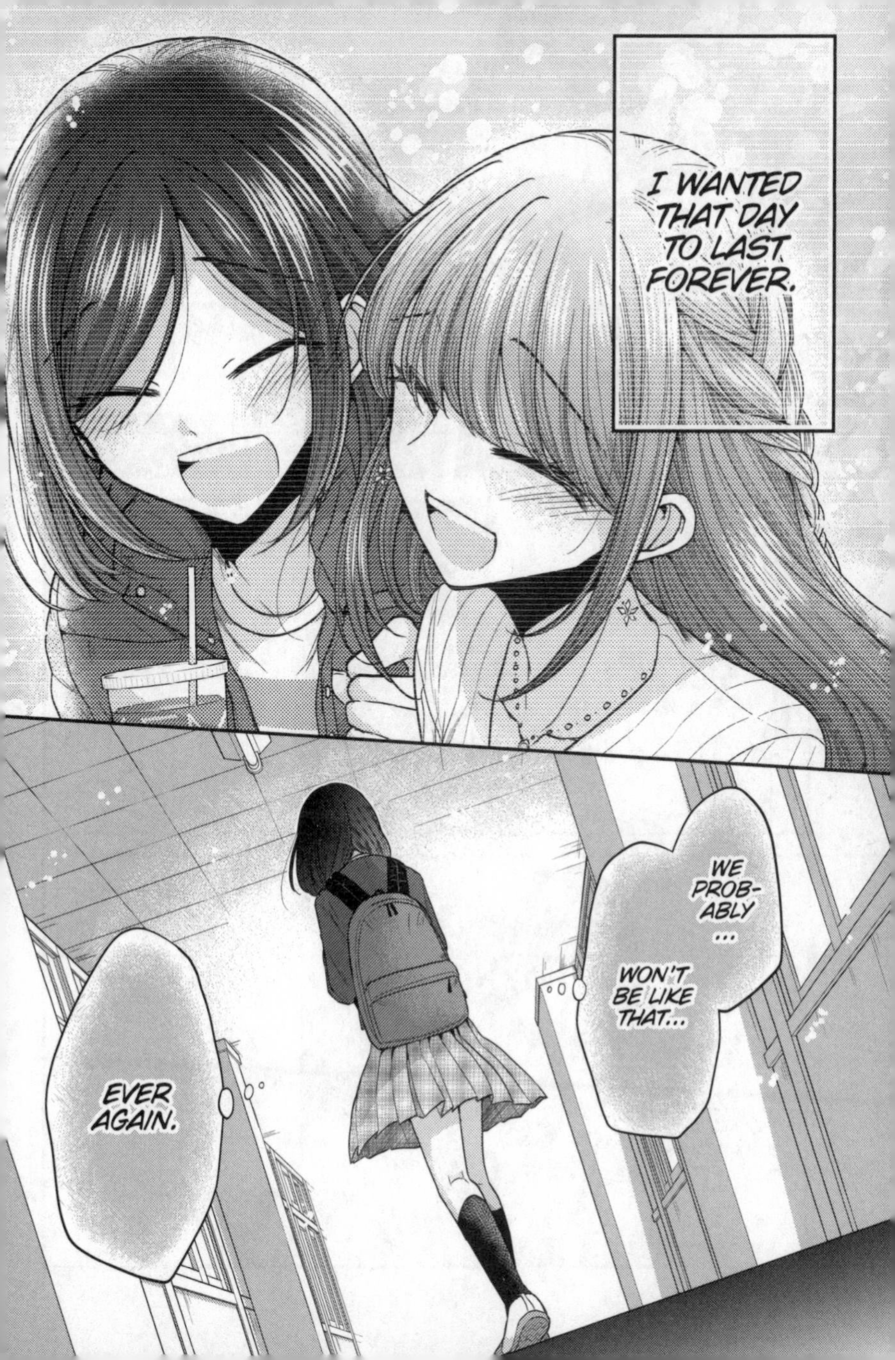
I WANTED THAT DAY TO LAST FOREVER.
WE PROB-ABLY ...
WON'T BE LIKE THAT...
EVER AGAIN.

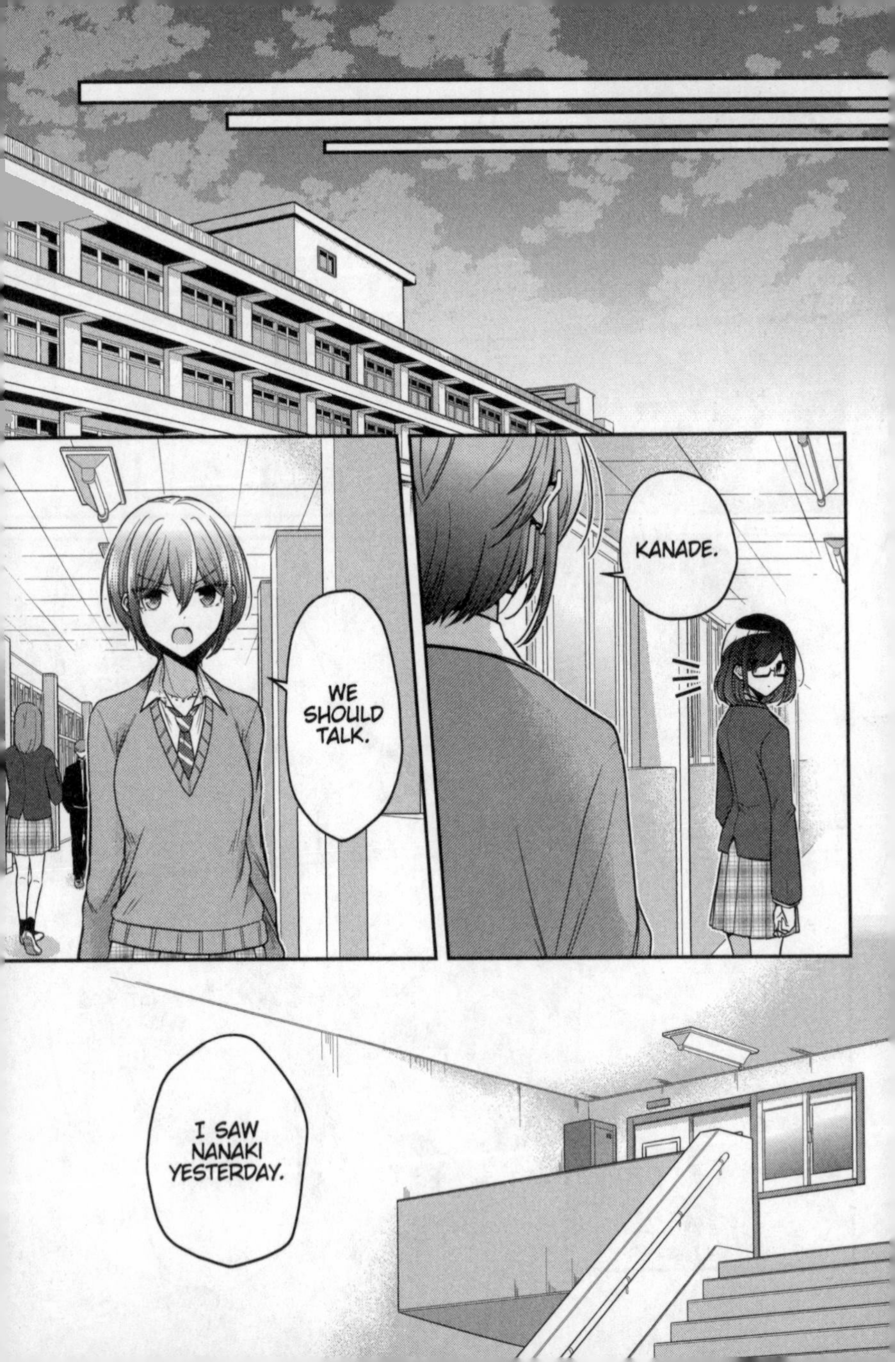
KANADE.
WE SHOULD TALK.
I SAW NANAKI YESTERDAY.

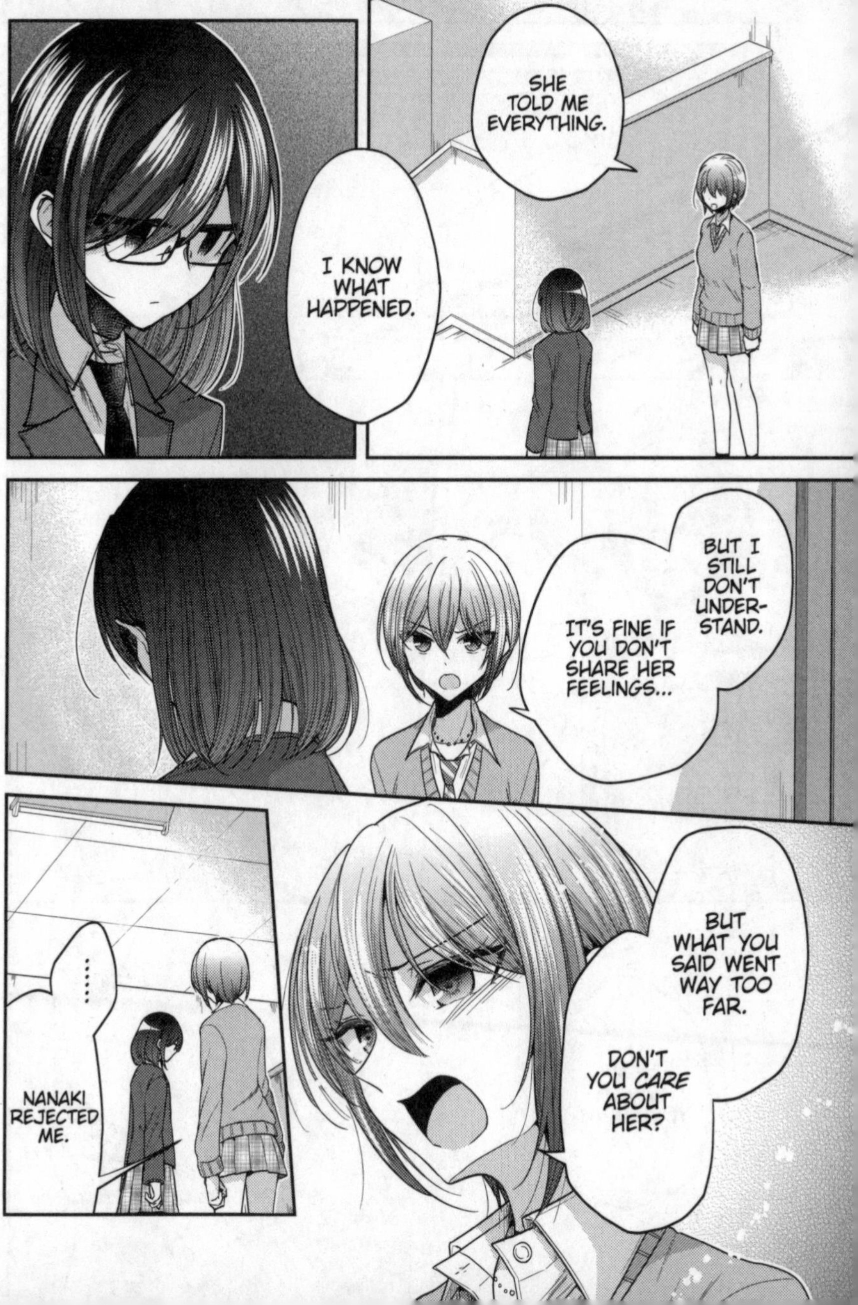
SHE TOLD ME EVERYTHING.
I KNOW WHAT HAPPENED.
BUT I STILL DON'T UNDER-STAND.
IT'S FINE IF YOU DON'T SHARE HER FEELINGS...
BUT WHAT YOU SAID WENT WAY TOO FAR.
DON'T YOU *CARE* ABOUT HER?
......
NANAKI REJECTED ME.

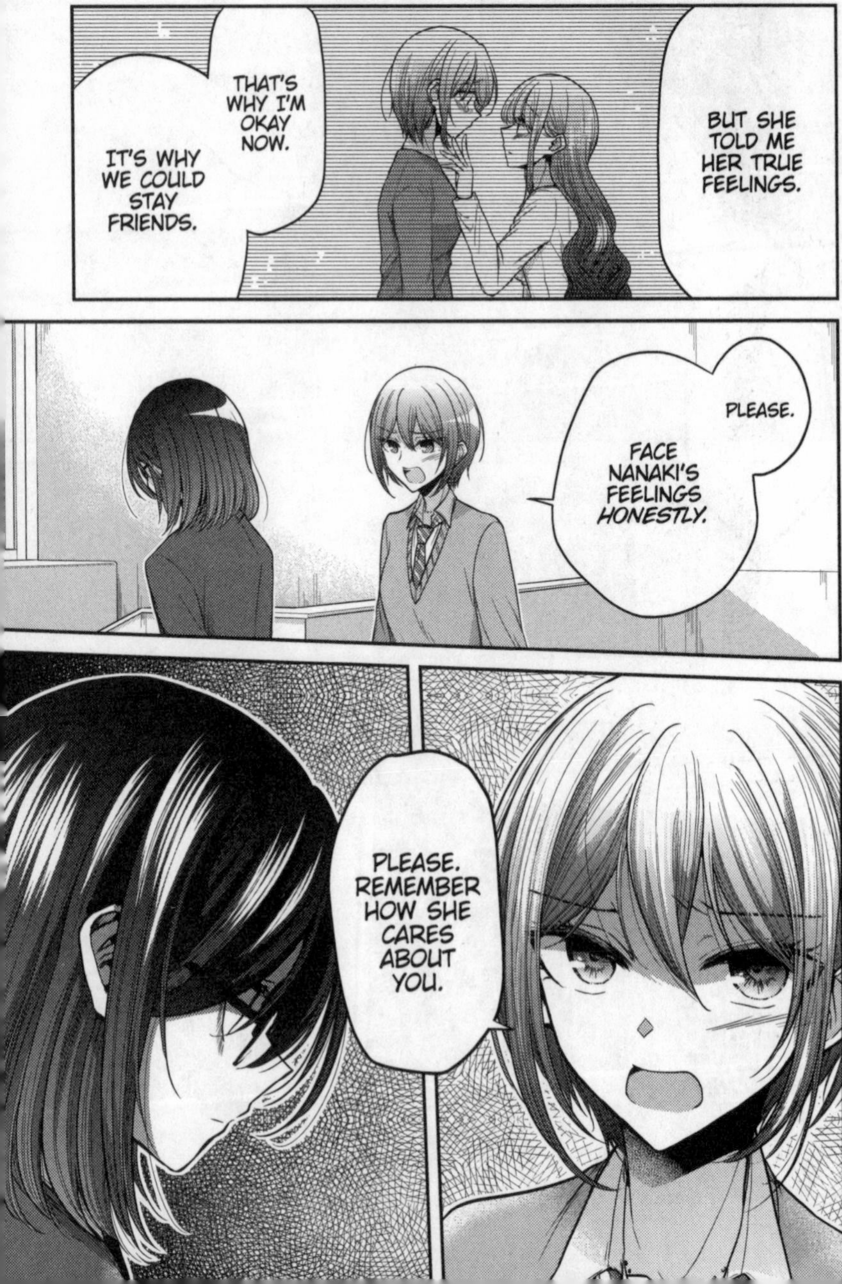
BUT SHE TOLD ME HER TRUE FEELINGS.
THAT'S WHY I'M OKAY NOW.
IT'S WHY WE COULD STAY FRIENDS.
PLEASE.
FACE NANAKI'S FEELINGS *HONESTLY.*
PLEASE. REMEMBER HOW SHE CARES ABOUT YOU.

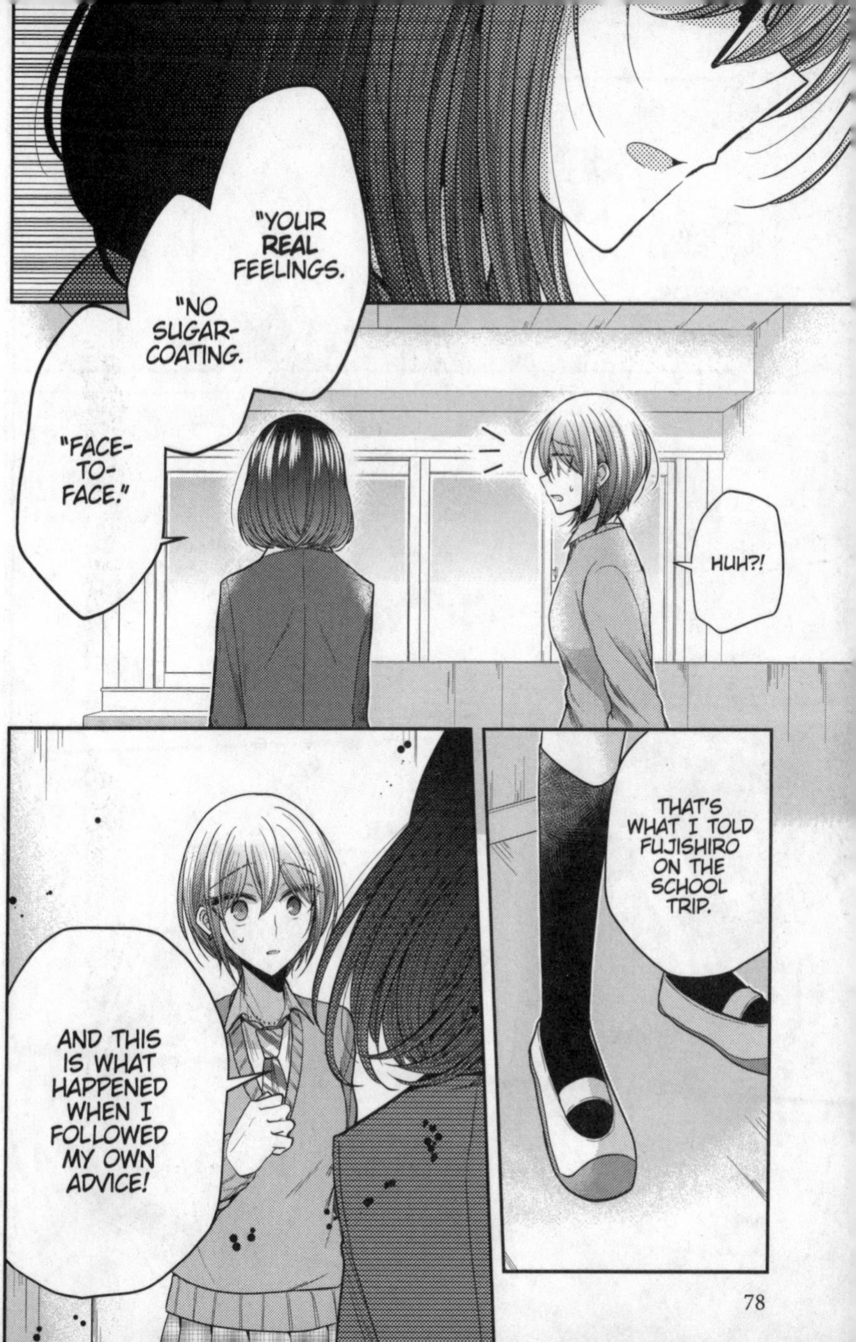
"YOUR REAL FEELINGS.
"NO SUGAR-COATING.
"FACE-TO-FACE."
HUH?!
THAT'S WHAT I TOLD FUJISHIRO ON THE SCHOOL TRIP.
AND THIS IS WHAT HAPPENED WHEN I FOLLOWED MY OWN ADVICE!

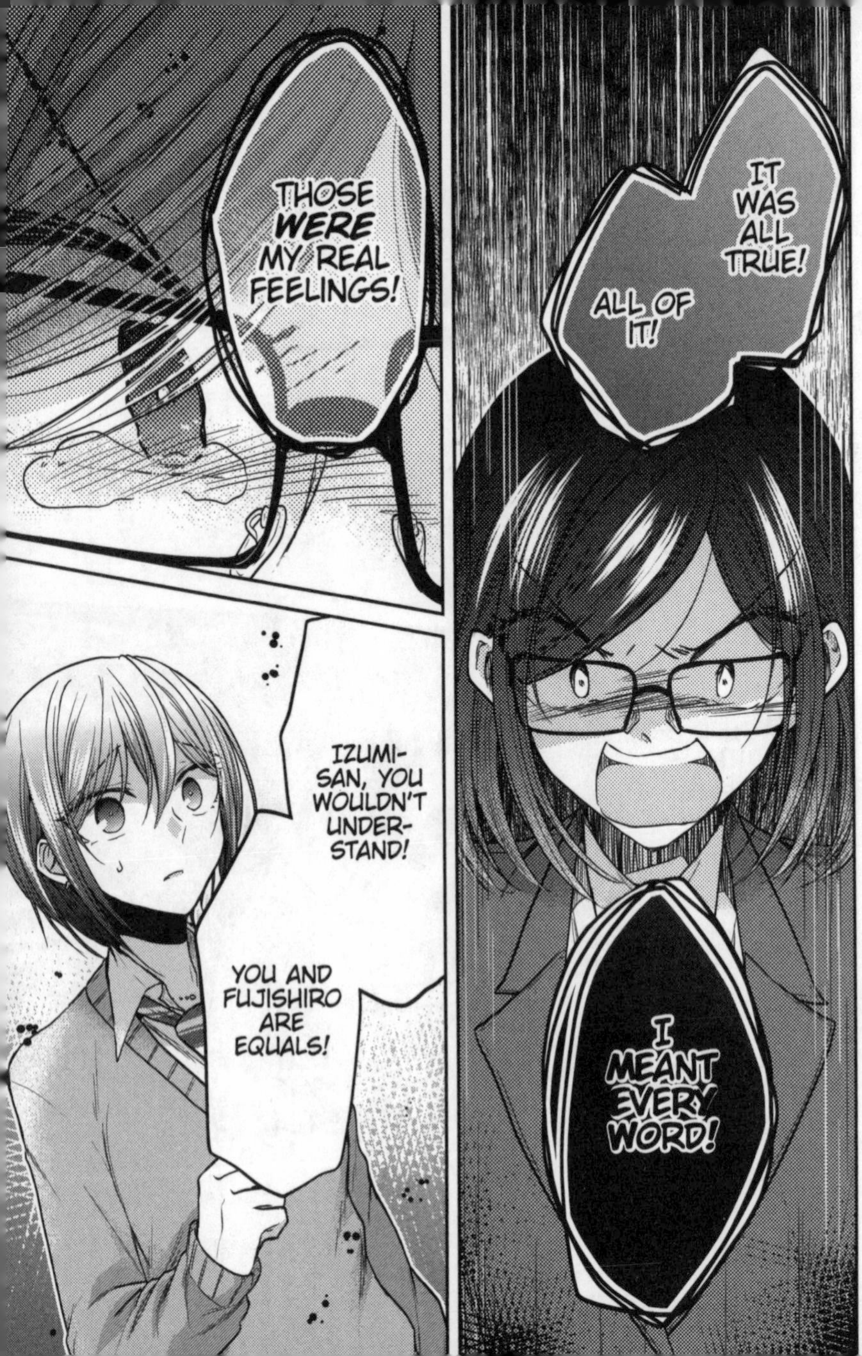
IT WAS ALL TRUE!
ALL OF IT!
I MEANT EVERY WORD!
THOSE WERE MY REAL FEELINGS!
IZUMI-SAN, YOU WOULDN'T UNDER-STAND!
YOU AND FUJISHIRO ARE EQUALS!

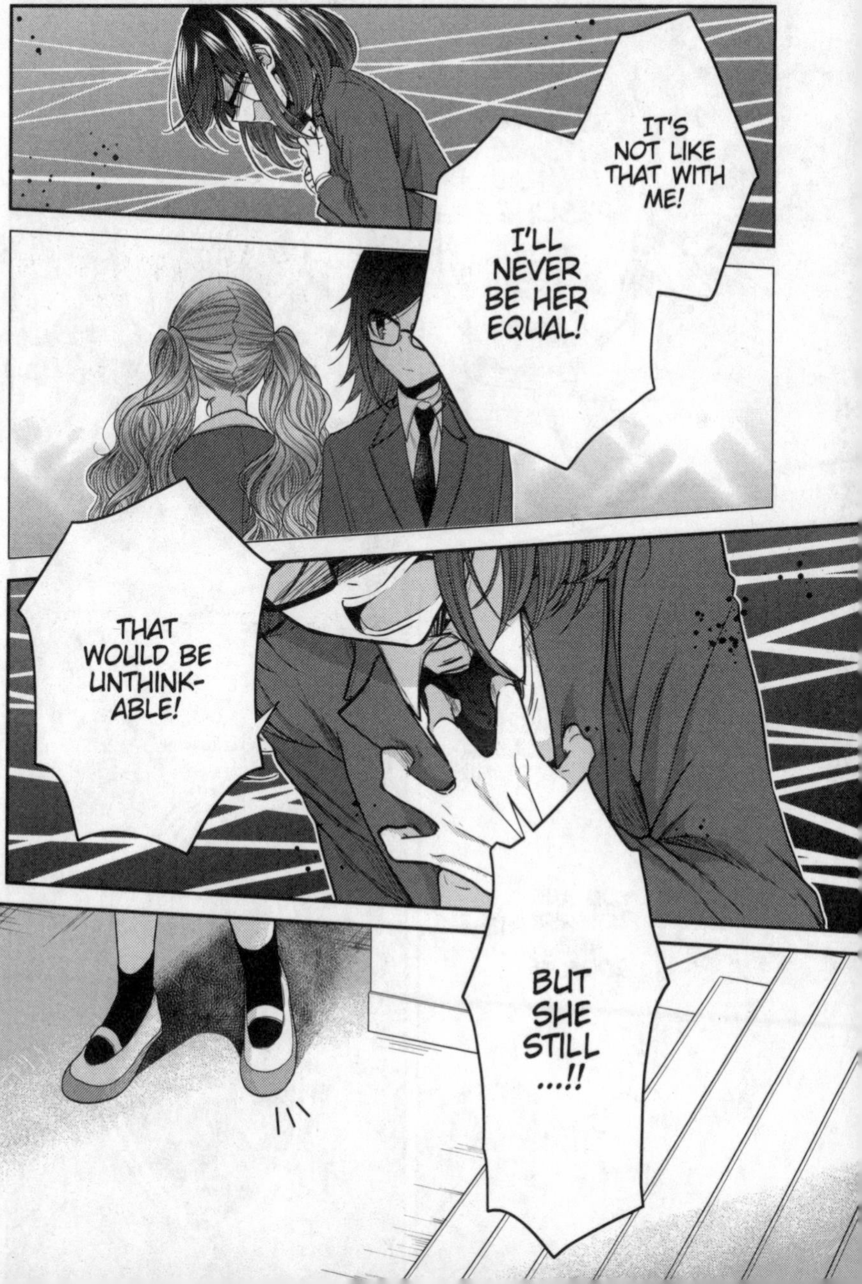
IT'S NOT LIKE THAT WITH ME!
I'LL NEVER BE HER EQUAL!
THAT WOULD BE UNTHINK-ABLE!
BUT SHE STILL ...!!

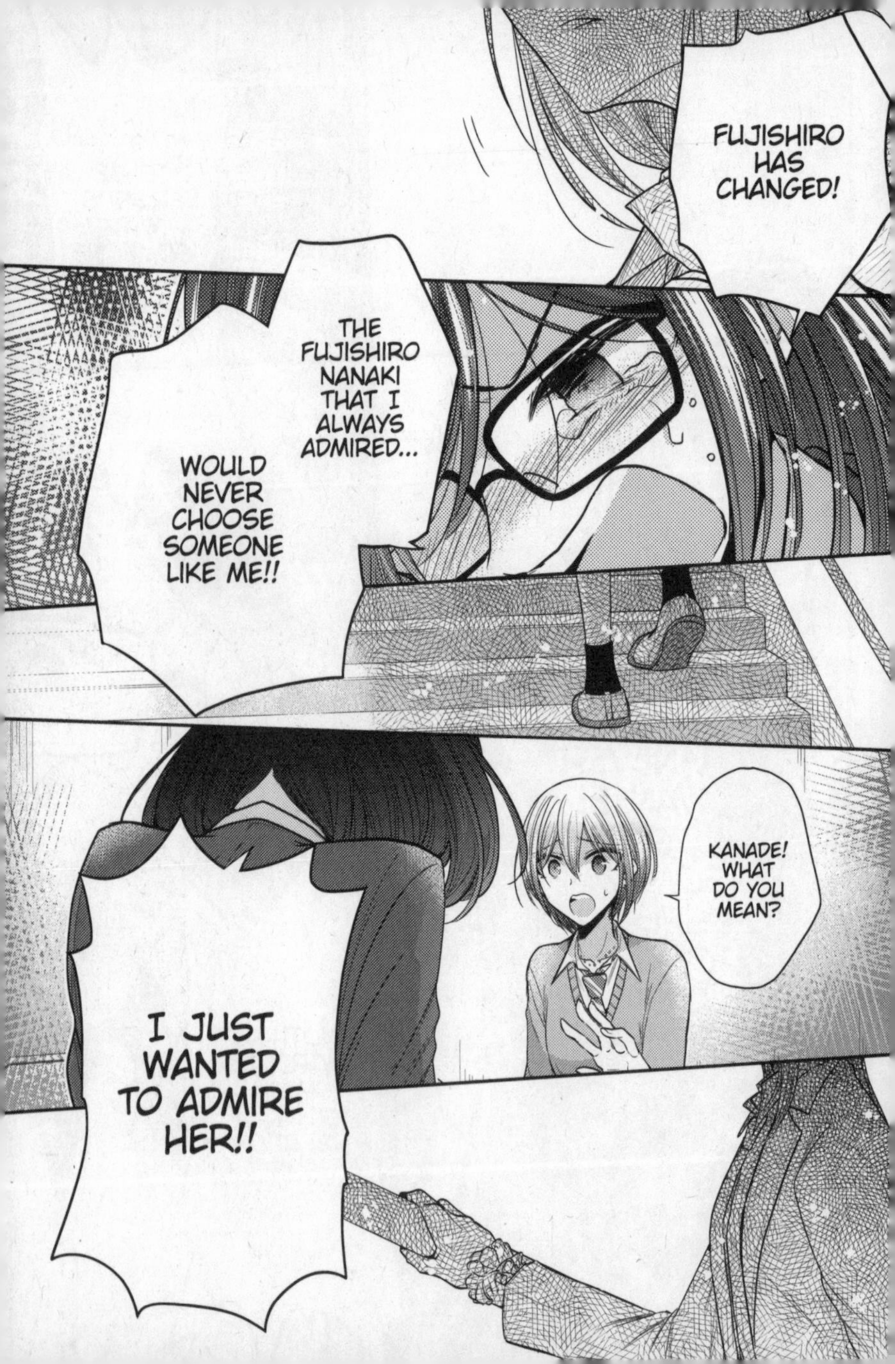
FUJISHIRO HAS CHANGED!
THE FUJISHIRO NANAKI THAT I ALWAYS ADMIRED...
WOULD NEVER CHOOSE SOMEONE LIKE ME!!
KANADE! WHAT DO YOU MEAN?
I JUST WANTED TO ADMIRE HER!!

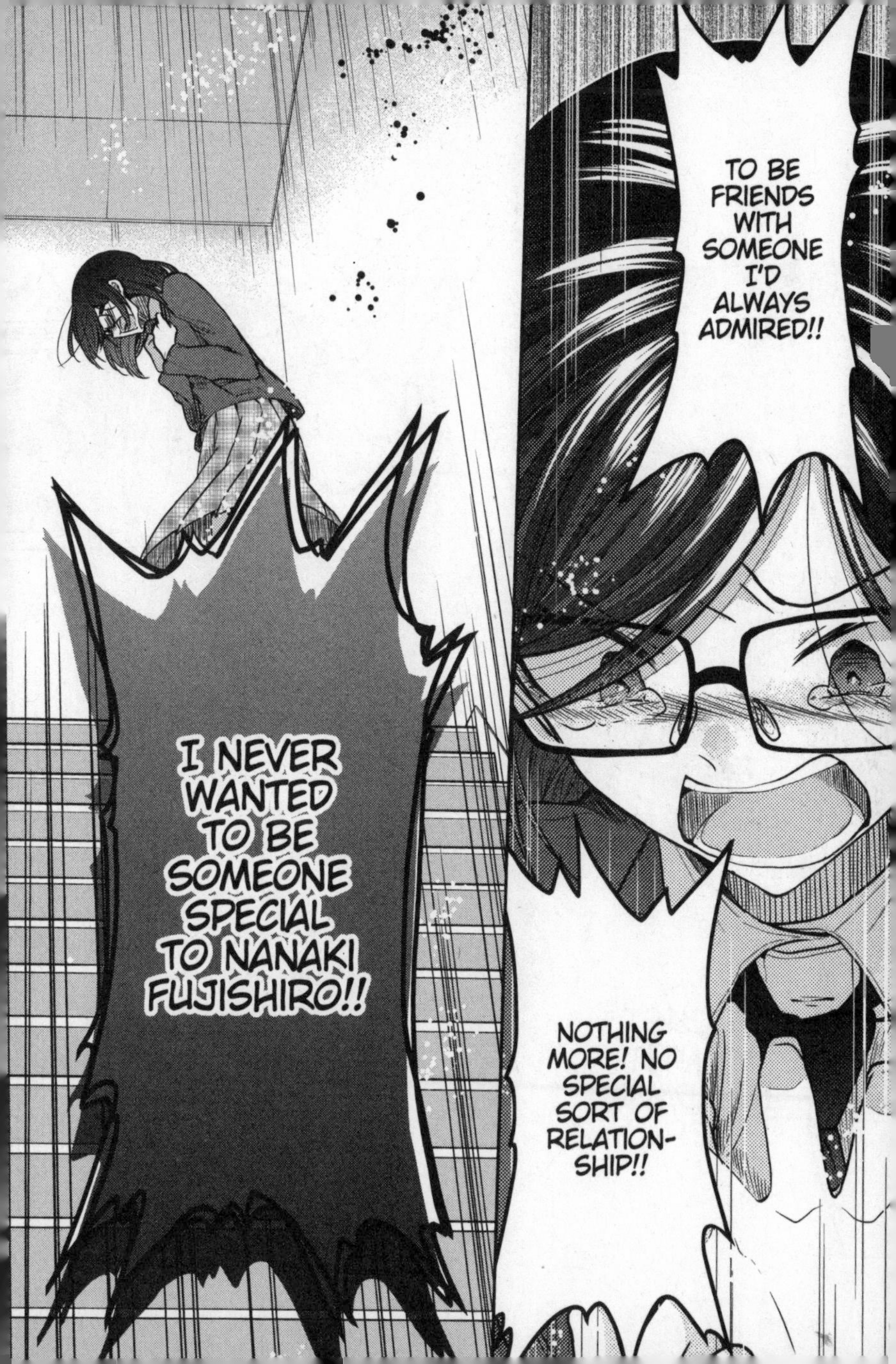

TO BE FRIENDS WITH SOMEONE I'D ALWAYS ADMIRED!!
NOTHING MORE! NO SPECIAL SORT OF RELATION-SHIP!!
I NEVER WANTED TO BE SOMEONE SPECIAL TO NANAKI FUJISHIRO!!

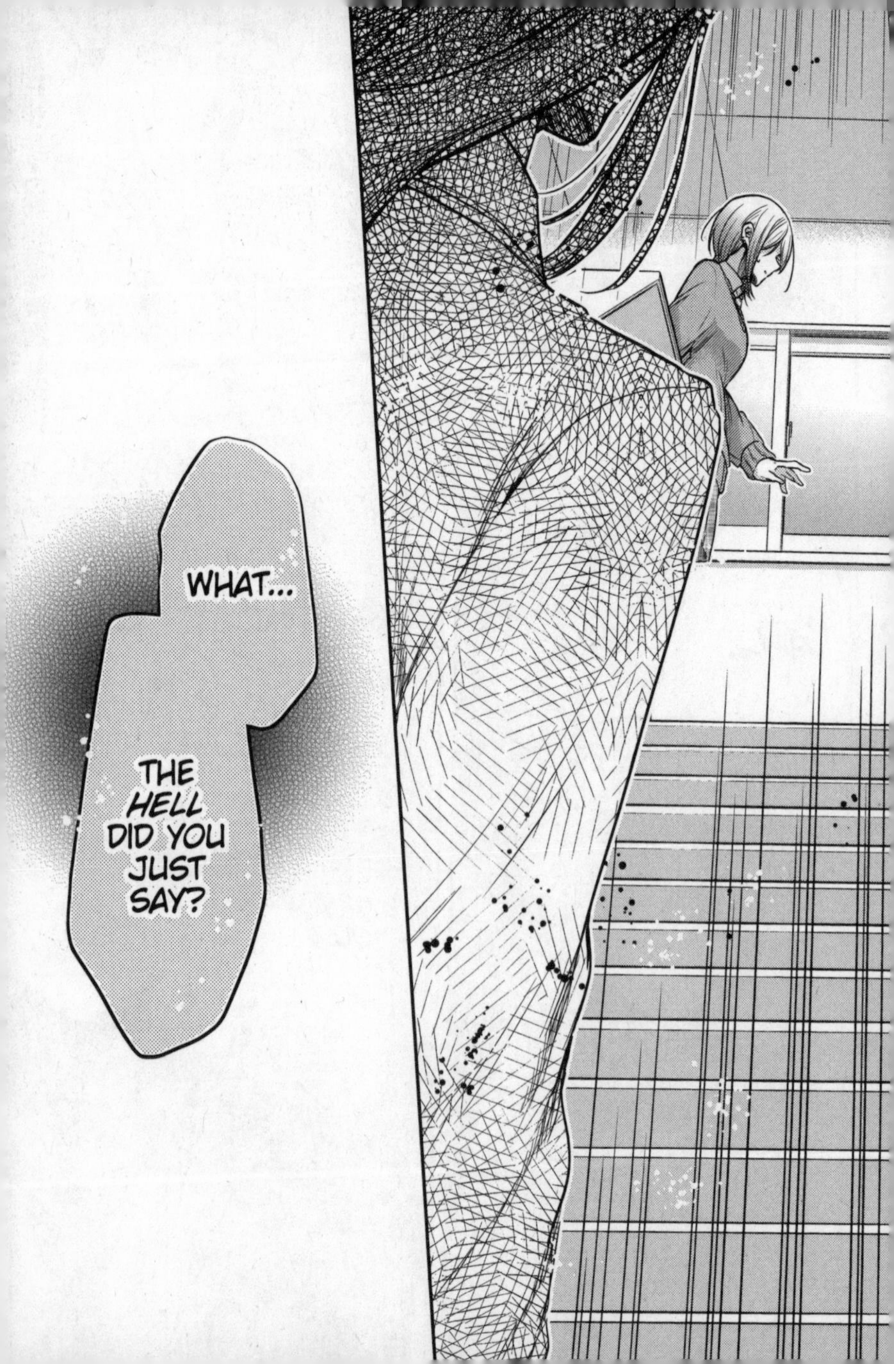
WHAT...
THE *HELL* DID YOU JUST SAY?

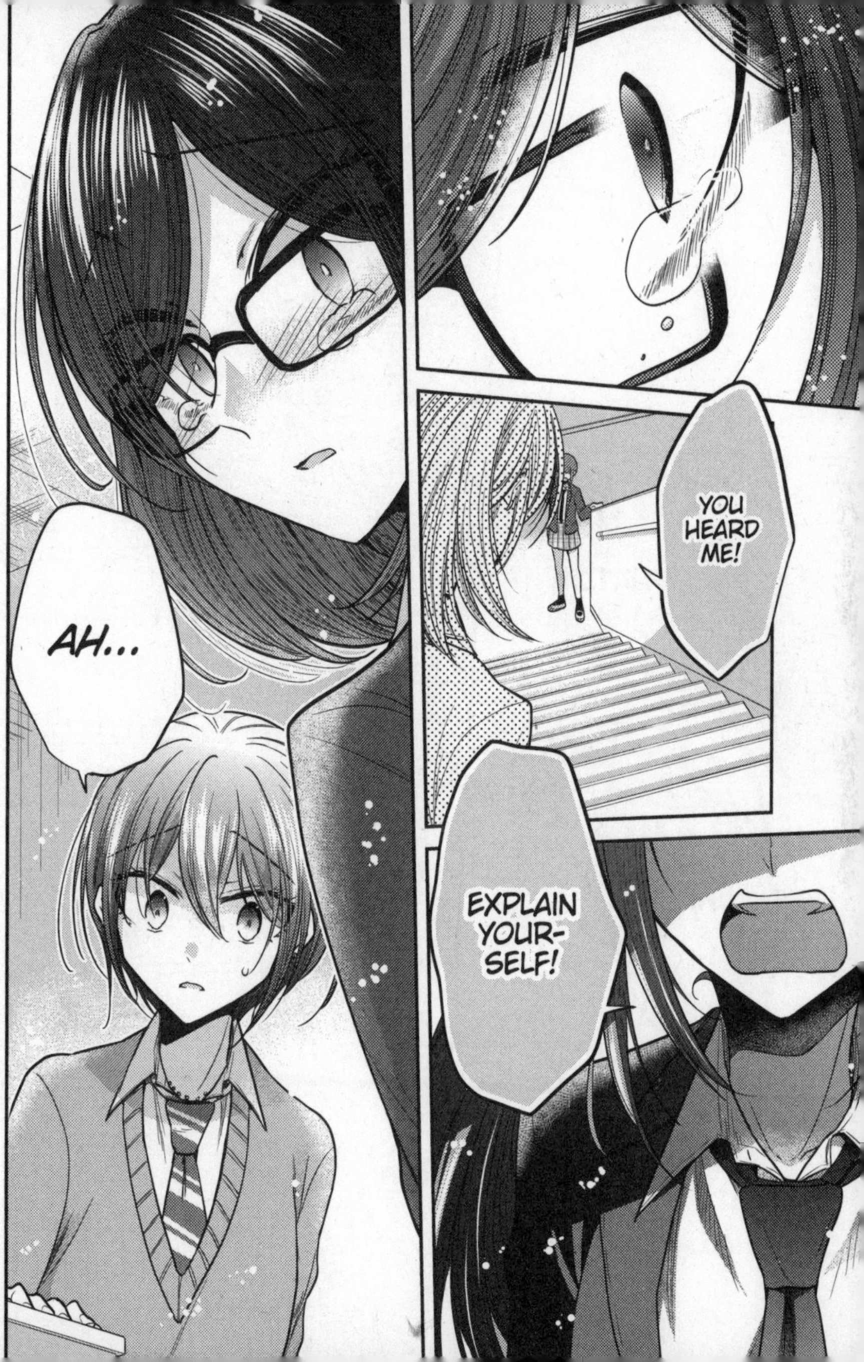
YOU HEARD ME!
EXPLAIN YOUR-SELF!
AH...

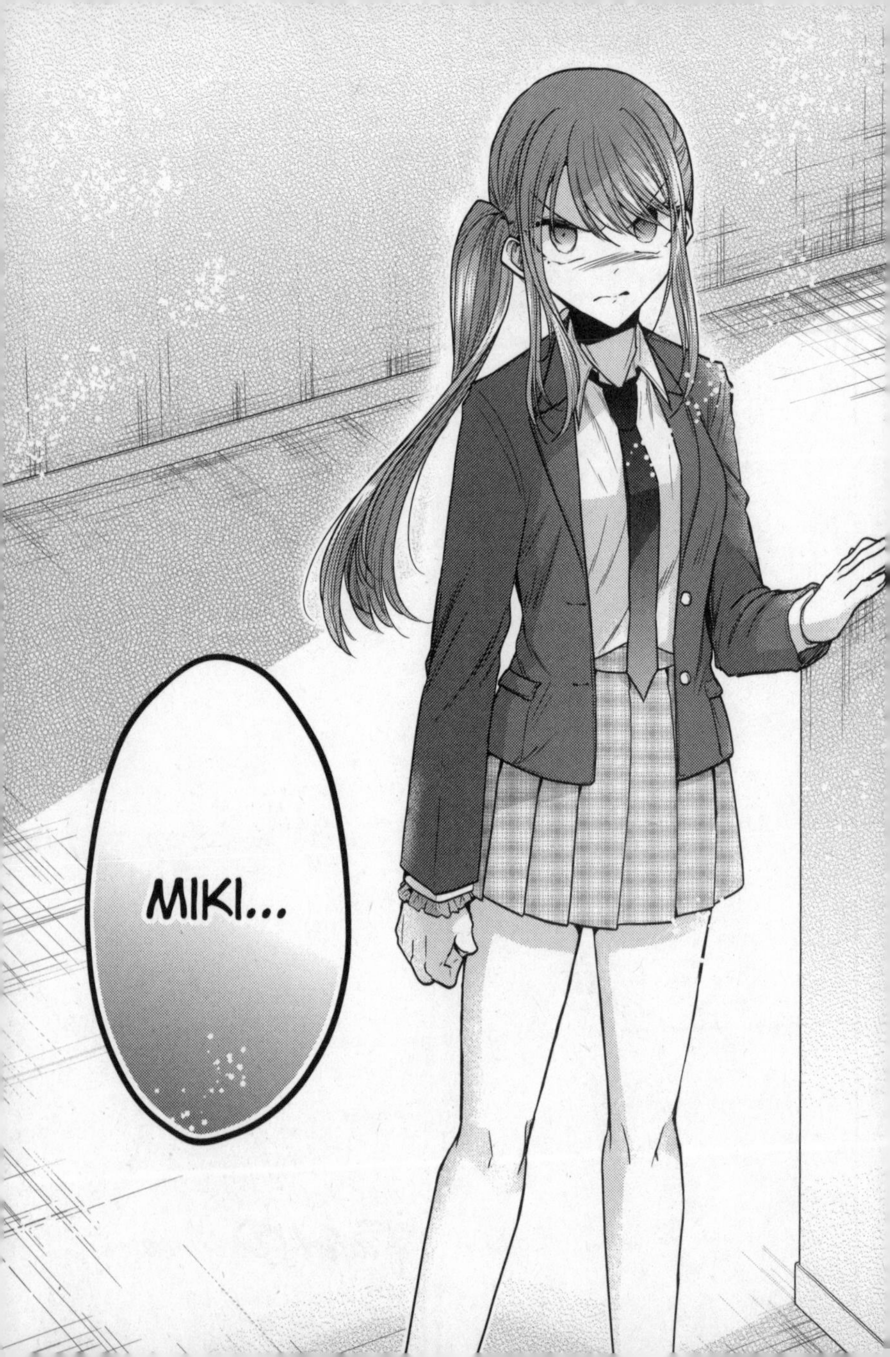
MIKI...

Failed Princesses

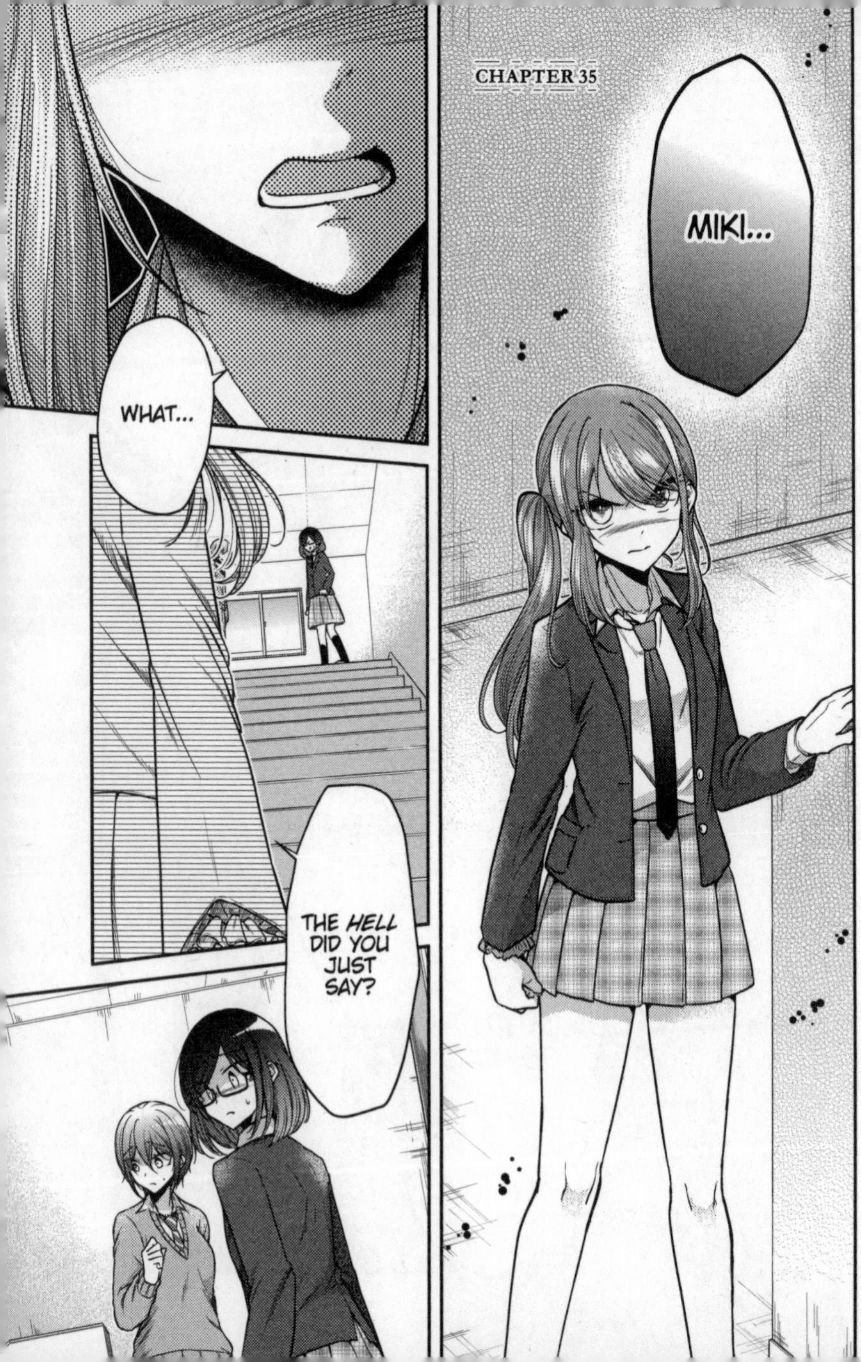
CHAPTER 35
MIKI...
WHAT...
THE *HELL* DID YOU JUST SAY?

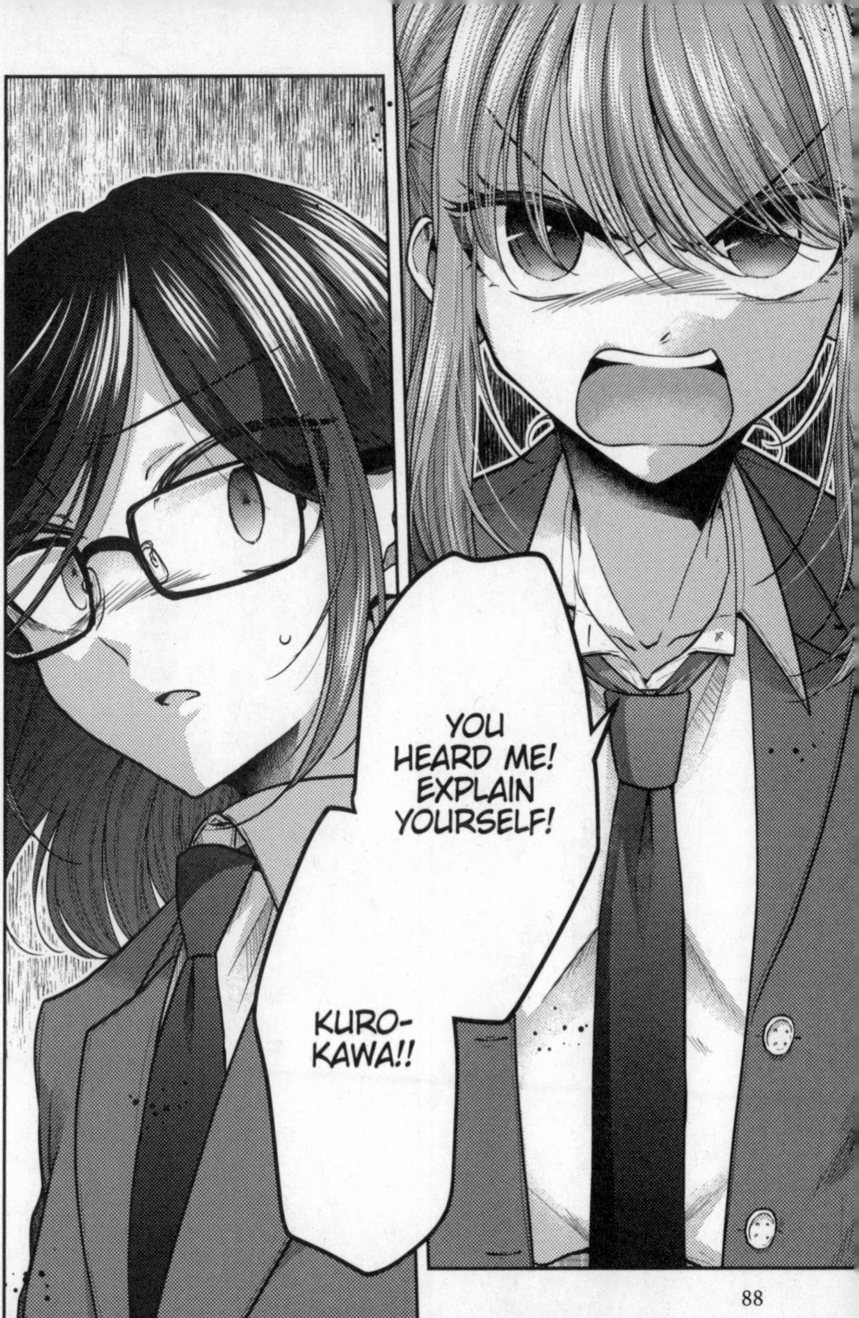
YOU HEARD ME! EXPLAIN YOURSELF!
KURO-KAWA!!

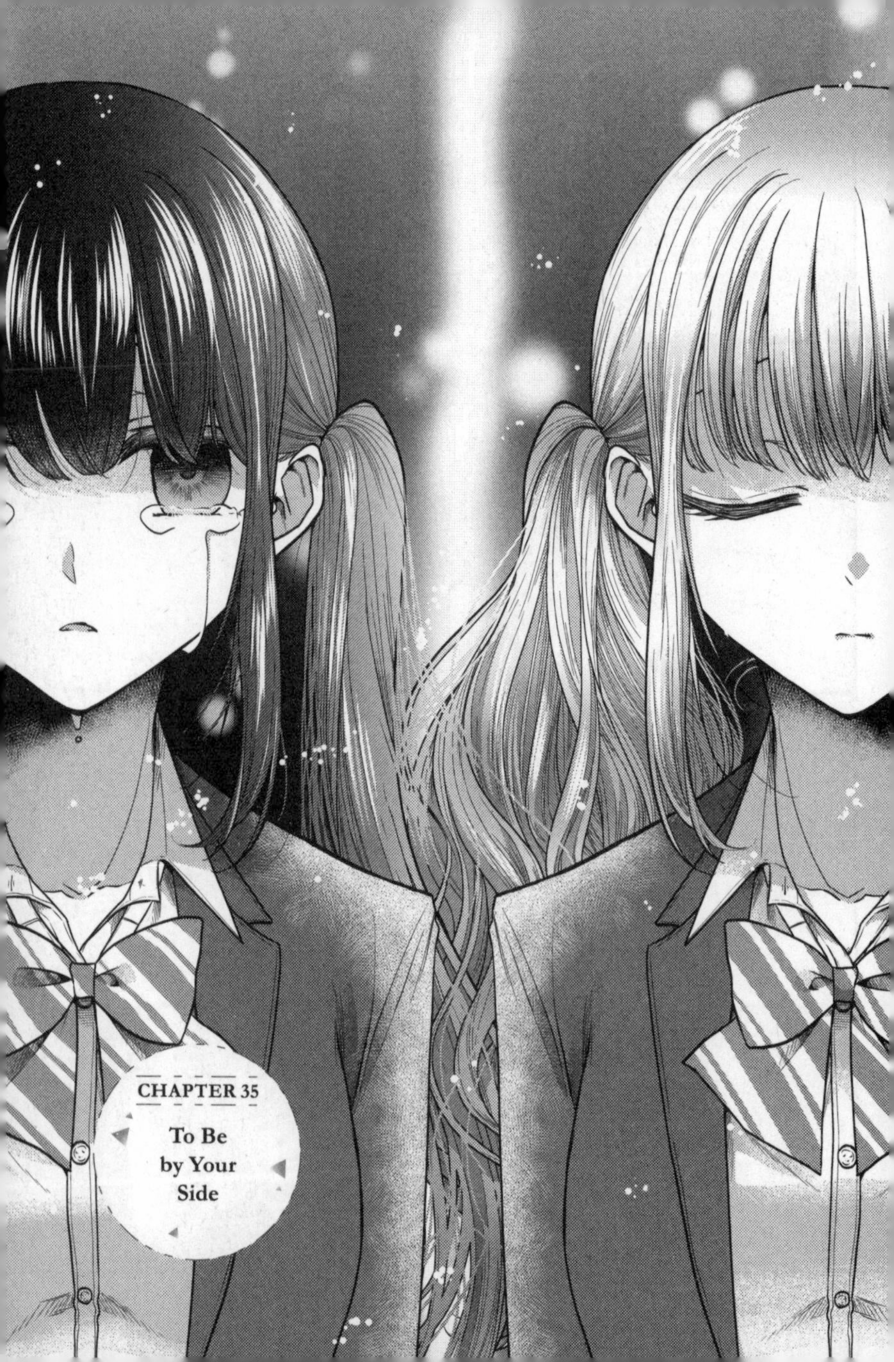
CHAPTER 35
To Be by Your Side

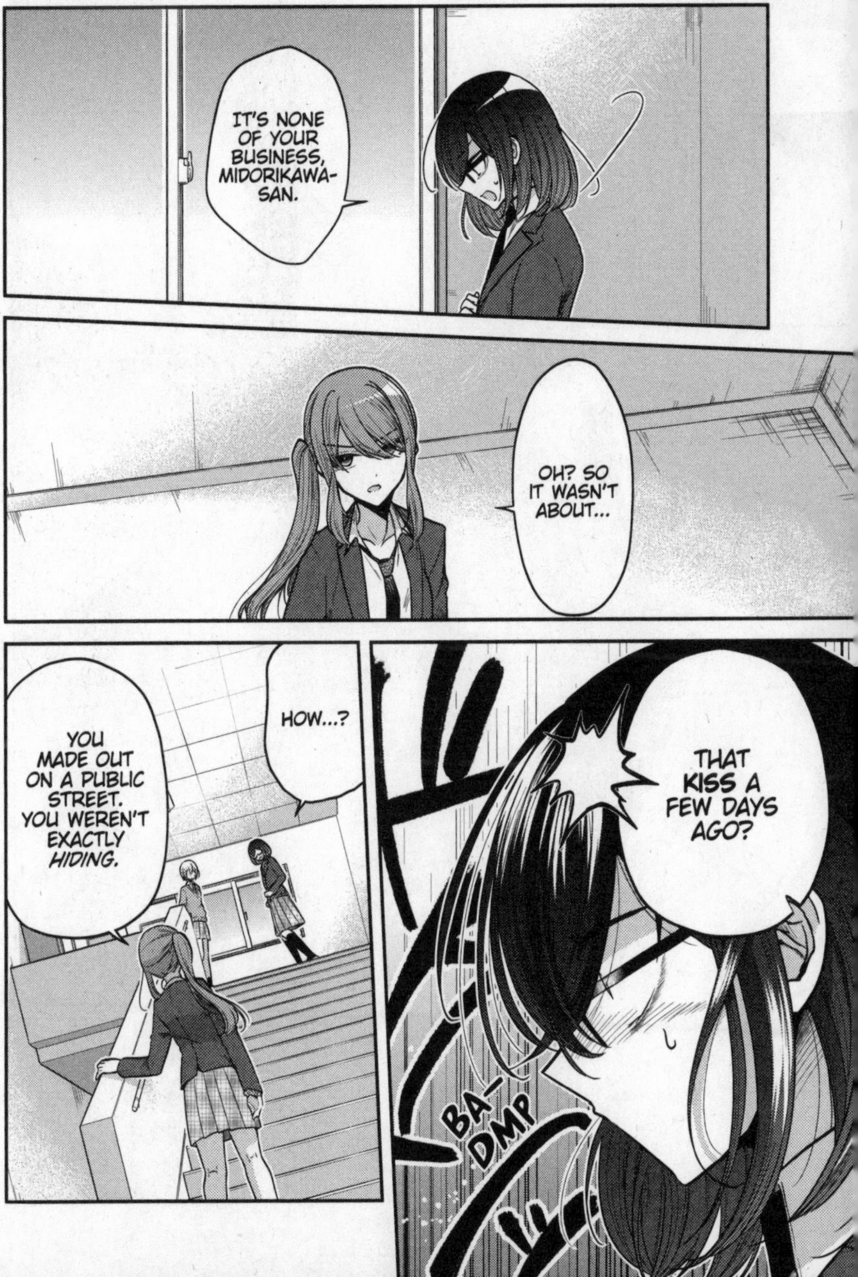
IT'S NONE OF YOUR BUSINESS, MIDORIKAWA-SAN.
OH? SO IT WASN'T ABOUT...
THAT KISS A FEW DAYS AGO?
BA-DMP
HOW...?
YOU MADE OUT ON A PUBLIC STREET. YOU WEREN'T EXACTLY *HIDING*.

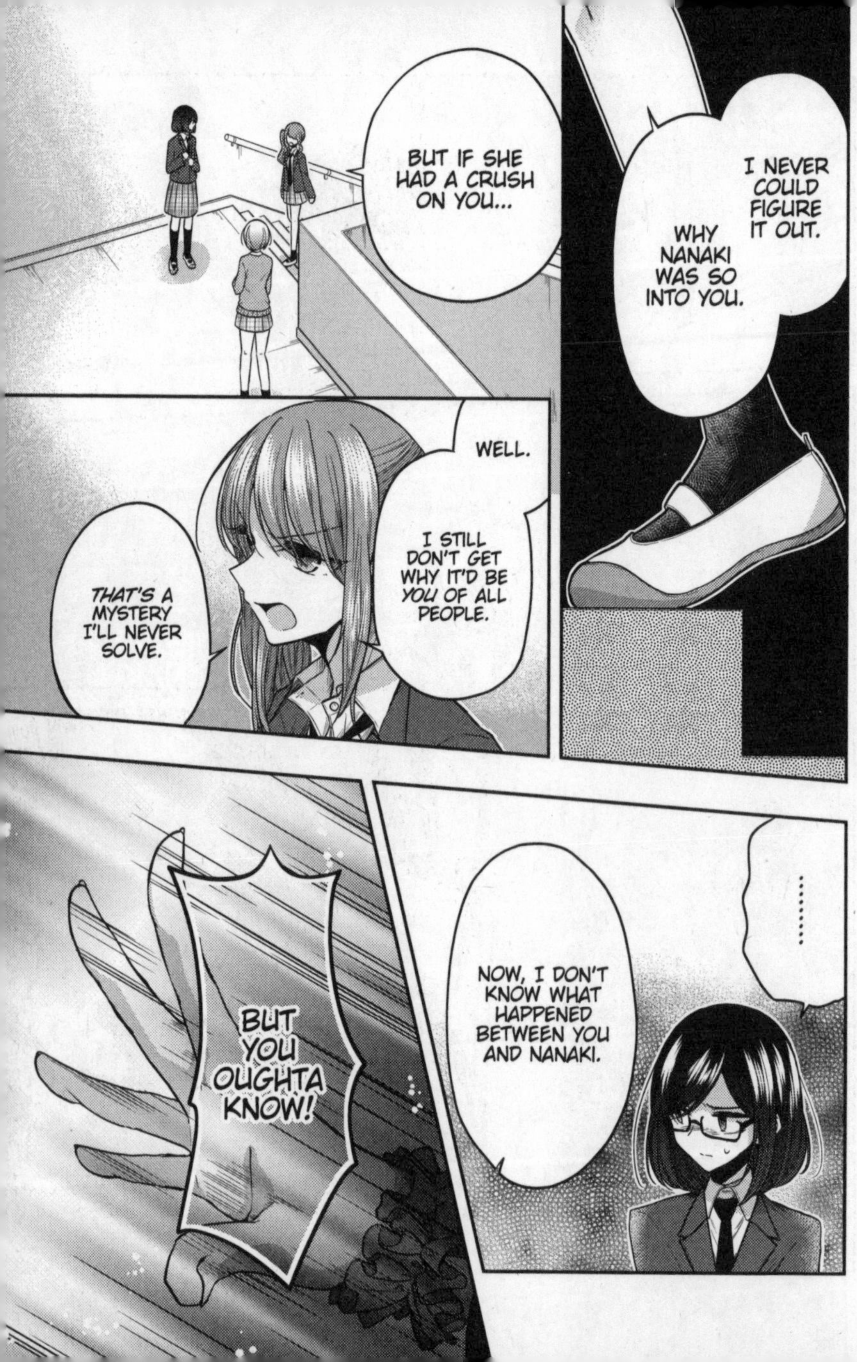
I NEVER COULD FIGURE IT OUT.
WHY NANAKI WAS SO INTO YOU.
BUT IF SHE HAD A CRUSH ON YOU...
WELL.
I STILL DON'T GET WHY IT'D BE *YOU* OF ALL PEOPLE.
THAT'S A MYSTERY I'LL NEVER SOLVE.
......
NOW, I DON'T KNOW WHAT HAPPENED BETWEEN YOU AND NANAKI.
BUT YOU OUGHTA KNOW!

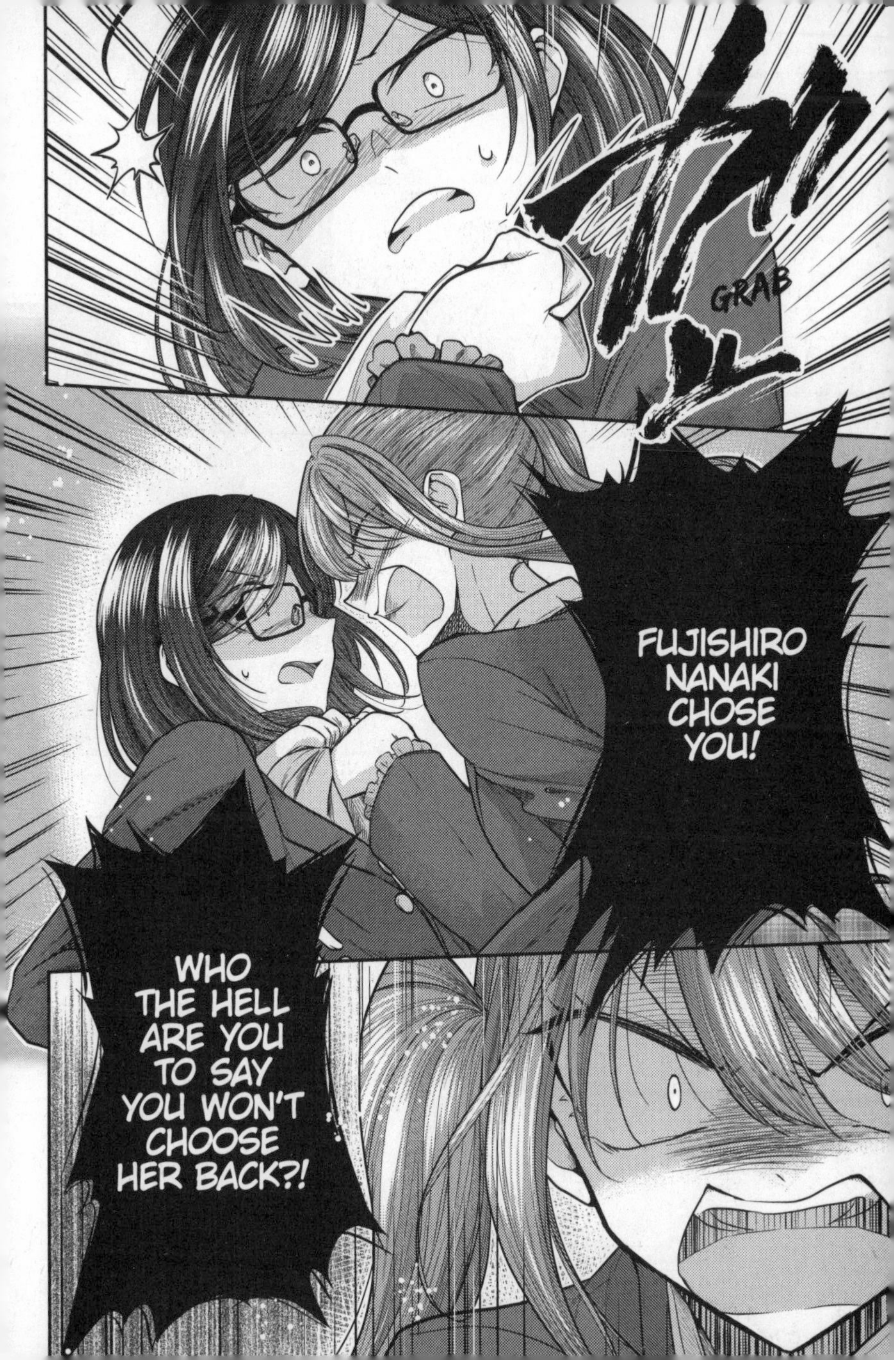
GRAB
FUJISHIRO NANAKI CHOSE YOU!
WHO THE HELL ARE YOU TO SAY YOU WON'T CHOOSE HER BACK?!

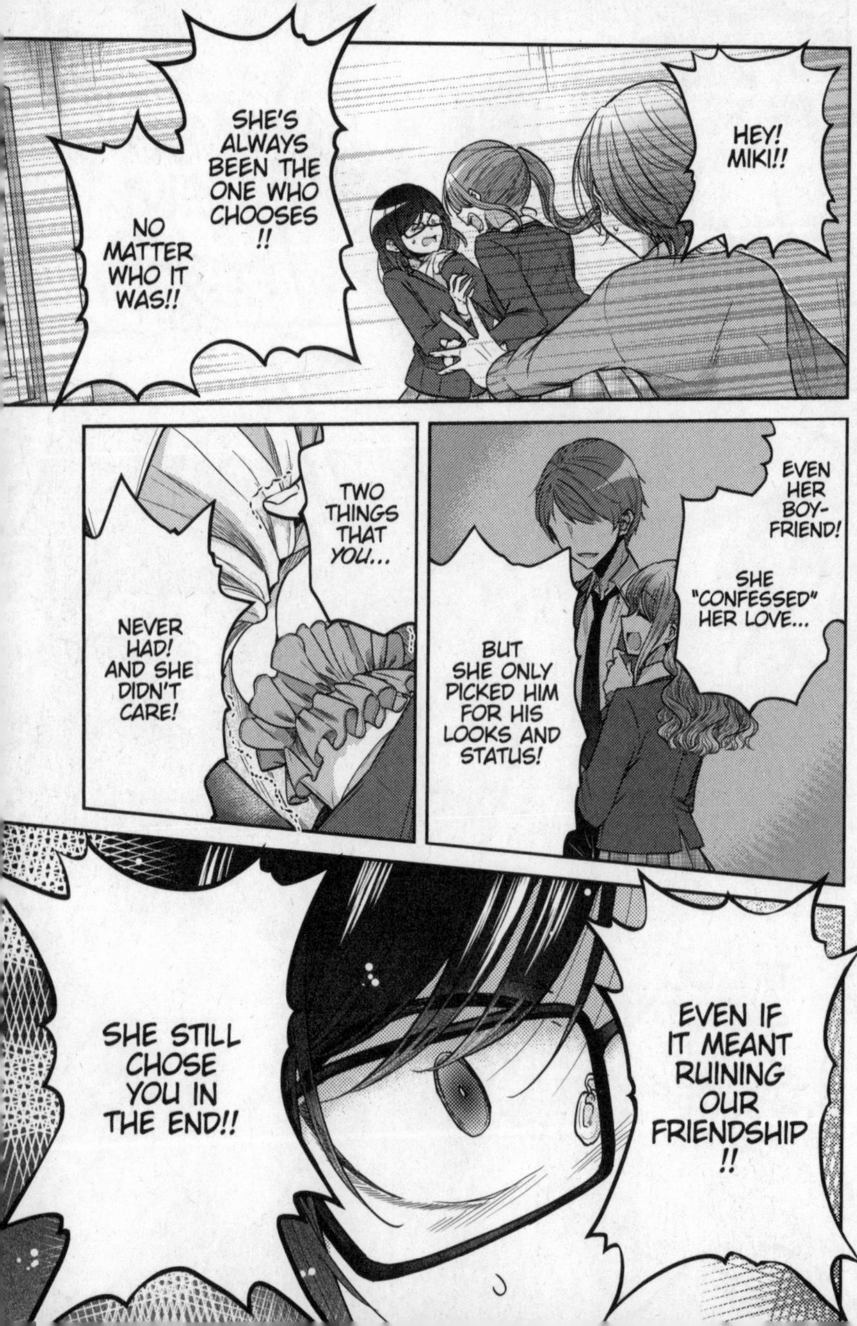
HEY! MIKI!!
SHE'S ALWAYS BEEN THE ONE WHO CHOOSES !!
NO MATTER WHO IT WAS!!
EVEN HER BOY-FRIEND!
SHE "CONFESSED" HER LOVE...
BUT SHE ONLY PICKED HIM FOR HIS LOOKS AND STATUS!
TWO THINGS THAT YOU...
NEVER HAD! AND SHE DIDN'T CARE!
EVEN IF IT MEANT RUINING OUR FRIENDSHIP !!
SHE STILL CHOSE YOU IN THE END!!

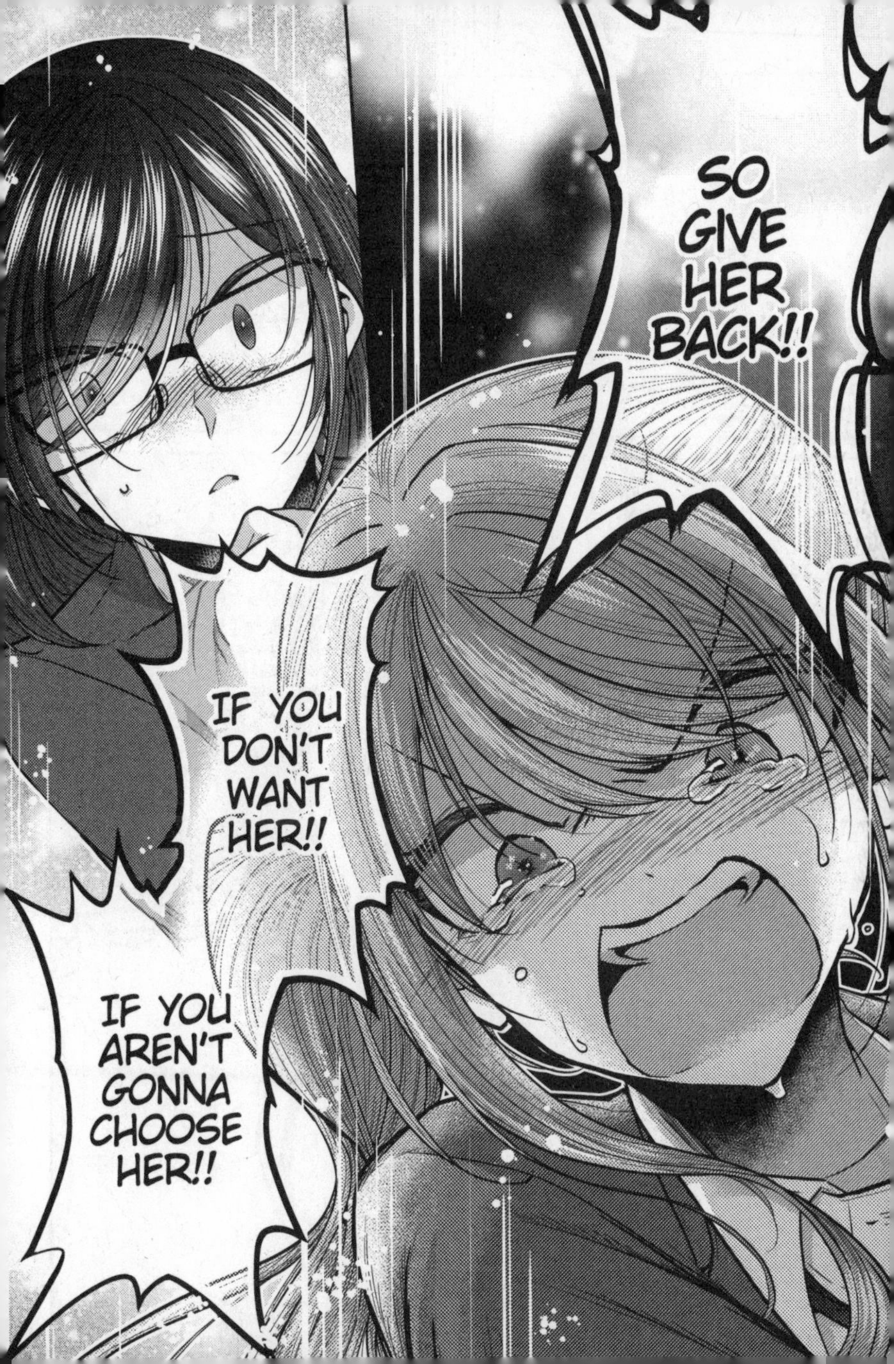
SO GIVE HER BACK!!
IF YOU DON'T WANT HER!!
IF YOU AREN'T GONNA CHOOSE HER!!

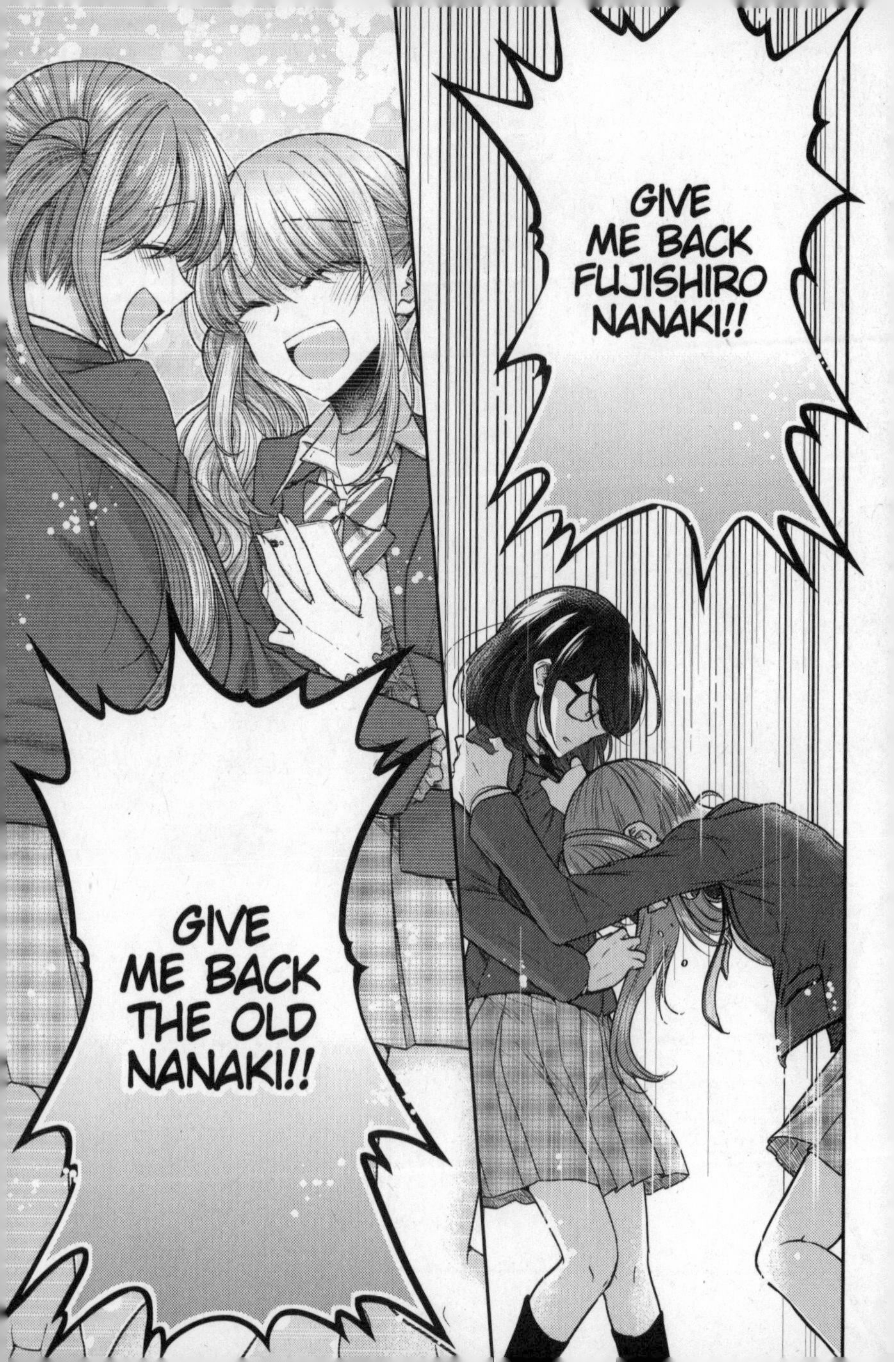
GIVE ME BACK FUJISHIRO NANAKI!!
GIVE ME BACK THE OLD NANAKI!!

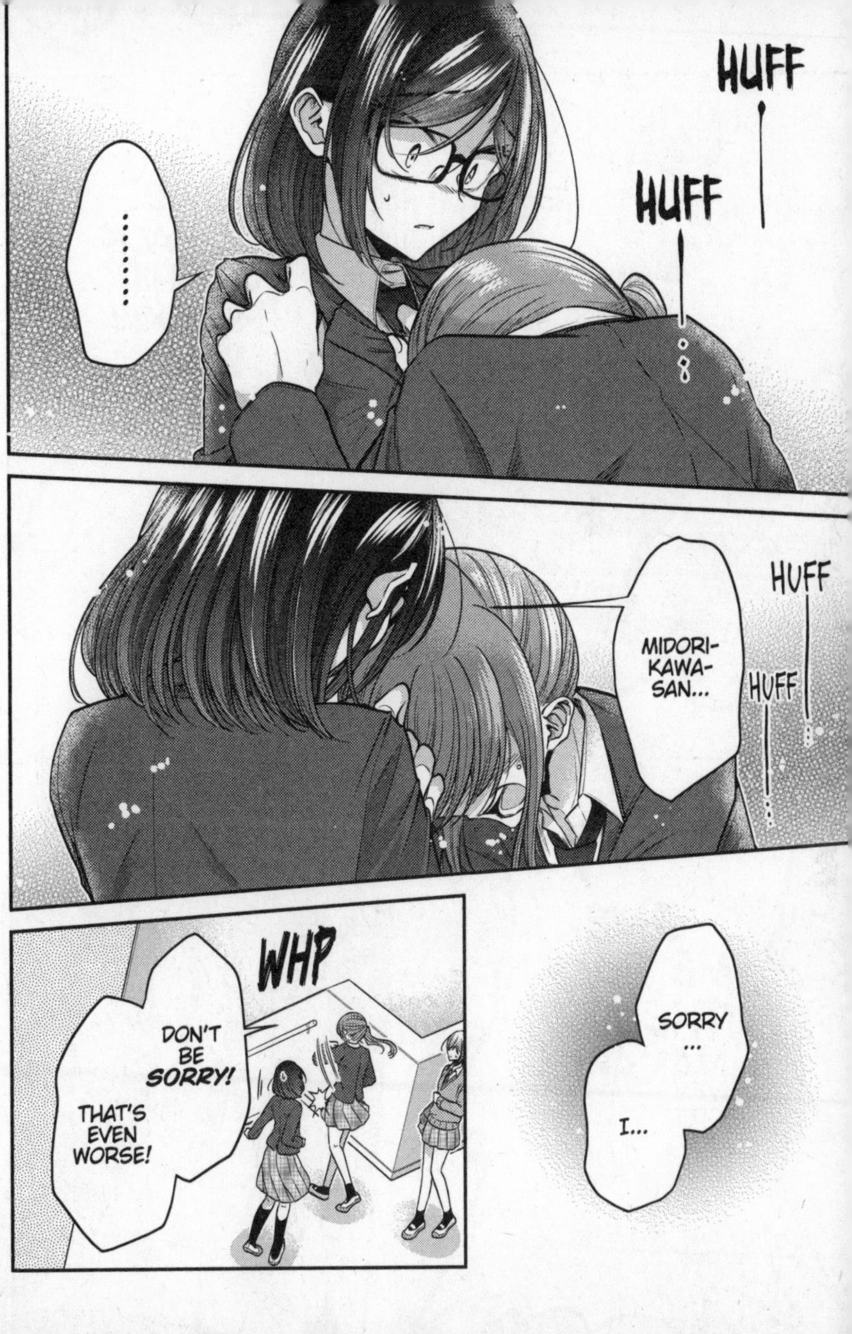
HUFF
HUFF
......
HUFF
HUFF
MIDORI-KAWA-SAN...
SORRY ...
I...
WHP
DON'T BE SORRY!
THAT'S EVEN WORSE!

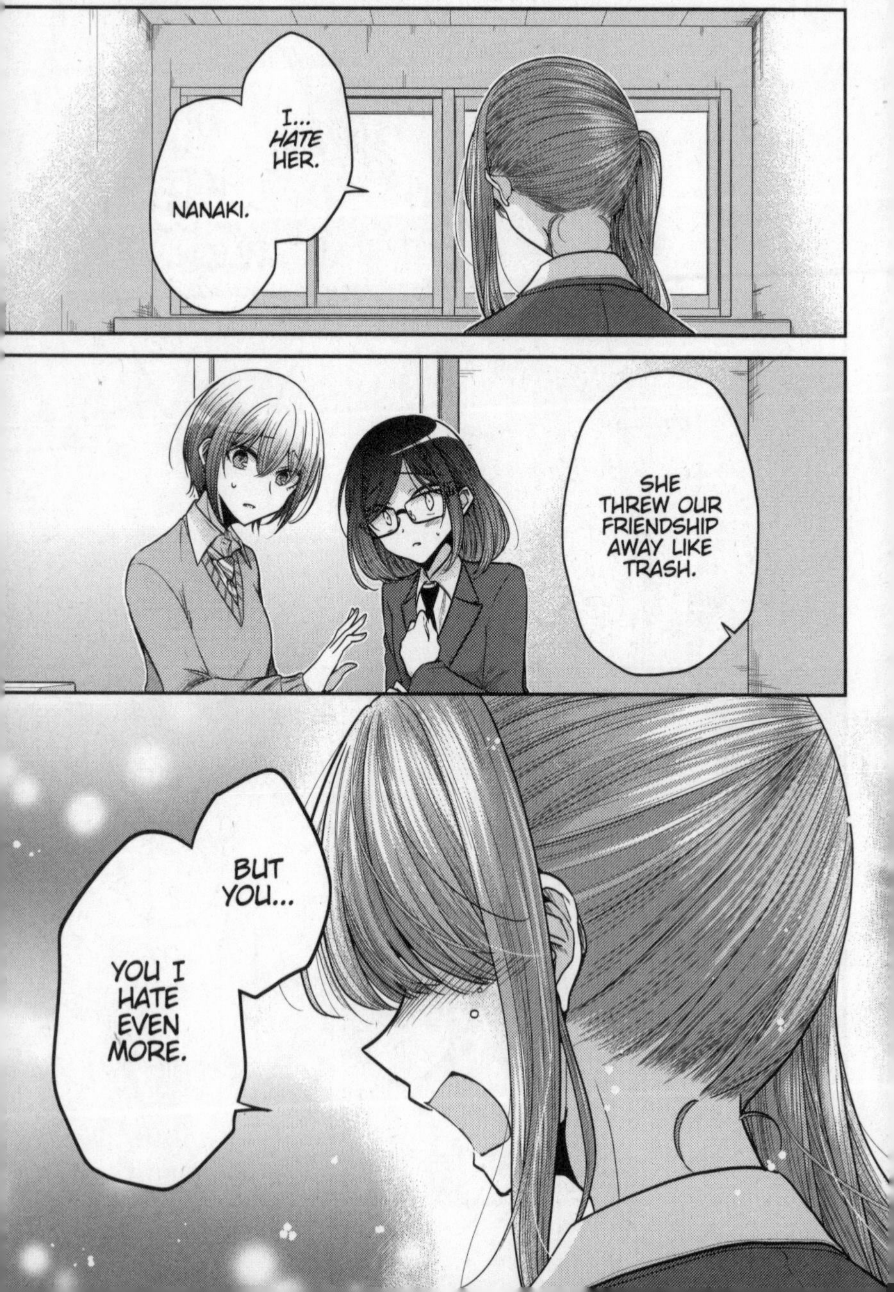
I... HATE HER.
NANAKI.
SHE THREW OUR FRIENDSHIP AWAY LIKE TRASH.
BUT YOU...
YOU I HATE EVEN MORE.

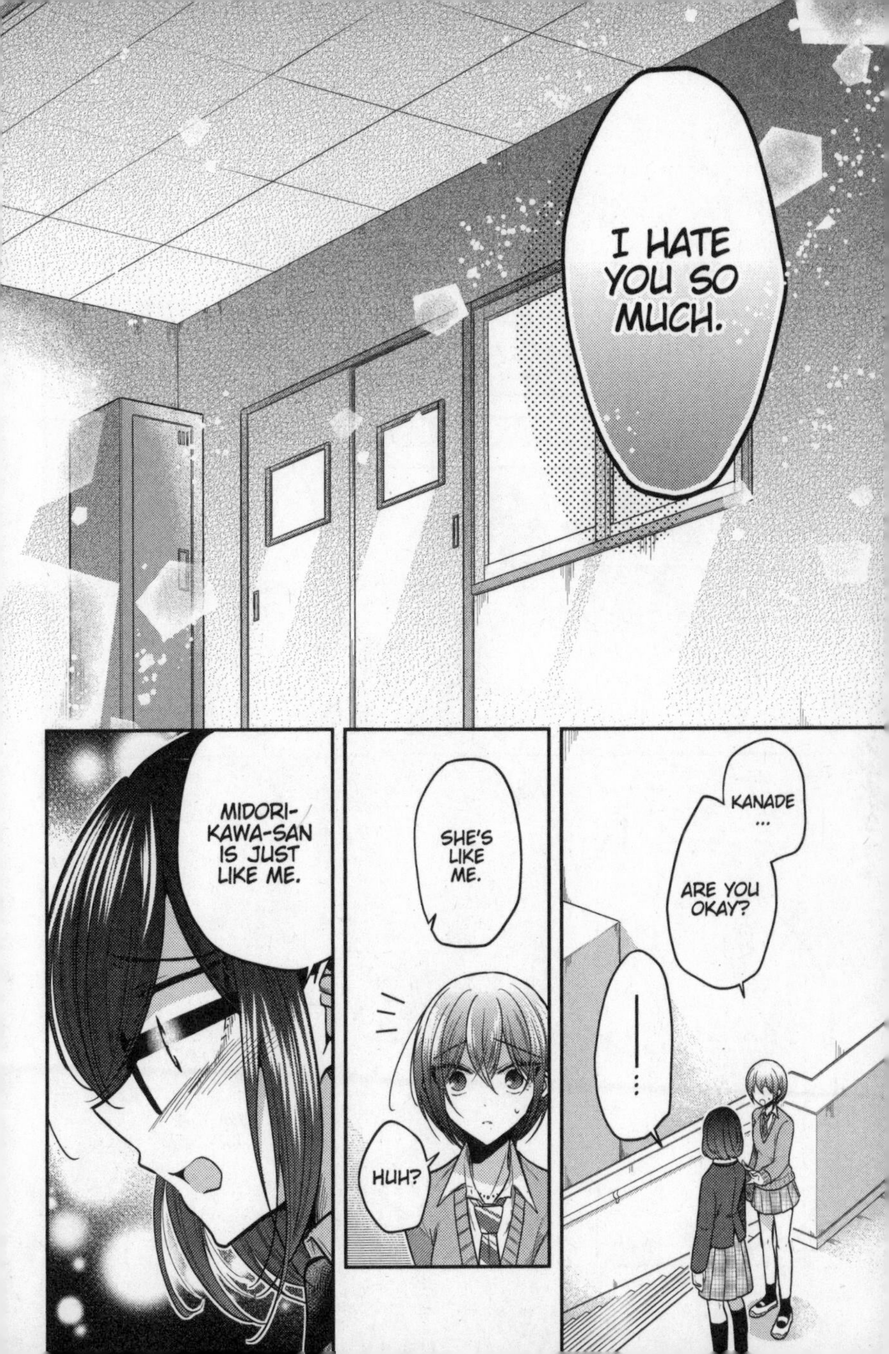
I HATE YOU SO MUCH.
KANADE ... ARE YOU OKAY?
—...
SHE'S LIKE ME.
HUH?
MIDORI-KAWA-SAN IS JUST LIKE ME.

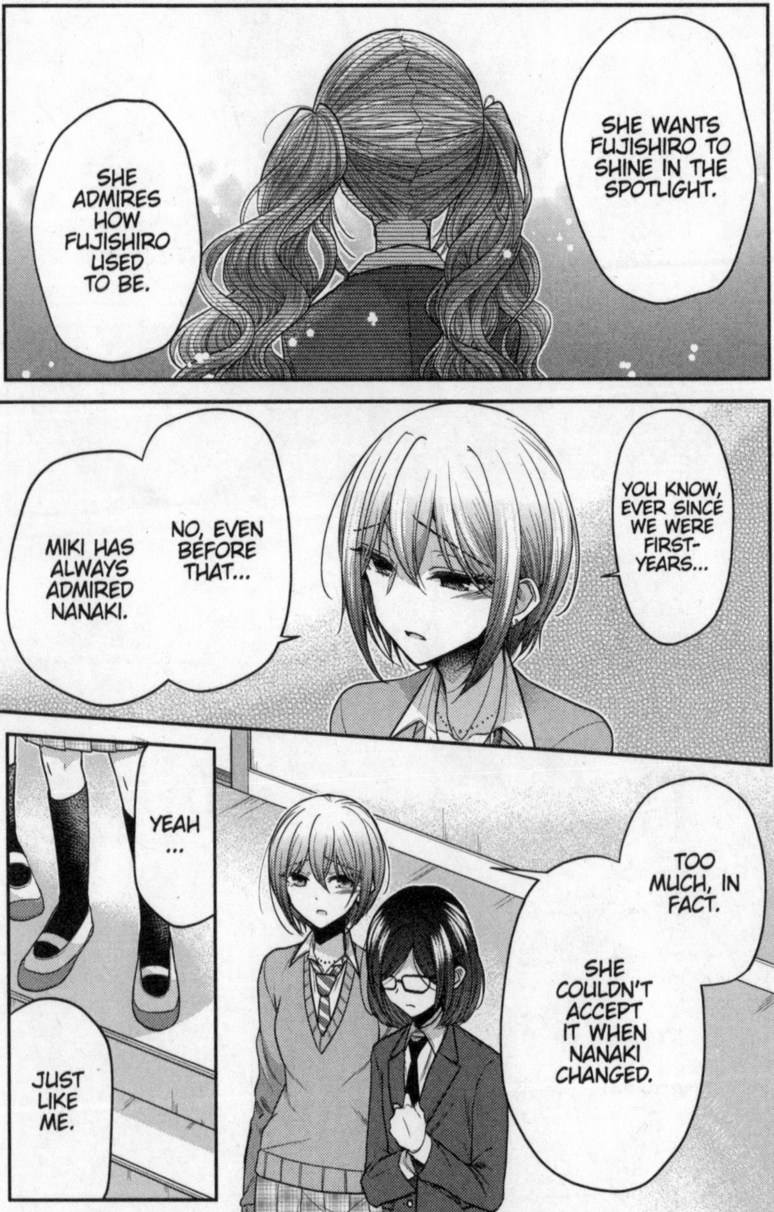
SHE WANTS FUJISHIRO TO SHINE IN THE SPOTLIGHT.
SHE ADMIRES HOW FUJISHIRO USED TO BE.
YOU KNOW, EVER SINCE WE WERE FIRST-YEARS...
NO, EVEN BEFORE THAT...
MIKI HAS ALWAYS ADMIRED NANAKI.
TOO MUCH, IN FACT.
SHE COULDN'T ACCEPT IT WHEN NANAKI CHANGED.
YEAH ...
JUST LIKE ME.

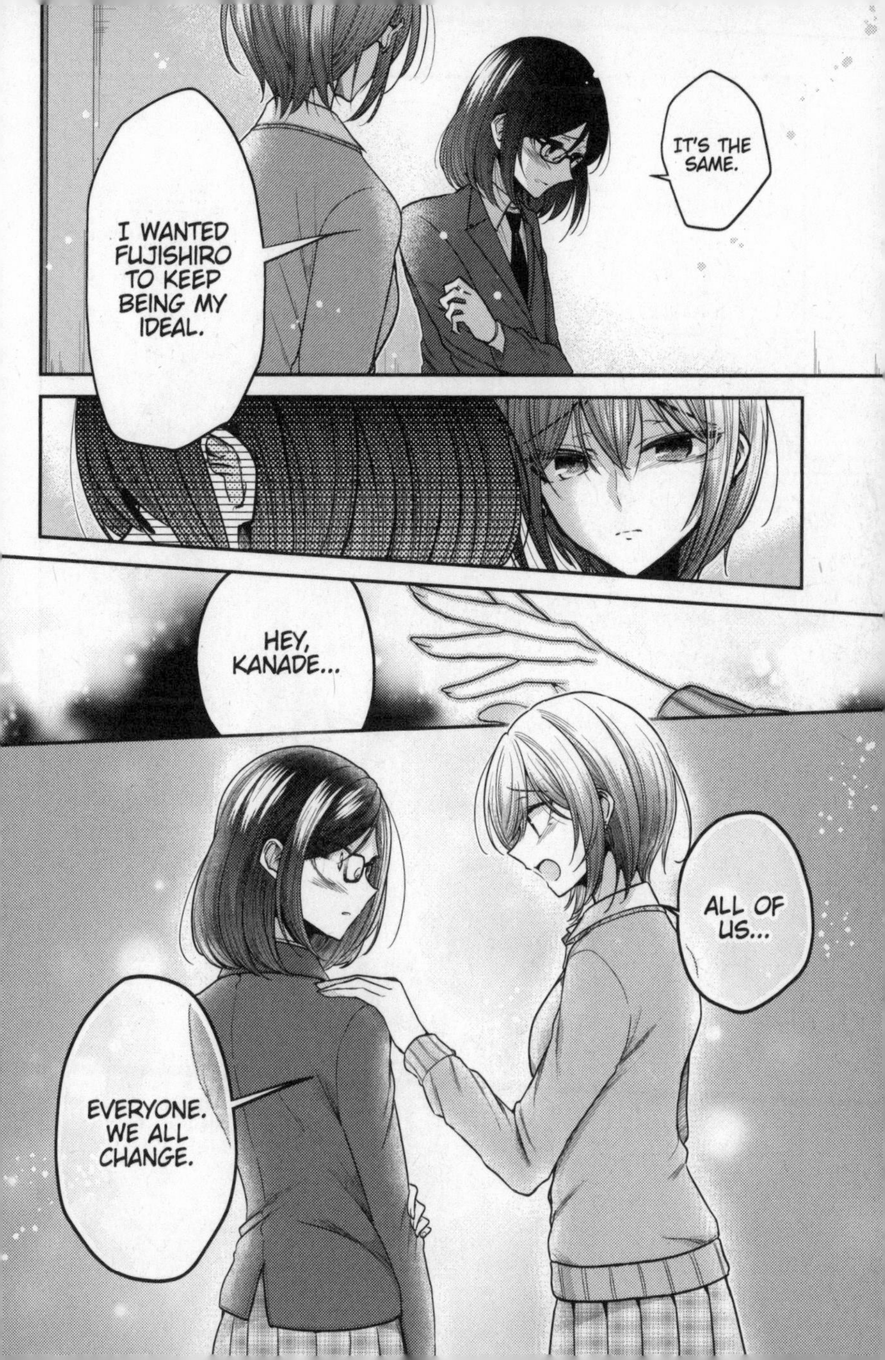
IT'S THE SAME.
I WANTED FUJISHIRO TO KEEP BEING MY IDEAL.
HEY, KANADE...
ALL OF US...
EVERYONE. WE ALL CHANGE.

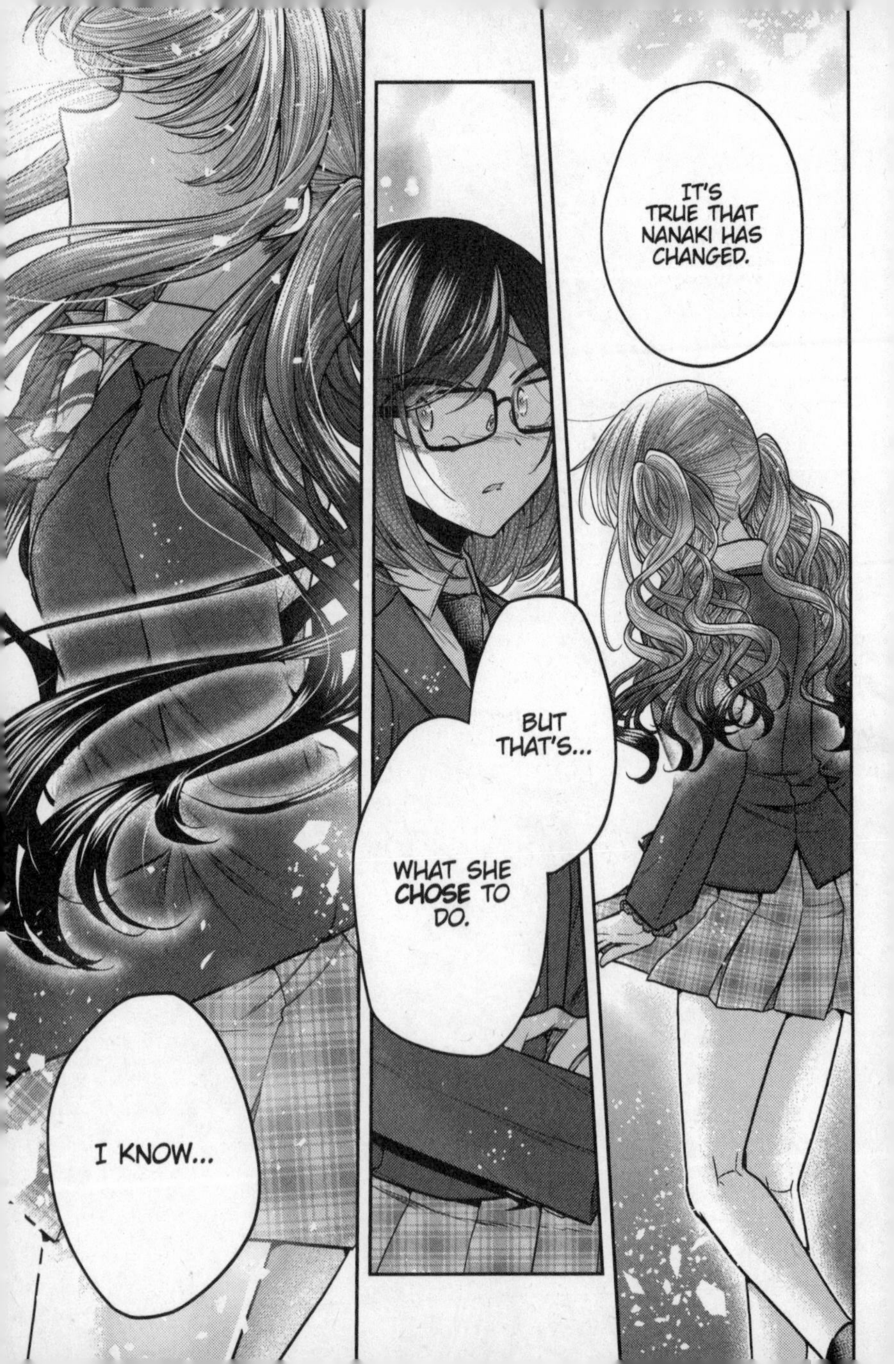
IT'S TRUE THAT NANAKI HAS CHANGED.
BUT THAT'S...
WHAT SHE CHOSE TO DO.
I KNOW...

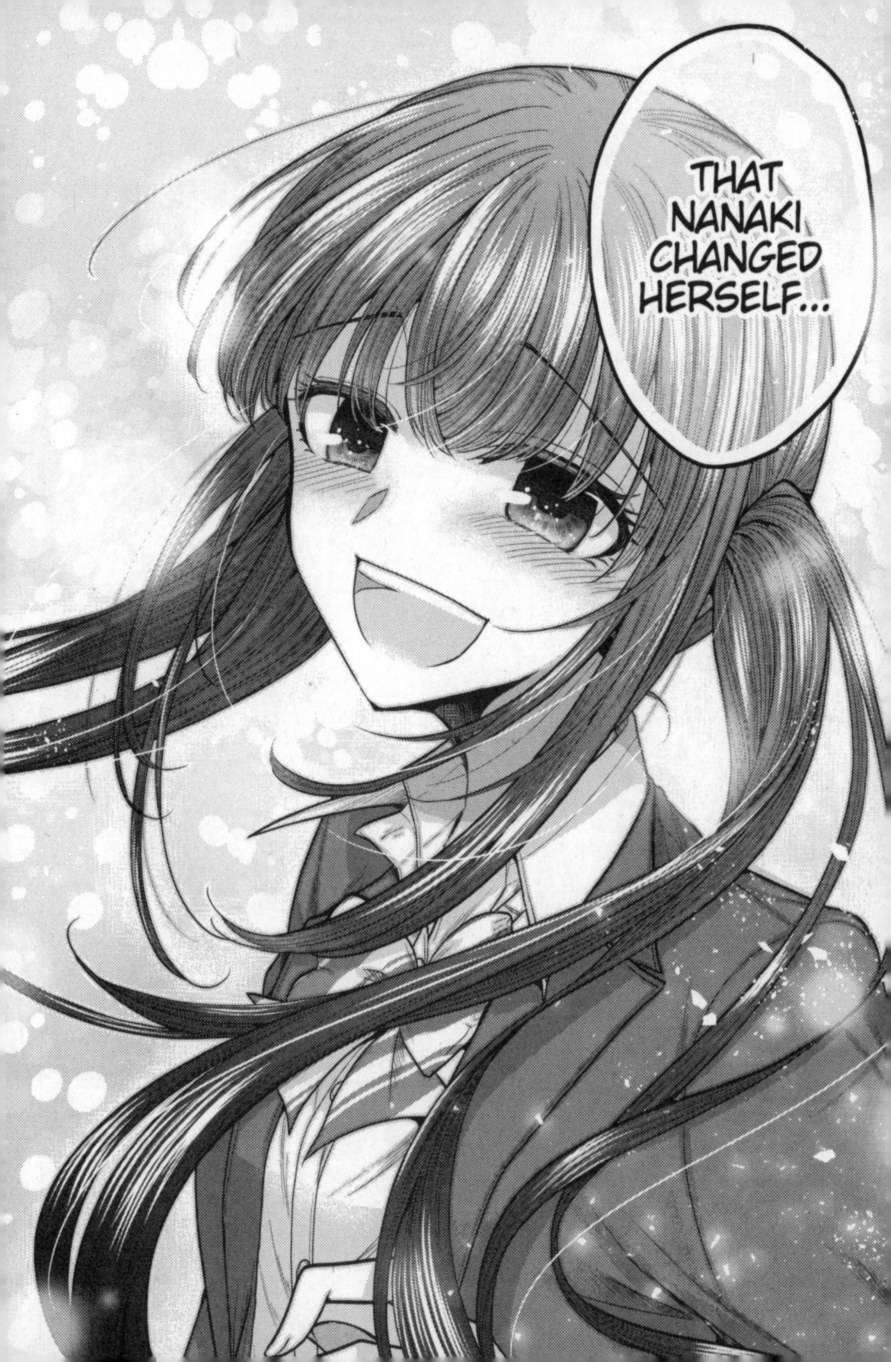
THAT NANAKI CHANGED HERSELF...

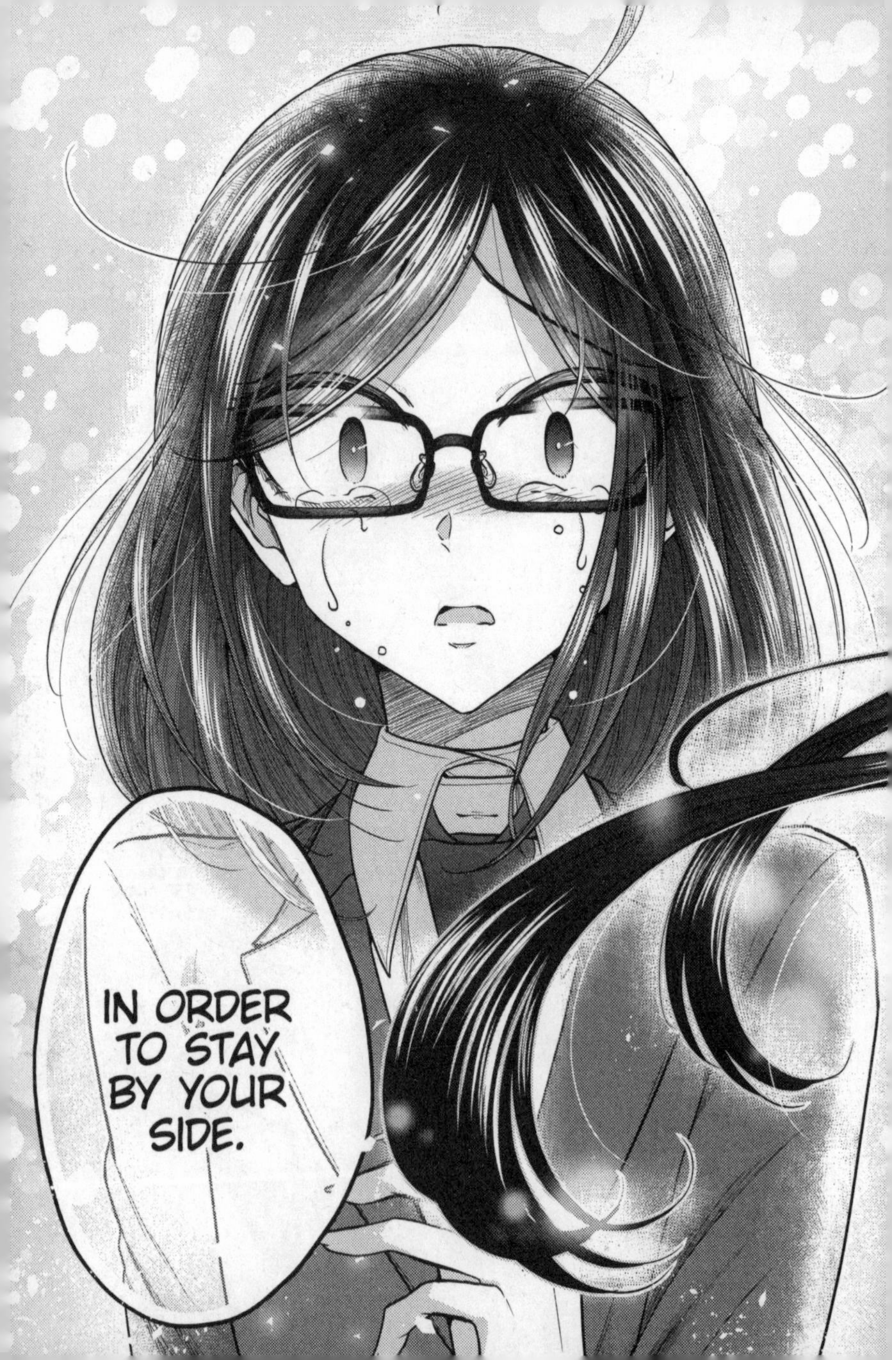
IN ORDER TO STAY BY YOUR SIDE.

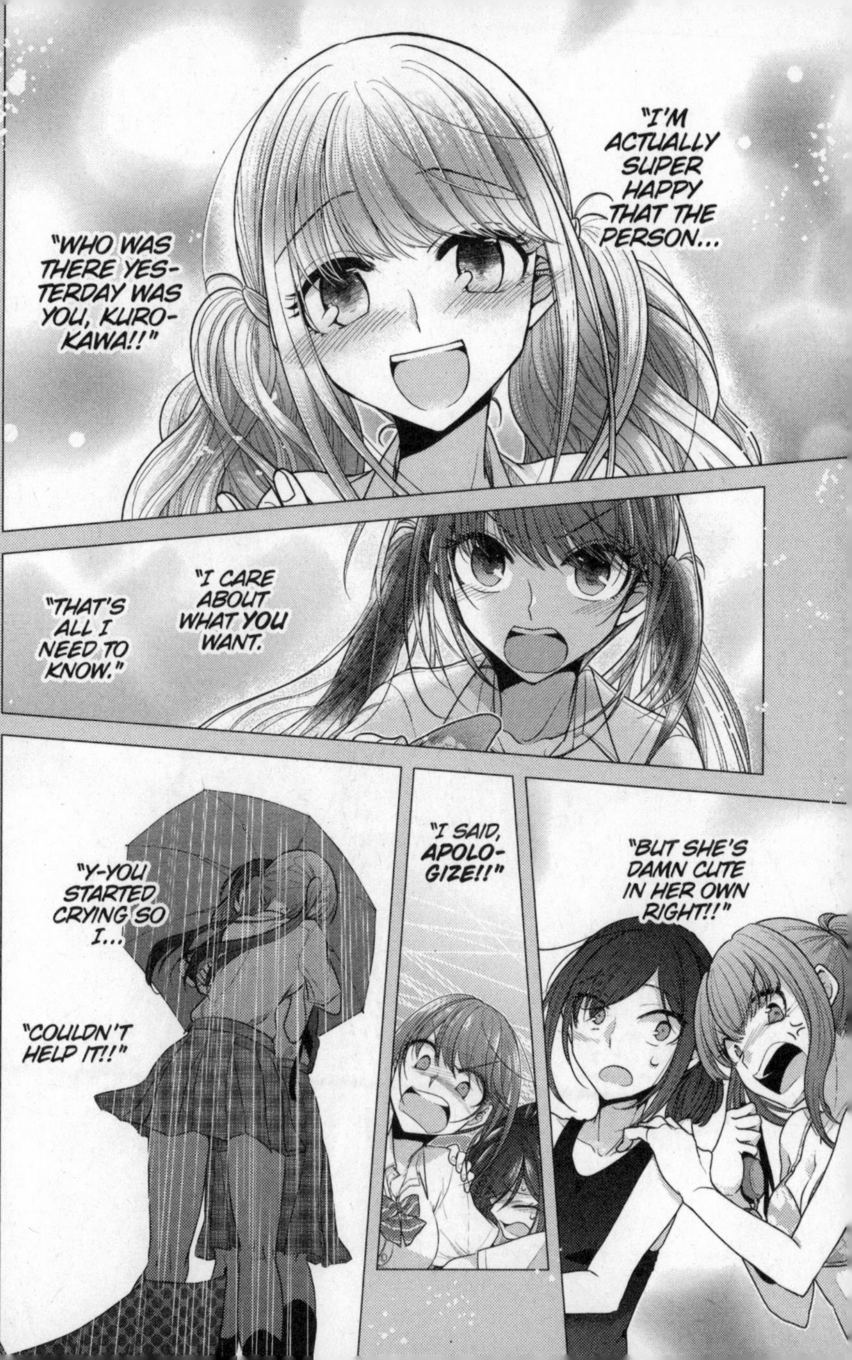
"I'M ACTUALLY SUPER HAPPY THAT THE PERSON...
"WHO WAS THERE YESTERDAY WAS YOU, KUROKAWA!!"
"I CARE ABOUT WHAT YOU WANT.
"THAT'S ALL I NEED TO KNOW."
"BUT SHE'S DAMN CUTE IN HER OWN RIGHT!!"
"I SAID, APOLOGIZE!!"
"Y-YOU STARTED CRYING SO I...
"COULDN'T HELP IT!!"

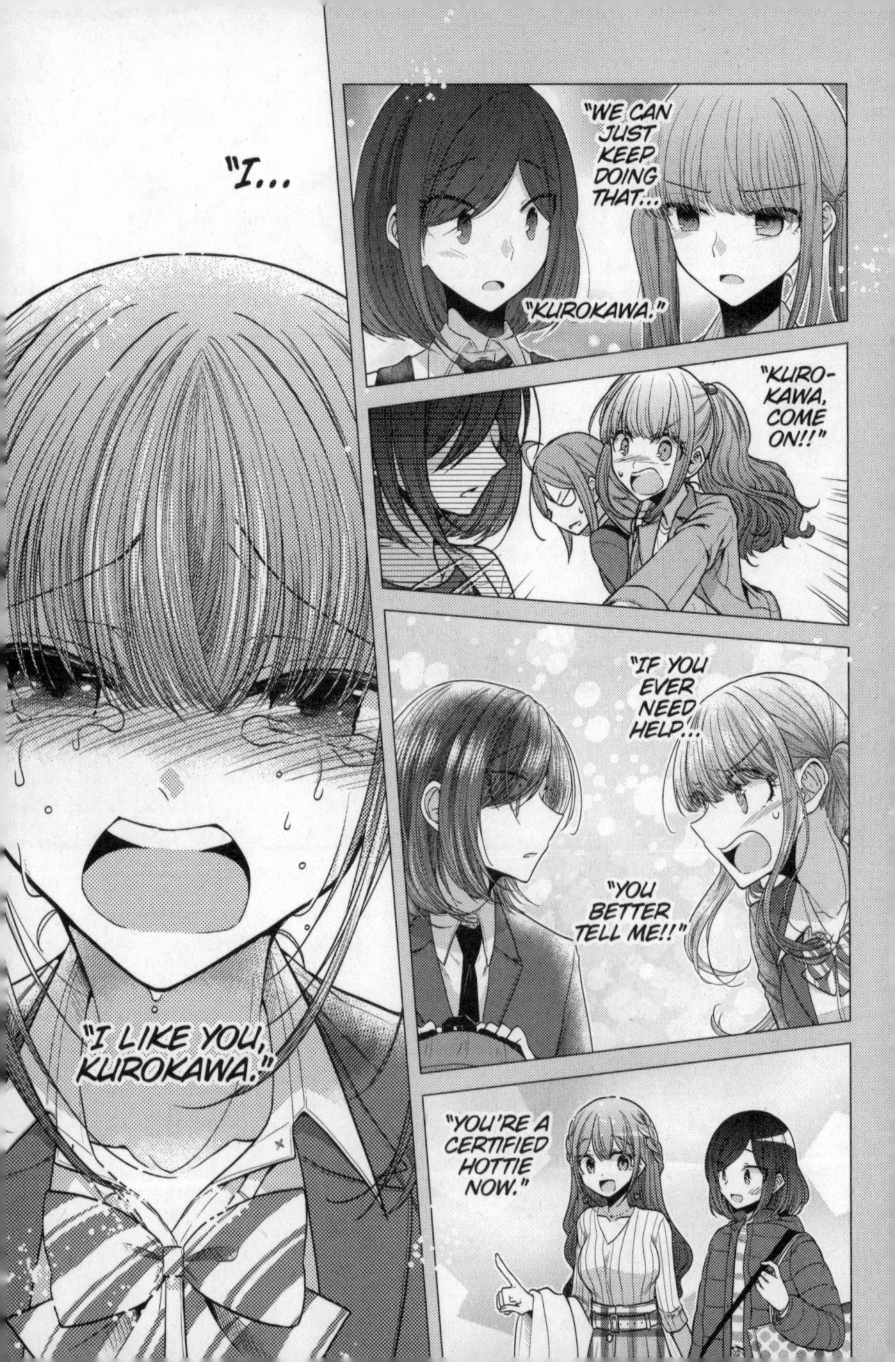
"WE CAN JUST KEEP DOING THAT...
"KUROKAWA."
"KURO-KAWA, COME ON!!"
"IF YOU EVER NEED HELP...
"YOU BETTER TELL ME!!"
"YOU'RE A CERTIFIED HOTTIE NOW."
"I...
"I LIKE YOU, KUROKAWA."

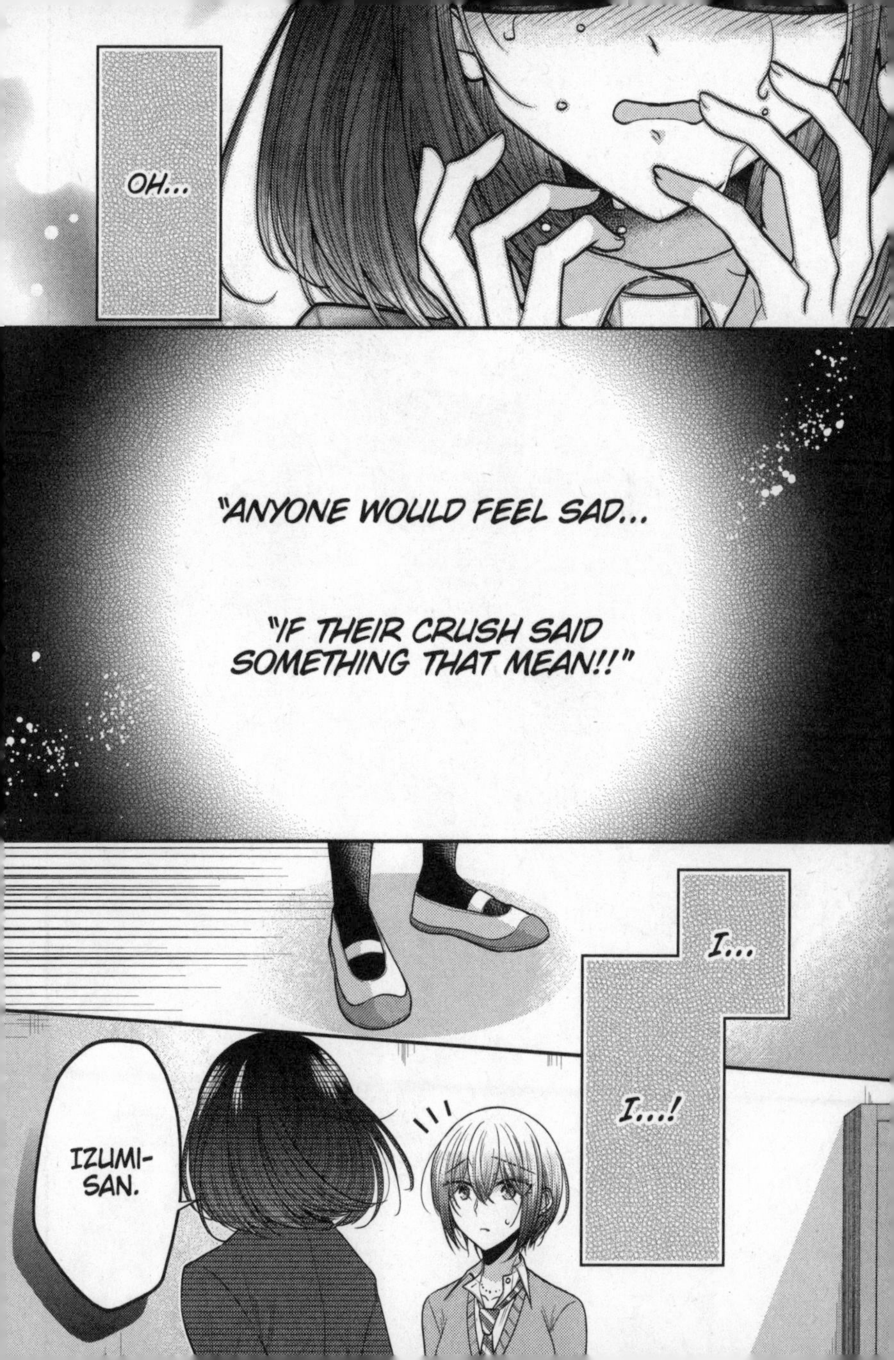
OH...
"ANYONE WOULD FEEL SAD...
"IF THEIR CRUSH SAID SOMETHING THAT MEAN!!"
I...
I...!
IZUMI-SAN.

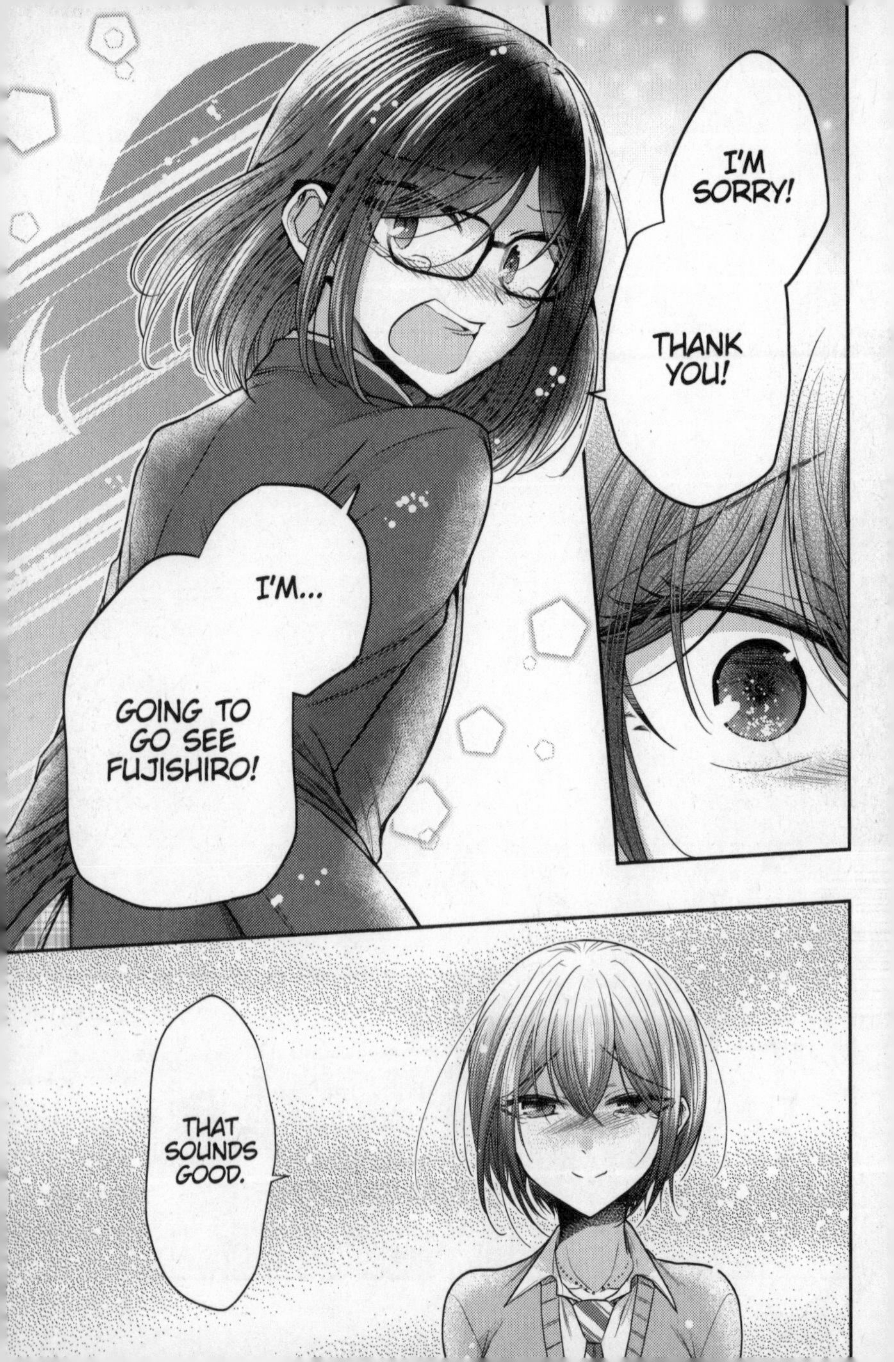
I'M SORRY!
THANK YOU!
I'M...
GOING TO GO SEE FUJISHIRO!
THAT SOUNDS GOOD.

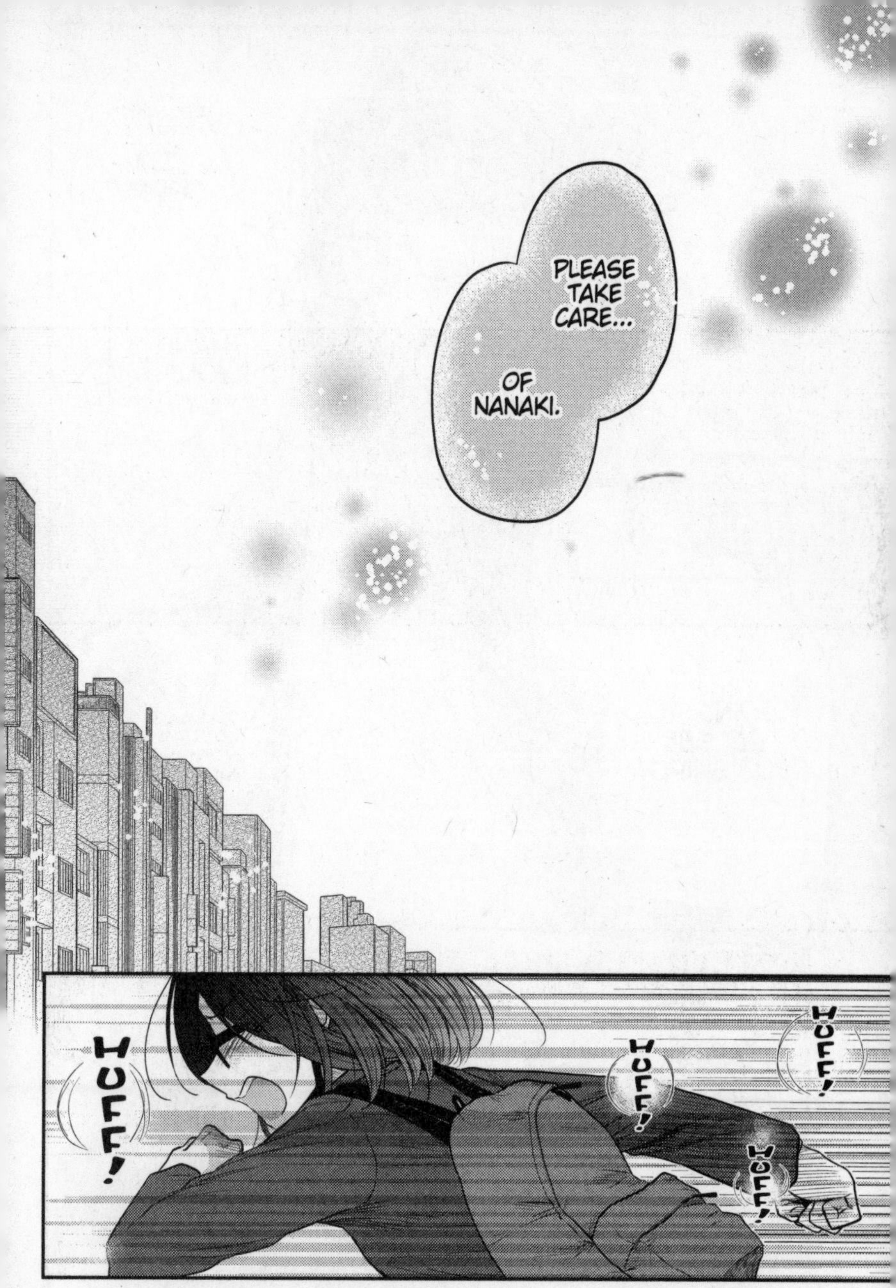
PLEASE TAKE CARE...
OF NANAKI.
HUFF!
HUFF!
HUFF!
HUFF!

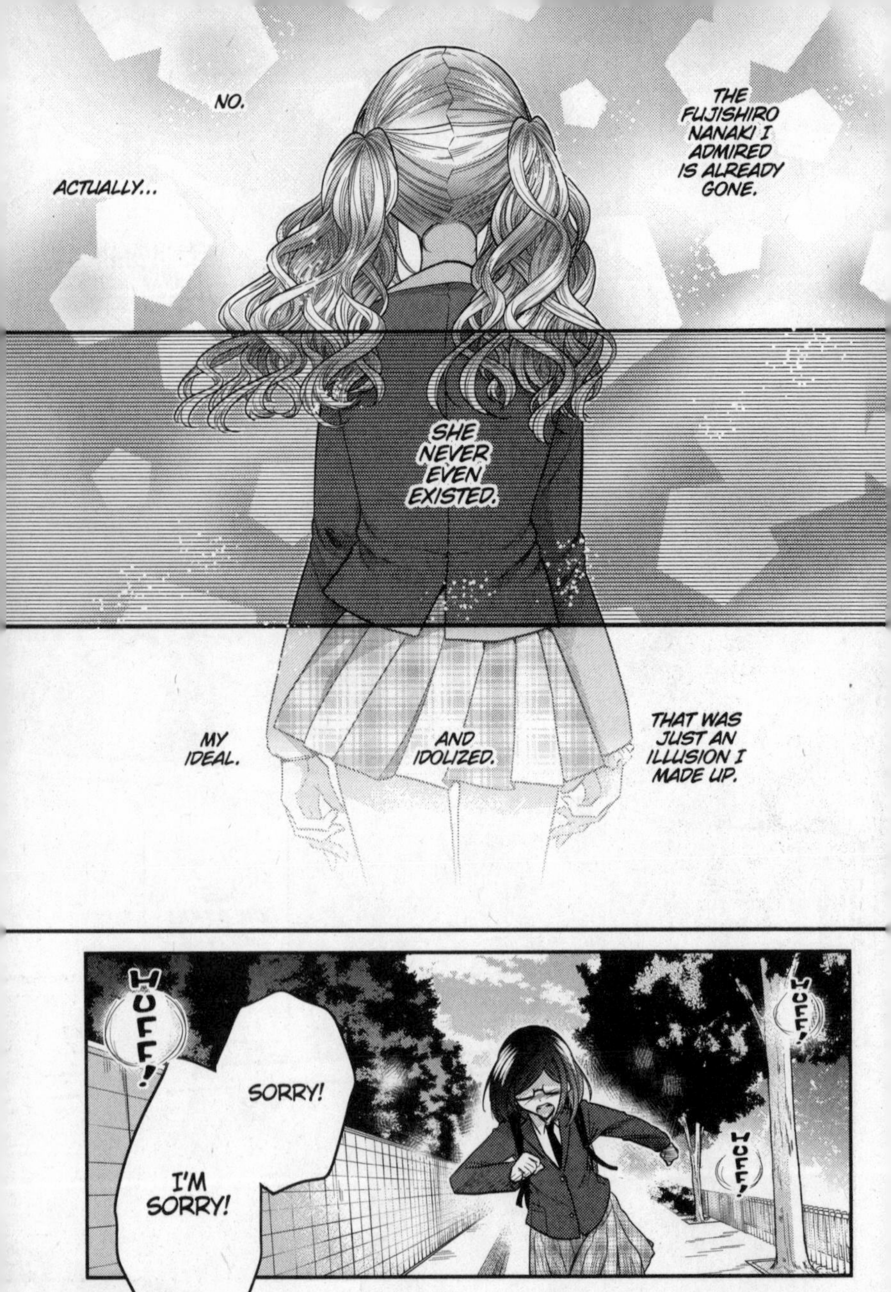
THE FUJISHIRO NANAKI I ADMIRED IS ALREADY GONE.
NO.
ACTUALLY...
SHE NEVER EVEN EXISTED.
THAT WAS JUST AN ILLUSION I MADE UP.
AND IDOLIZED.
MY IDEAL.
HUFF!
HUFF!
SORRY!
I'M SORRY!
HUFF!

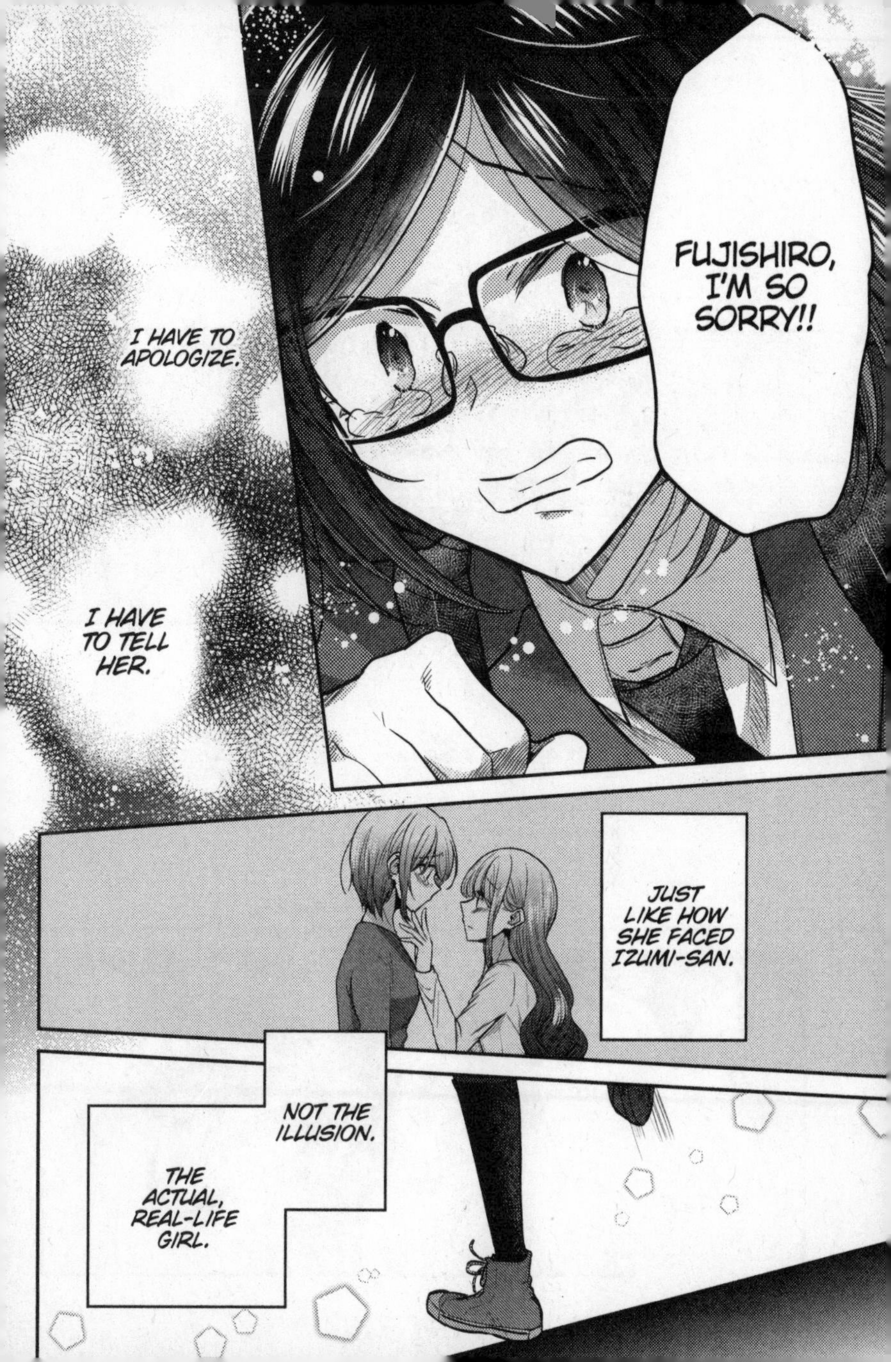
FUJISHIRO, I'M SO SORRY!!
I HAVE TO APOLOGIZE.
I HAVE TO TELL HER.
JUST LIKE HOW SHE FACED IZUMI-SAN.
NOT THE ILLUSION.
THE ACTUAL, REAL-LIFE GIRL.

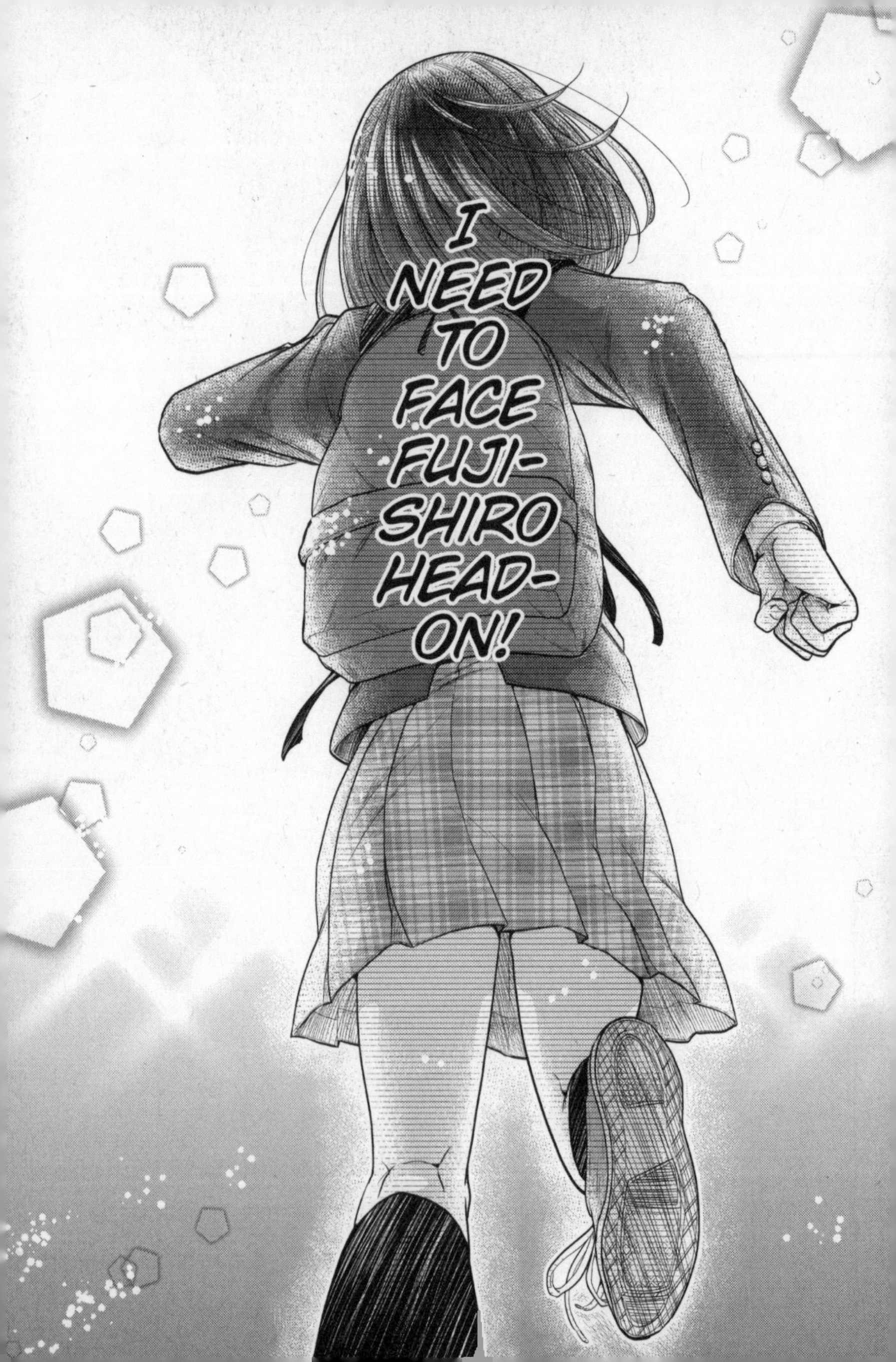
I NEED TO FACE FUJI-SHIRO HEAD-ON!

Failed Princesses

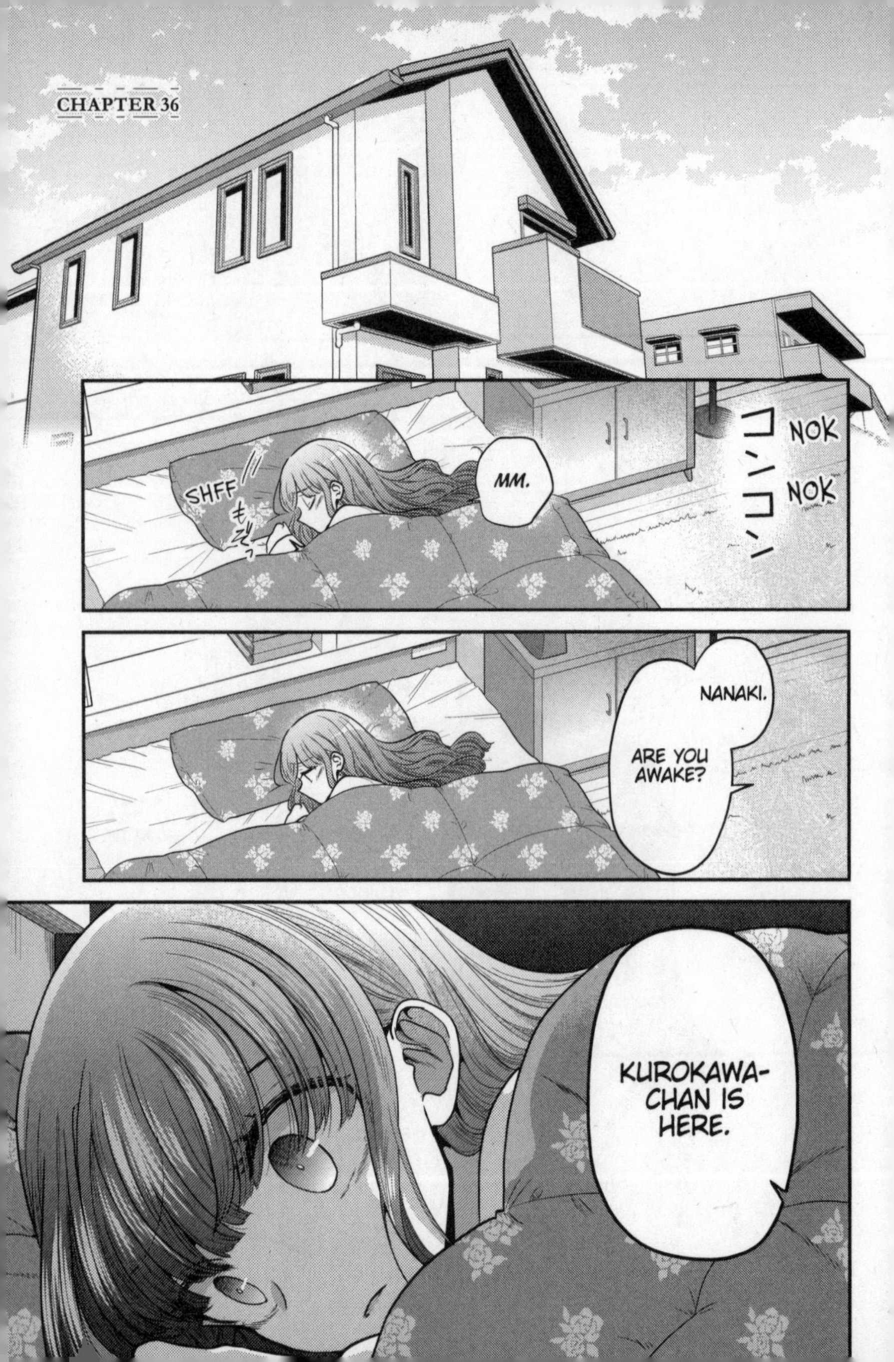
CHAPTER 36
コンコン
NOK NOK
MM.
SHFF もぞっ
NANAKI.
ARE YOU AWAKE?
KUROKAWA-CHAN IS HERE.

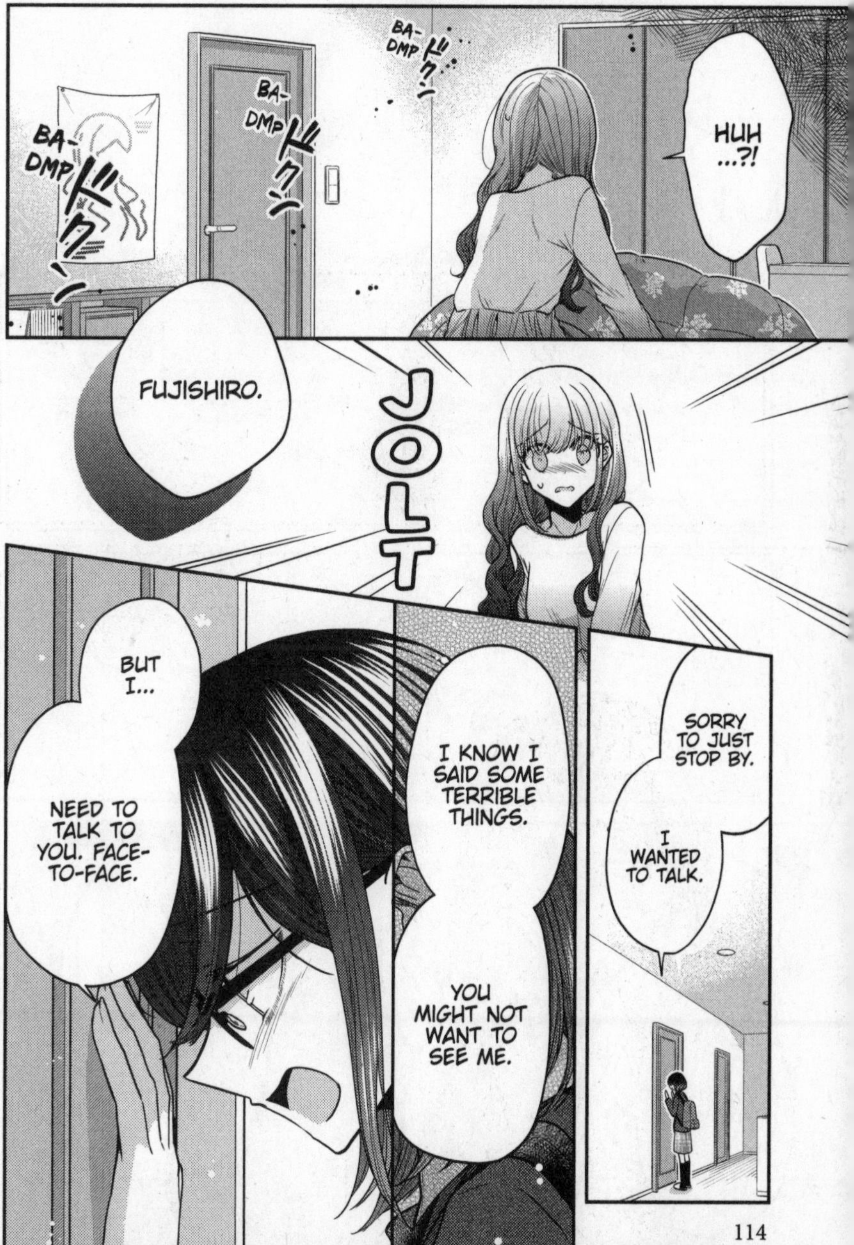
HUH ...?!
BA-DMP ドクン
BA-DMP ドクン
BA-DMP ドクン
FUJISHIRO.
JOLT
SORRY TO JUST STOP BY.
I WANTED TO TALK.
I KNOW I SAID SOME TERRIBLE THINGS.
YOU MIGHT NOT WANT TO SEE ME.
BUT I...
NEED TO TALK TO YOU. FACE-TO-FACE.

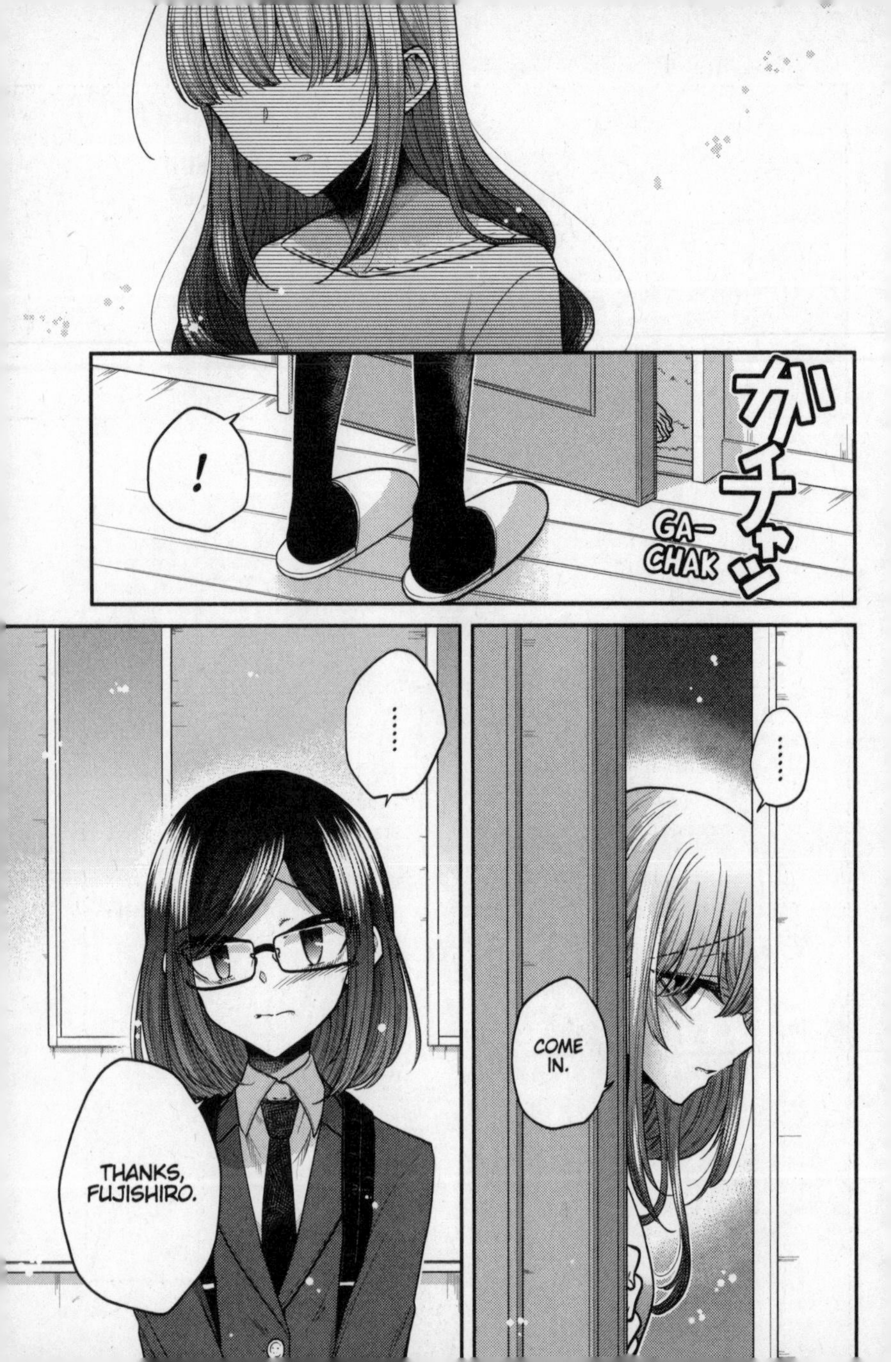
ガチャッ
GA-CHAK
!
......
COME IN.
......
THANKS, FUJISHIRO.

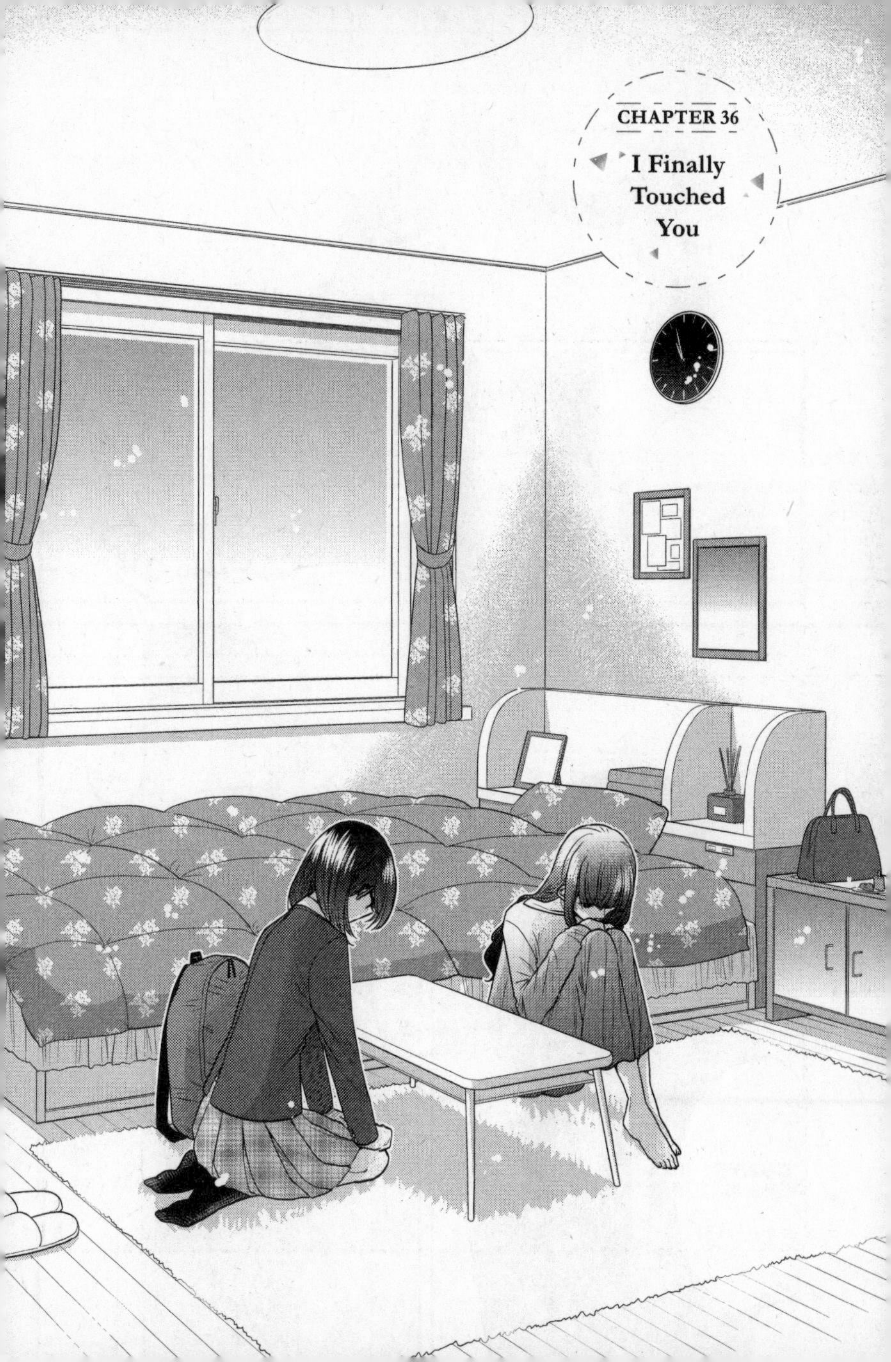
CHAPTER 36
I Finally Touched You

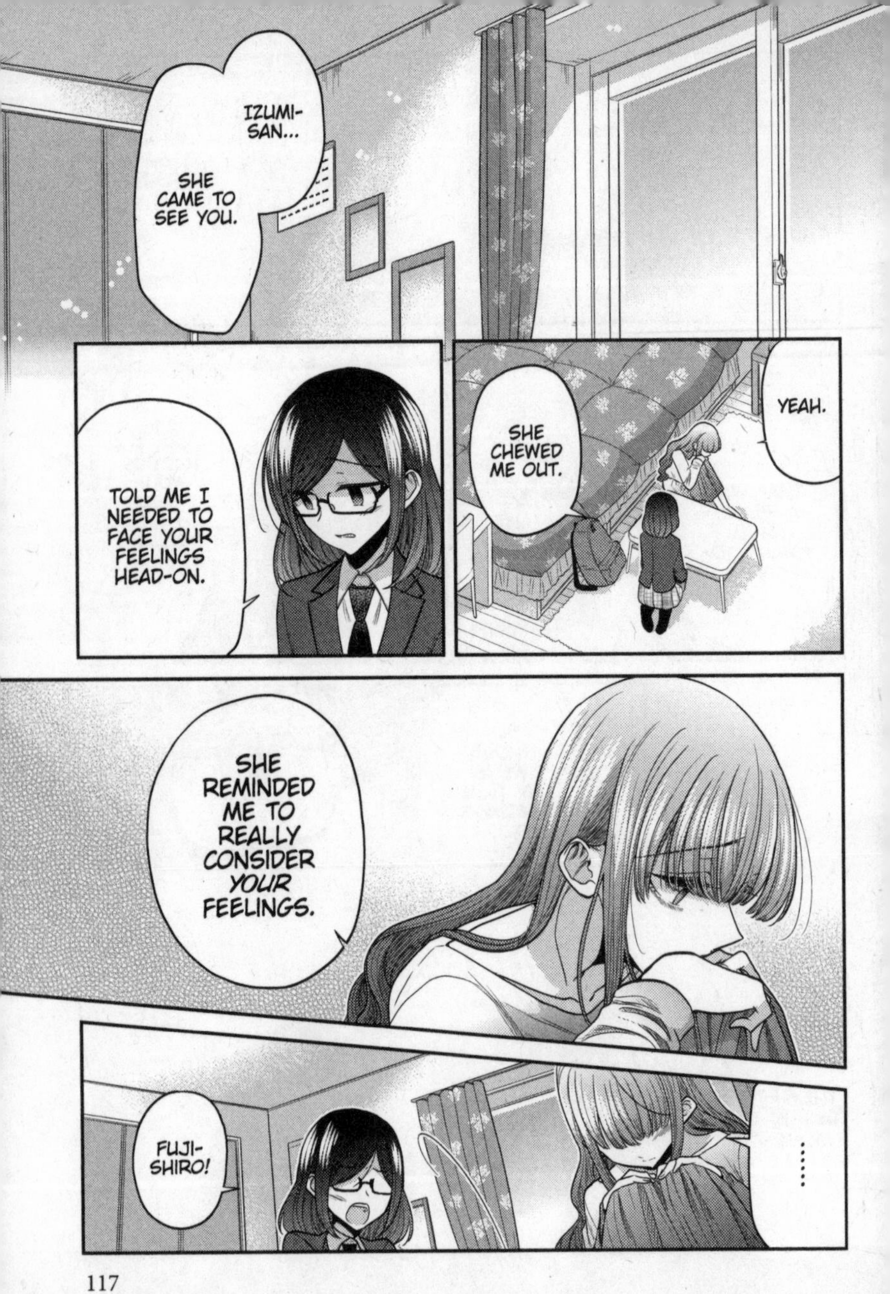
IZUMI-SAN...
SHE CAME TO SEE YOU.
YEAH.
SHE CHEWED ME OUT.
TOLD ME I NEEDED TO FACE YOUR FEELINGS HEAD-ON.
SHE REMINDED ME TO REALLY CONSIDER *YOUR* FEELINGS.
......
FUJI-SHIRO!

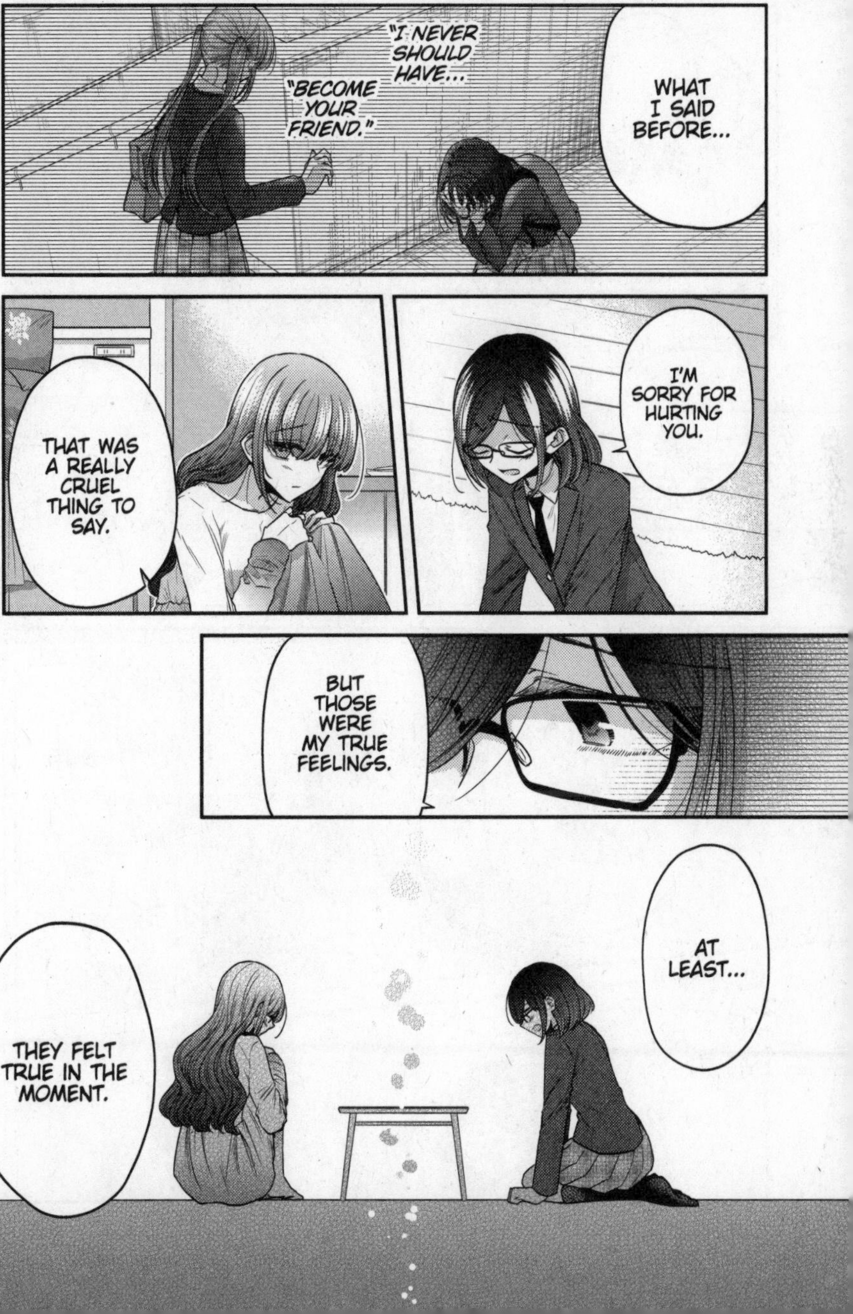
WHAT I SAID BEFORE...
"I NEVER SHOULD HAVE...
"BECOME YOUR FRIEND."
I'M SORRY FOR HURTING YOU.
THAT WAS A REALLY CRUEL THING TO SAY.
BUT THOSE WERE MY TRUE FEELINGS.
AT LEAST...
THEY FELT TRUE IN THE MOMENT.

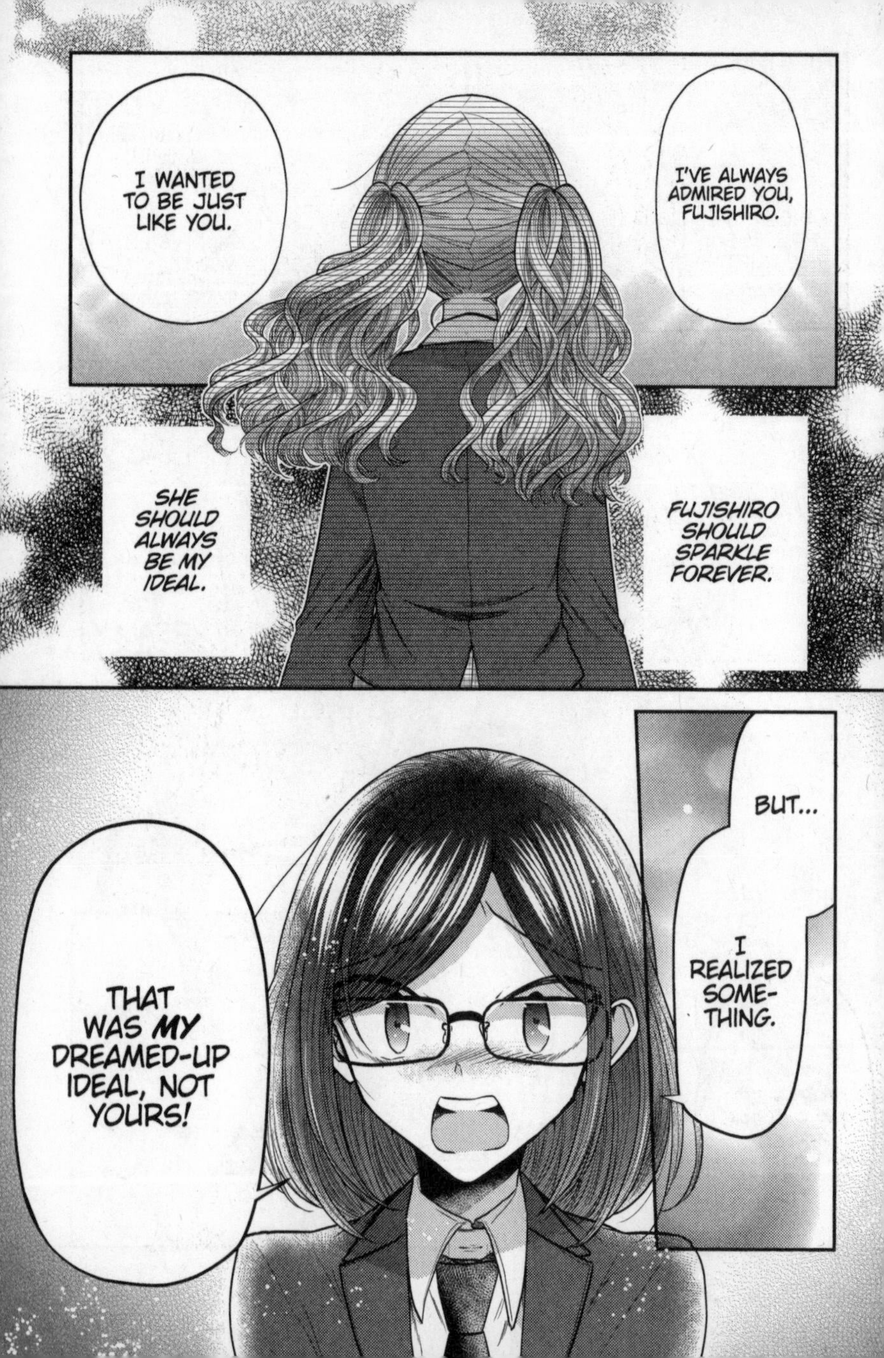
I'VE ALWAYS ADMIRED YOU, FUJISHIRO.
I WANTED TO BE JUST LIKE YOU.
FUJISHIRO SHOULD SPARKLE FOREVER.
SHE SHOULD ALWAYS BE MY IDEAL.
BUT...
I REALIZED SOME-THING.
THAT WAS MY DREAMED-UP IDEAL, NOT YOURS!

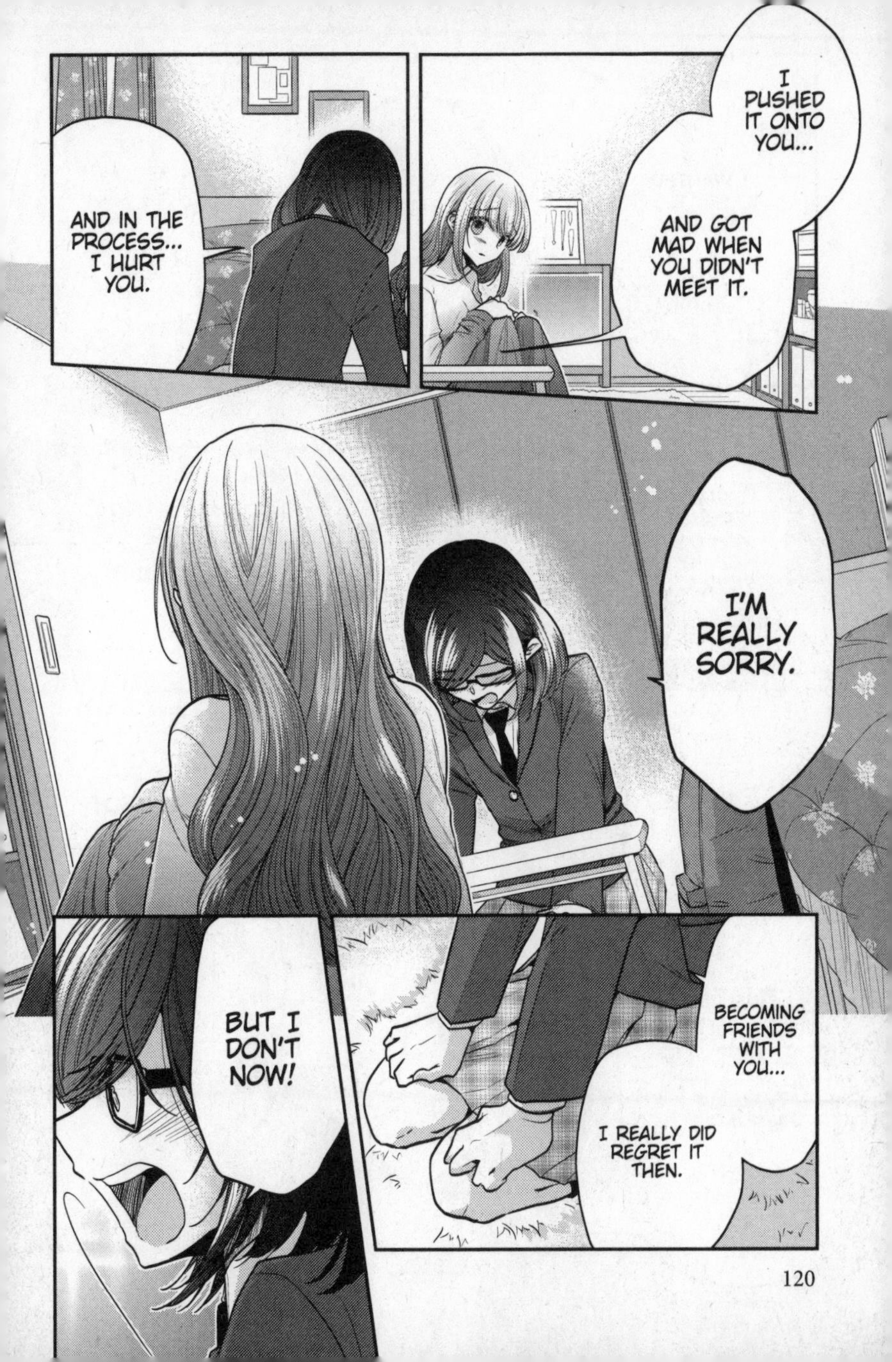

I PUSHED IT ONTO YOU...
AND GOT MAD WHEN YOU DIDN'T MEET IT.
AND IN THE PROCESS... I HURT YOU.
I'M REALLY SORRY.
BECOMING FRIENDS WITH YOU...
I REALLY DID REGRET IT THEN.
BUT I DON'T NOW!

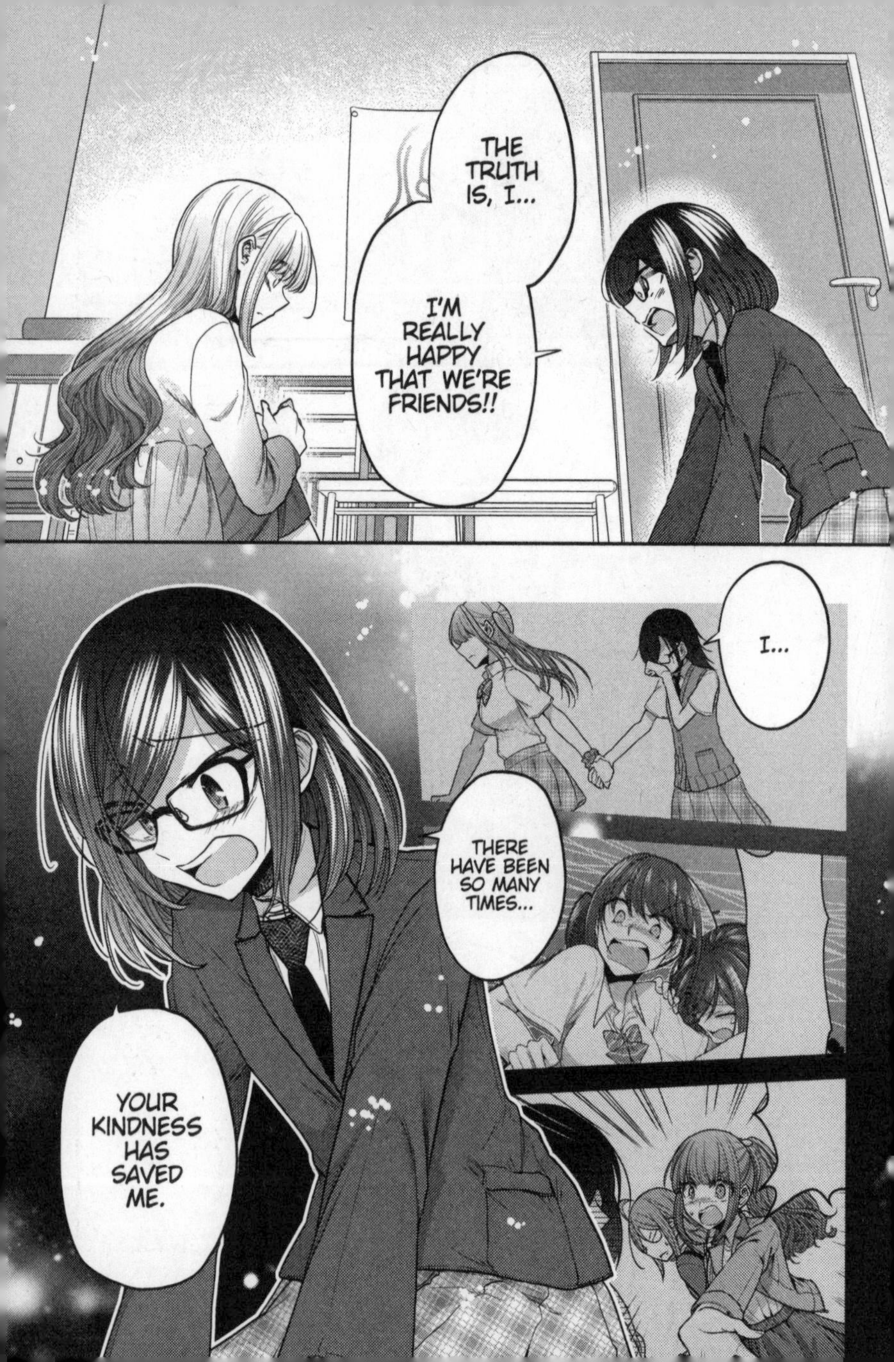
THE TRUTH IS, I...
I'M REALLY HAPPY THAT WE'RE FRIENDS!!
I...
THERE HAVE BEEN SO MANY TIMES...
YOUR KINDNESS HAS SAVED ME.

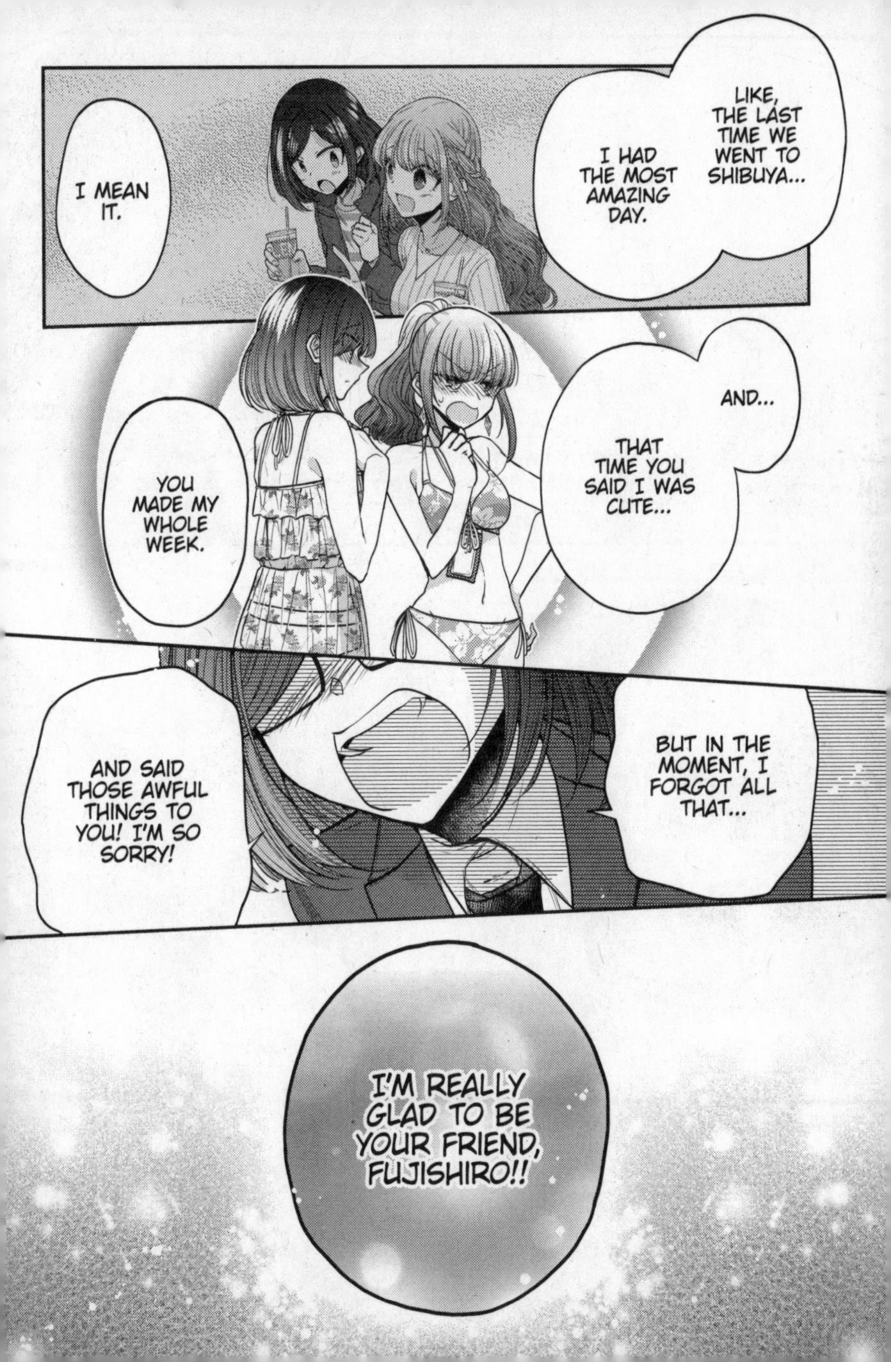
LIKE, THE LAST TIME WE WENT TO SHIBUYA...
I HAD THE MOST AMAZING DAY.
I MEAN IT.
AND...
THAT TIME YOU SAID I WAS CUTE...
YOU MADE MY WHOLE WEEK.
BUT IN THE MOMENT, I FORGOT ALL THAT...
AND SAID THOSE AWFUL THINGS TO YOU! I'M SO SORRY!
I'M REALLY GLAD TO BE YOUR FRIEND, FUJISHIRO!!

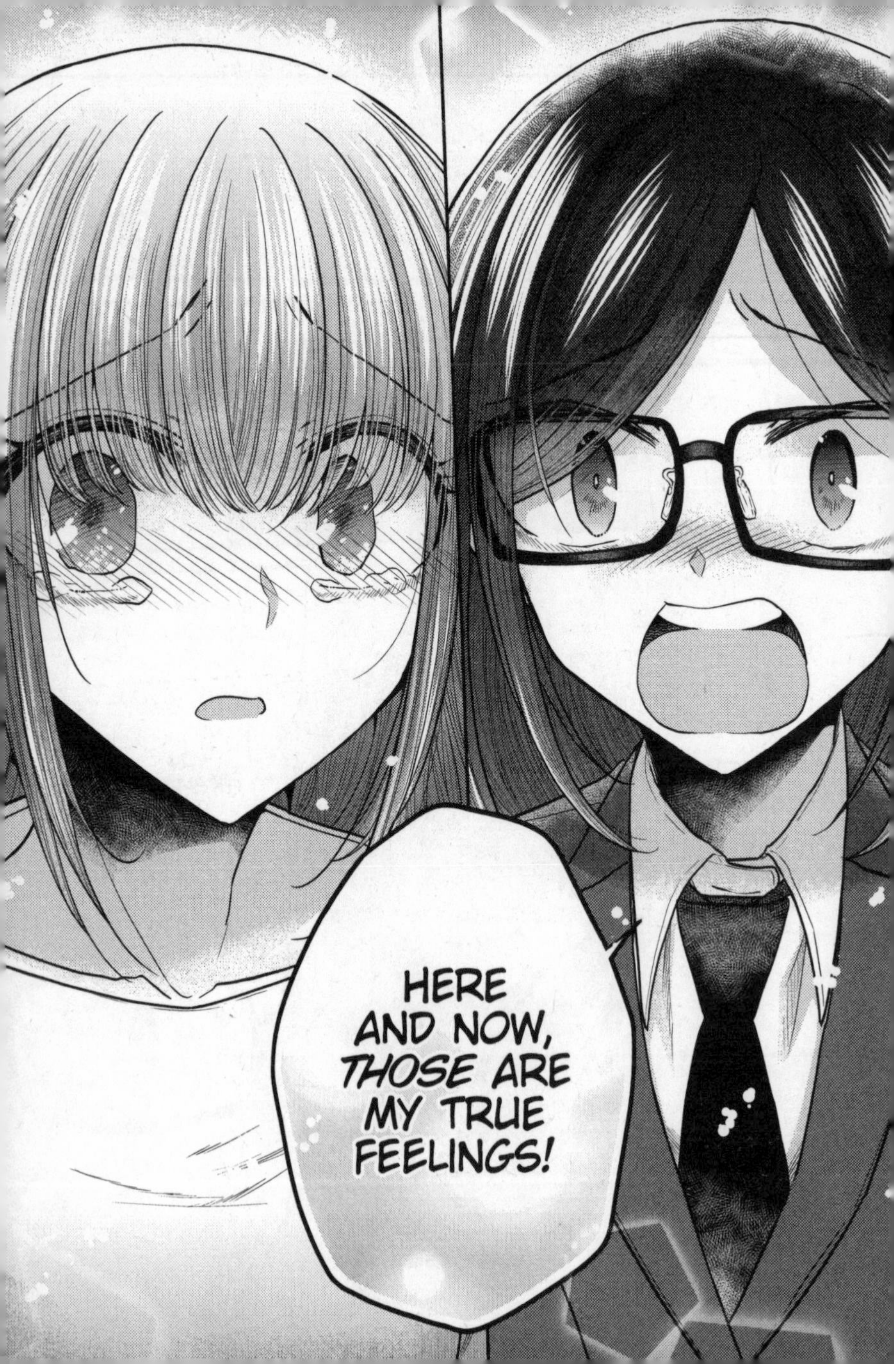
HERE AND NOW, *THOSE* ARE MY TRUE FEELINGS!

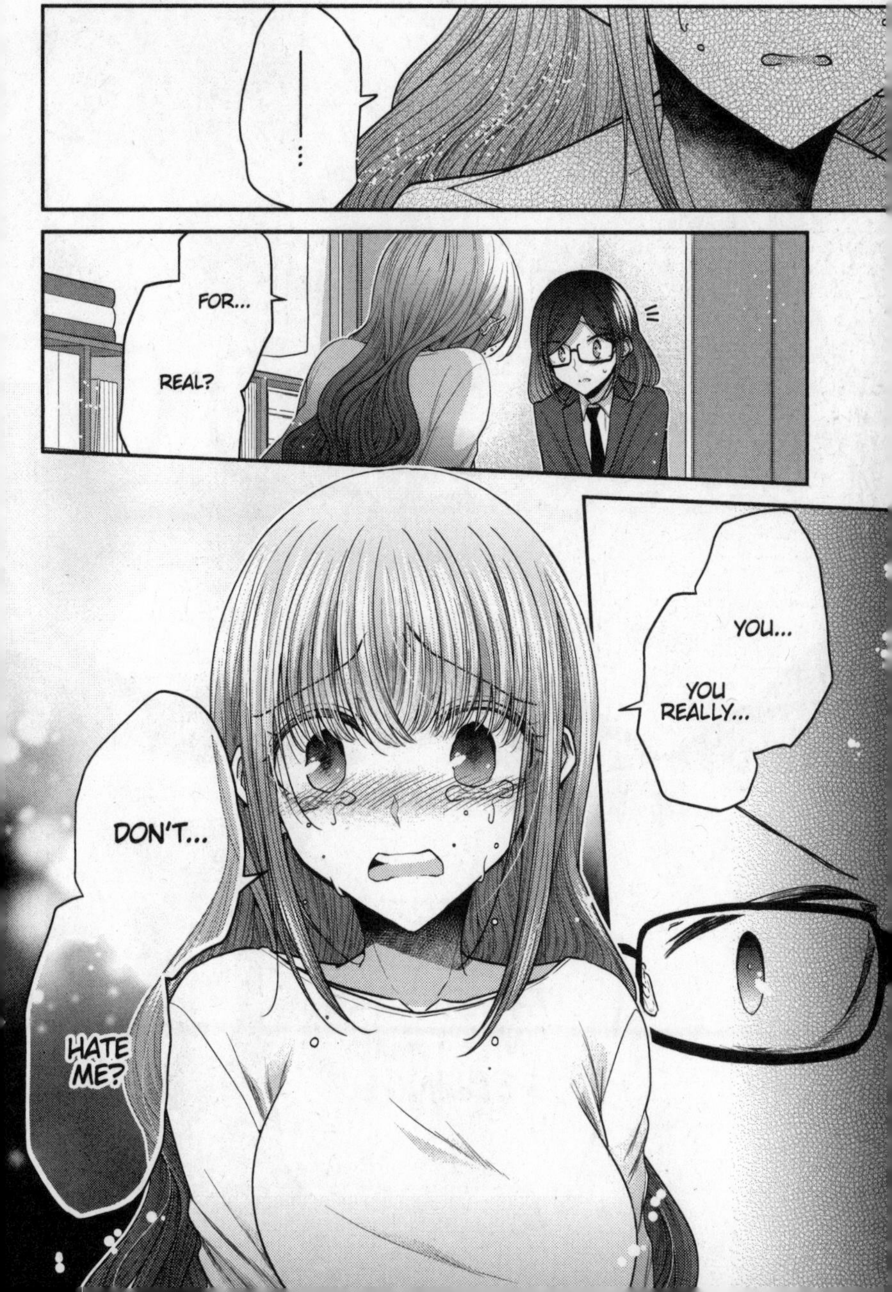

—…
FOR... REAL?
YOU... YOU REALLY...
DON'T... HATE ME?

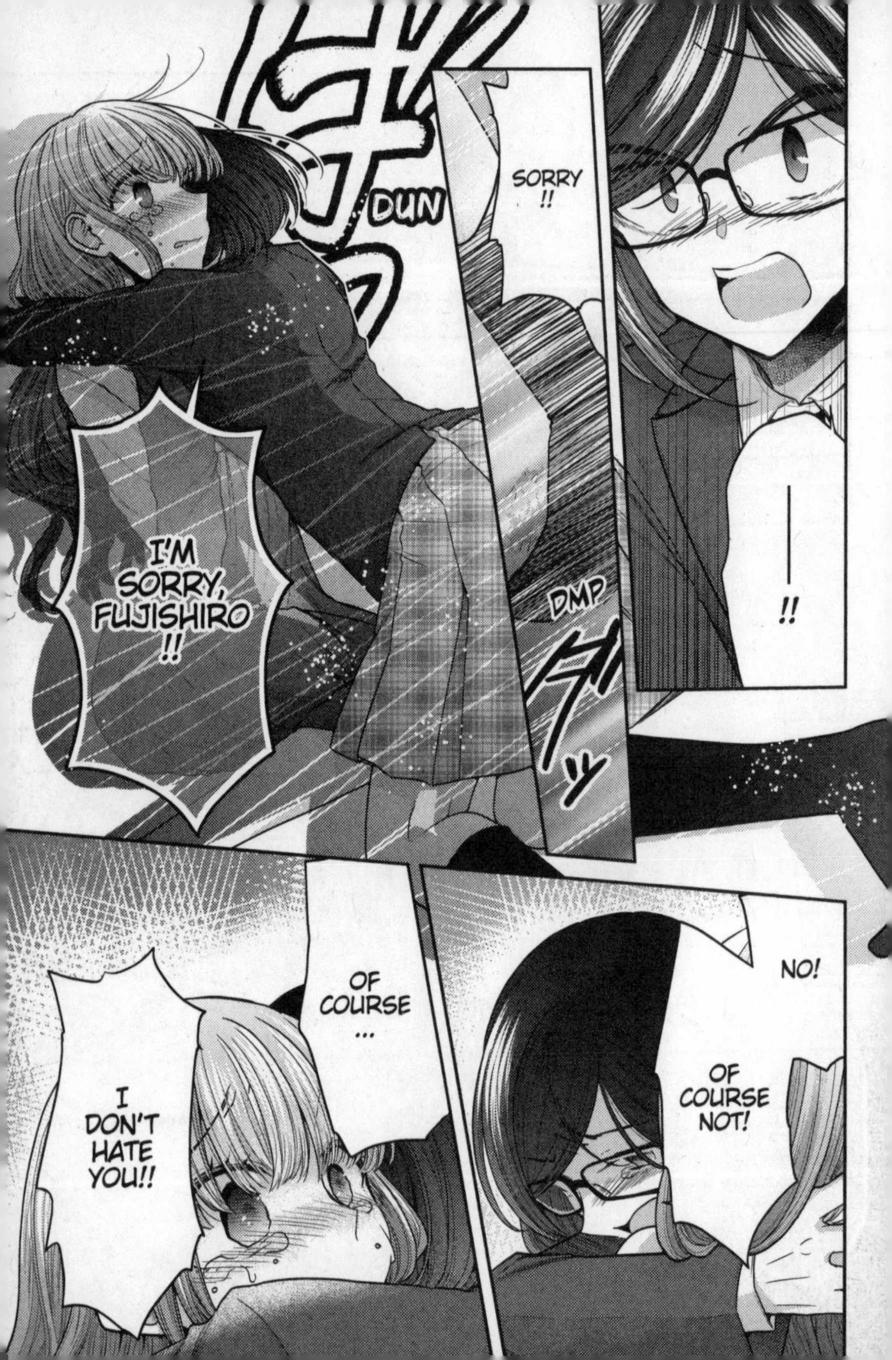

—!!
SORRY !!
DMP
DUN
I'M SORRY, FUJISHIRO !!
NO!
OF COURSE NOT!
OF COURSE ...
I DON'T HATE YOU!!

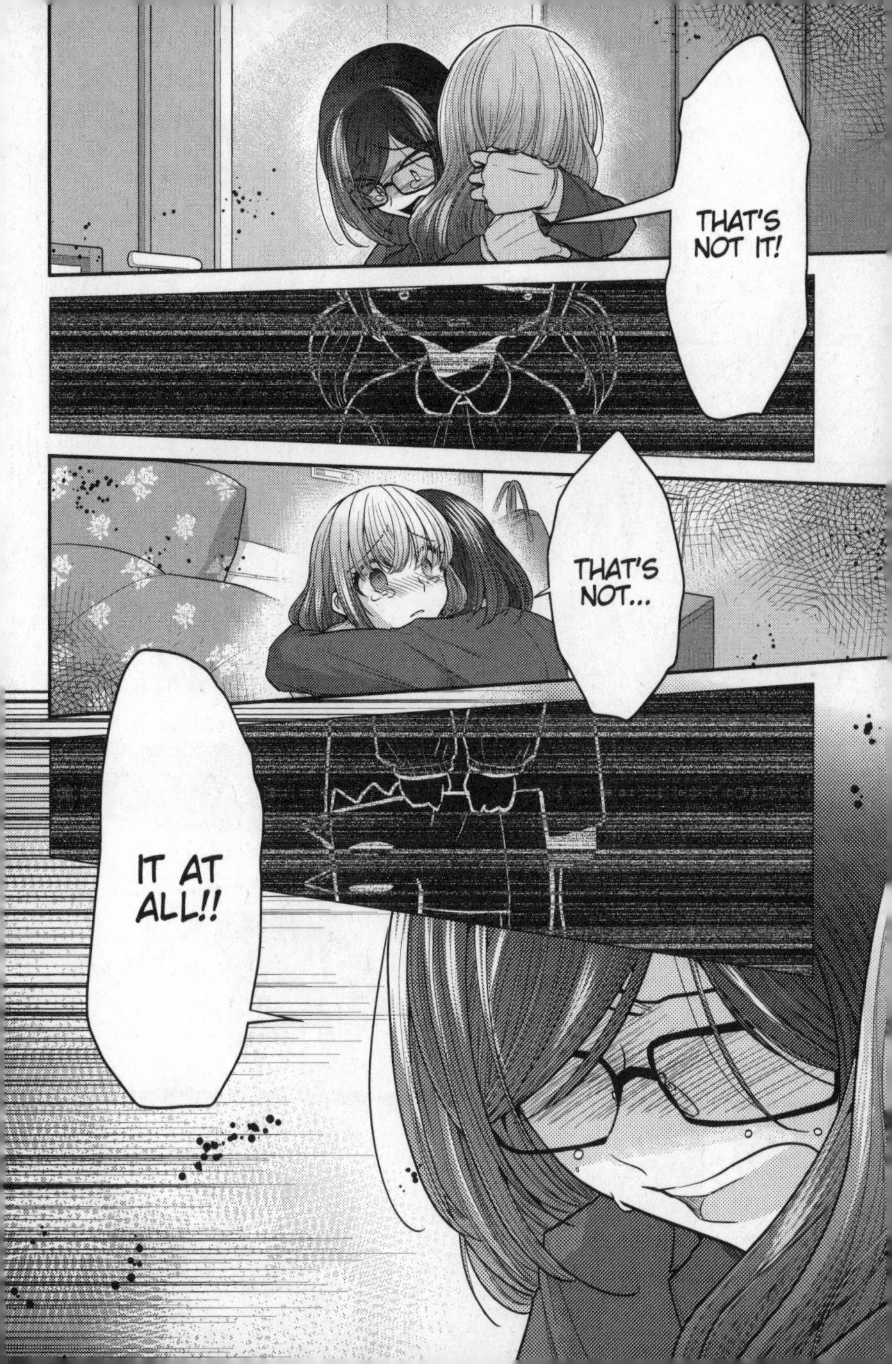
THAT'S NOT IT!
THAT'S NOT...
IT AT ALL!!

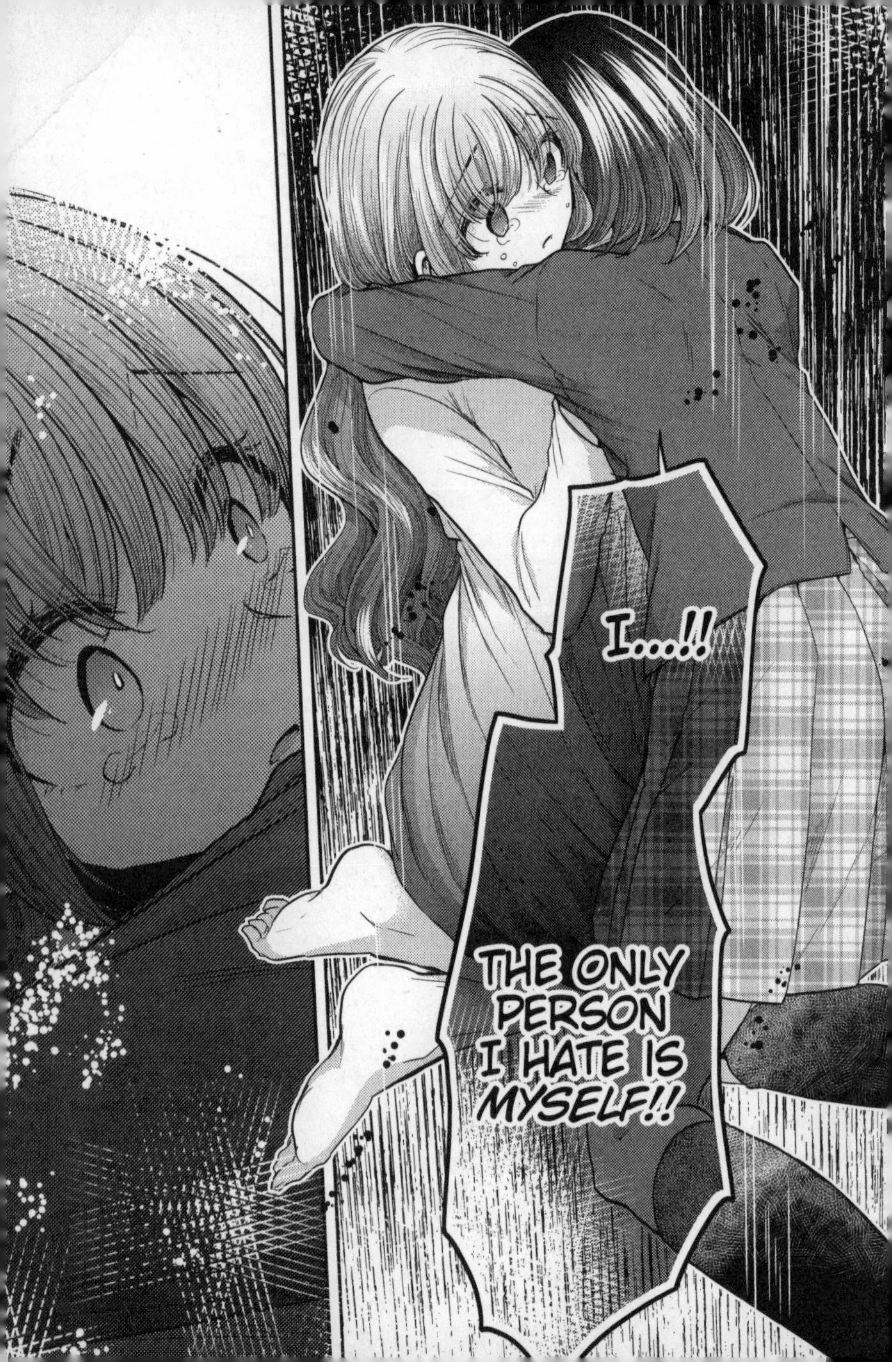
I...!!
THE ONLY PERSON I HATE IS MYSELF!!

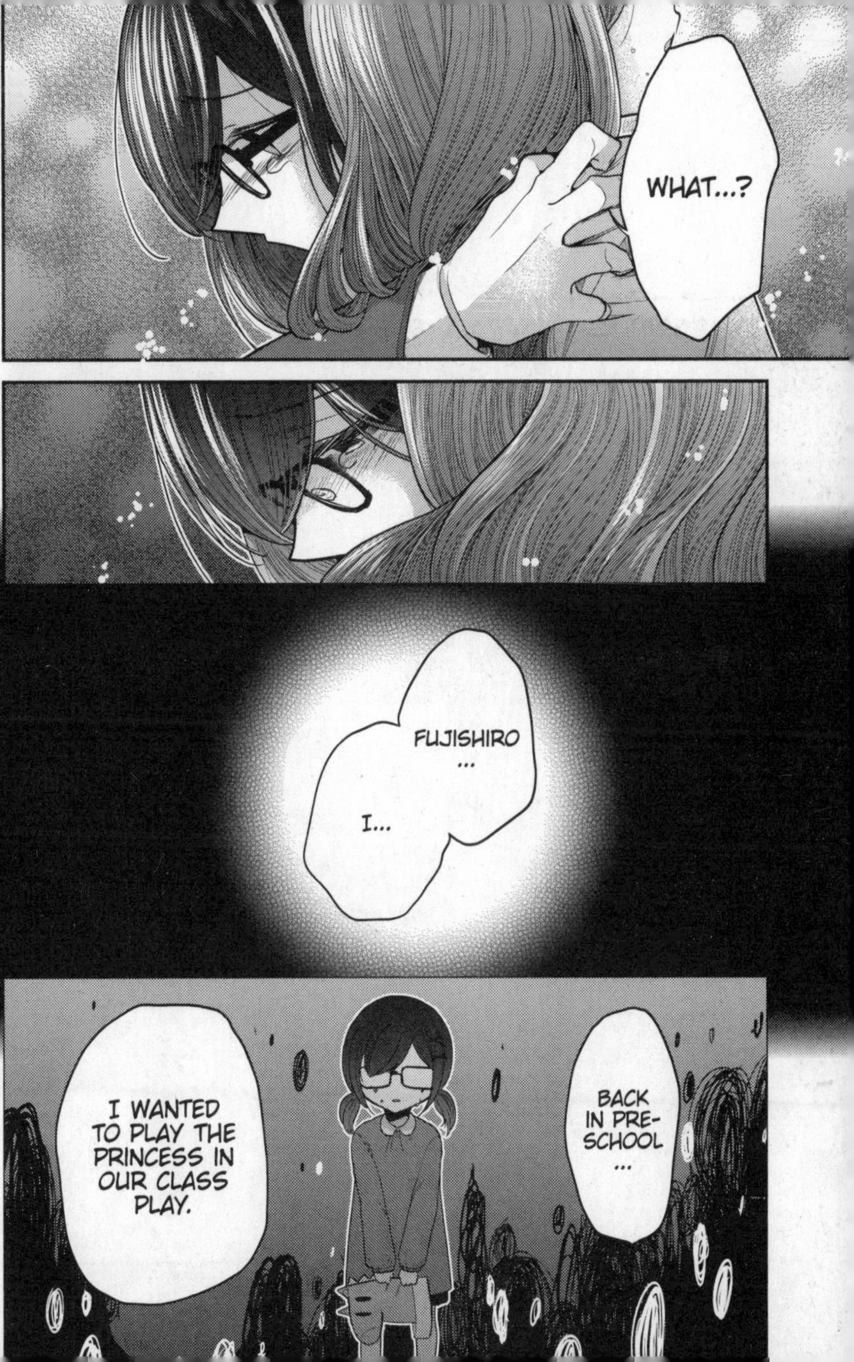
WHAT...?
FUJISHIRO ...
I...
BACK IN PRE-SCHOOL ...
I WANTED TO PLAY THE PRINCESS IN OUR CLASS PLAY.

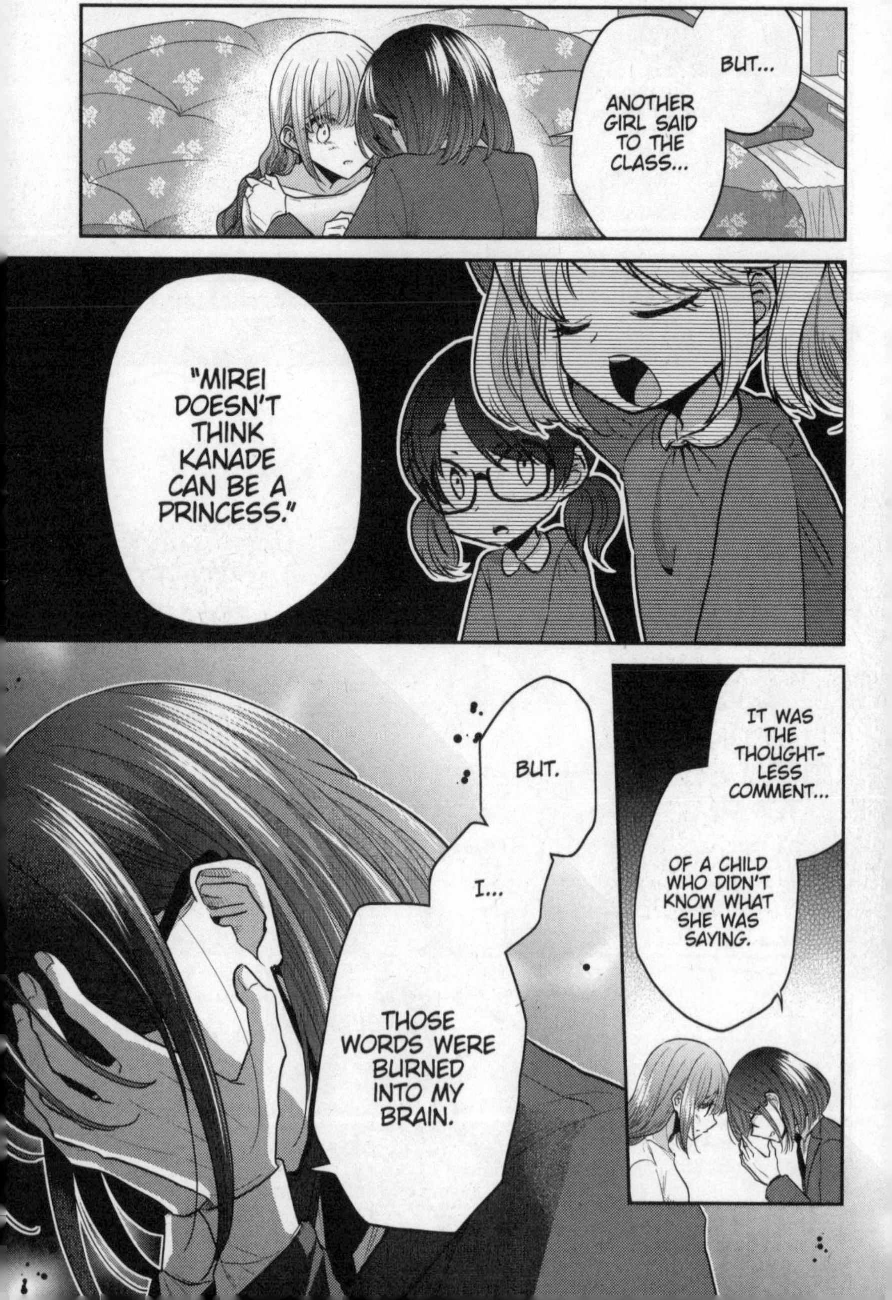
BUT...
ANOTHER GIRL SAID TO THE CLASS...
"MIREI DOESN'T THINK KANADE CAN BE A PRINCESS."
IT WAS THE THOUGHT-LESS COMMENT...
OF A CHILD WHO DIDN'T KNOW WHAT SHE WAS SAYING.
BUT.
I...
THOSE WORDS WERE BURNED INTO MY BRAIN.

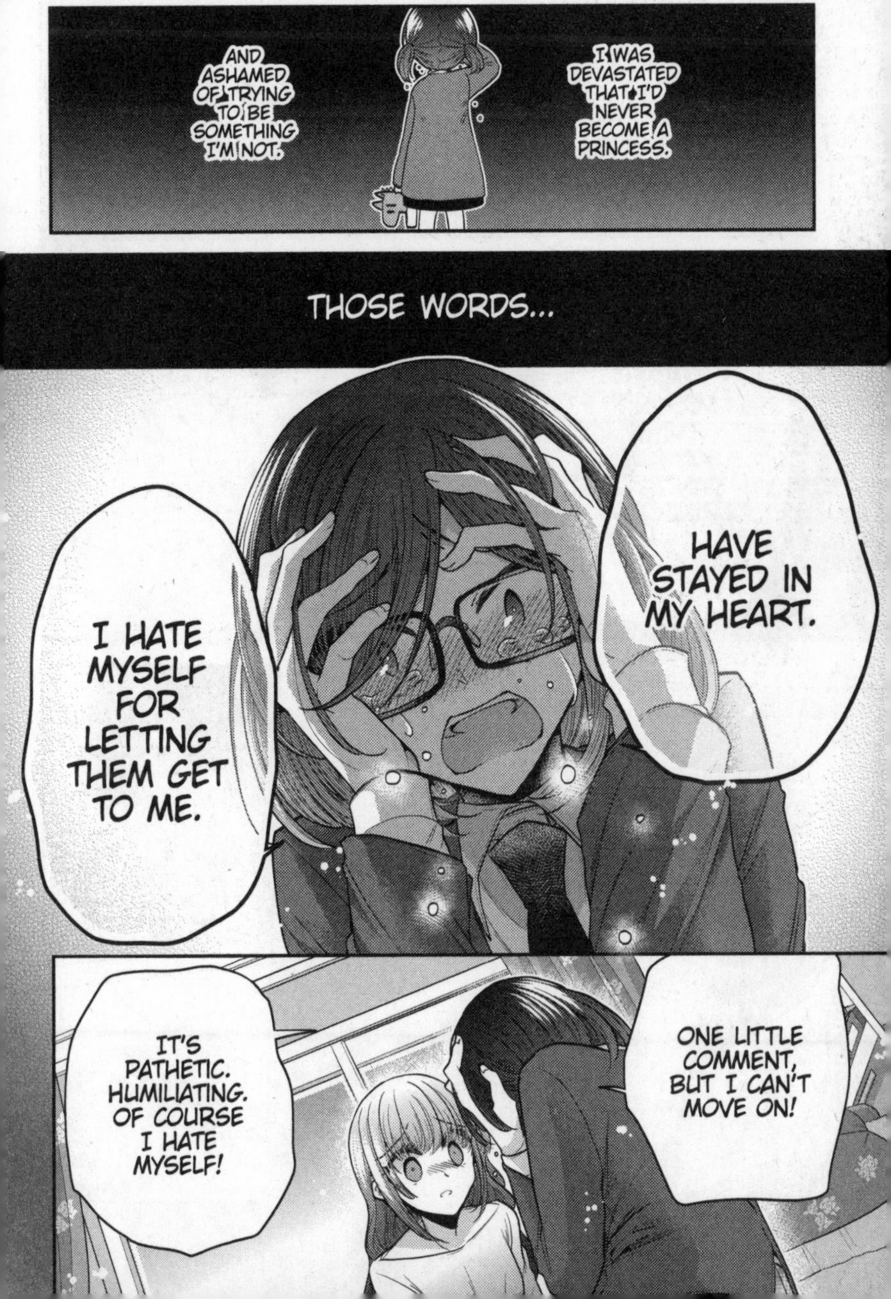
I WAS DEVASTATED THAT I'D NEVER BECOME A PRINCESS.
AND ASHAMED OF TRYING TO BE SOMETHING I'M NOT.
THOSE WORDS...
HAVE STAYED IN MY HEART.
I HATE MYSELF FOR LETTING THEM GET TO ME.
ONE LITTLE COMMENT, BUT I CAN'T MOVE ON!
IT'S PATHETIC. HUMILIATING. OF COURSE I HATE MYSELF!

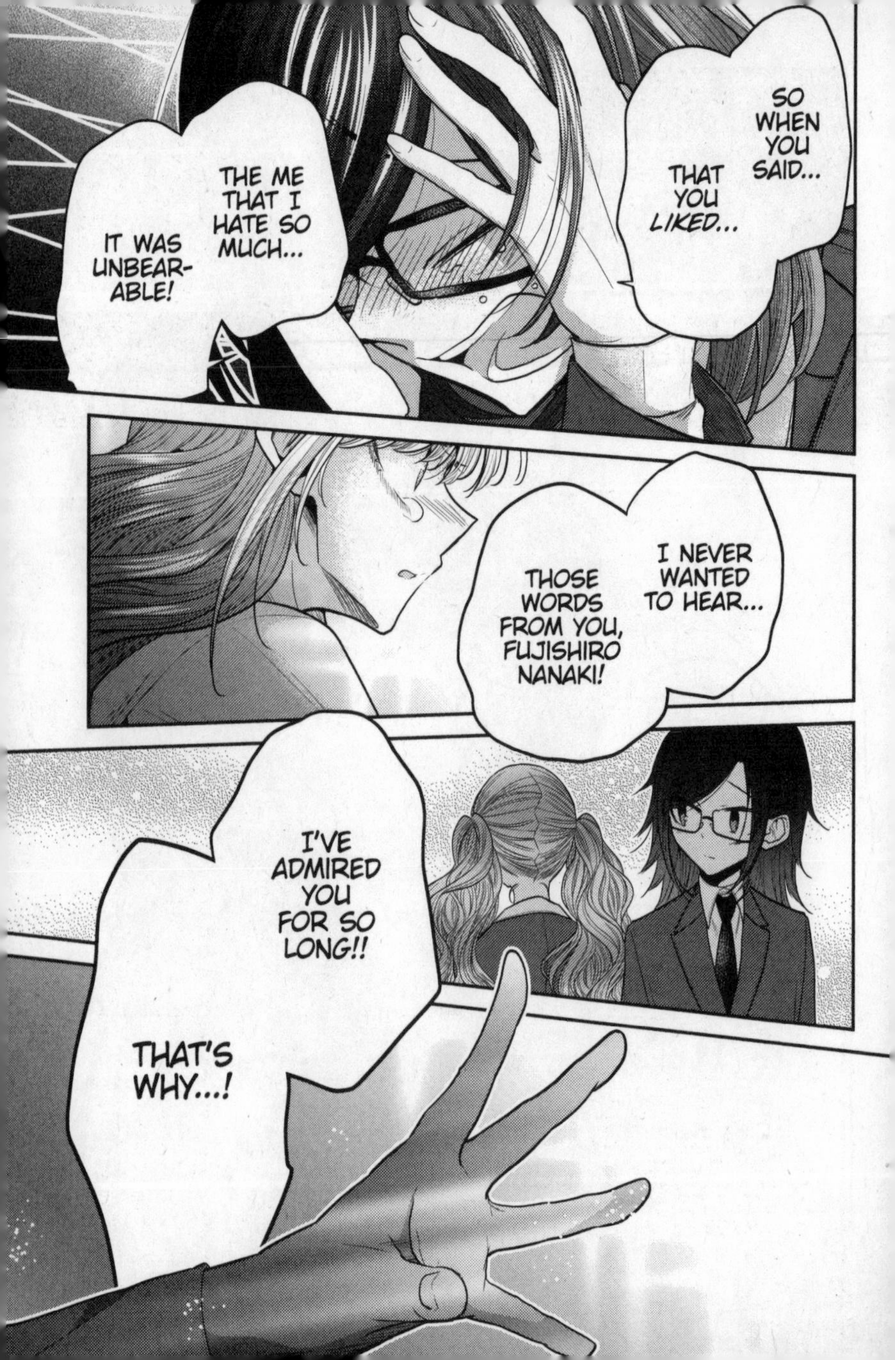
SO WHEN YOU SAID...
THAT YOU LIKED...
THE ME THAT I HATE SO MUCH...
IT WAS UNBEARABLE!
I NEVER WANTED TO HEAR...
THOSE WORDS FROM YOU, FUJISHIRO NANAKI!
I'VE ADMIRED YOU FOR SO LONG!!
THAT'S WHY...!

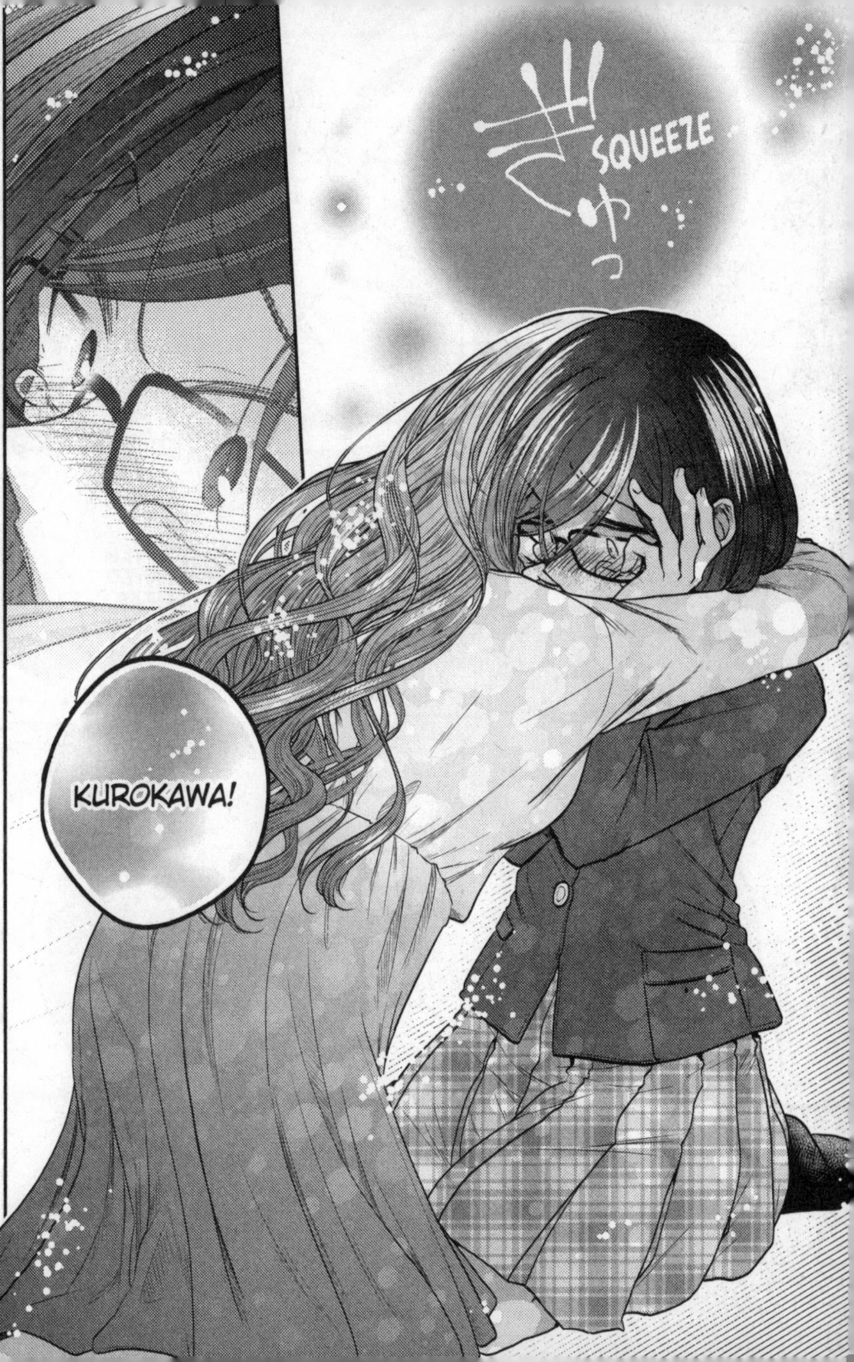
ぎゅっ
SQUEEZE
KUROKAWA!

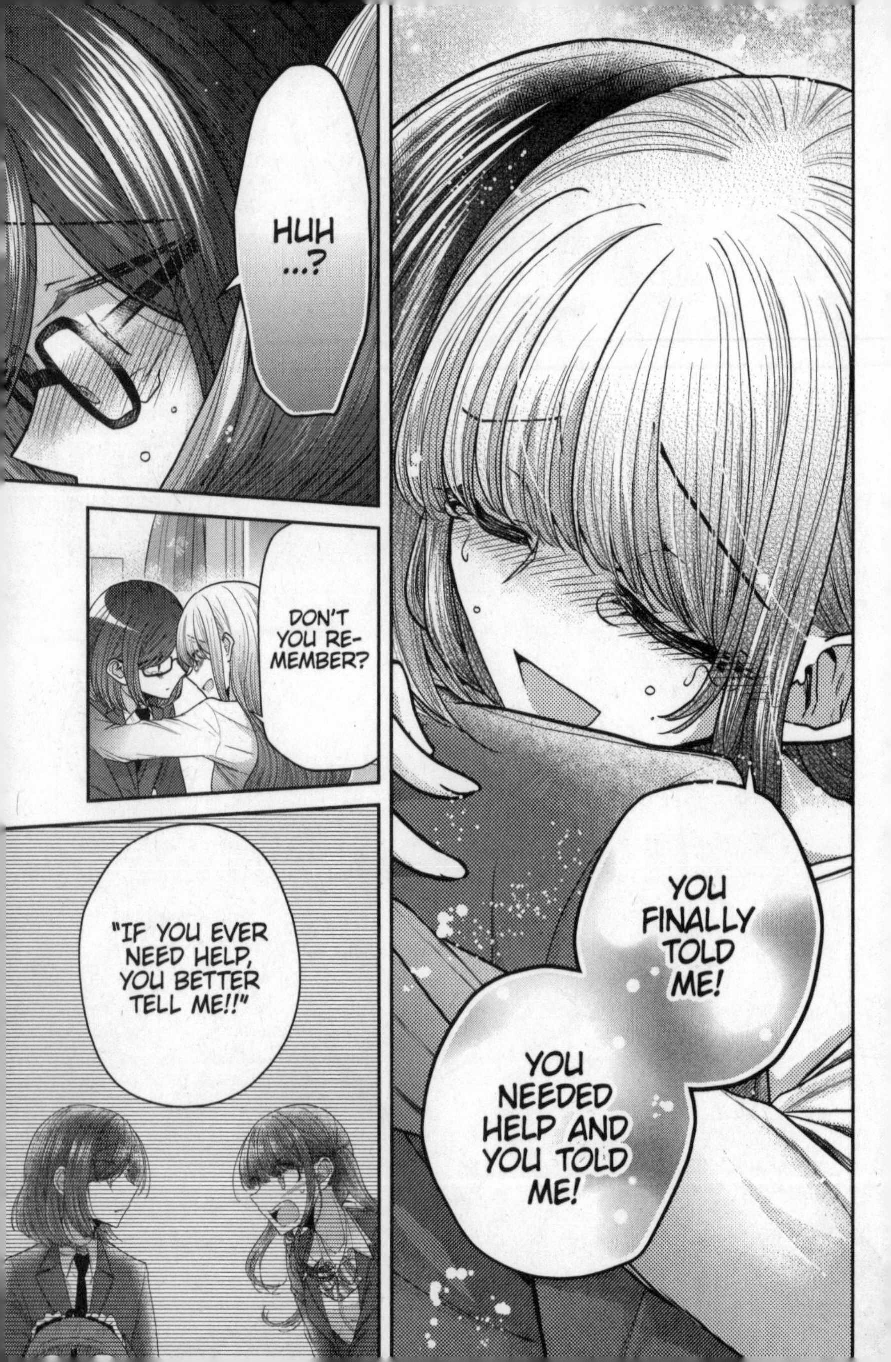
YOU FINALLY TOLD ME!
YOU NEEDED HELP AND YOU TOLD ME!
HUH ...?
DON'T YOU RE-MEMBER?
"IF YOU EVER NEED HELP, YOU BETTER TELL ME!!"

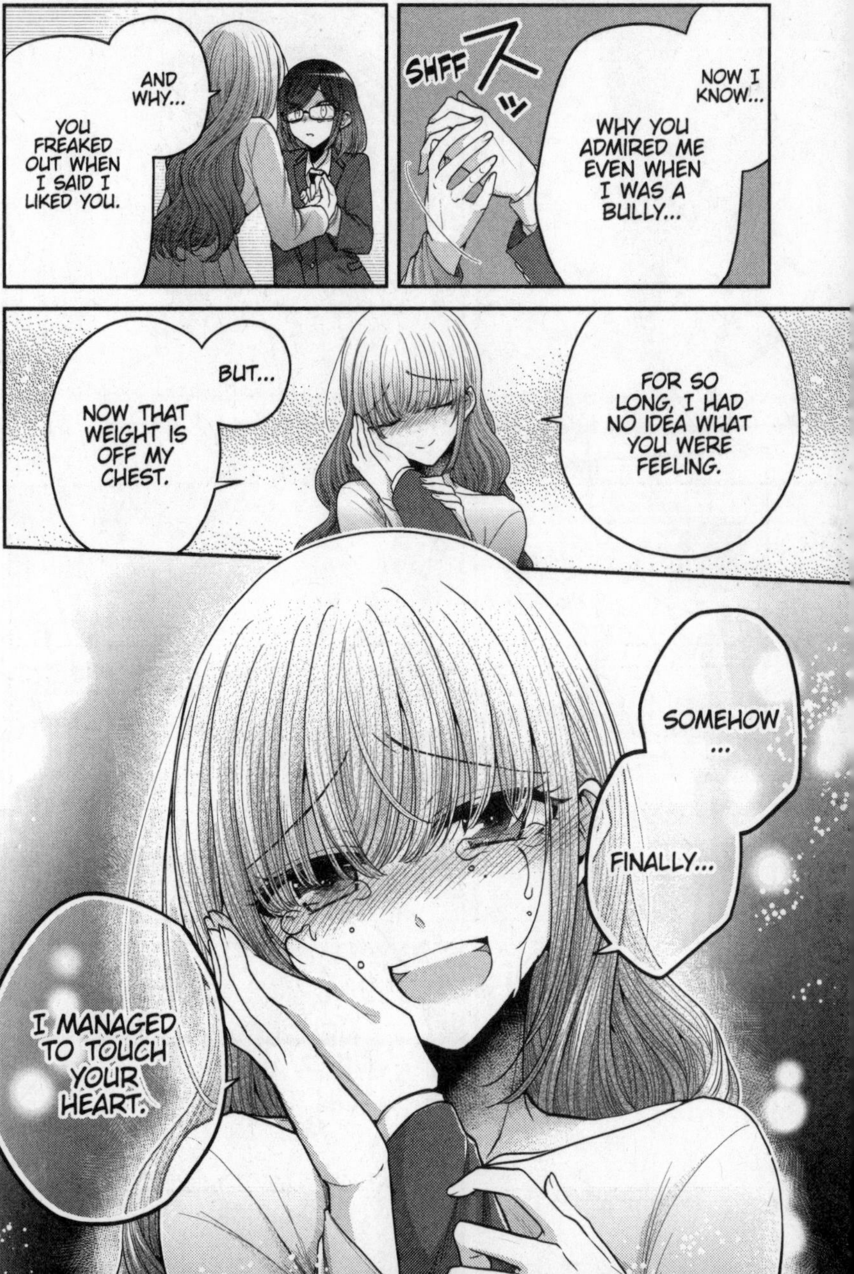
SHFF
スッ
NOW I KNOW...
WHY YOU ADMIRED ME EVEN WHEN I WAS A BULLY...
AND WHY...
YOU FREAKED OUT WHEN I SAID I LIKED YOU.
FOR SO LONG, I HAD NO IDEA WHAT YOU WERE FEELING.
BUT...
NOW THAT WEIGHT IS OFF MY CHEST.
SOMEHOW...
FINALLY...
I MANAGED TO TOUCH YOUR HEART.

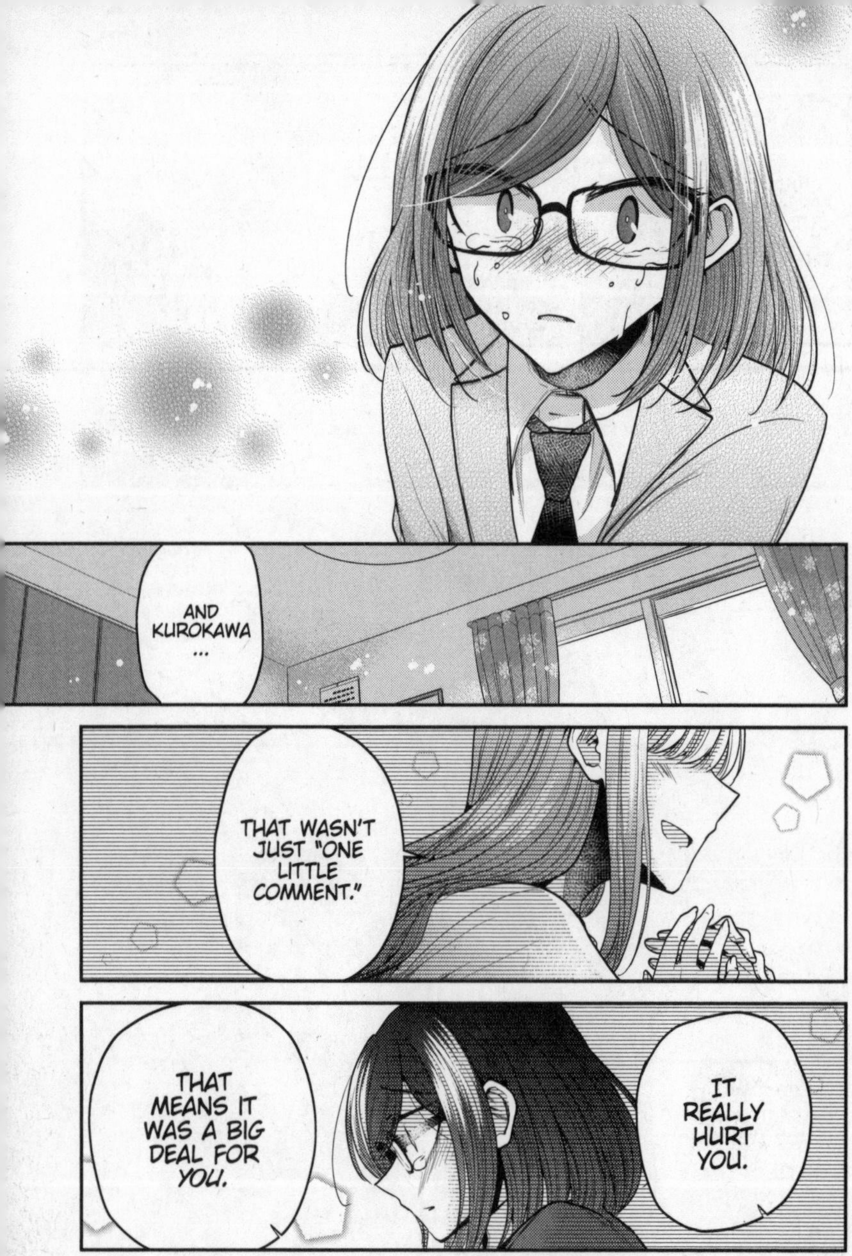
AND KUROKAWA ...
THAT WASN'T JUST "ONE LITTLE COMMENT."
IT REALLY HURT YOU.
THAT MEANS IT WAS A BIG DEAL FOR YOU.

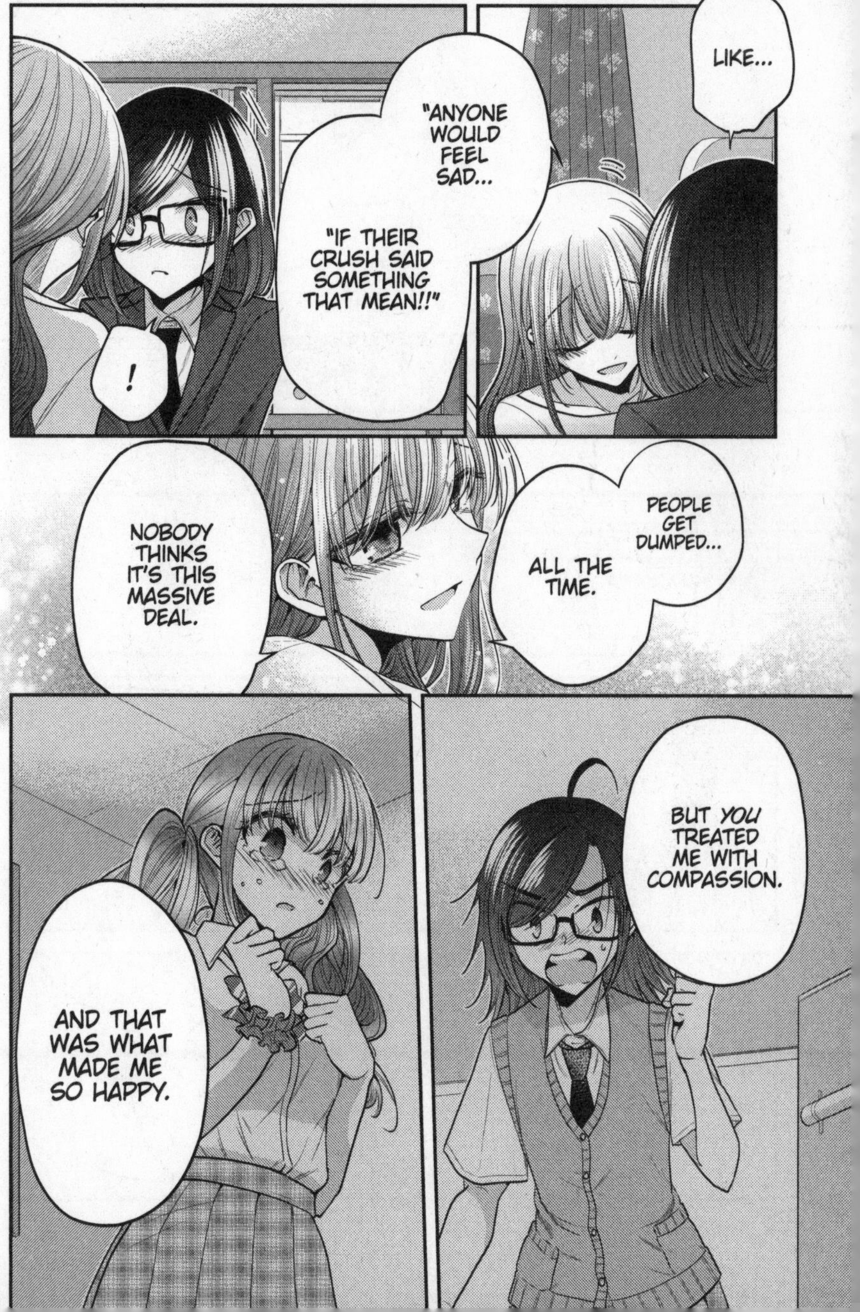
LIKE...
"ANYONE WOULD FEEL SAD...
"IF THEIR CRUSH SAID SOMETHING THAT MEAN!!"
!
PEOPLE GET DUMPED...
ALL THE TIME.
NOBODY THINKS IT'S THIS MASSIVE DEAL.
BUT *YOU* TREATED ME WITH COMPASSION.
AND THAT WAS WHAT MADE ME SO HAPPY.

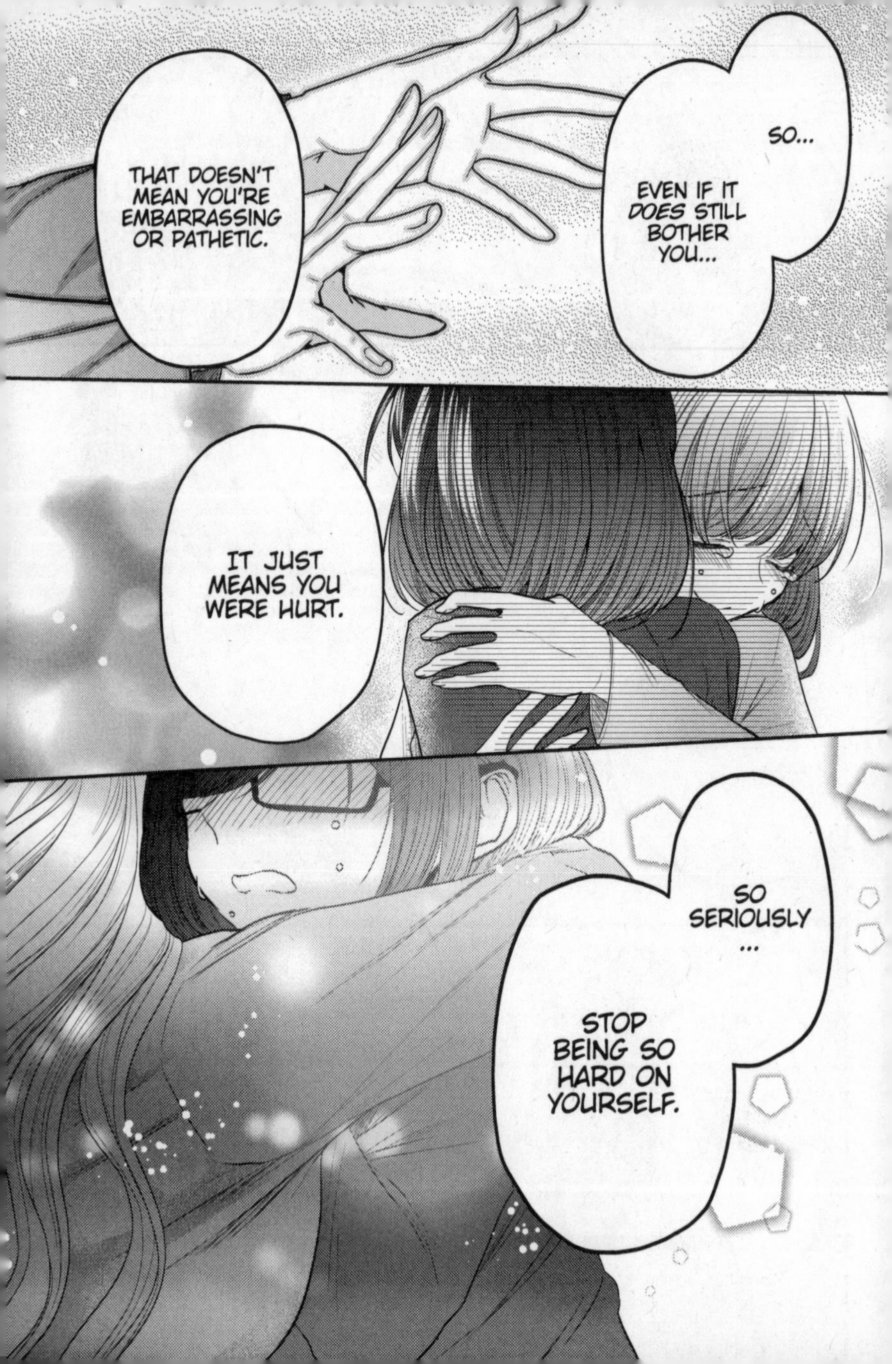
SO...
EVEN IF IT *DOES* STILL BOTHER YOU...
THAT DOESN'T MEAN YOU'RE EMBARRASSING OR PATHETIC.
IT JUST MEANS YOU WERE HURT.
SO SERIOUSLY ...
STOP BEING SO HARD ON YOURSELF.

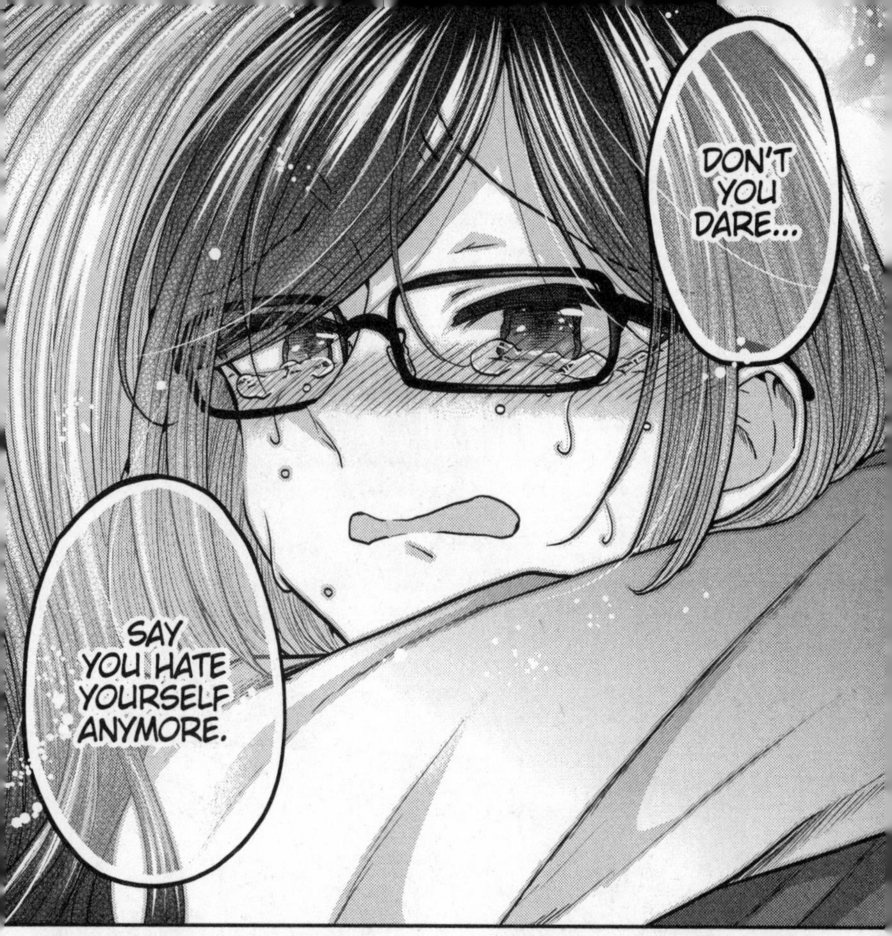
DON'T YOU DARE...
SAY YOU HATE YOURSELF ANYMORE.
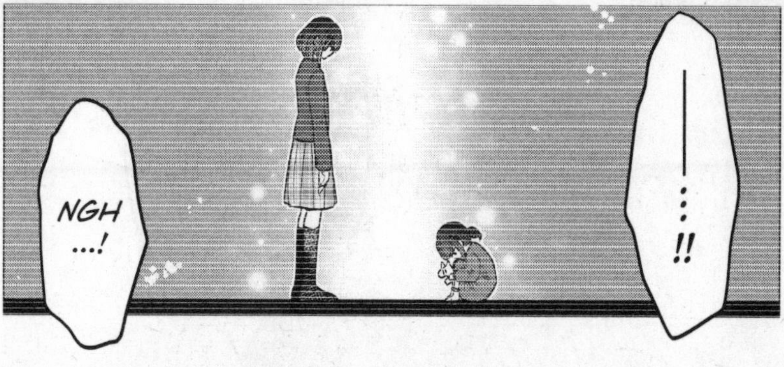
——...!!
NGH ...!

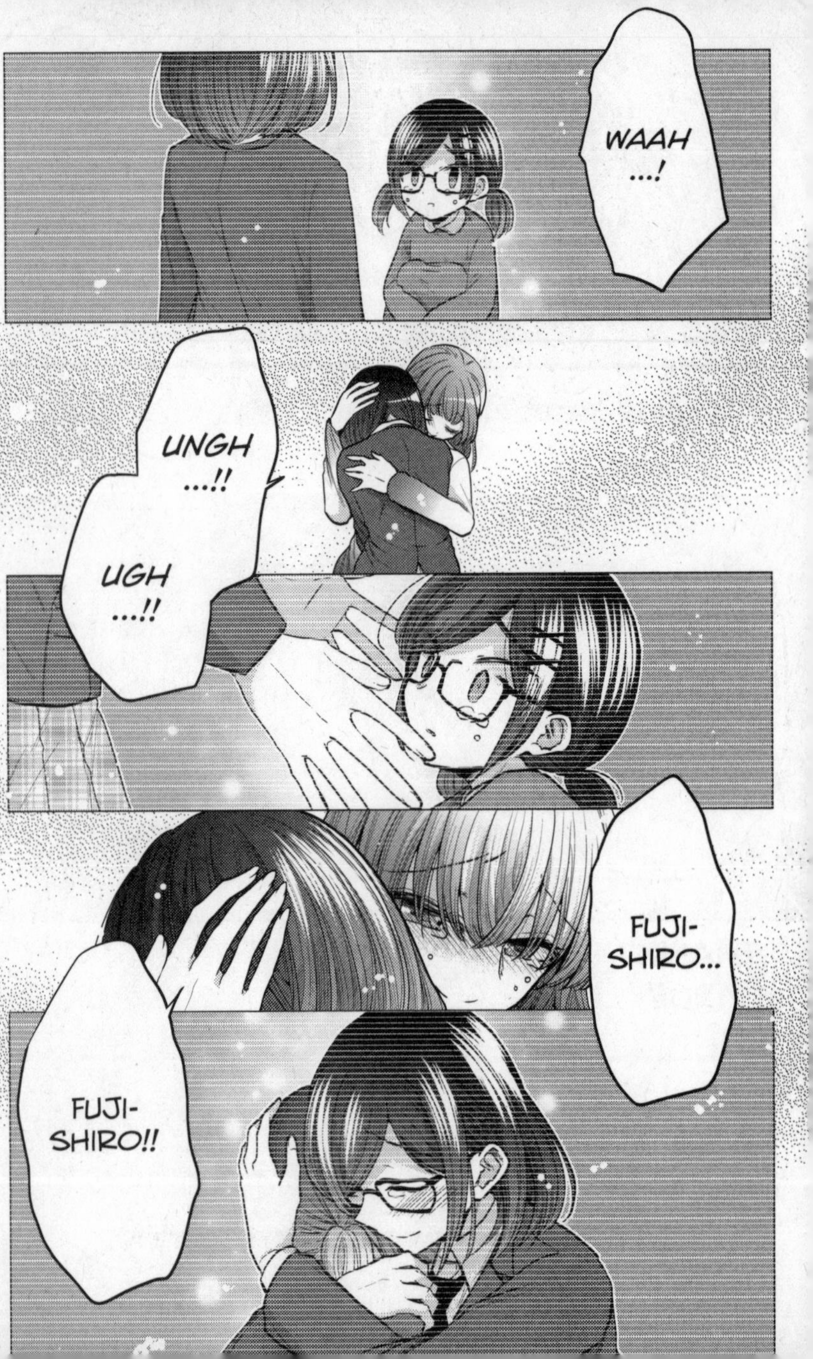
WAAH ...!
UNGH ...!!
UGH ...!!
FUJI-SHIRO...
FUJI-SHIRO!!

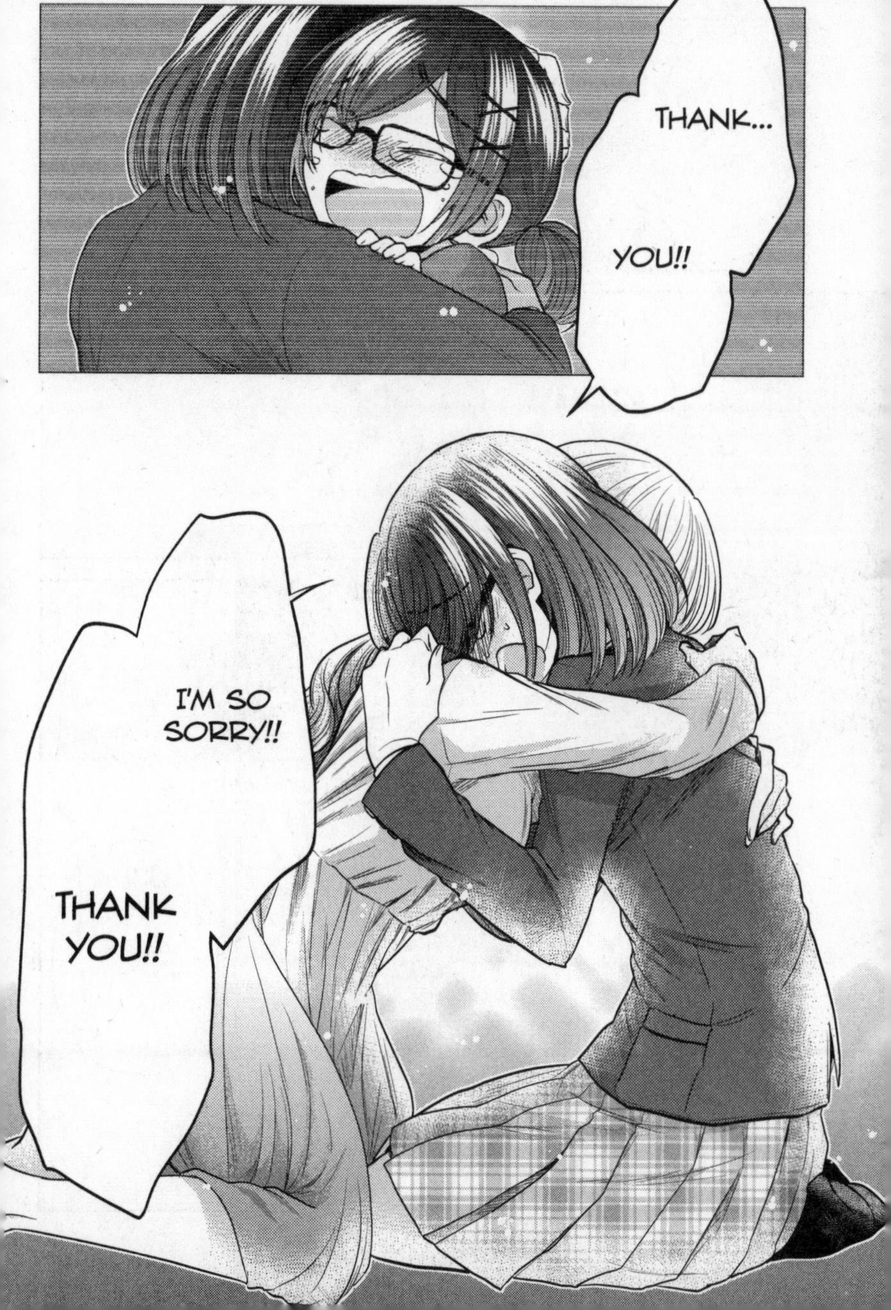
THANK...
YOU!!
I'M SO SORRY!!
THANK YOU!!

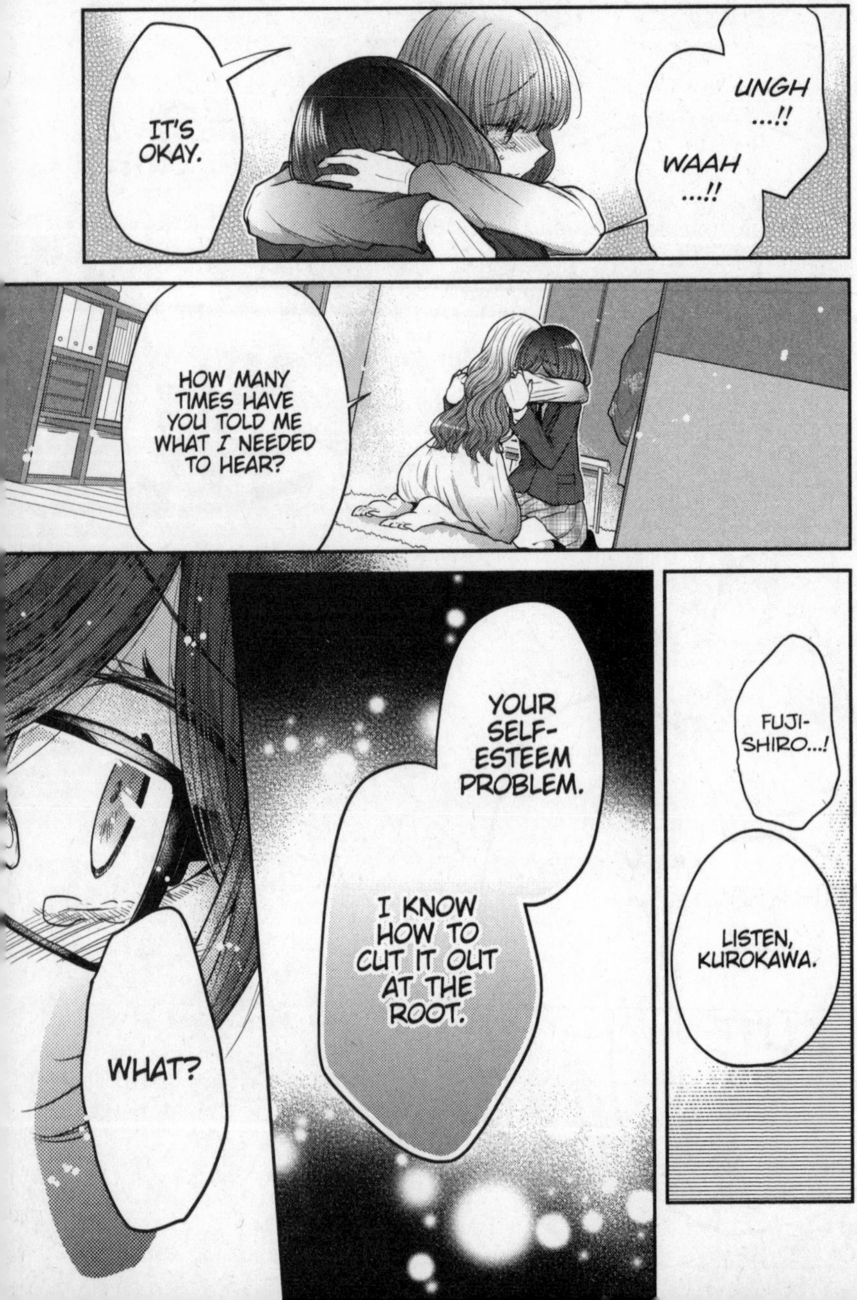
UNGH ...!!
WAAH ...!!
IT'S OKAY.
HOW MANY TIMES HAVE YOU TOLD ME WHAT I NEEDED TO HEAR?
FUJI-SHIRO...!
LISTEN, KUROKAWA.
YOUR SELF-ESTEEM PROBLEM.
I KNOW HOW TO CUT IT OUT AT THE ROOT.
WHAT?

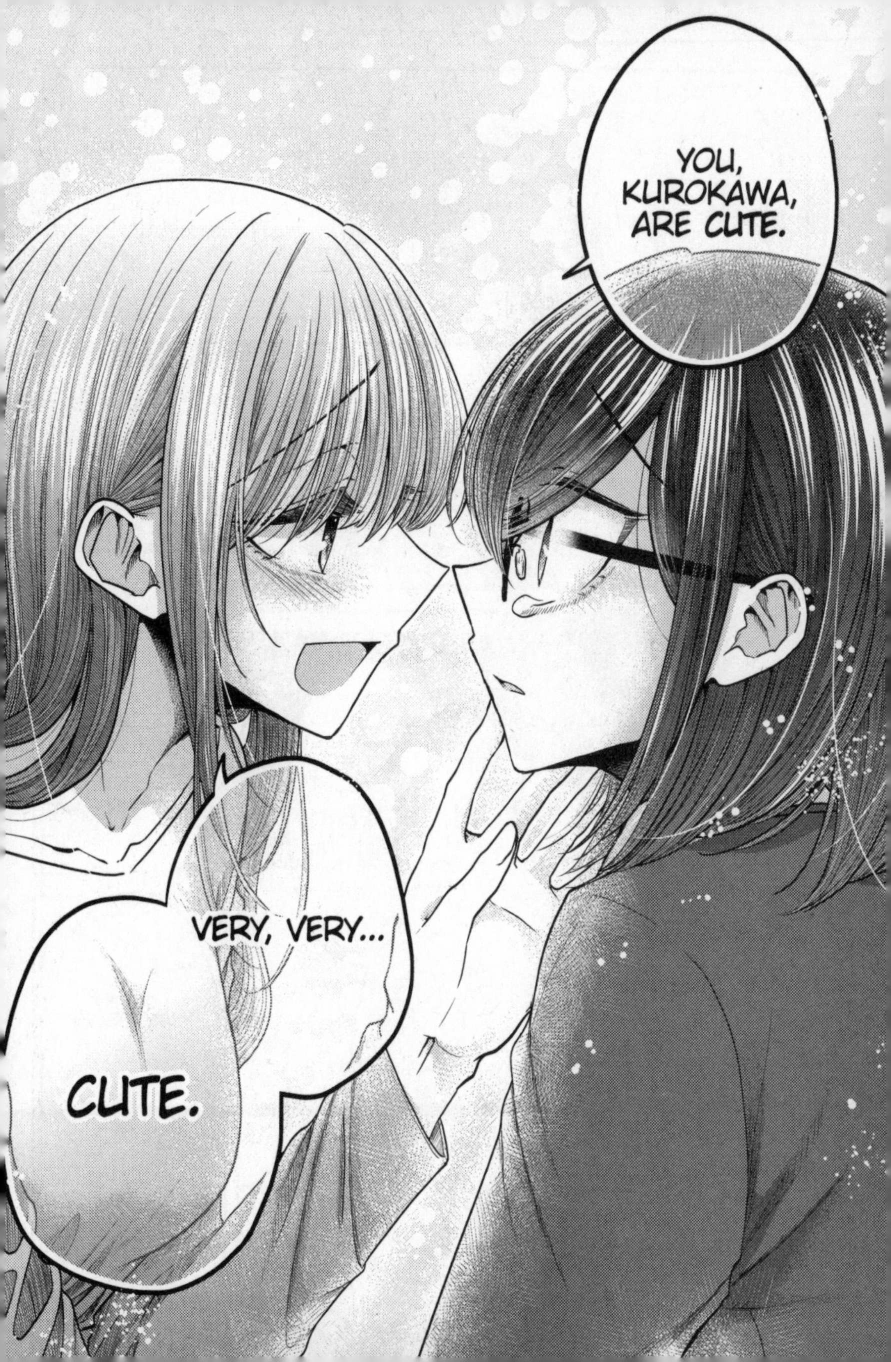
YOU, KUROKAWA, ARE CUTE.
VERY, VERY...
CUTE.

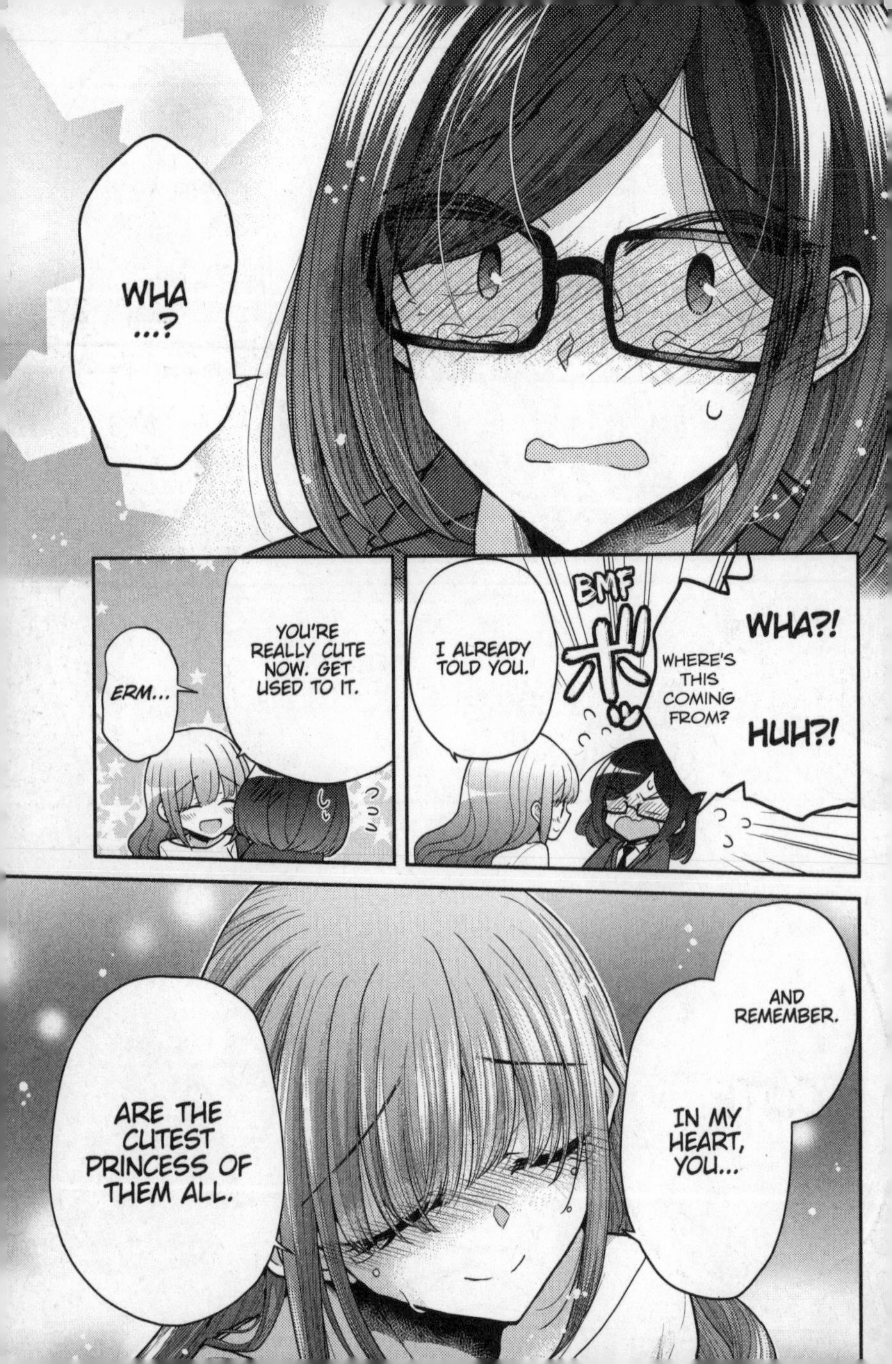
WHA ...?
WHA?!
BMF
I ALREADY TOLD YOU.
WHERE'S THIS COMING FROM?
HUH?!
YOU'RE REALLY CUTE NOW. GET USED TO IT.
ERM...
AND REMEMBER.
IN MY HEART, YOU...
ARE THE CUTEST PRINCESS OF THEM ALL.

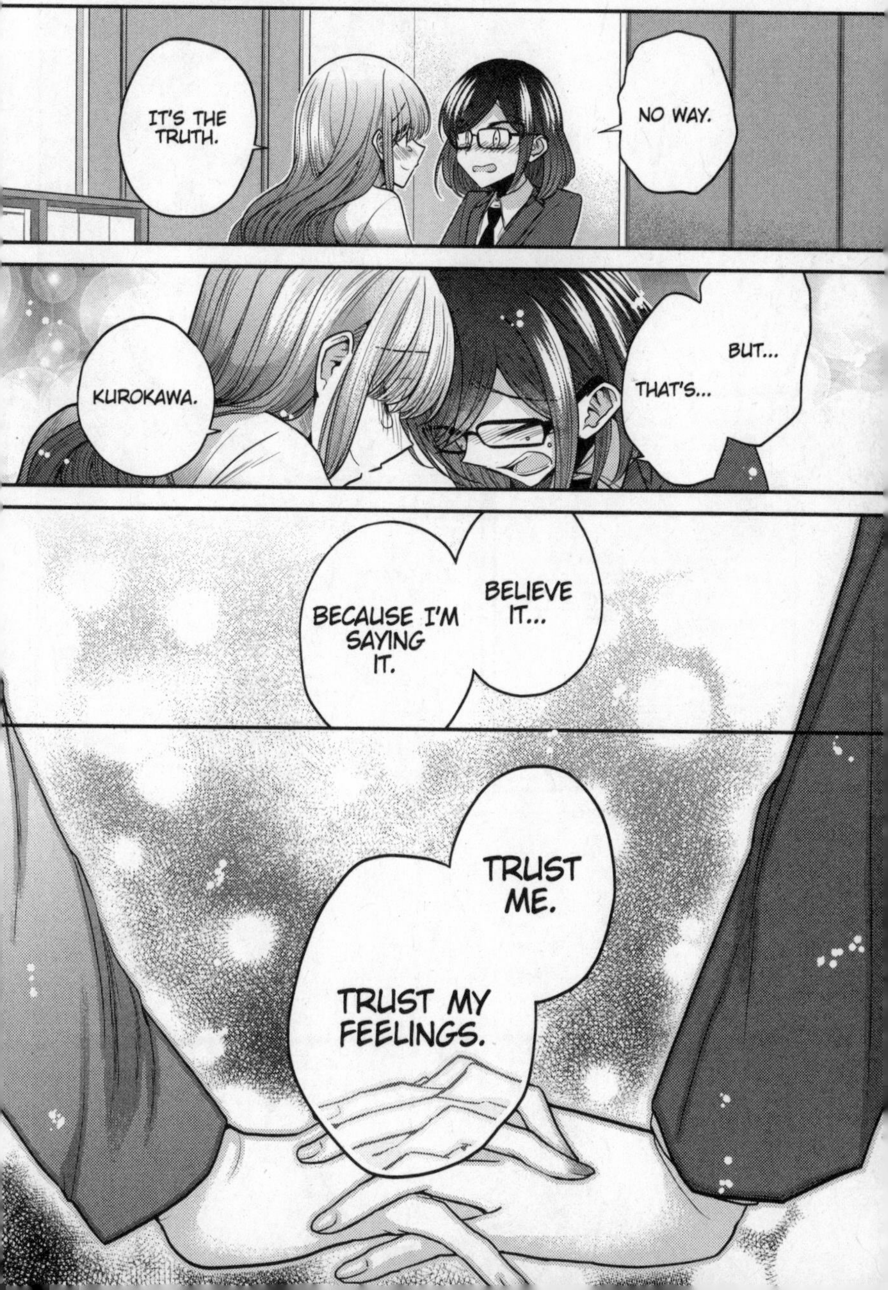
NO WAY.
IT'S THE TRUTH.
BUT...
THAT'S...
KUROKAWA.
BELIEVE IT...
BECAUSE I'M SAYING IT.
TRUST ME.
TRUST MY FEELINGS.

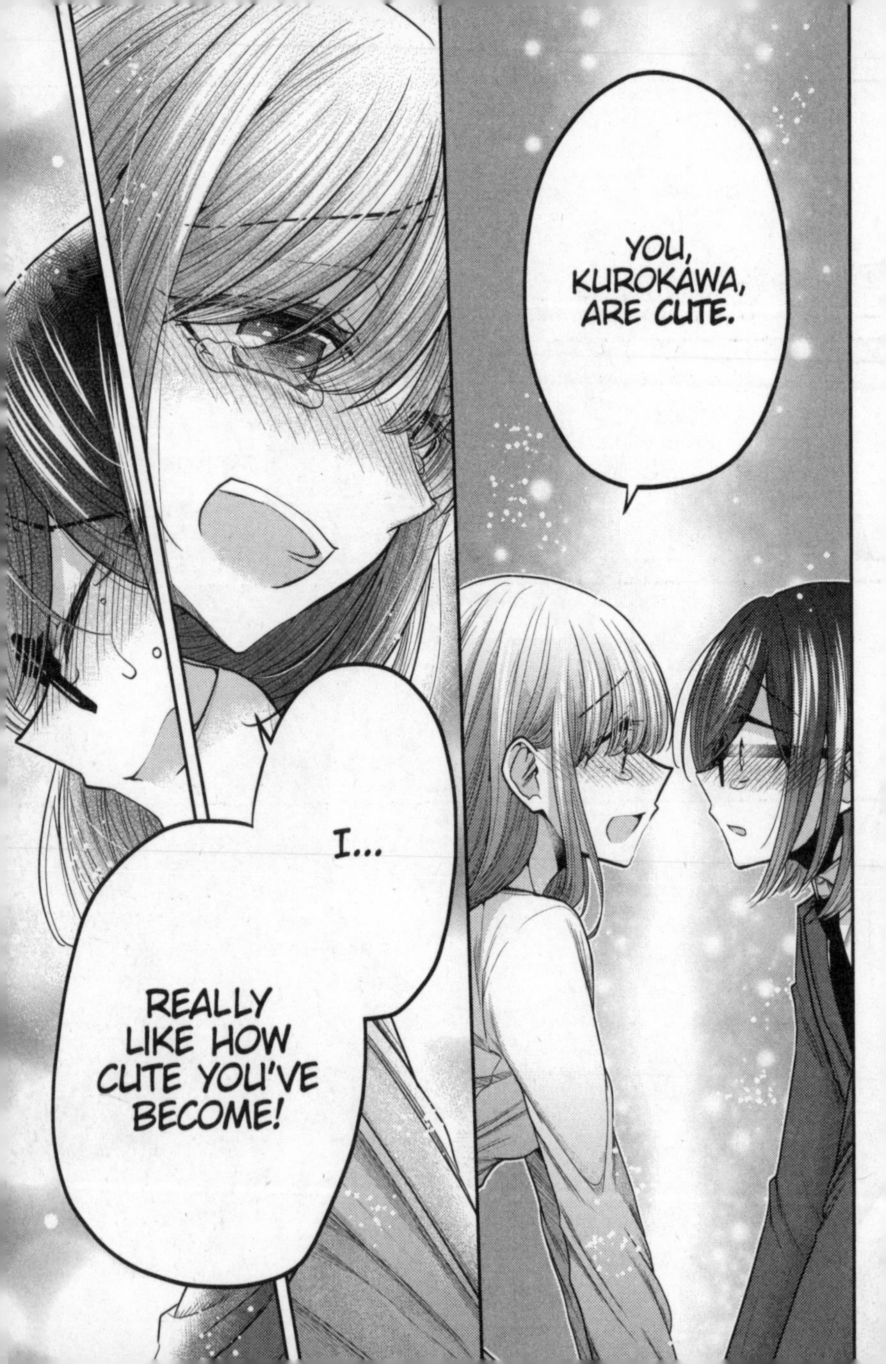
YOU, KUROKAWA, ARE CUTE.
I...
REALLY LIKE HOW CUTE YOU'VE BECOME!

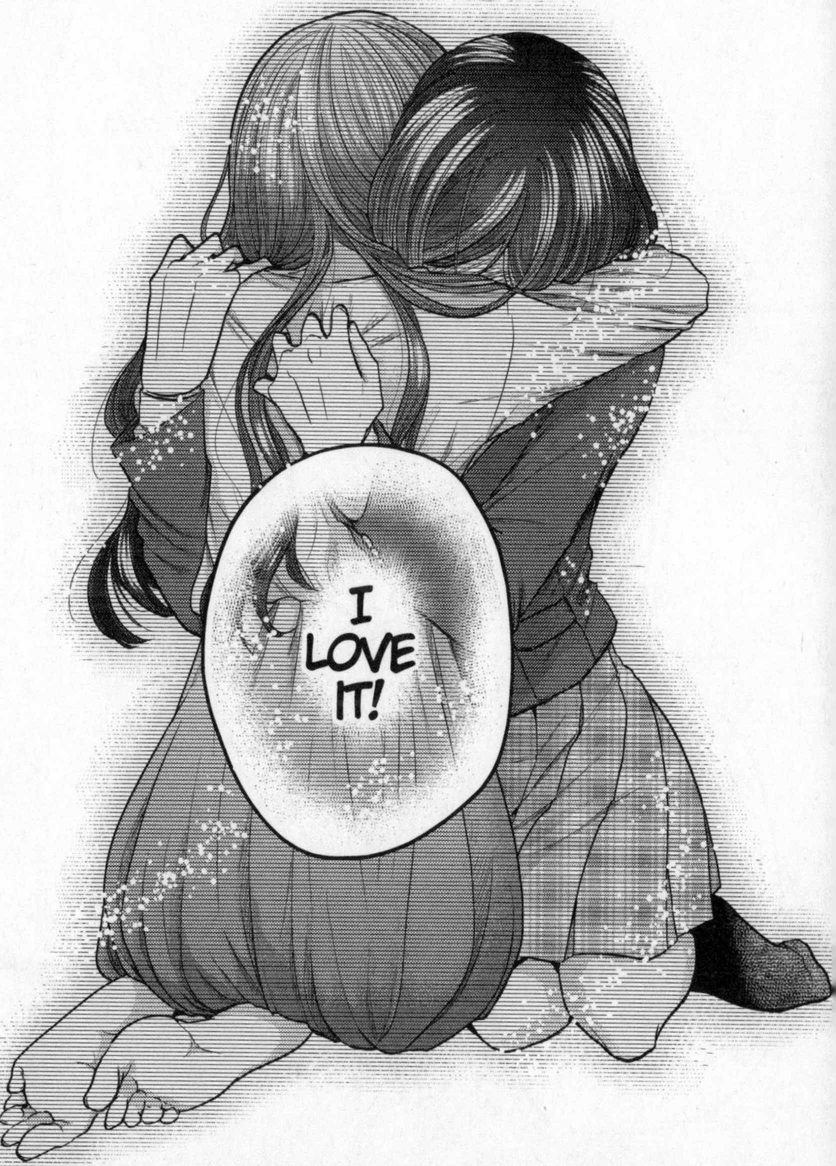
I LOVE IT!

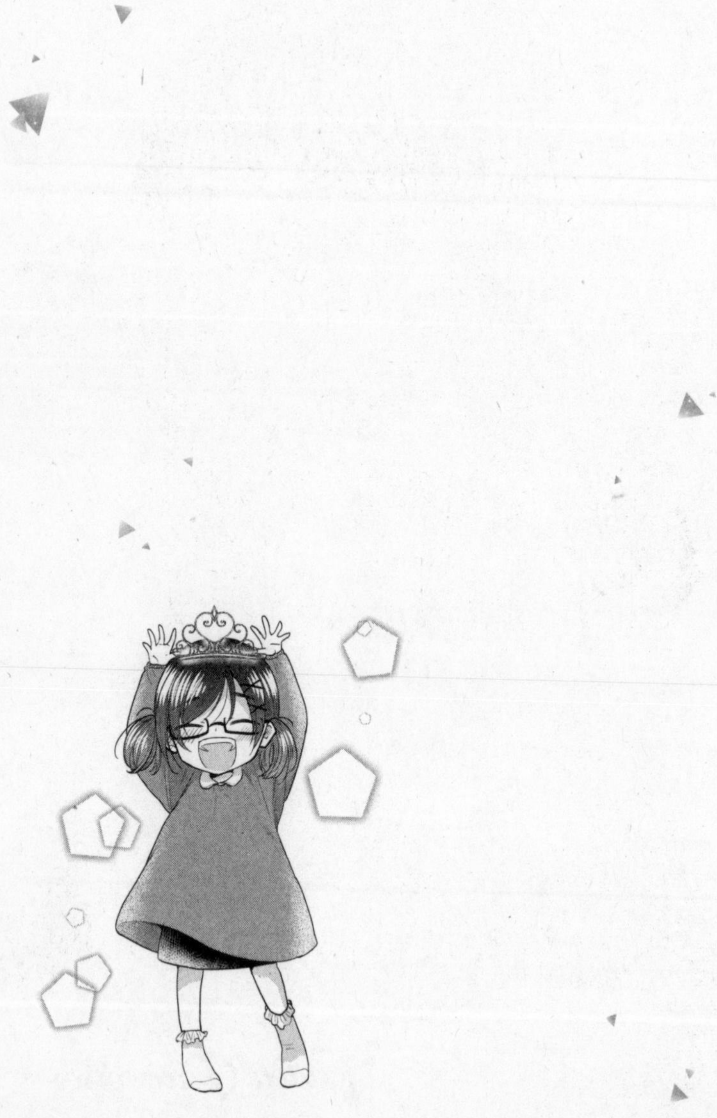

Failed Princesses

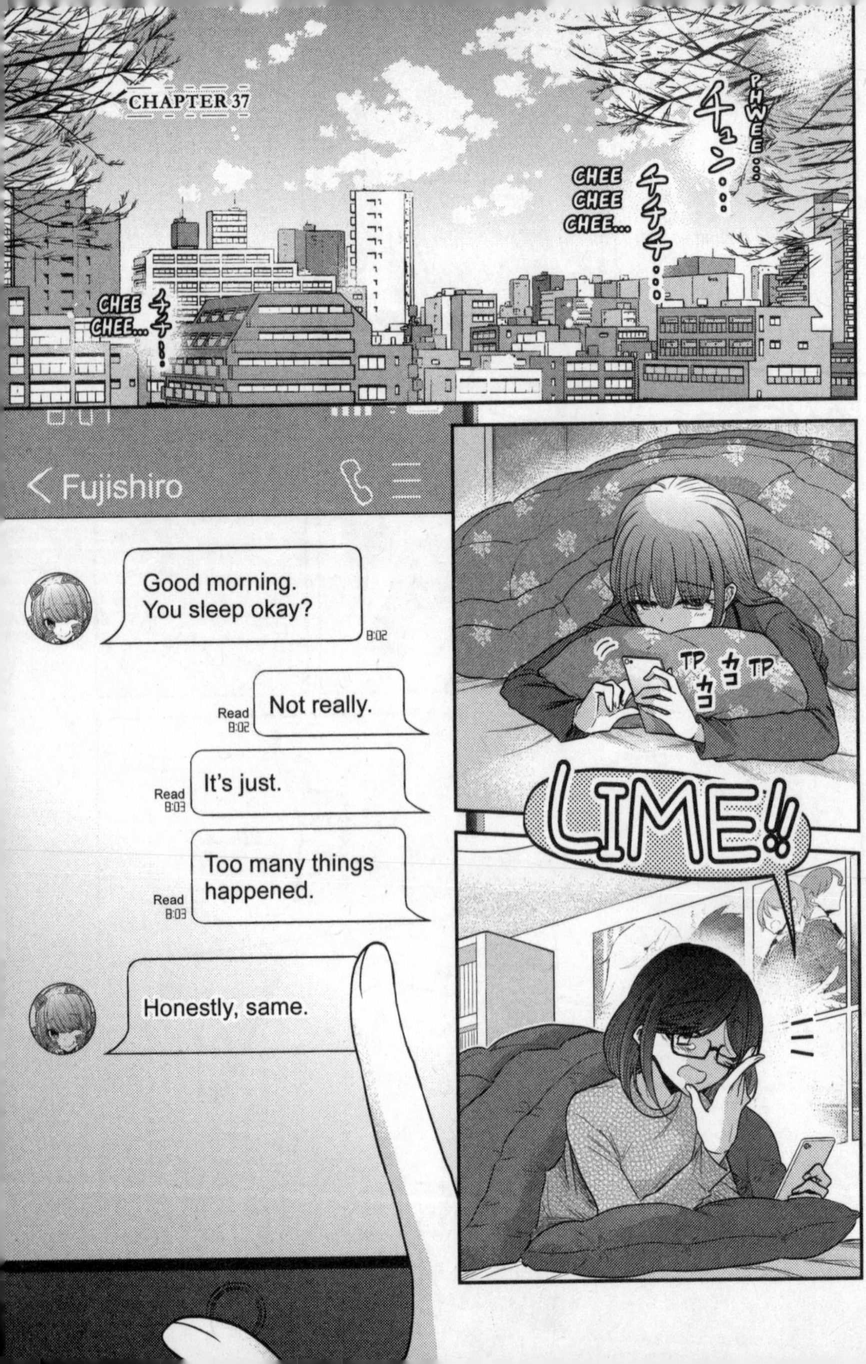
CHAPTER 37
PHWEE...
チュン...
CHEE CHEE CHEE...
チチチ...
CHEE CHEE...
チチ...
TP
カコ
TP
カコ
LIME!!
Fujishiro
Good morning. You sleep okay?
8:02
Read 8:02
Not really.
Read 8:03
It's just.
Read 8:03
Too many things happened.
Honestly, same.

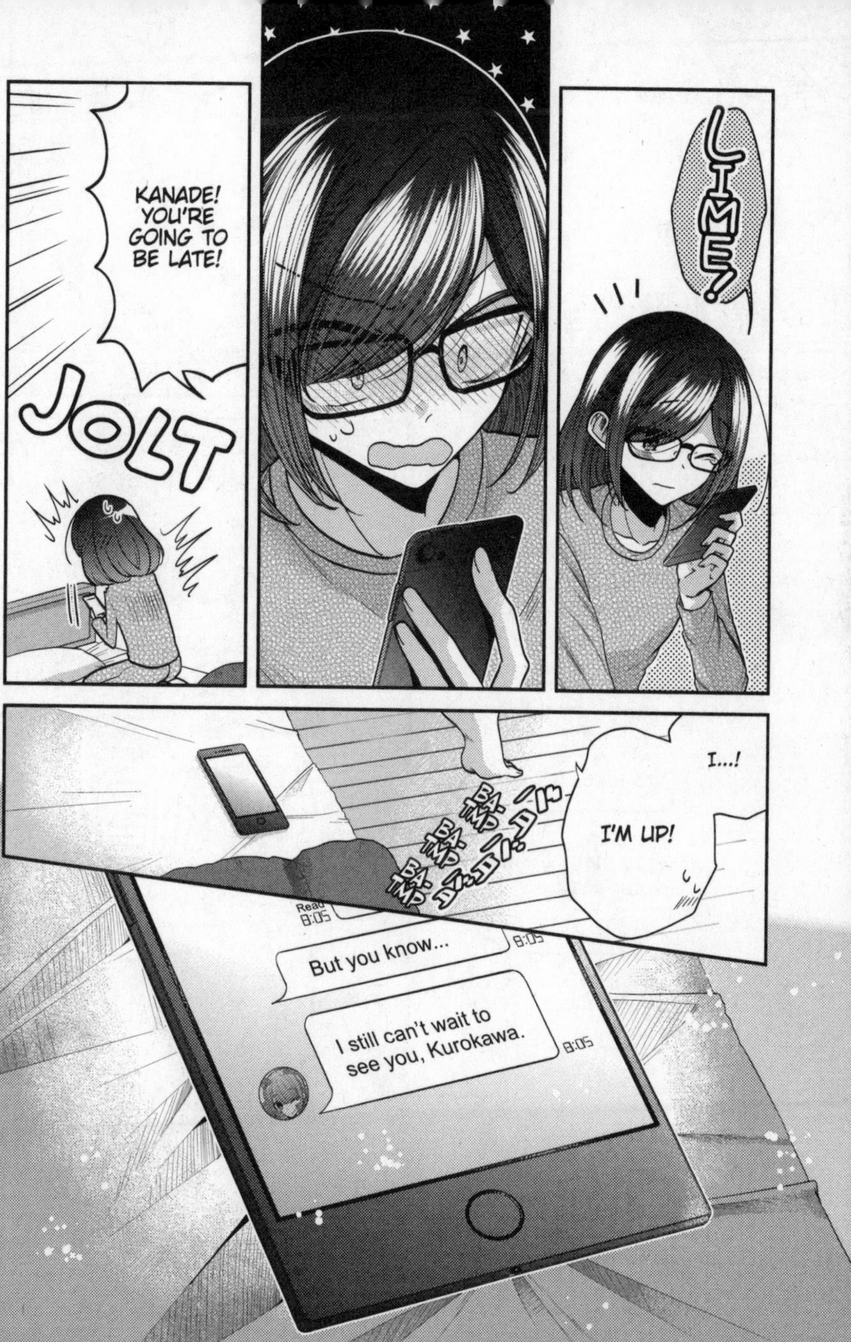
LIME!
KANADE! YOU'RE GOING TO BE LATE!
JOLT
I...!
I'M UP!
BA-TMP
BA-TMP
BA-TMP
Read
8:05
8:05
But you know...
I still can't wait to see you, Kurokawa.
8:05

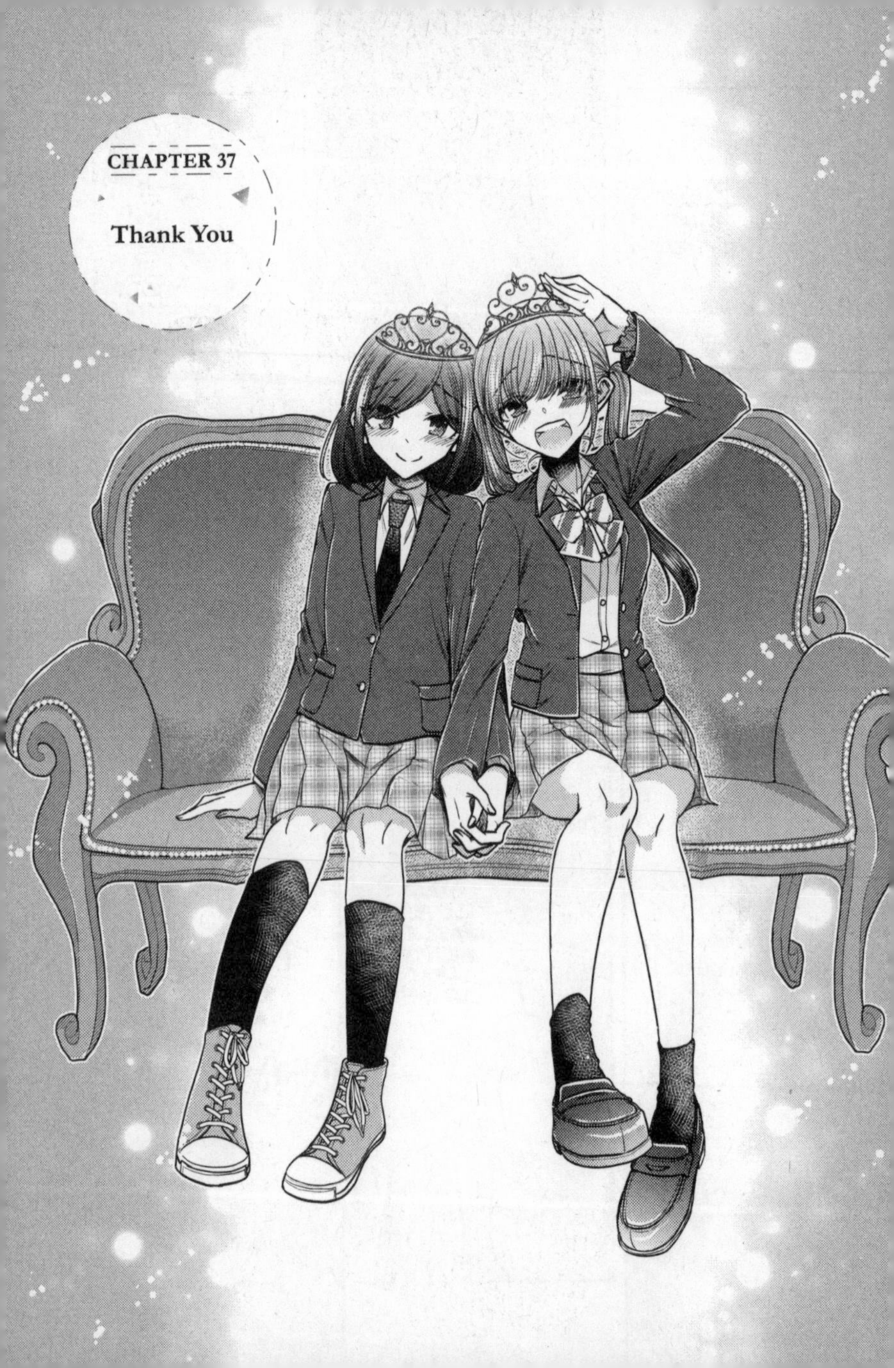
CHAPTER 37
Thank You

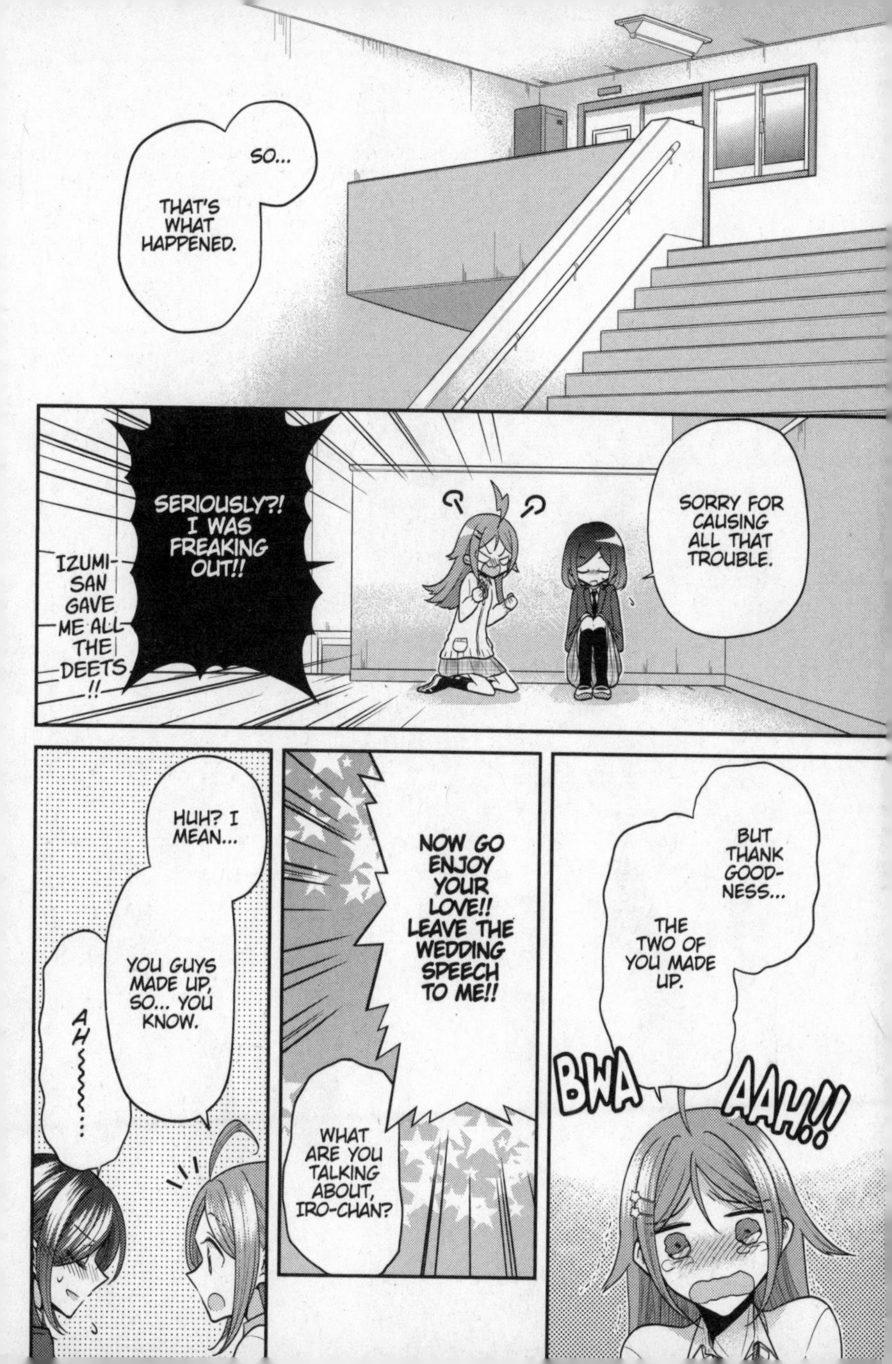
SO...
THAT'S WHAT HAPPENED.
SORRY FOR CAUSING ALL THAT TROUBLE.
SERIOUSLY?! I WAS FREAKING OUT!!
IZUMI-SAN GAVE ME ALL THE DEETS!!
BUT THANK GOODNESS...
THE TWO OF YOU MADE UP.
BWAAAH!!
NOW GO ENJOY YOUR LOVE!! LEAVE THE WEDDING SPEECH TO ME!!
WHAT ARE YOU TALKING ABOUT, IRO-CHAN?
HUH? I MEAN...
YOU GUYS MADE UP, SO... YOU KNOW.
AH~~~...

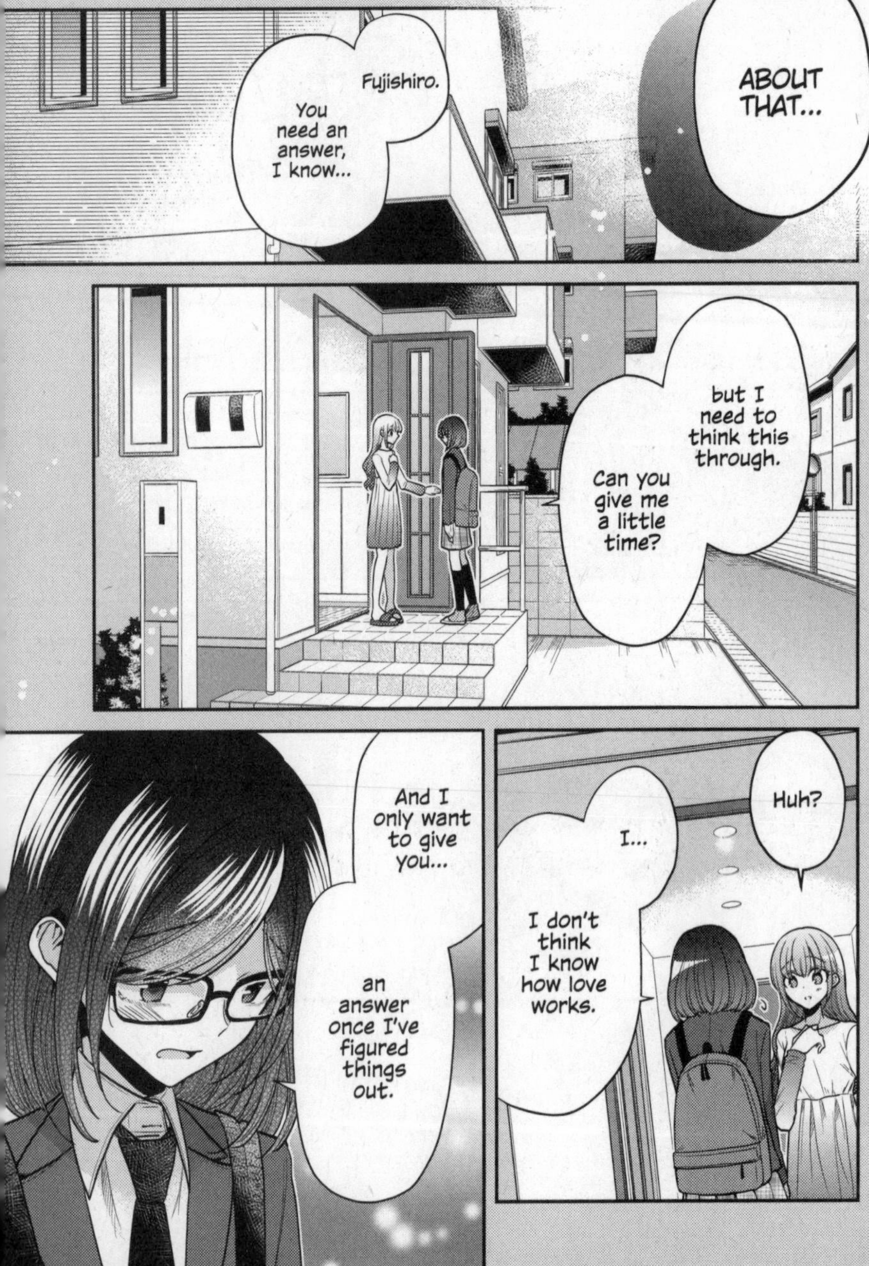
ABOUT THAT...
Fujishiro.
You need an answer, I know...
but I need to think this through.
Can you give me a little time?
Huh?
I...
I don't think I know how love works.
And I only want to give you...
an answer once I've figured things out.

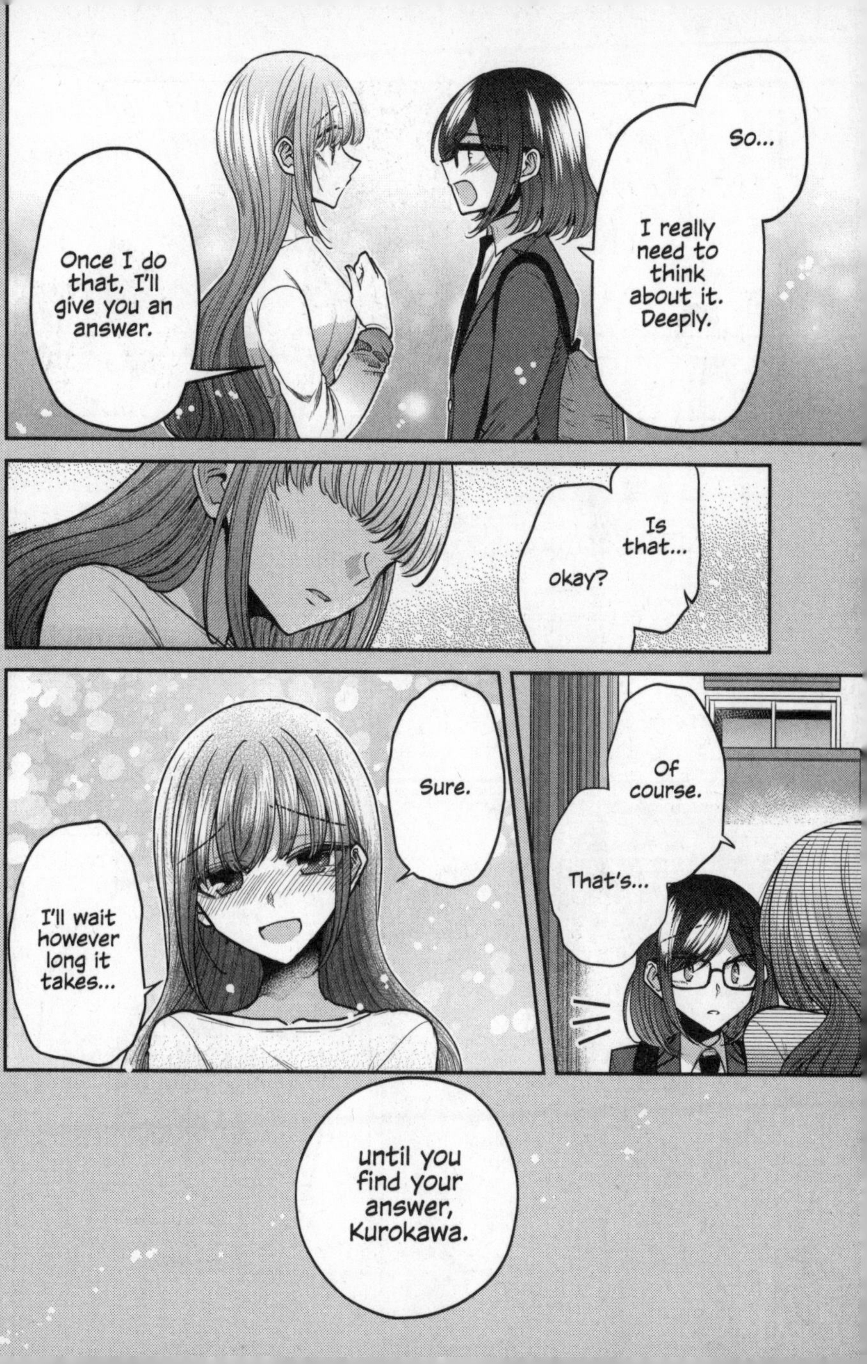
So...
I really need to think about it. Deeply.
Once I do that, I'll give you an answer.
Is that...
okay?
Of course.
That's...
Sure.
I'll wait however long it takes...
until you find your answer, Kurokawa.

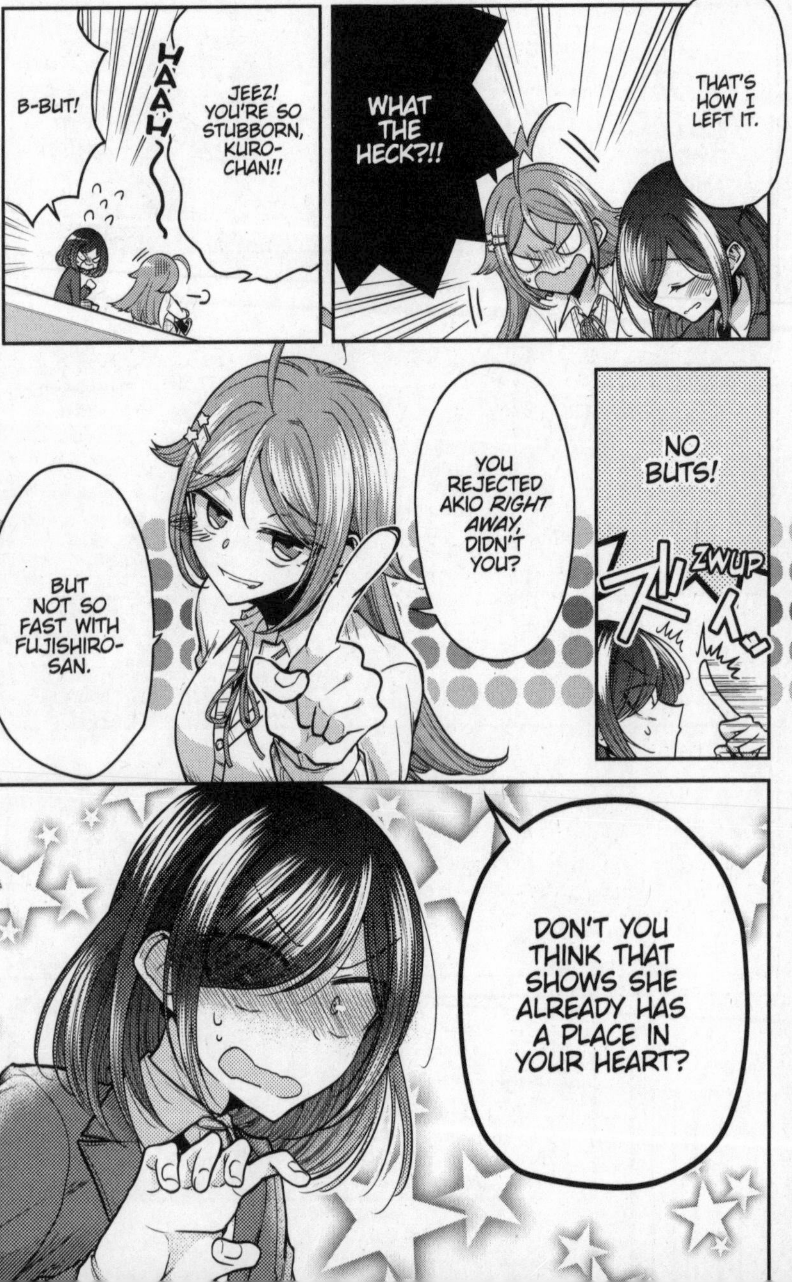
THAT'S HOW I LEFT IT.
WHAT THE HECK?!!
JEEZ! YOU'RE SO STUBBORN, KURO-CHAN!!
HAAAH
B-BUT!
NO BUTS!
ZWUP
YOU REJECTED AKIO *RIGHT AWAY*, DIDN'T YOU?
BUT NOT SO FAST WITH FUJISHIRO-SAN.
DON'T YOU THINK THAT SHOWS SHE ALREADY HAS A PLACE IN YOUR HEART?

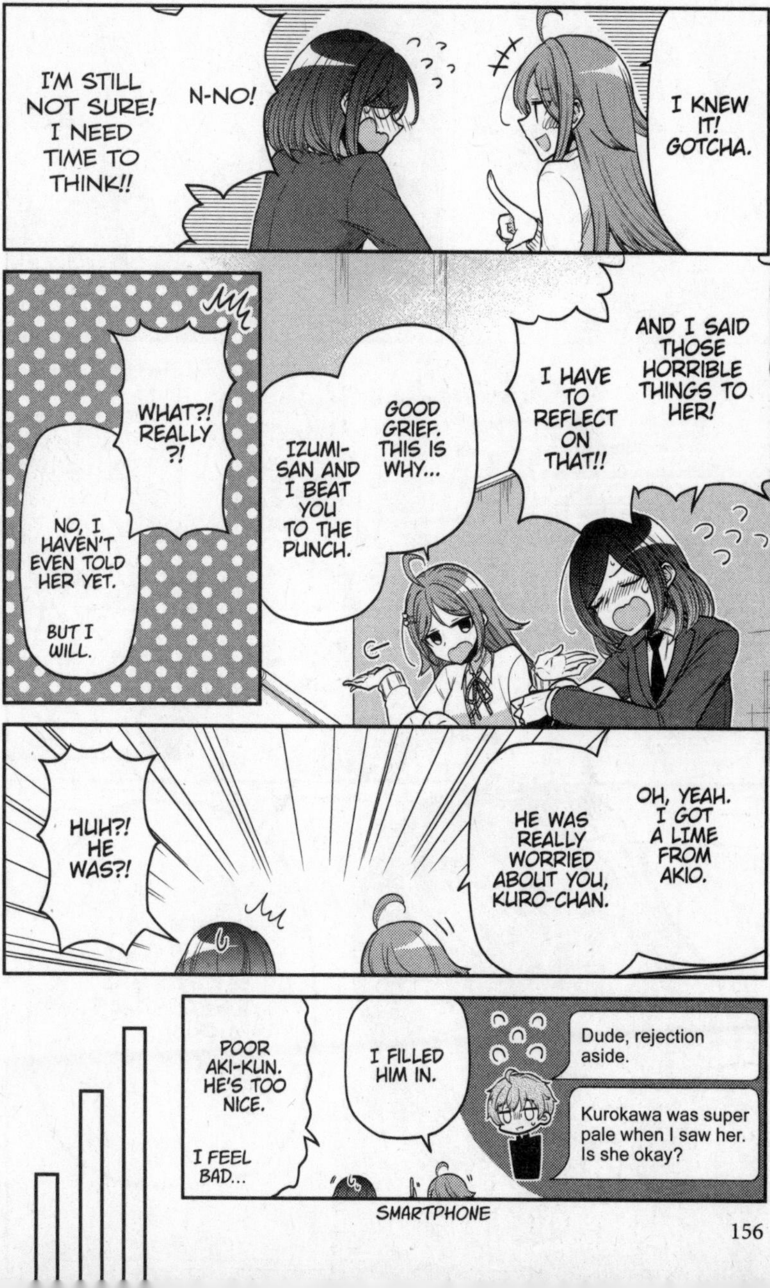
I KNEW IT! GOTCHA.
N-NO!
I'M STILL NOT SURE! I NEED TIME TO THINK!!
AND I SAID THOSE HORRIBLE THINGS TO HER!
I HAVE TO REFLECT ON THAT!!
GOOD GRIEF. THIS IS WHY...
IZUMI-SAN AND I BEAT YOU TO THE PUNCH.
WHAT?! REALLY?!
NO, I HAVEN'T EVEN TOLD HER YET.
BUT I WILL.
OH, YEAH. I GOT A LIME FROM AKIO.
HE WAS REALLY WORRIED ABOUT YOU, KURO-CHAN.
HUH?! HE WAS?!
Dude, rejection aside.
Kurokawa was super pale when I saw her. Is she okay?
I FILLED HIM IN.
POOR AKI-KUN. HE'S TOO NICE.
I FEEL BAD...
SMARTPHONE

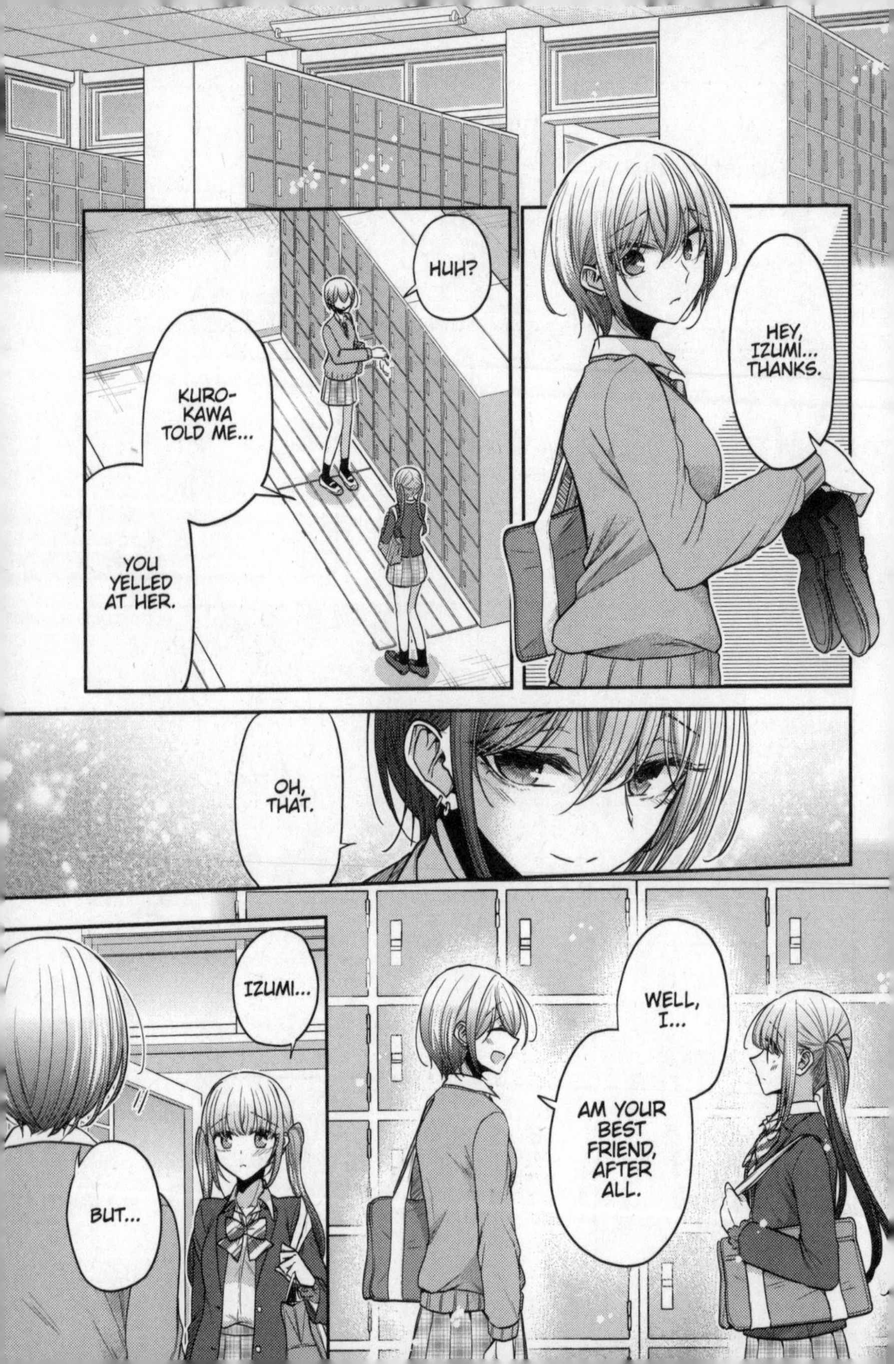
HEY, IZUMI... THANKS.
HUH?
KURO-KAWA TOLD ME...
YOU YELLED AT HER.
OH, THAT.
WELL, I...
AM YOUR BEST FRIEND, AFTER ALL.
IZUMI...
BUT...

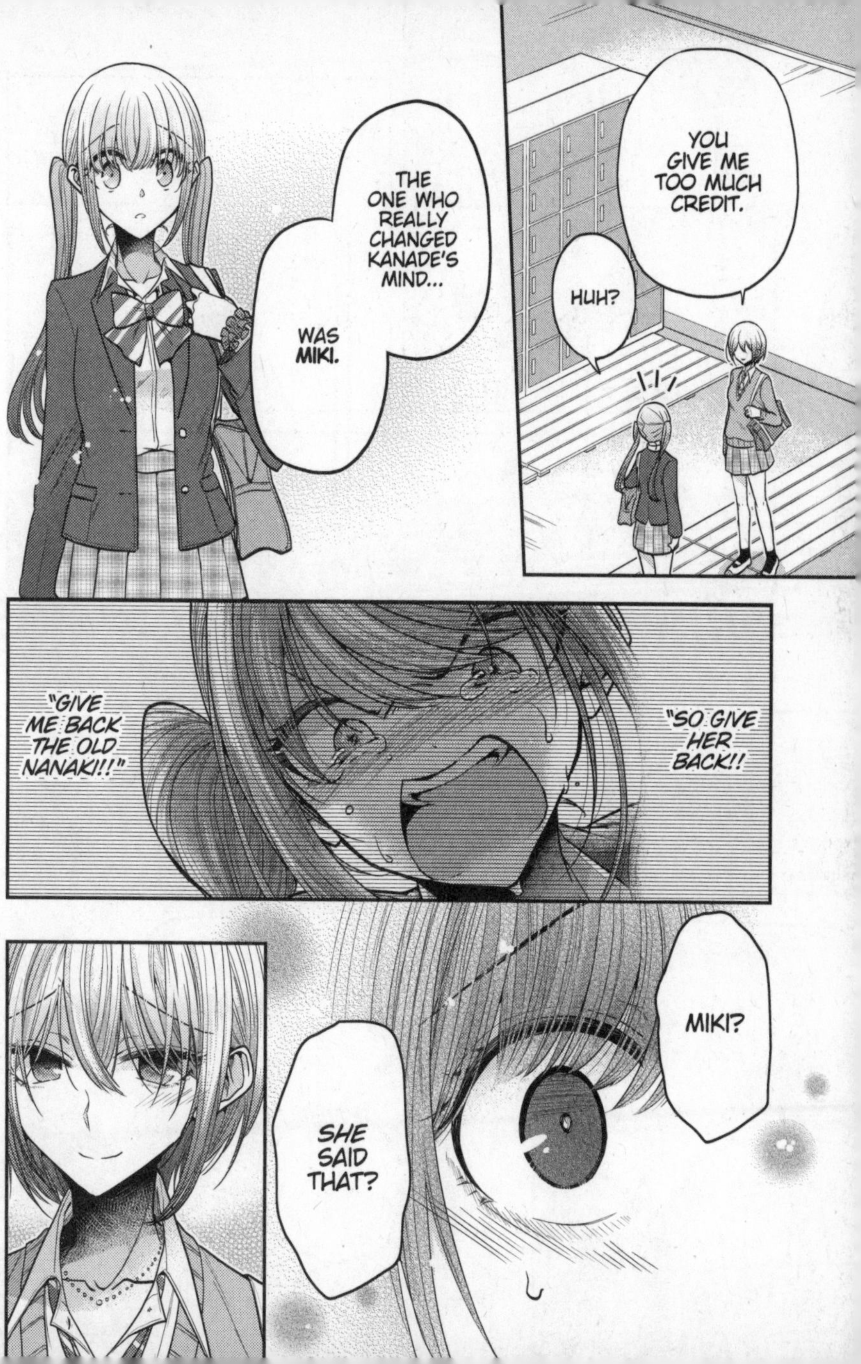
YOU GIVE ME TOO MUCH CREDIT.
HUH?
THE ONE WHO REALLY CHANGED KANADE'S MIND...
WAS MIKI.
"SO GIVE HER BACK!!
"GIVE ME BACK THE OLD NANAKI!!!"
MIKI?
SHE SAID THAT?

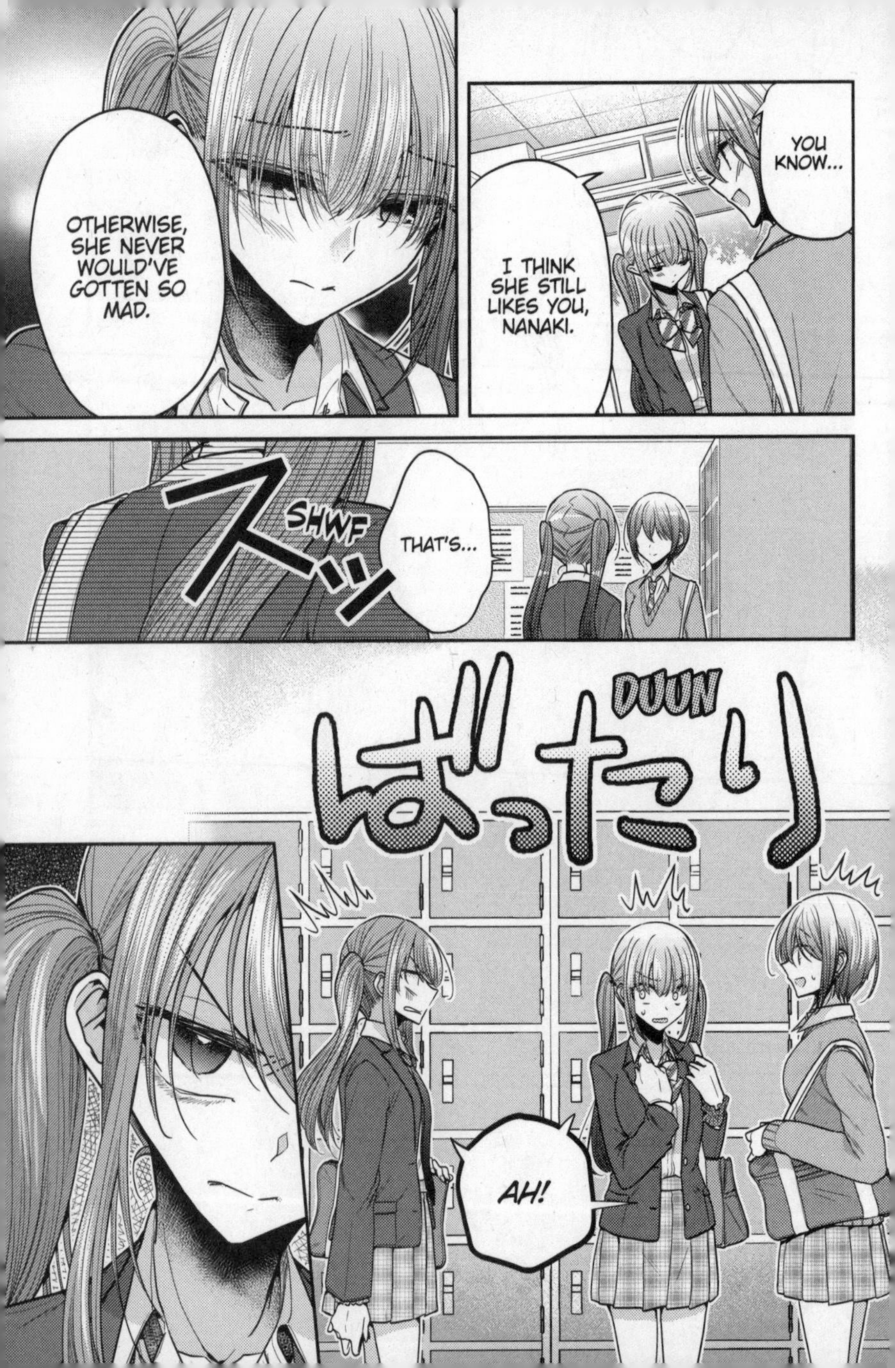
YOU KNOW...
I THINK SHE STILL LIKES YOU, NANAKI.
OTHERWISE, SHE NEVER WOULD'VE GOTTEN SO MAD.
THAT'S...
SHWF
スッ
ぱったり
DUUN
AH!

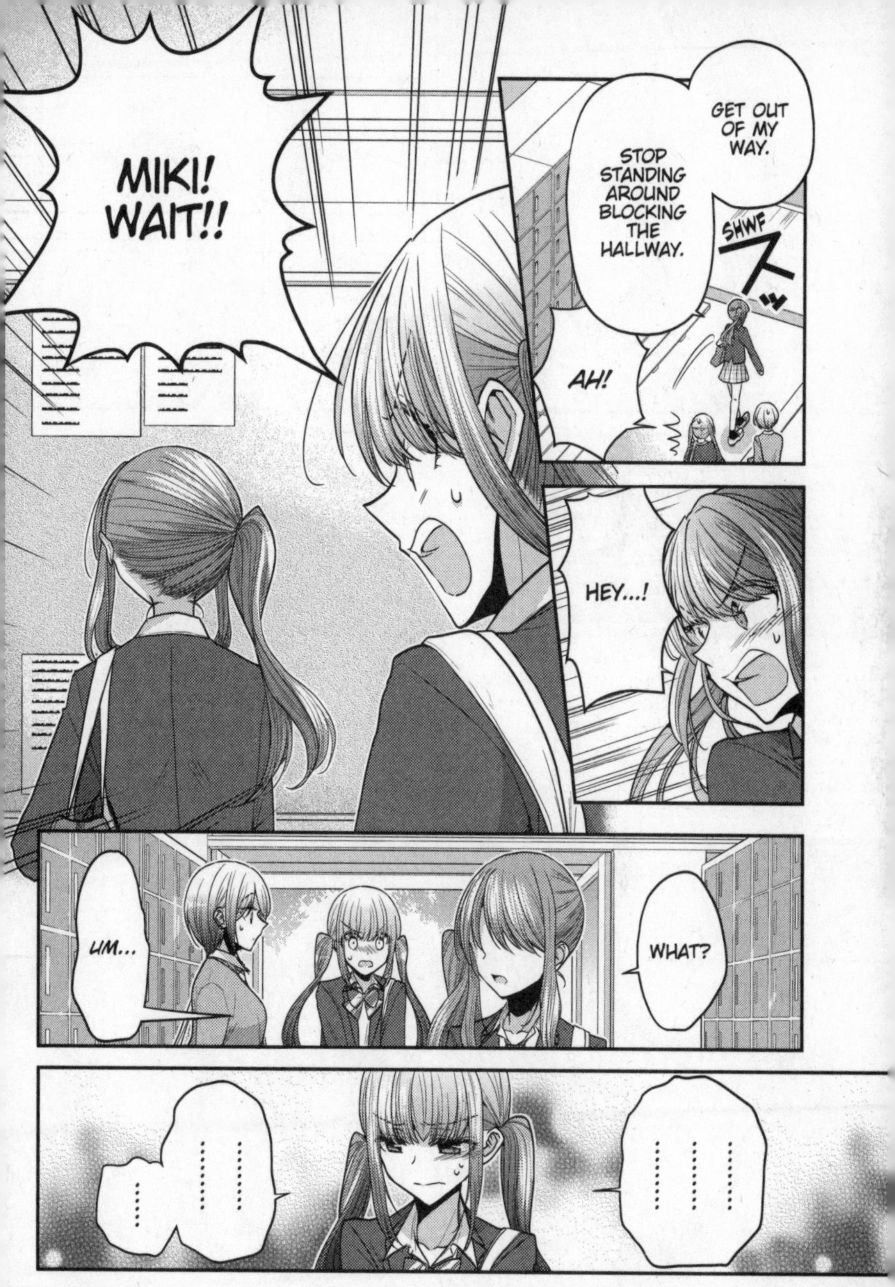
GET OUT OF MY WAY.
STOP STANDING AROUND BLOCKING THE HALLWAY.
SHWF
AH!
HEY...!
MIKI! WAIT!!
WHAT?
UM...
......
......

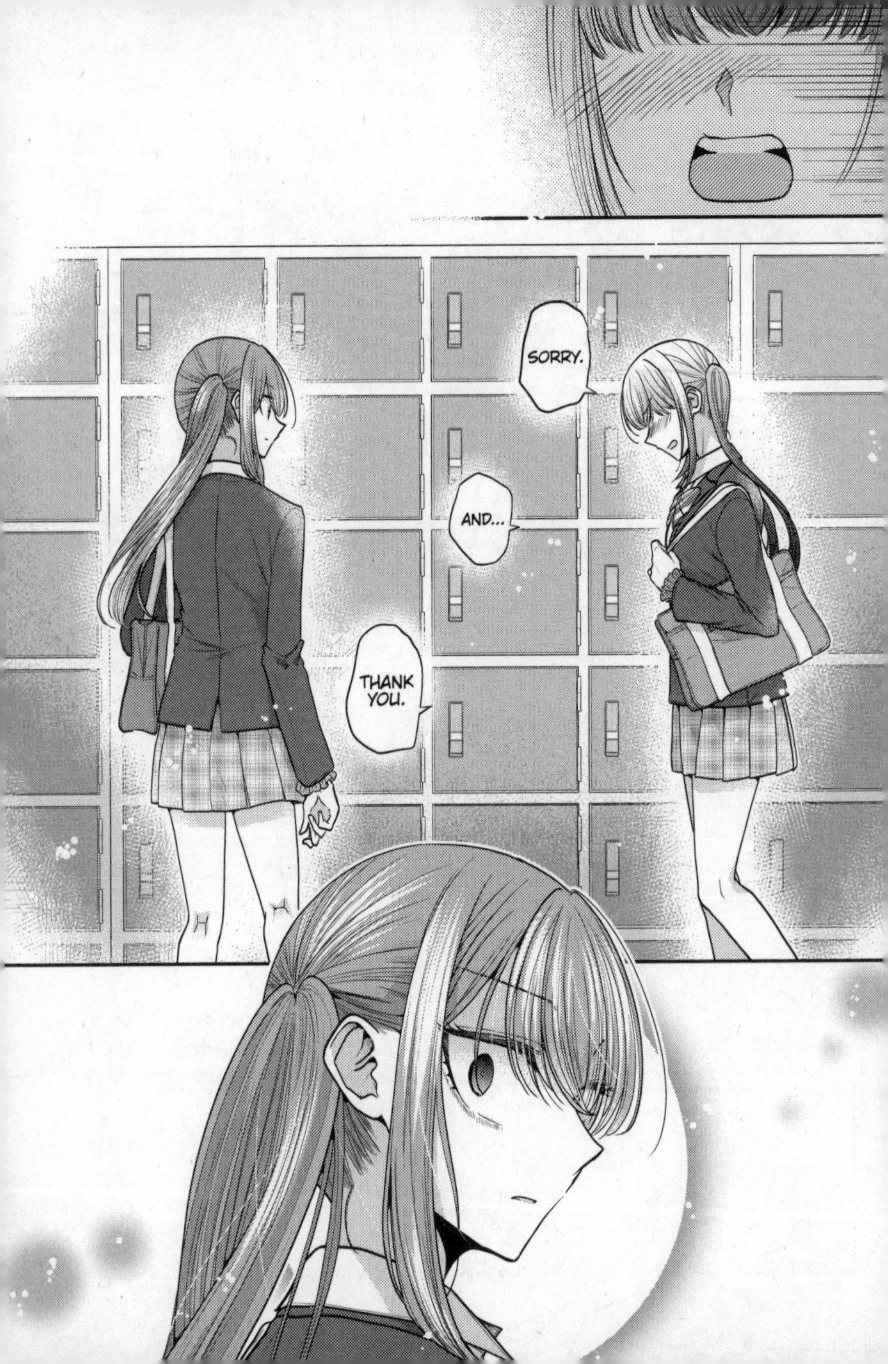
SORRY.
AND...
THANK YOU.

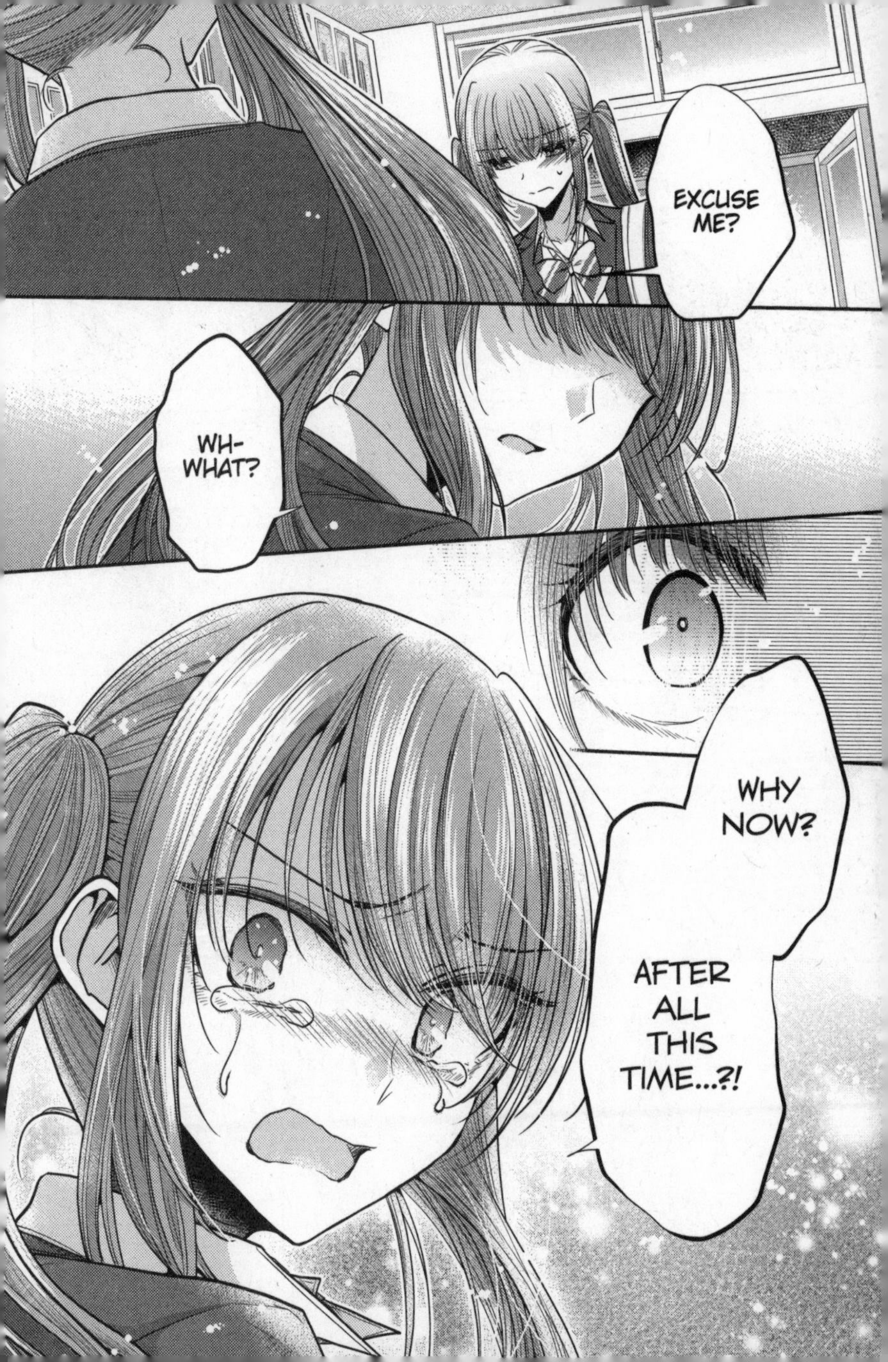
EXCUSE ME?
WH- WHAT?
WHY NOW?
AFTER ALL THIS TIME...?!

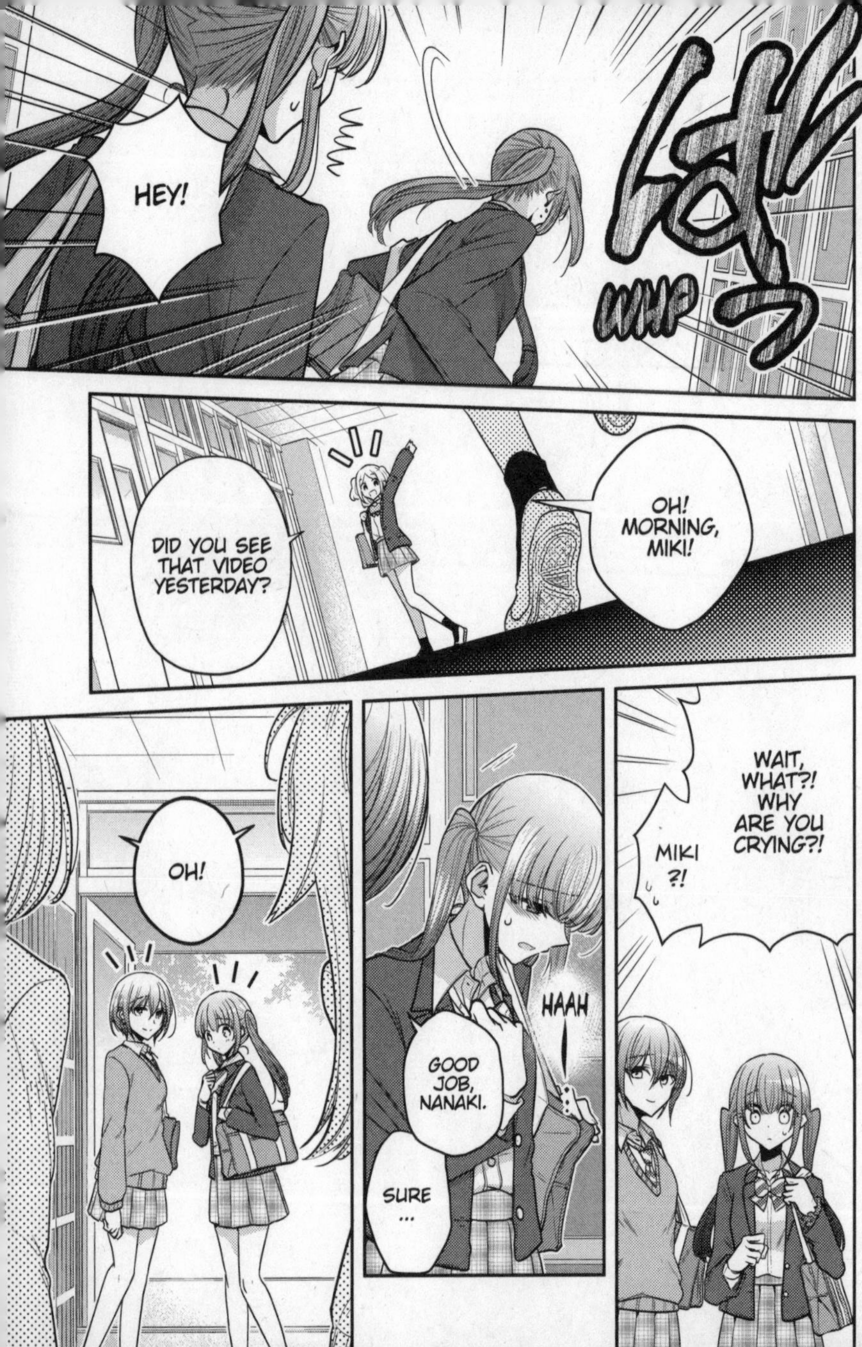
WHIP
HEY!
OH! MORNING, MIKI!
DID YOU SEE THAT VIDEO YESTERDAY?
WAIT, WHAT?! WHY ARE YOU CRYING?!
MIKI ?!
HAAH
GOOD JOB, NANAKI.
SURE ...
OH!

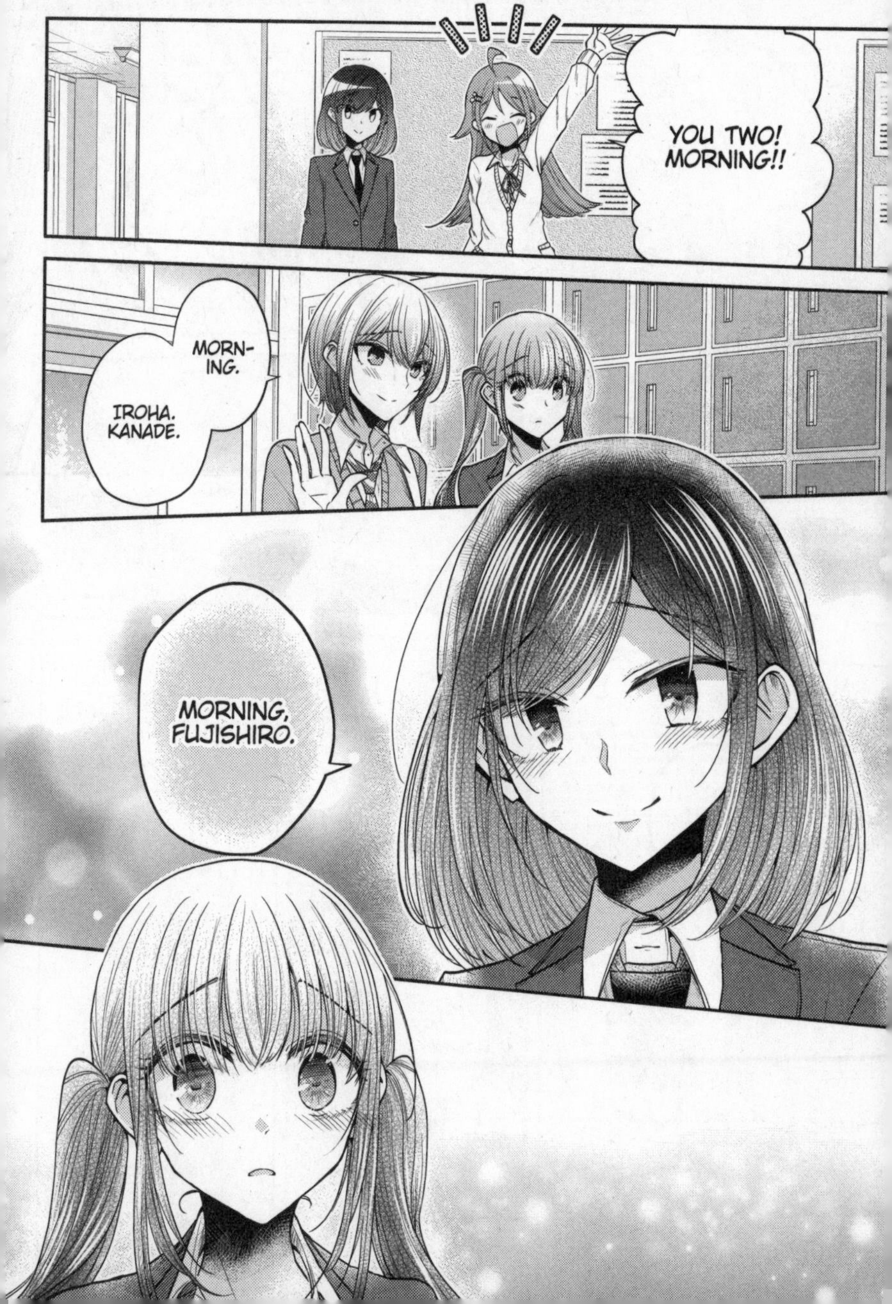
YOU TWO! MORNING!!
MORN-ING.
IROHA. KANADE.
MORNING, FUJISHIRO.

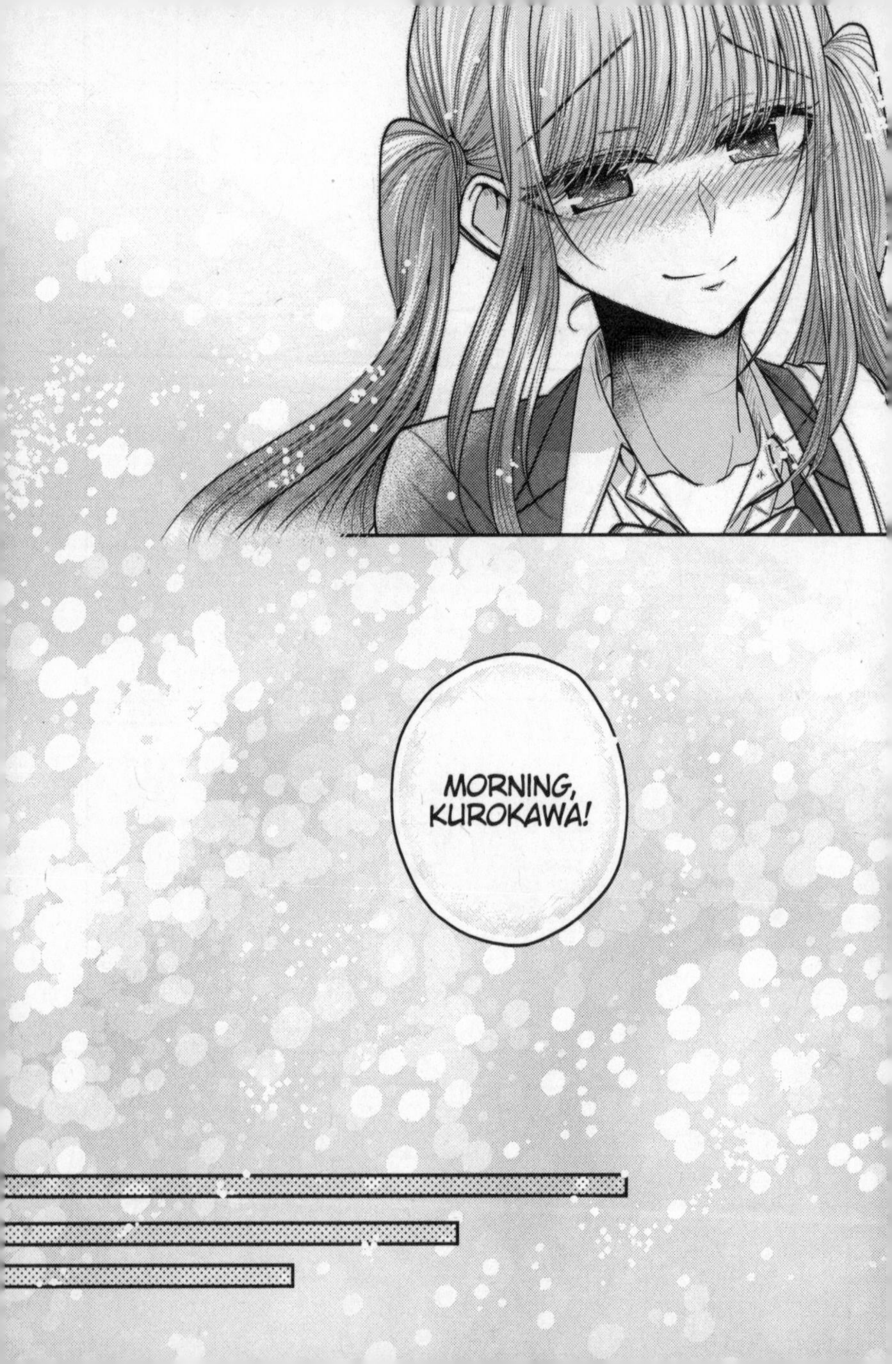
MORNING, KUROKAWA!

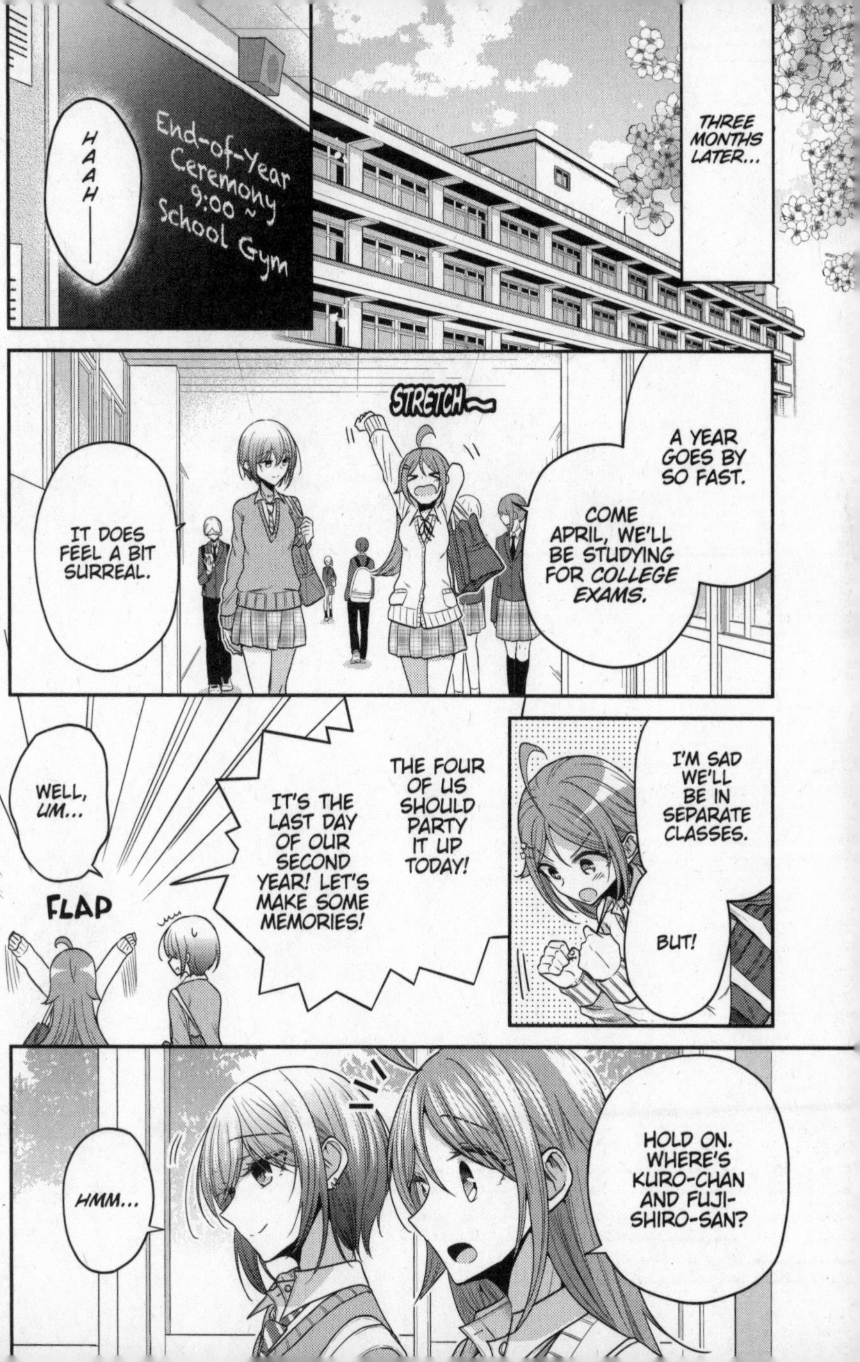
THREE MONTHS LATER...
End-of-Year Ceremony 9:00 ~ School Gym
HAAH—
STRETCH~
A YEAR GOES BY SO FAST.
COME APRIL, WE'LL BE STUDYING FOR COLLEGE EXAMS.
IT DOES FEEL A BIT SURREAL.
I'M SAD WE'LL BE IN SEPARATE CLASSES.
BUT!
THE FOUR OF US SHOULD PARTY IT UP TODAY!
IT'S THE LAST DAY OF OUR SECOND YEAR! LET'S MAKE SOME MEMORIES!
FLAP
WELL, UM...
HOLD ON. WHERE'S KURO-CHAN AND FUJI-SHIRO-SAN?
HMM...

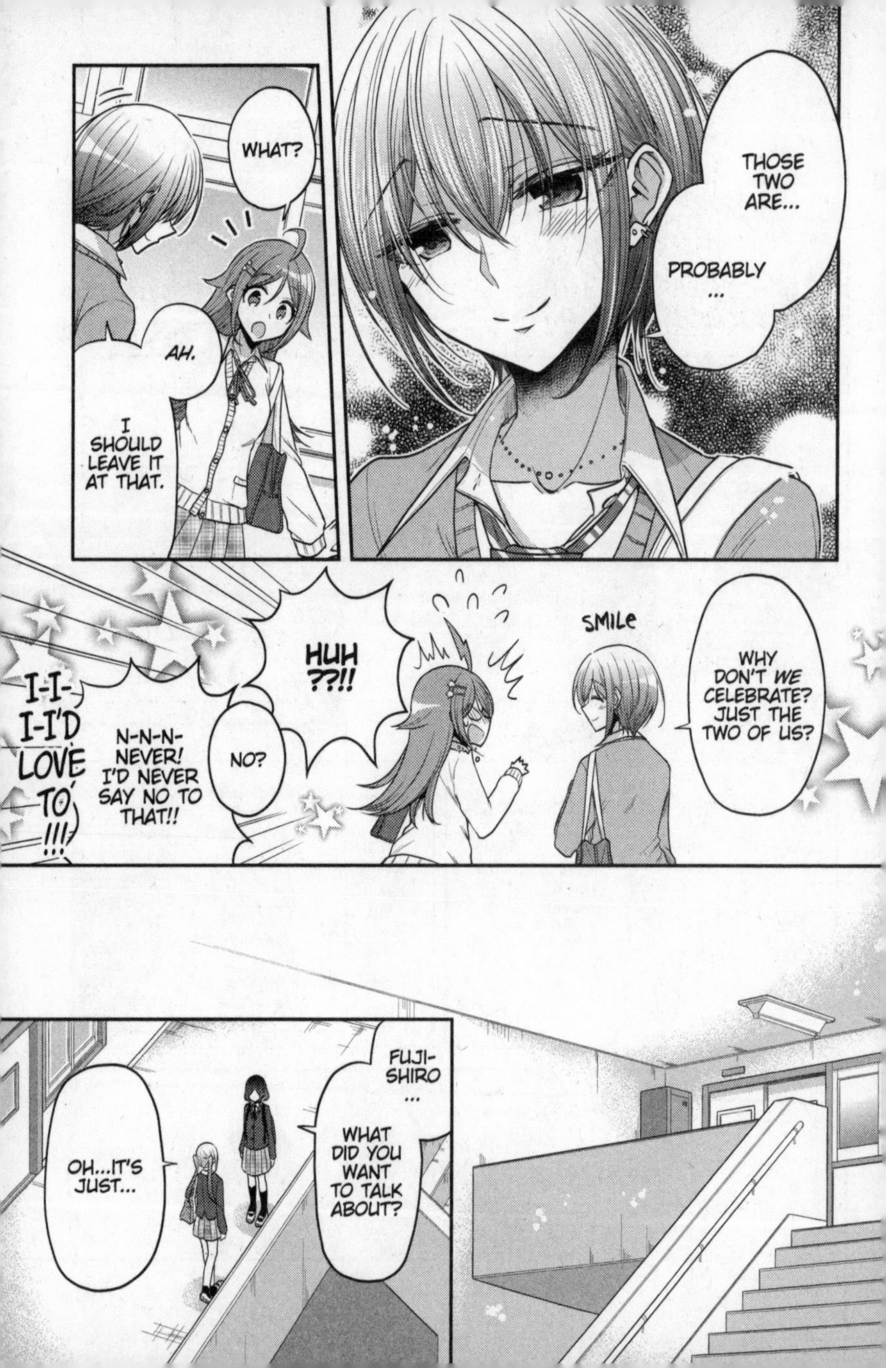
THOSE TWO ARE...
PROBABLY ...
WHAT?
AH.
I SHOULD LEAVE IT AT THAT.
SMILE
WHY DON'T *WE* CELEBRATE? JUST THE TWO OF US?
HUH ??!!
NO?
N-N-N-NEVER! I'D NEVER SAY NO TO THAT!!
I-I-I-I'D LOVE TO!!!
FUJI-SHIRO ...
WHAT DID YOU WANT TO TALK ABOUT?
OH...IT'S JUST...

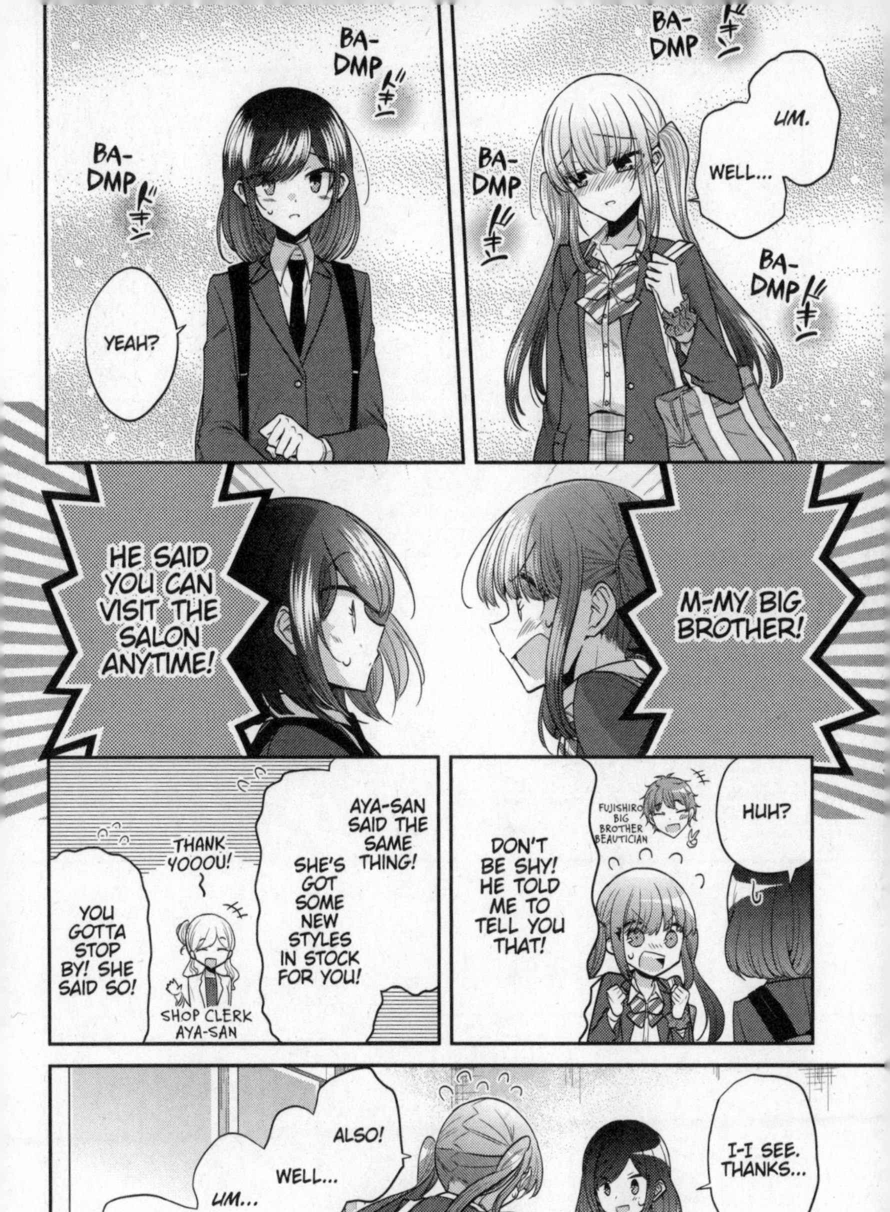
BA-DMP ドキン
UM.
WELL...
BA-DMP ドキン
BA-DMP ドキン
BA-DMP ドキン
BA-DMP ドキン
YEAH?
M-MY BIG BROTHER!
HE SAID YOU CAN VISIT THE SALON ANYTIME!
HUH?
FUJISHIRO BIG BROTHER BEAUTICIAN
DON'T BE SHY! HE TOLD ME TO TELL YOU THAT!
AYA-SAN SAID THE SAME THING!
SHE'S GOT SOME NEW STYLES IN STOCK FOR YOU!
THANK YOOOU!
YOU GOTTA STOP BY! SHE SAID SO!
SHOP CLERK AYA-SAN
I-I SEE. THANKS...
ALSO!
WELL...
UM...
......

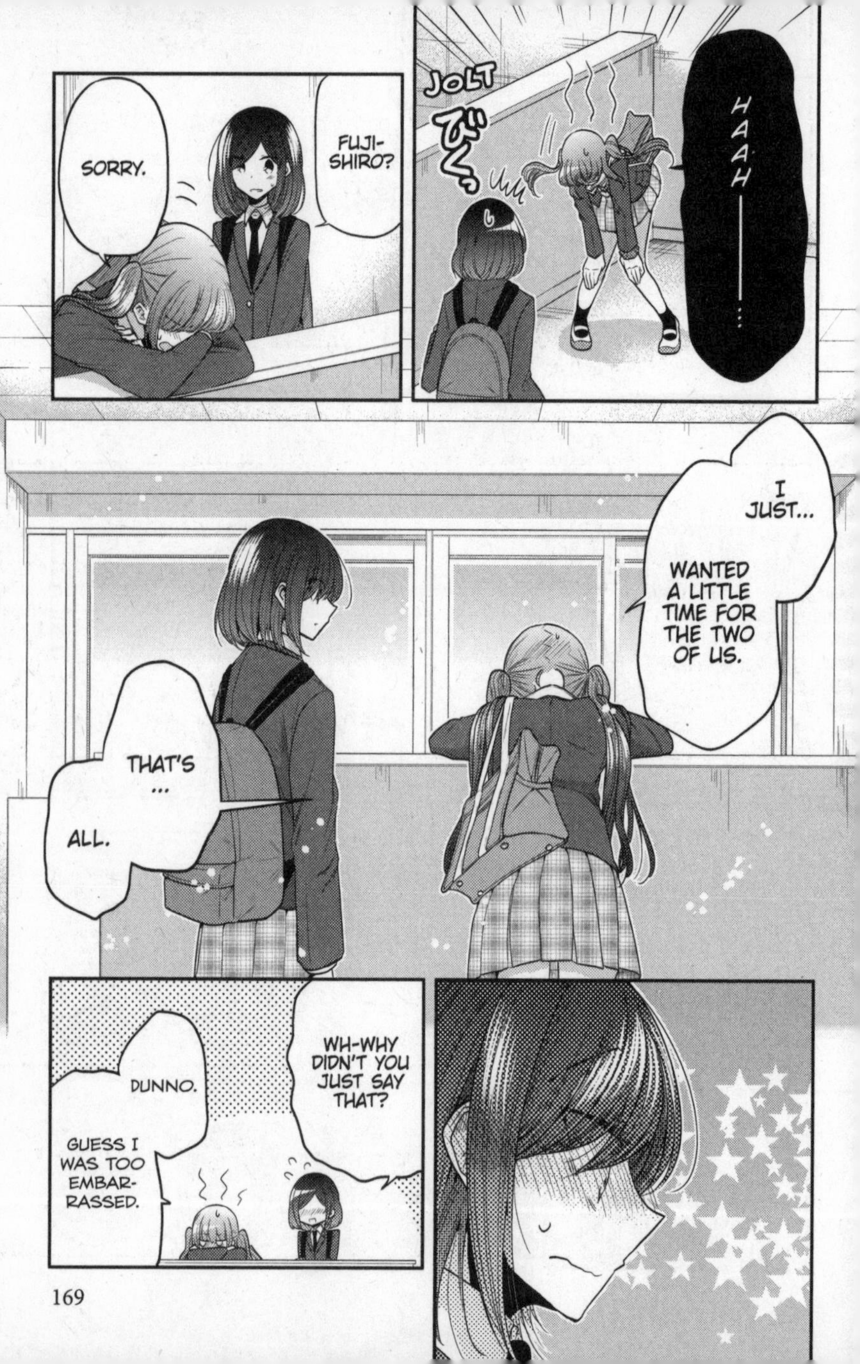
HAAAH——...
JOLT
びくっ
FUJI-SHIRO?
SORRY.
I JUST...
WANTED A LITTLE TIME FOR THE TWO OF US.
THAT'S ... ALL.
WH-WHY DIDN'T YOU JUST SAY THAT?
DUNNO.
GUESS I WAS TOO EMBAR-RASSED.

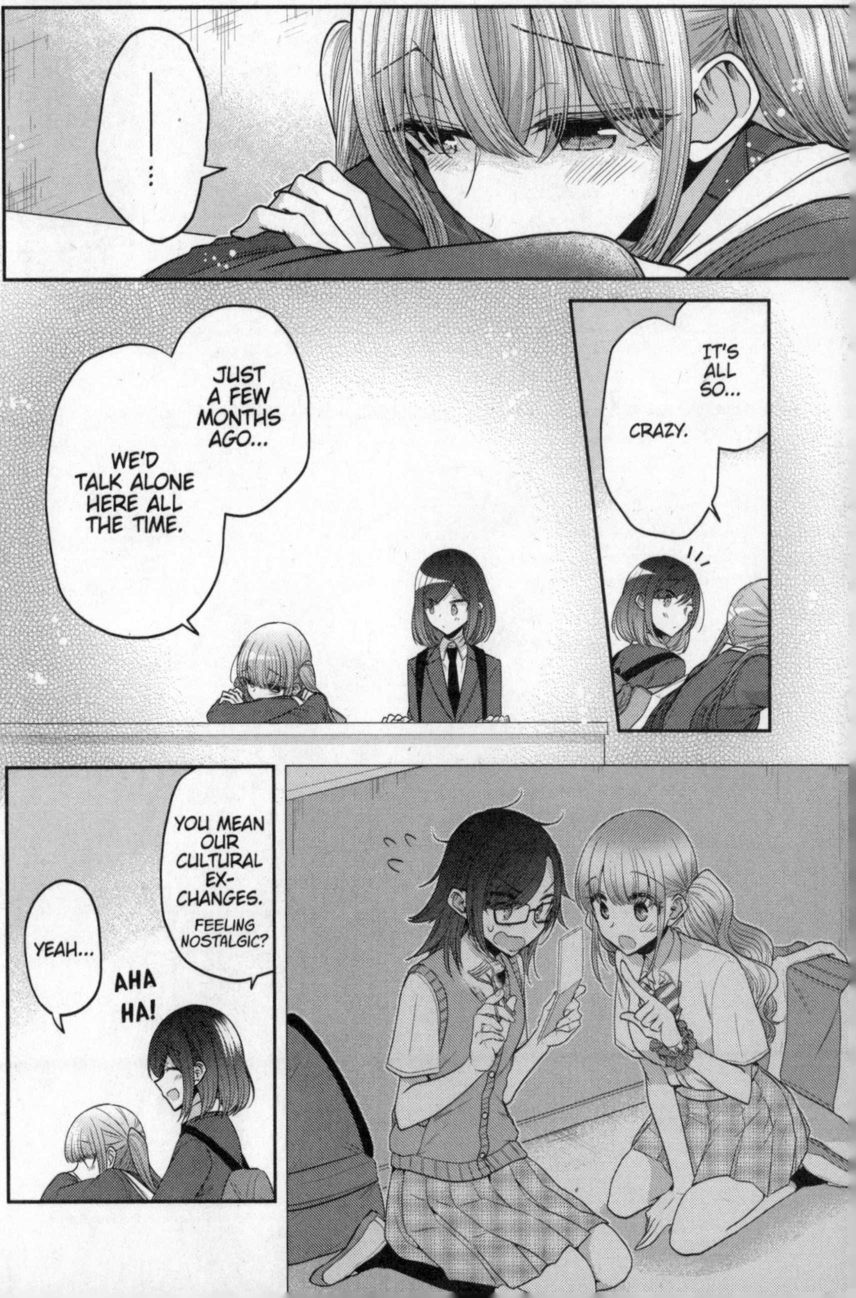
—...
IT'S ALL SO...
CRAZY.
JUST A FEW MONTHS AGO...
WE'D TALK ALONE HERE ALL THE TIME.
YOU MEAN OUR CULTURAL EX-CHANGES.
FEELING NOSTALGIC?
YEAH...
AHA HA!

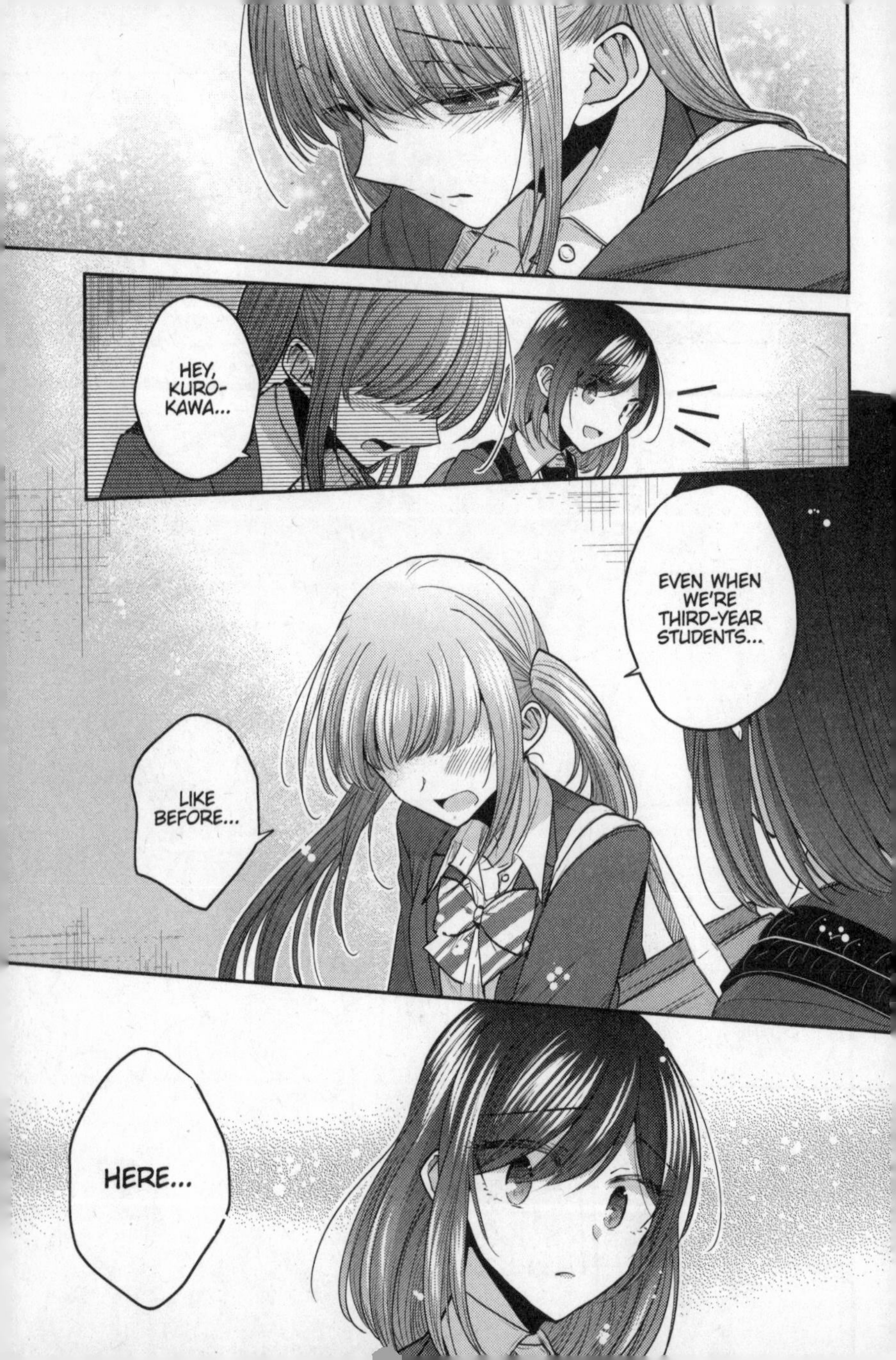
HEY, KURO-KAWA...
EVEN WHEN WE'RE THIRD-YEAR STUDENTS...
LIKE BEFORE...
HERE...

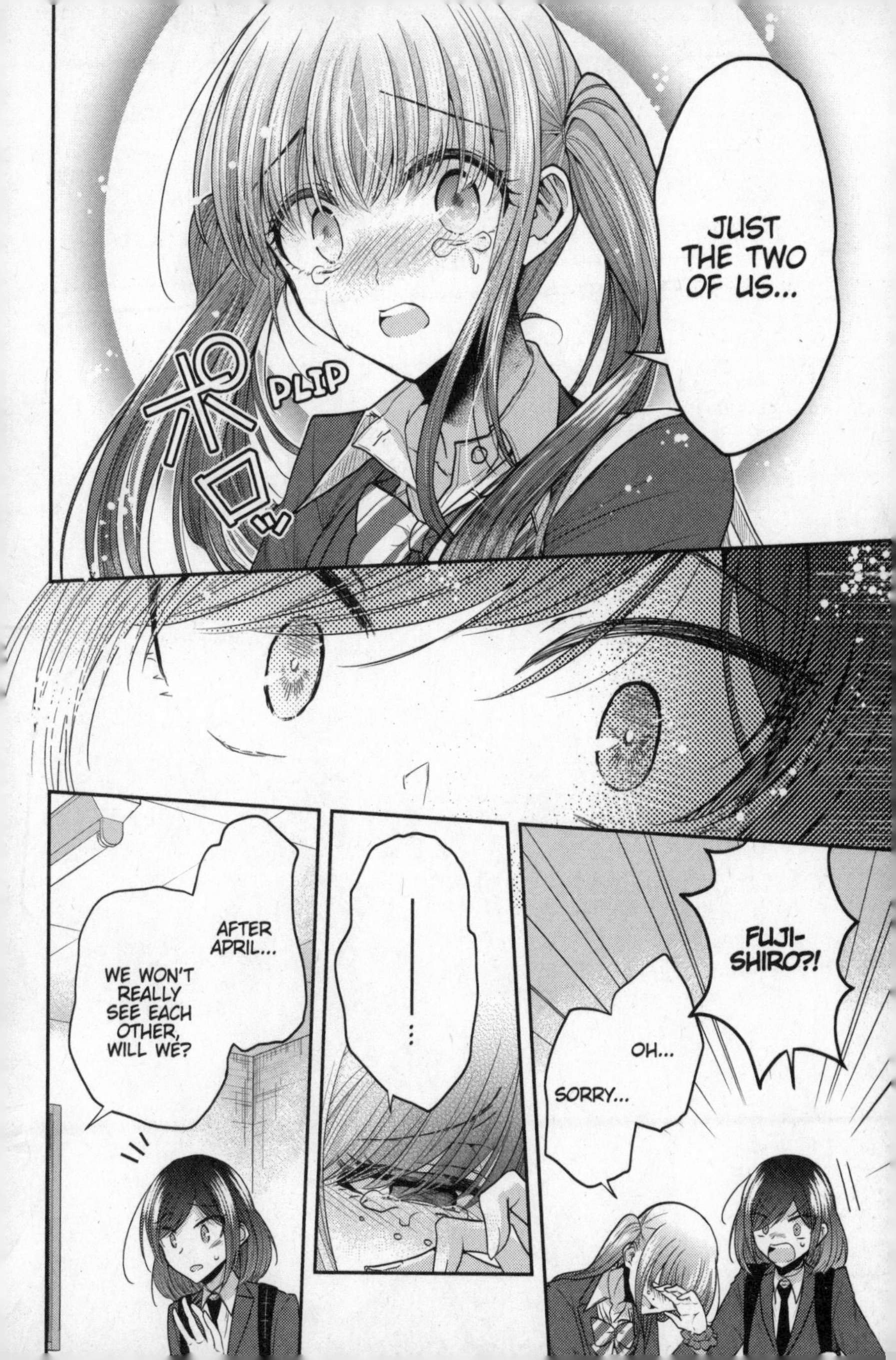
JUST THE TWO OF US...
PLIP
FUJI-SHIRO?!
OH...
SORRY...
—
...
AFTER APRIL...
WE WON'T REALLY SEE EACH OTHER, WILL WE?

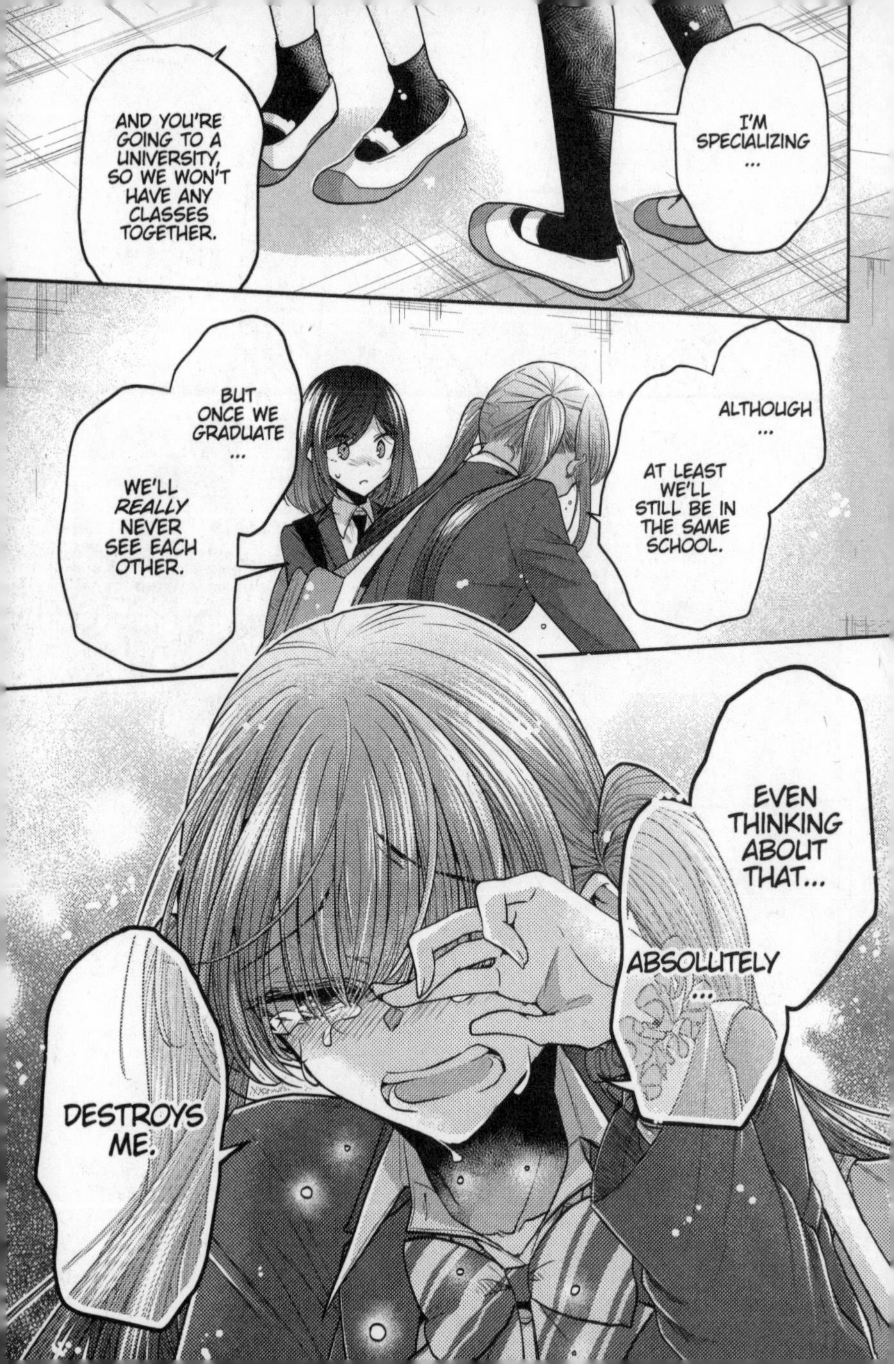
I'M SPECIALIZING ...
AND YOU'RE GOING TO A UNIVERSITY, SO WE WON'T HAVE ANY CLASSES TOGETHER.
ALTHOUGH ...
AT LEAST WE'LL STILL BE IN THE SAME SCHOOL.
BUT ONCE WE GRADUATE ...
WE'LL *REALLY* NEVER SEE EACH OTHER.
EVEN THINKING ABOUT THAT...
ABSOLUTELY ...
DESTROYS ME.

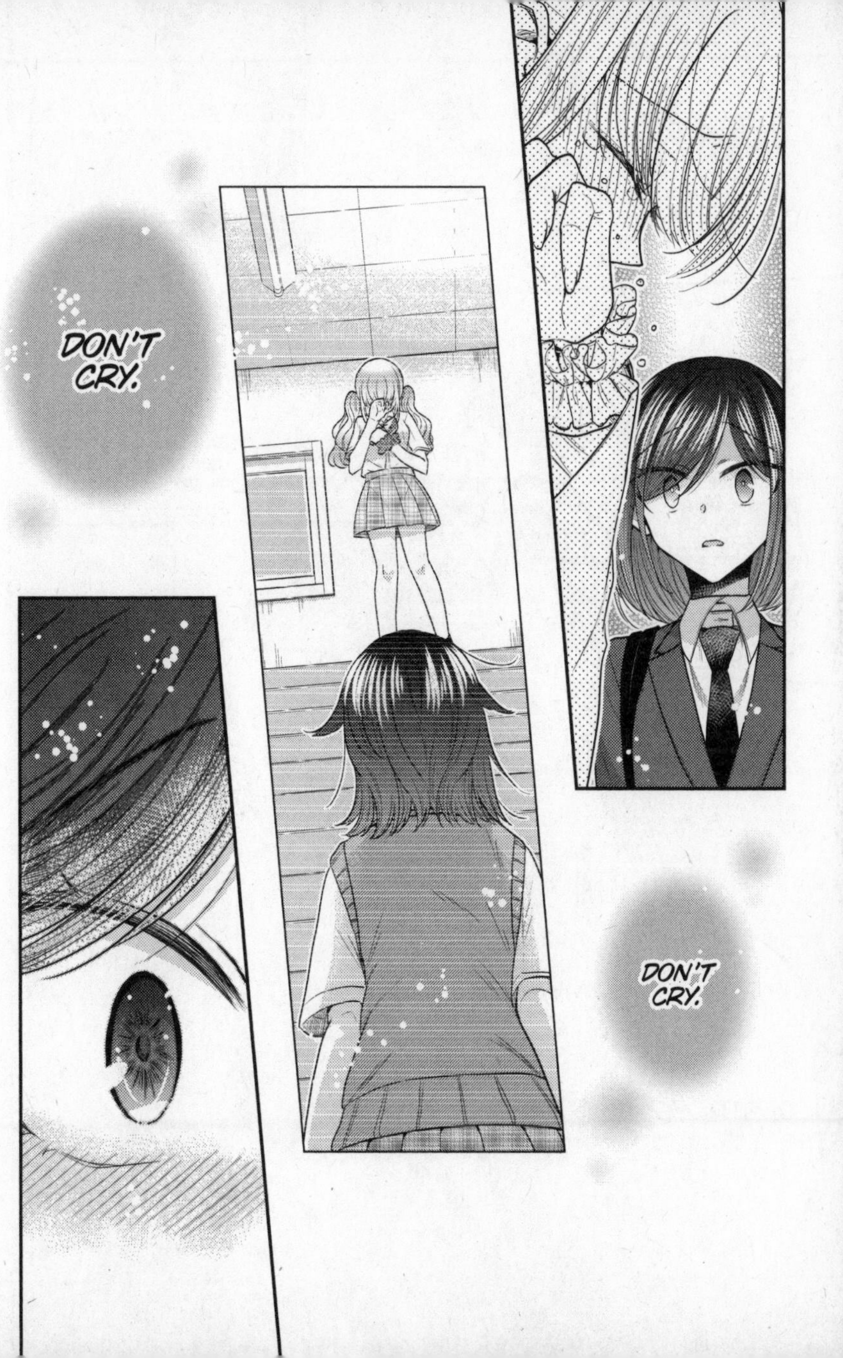
DON'T CRY.
DON'T CRY.

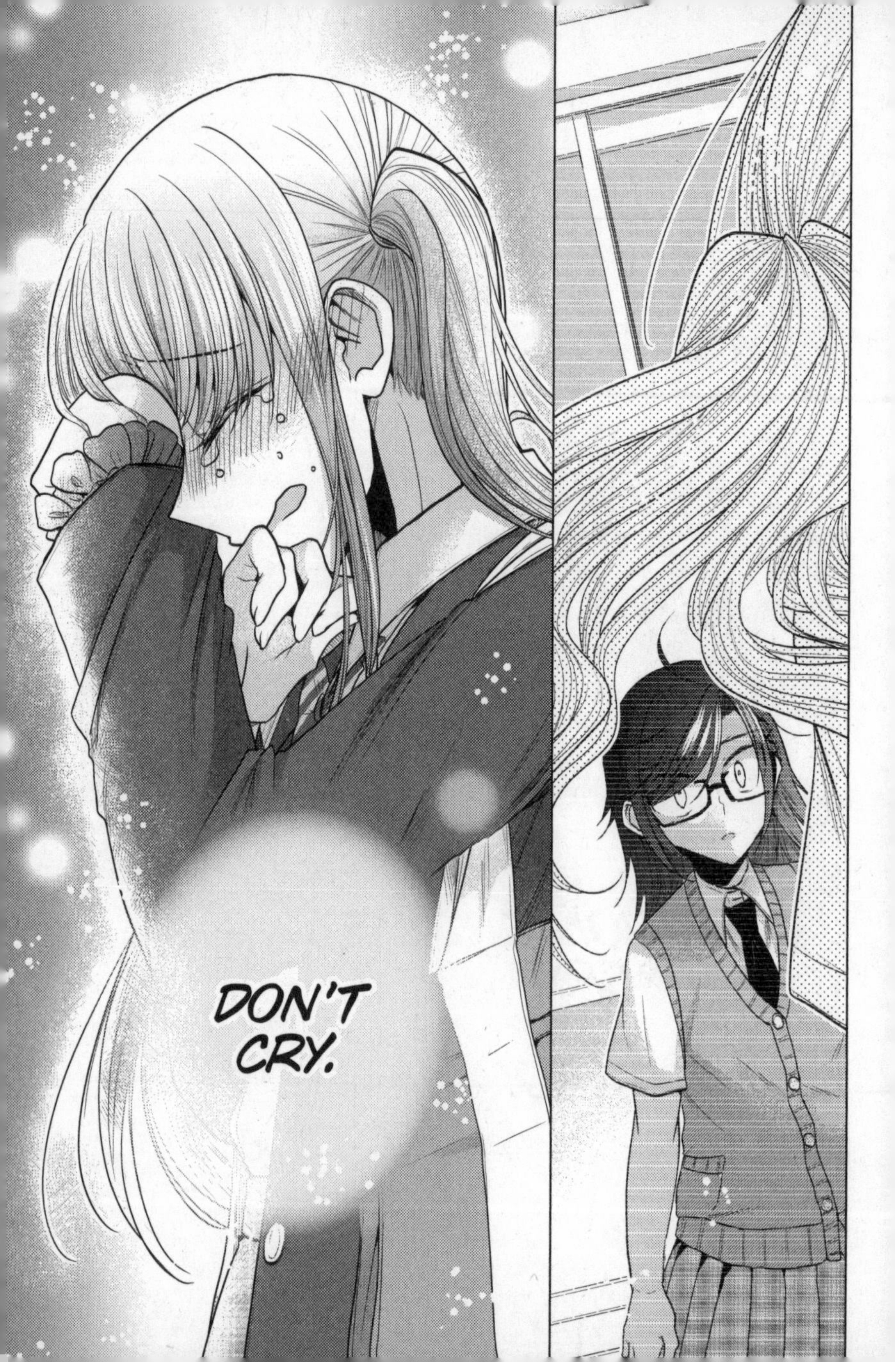
DON'T
CRY.

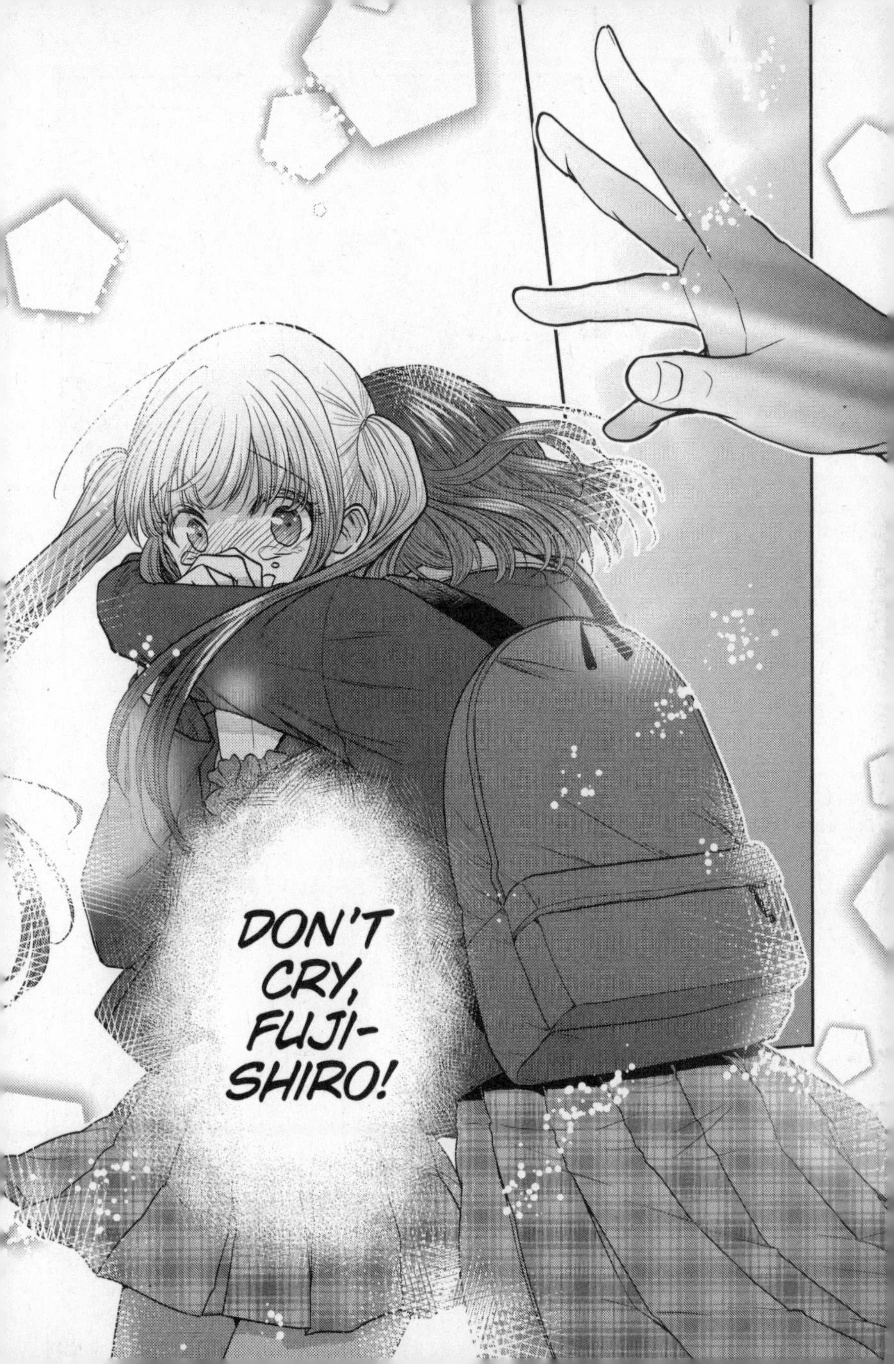
DON'T CRY, FUJI-SHIRO!

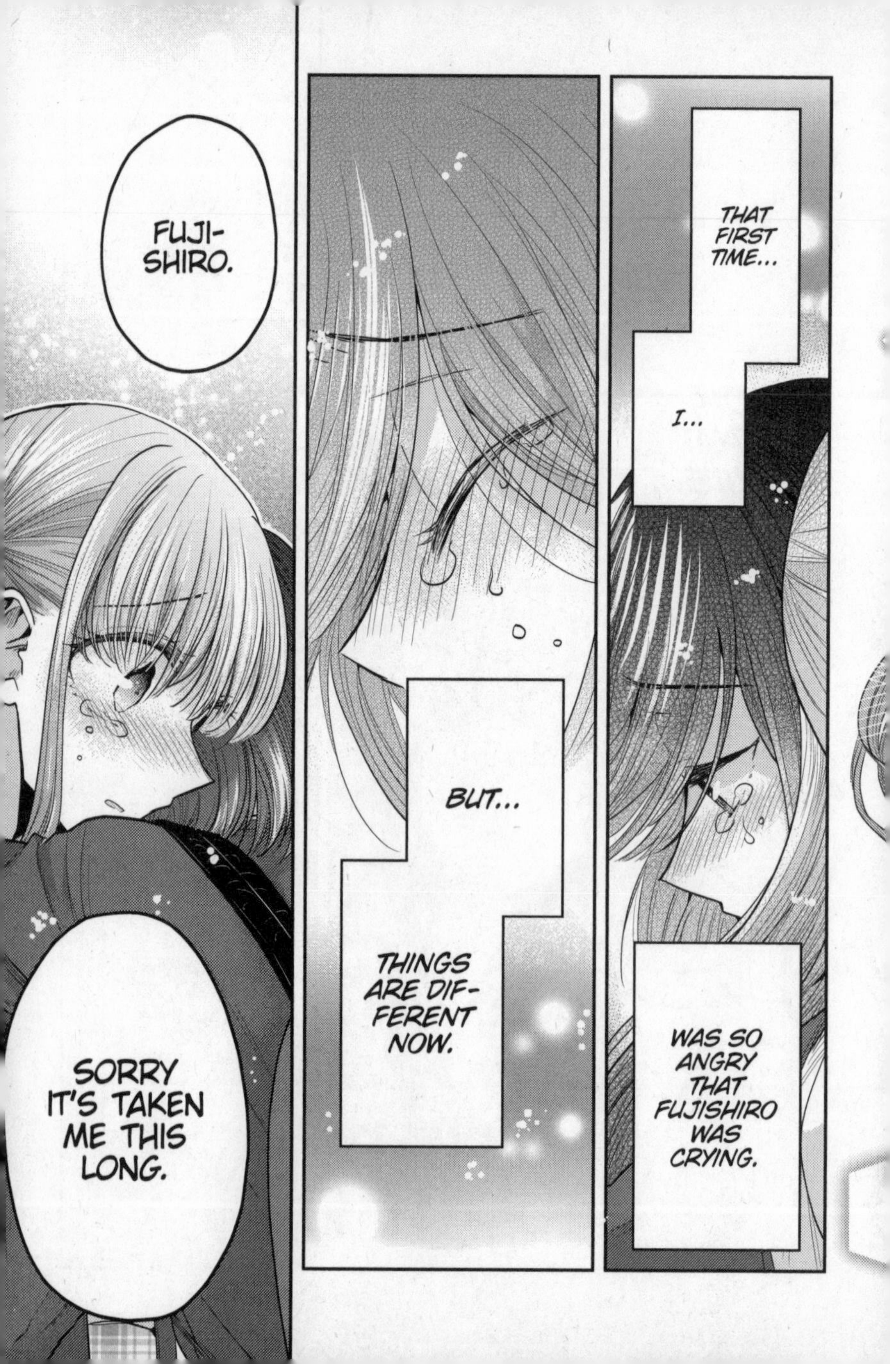
THAT FIRST TIME...
I...
WAS SO ANGRY THAT FUJISHIRO WAS CRYING.
BUT...
THINGS ARE DIF-FERENT NOW.
FUJI-SHIRO.
SORRY IT'S TAKEN ME THIS LONG.

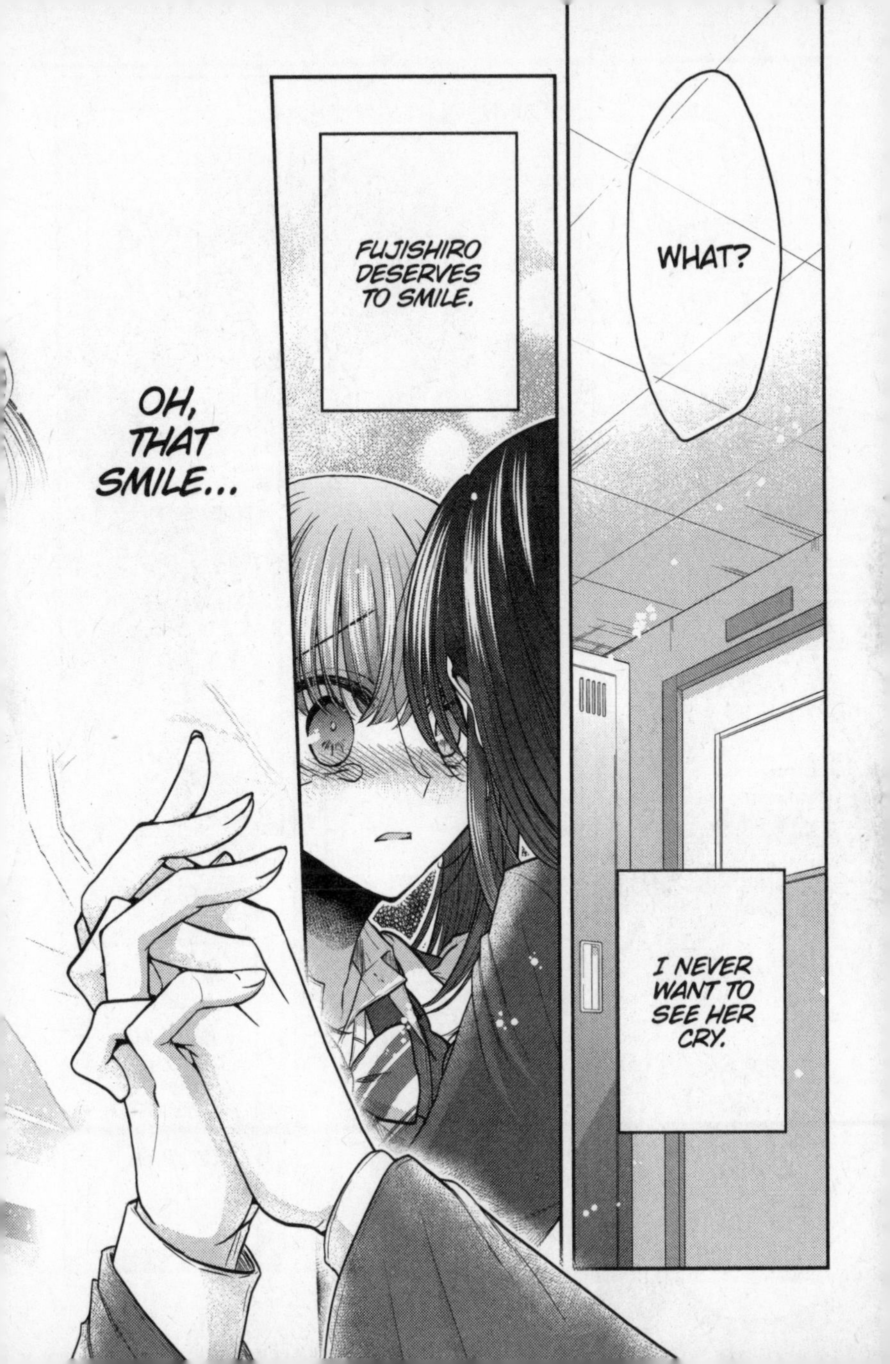
WHAT?
I NEVER WANT TO SEE HER CRY.
FUJISHIRO DESERVES TO SMILE.
OH, THAT SMILE...

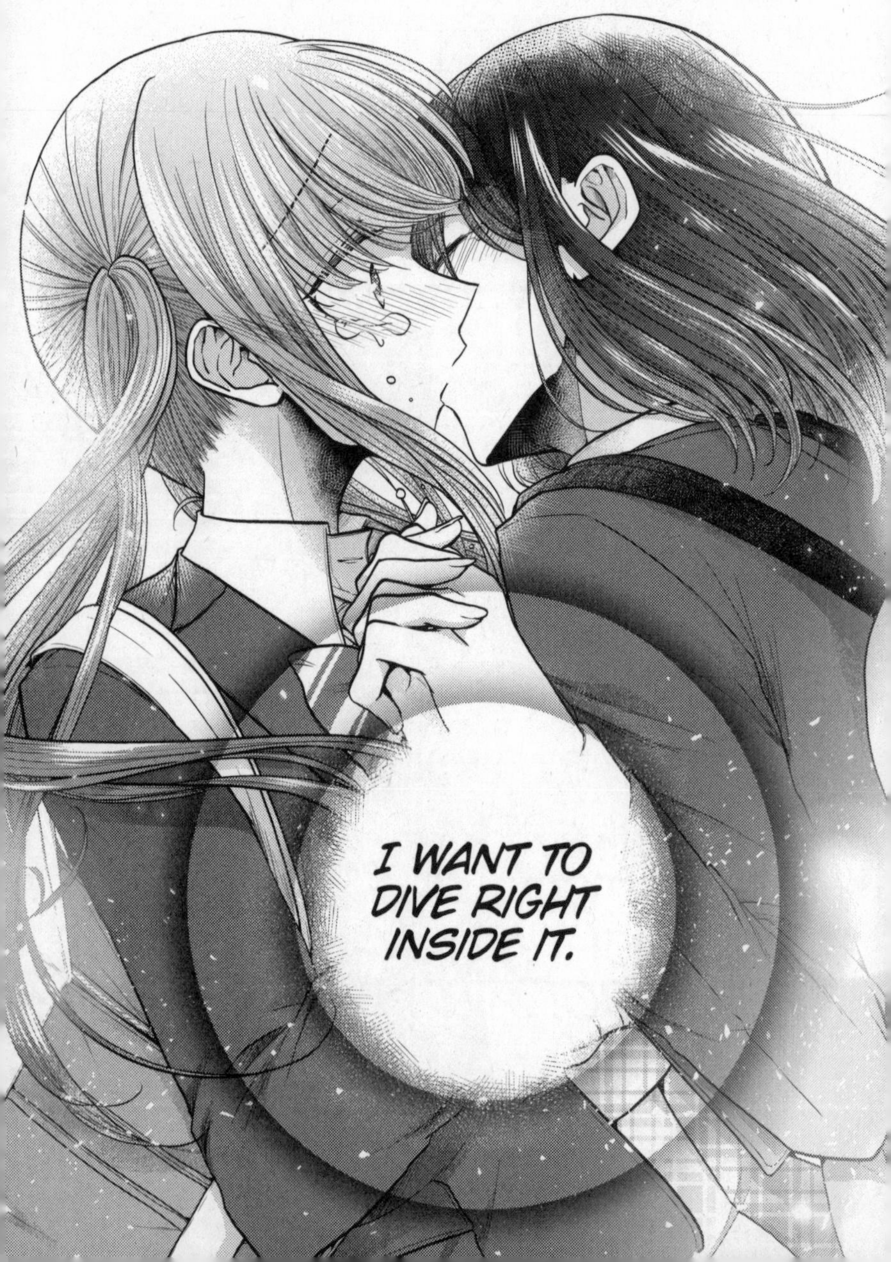
I WANT TO DIVE RIGHT INSIDE IT.

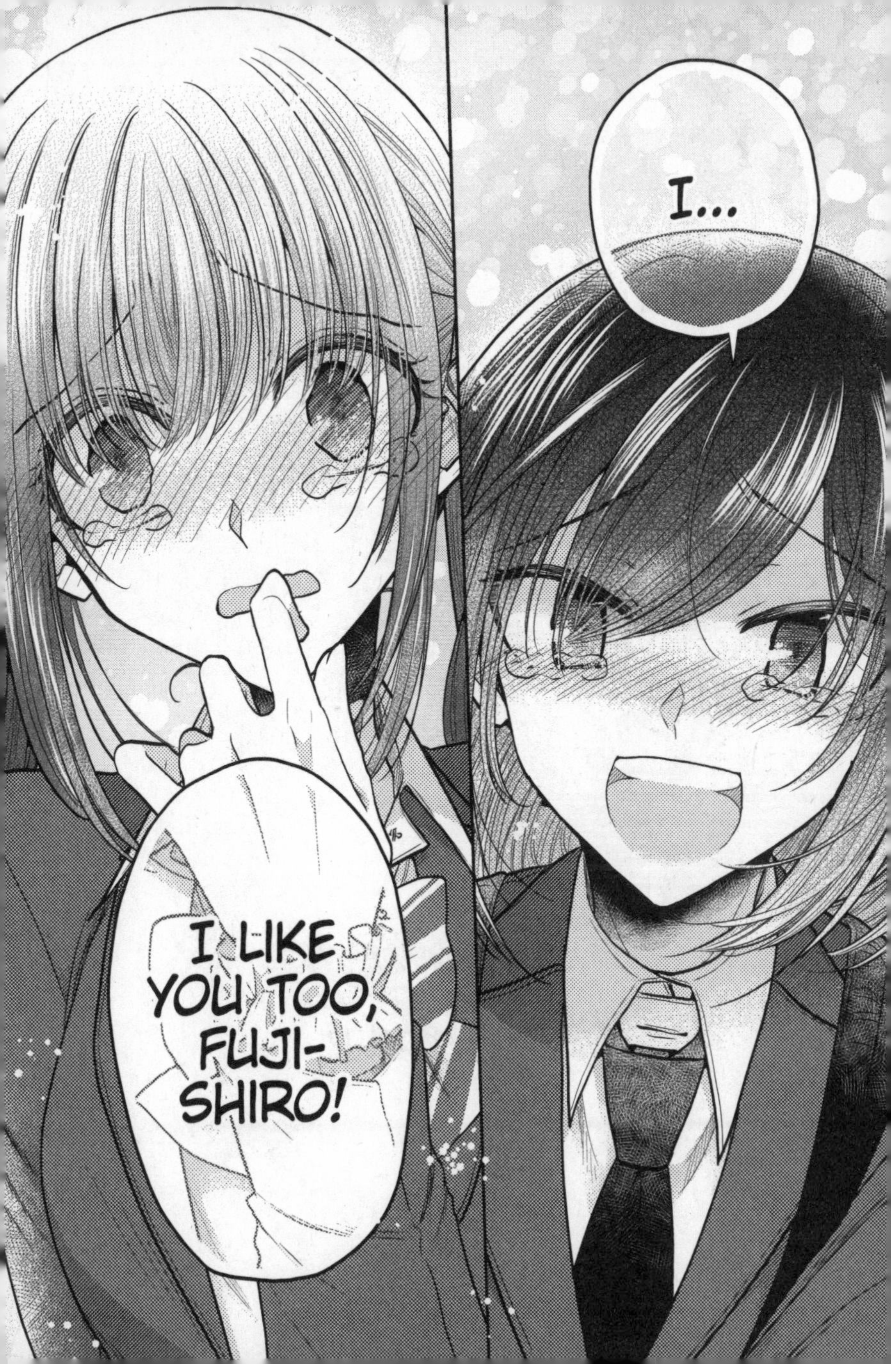
I...
I LIKE YOU TOO, FUJI-SHIRO!

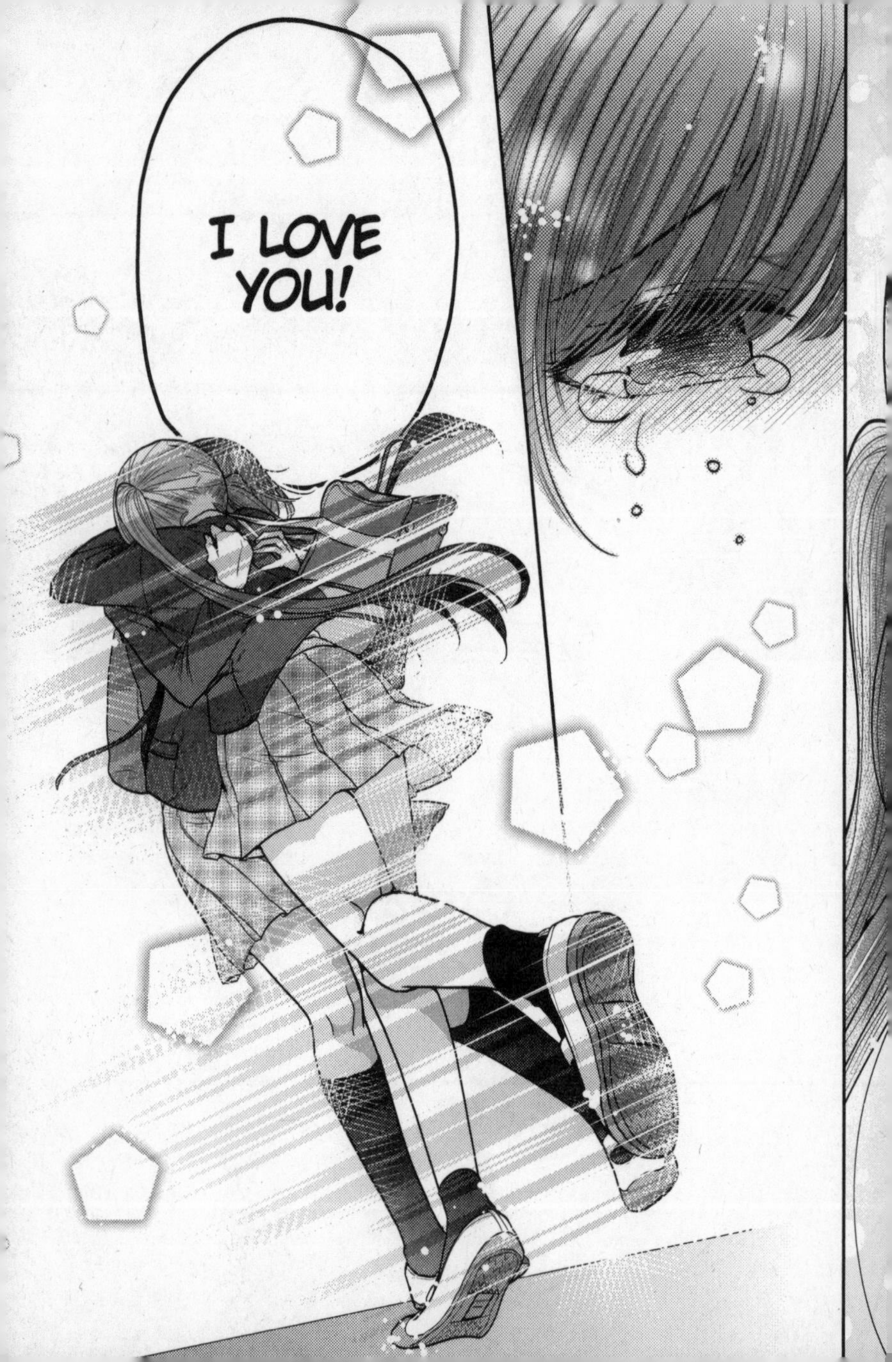
I LOVE YOU!

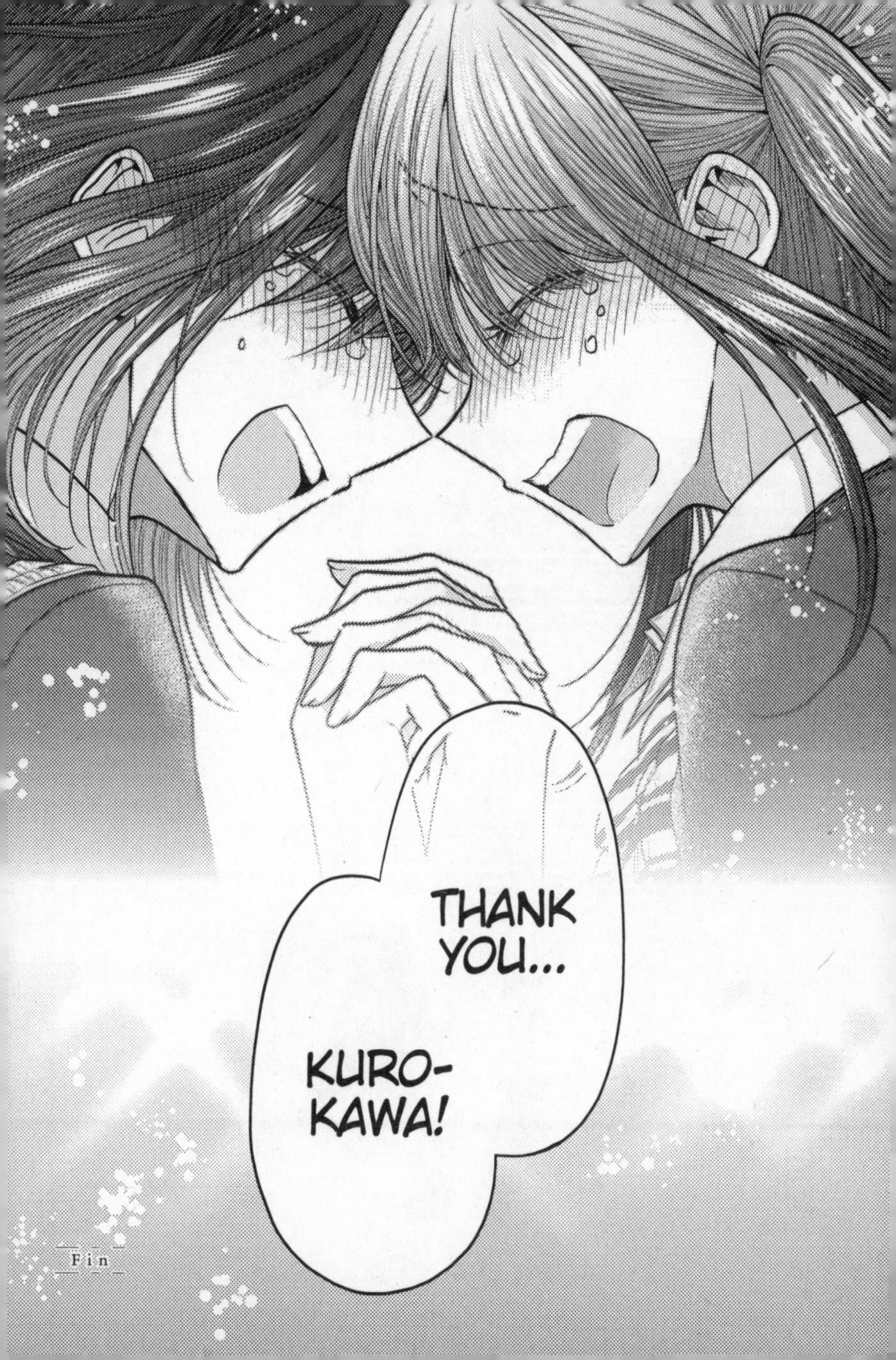
THANK YOU... KURO-KAWA!
Fin

Failed Princesses

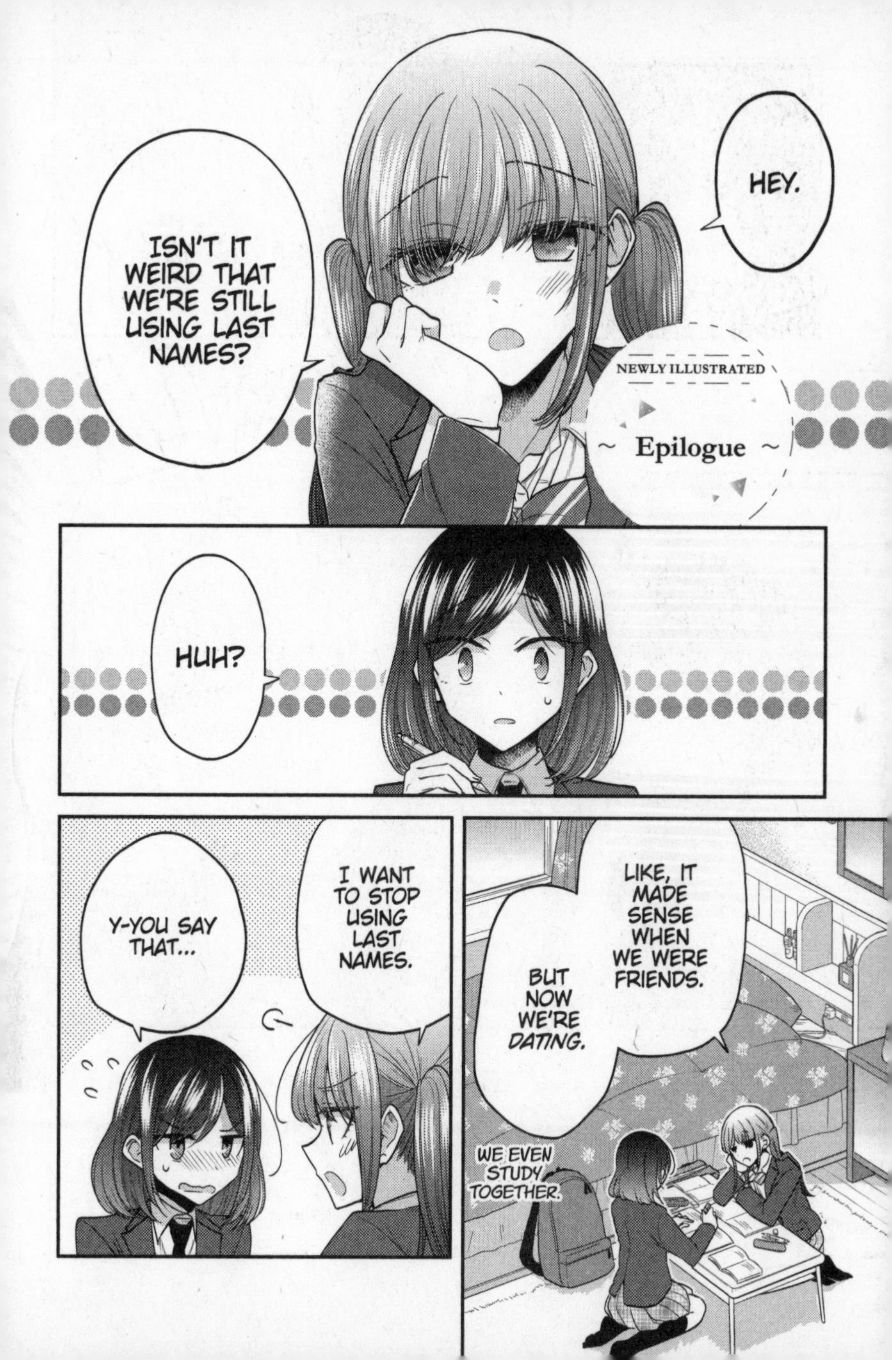
NEWLY ILLUSTRATED
~ Epilogue ~
HEY.
ISN'T IT WEIRD THAT WE'RE STILL USING LAST NAMES?
HUH?
LIKE, IT MADE SENSE WHEN WE WERE FRIENDS.
BUT NOW WE'RE DATING.
WE EVEN STUDY TOGETHER.
I WANT TO STOP USING LAST NAMES.
Y-YOU SAY THAT...

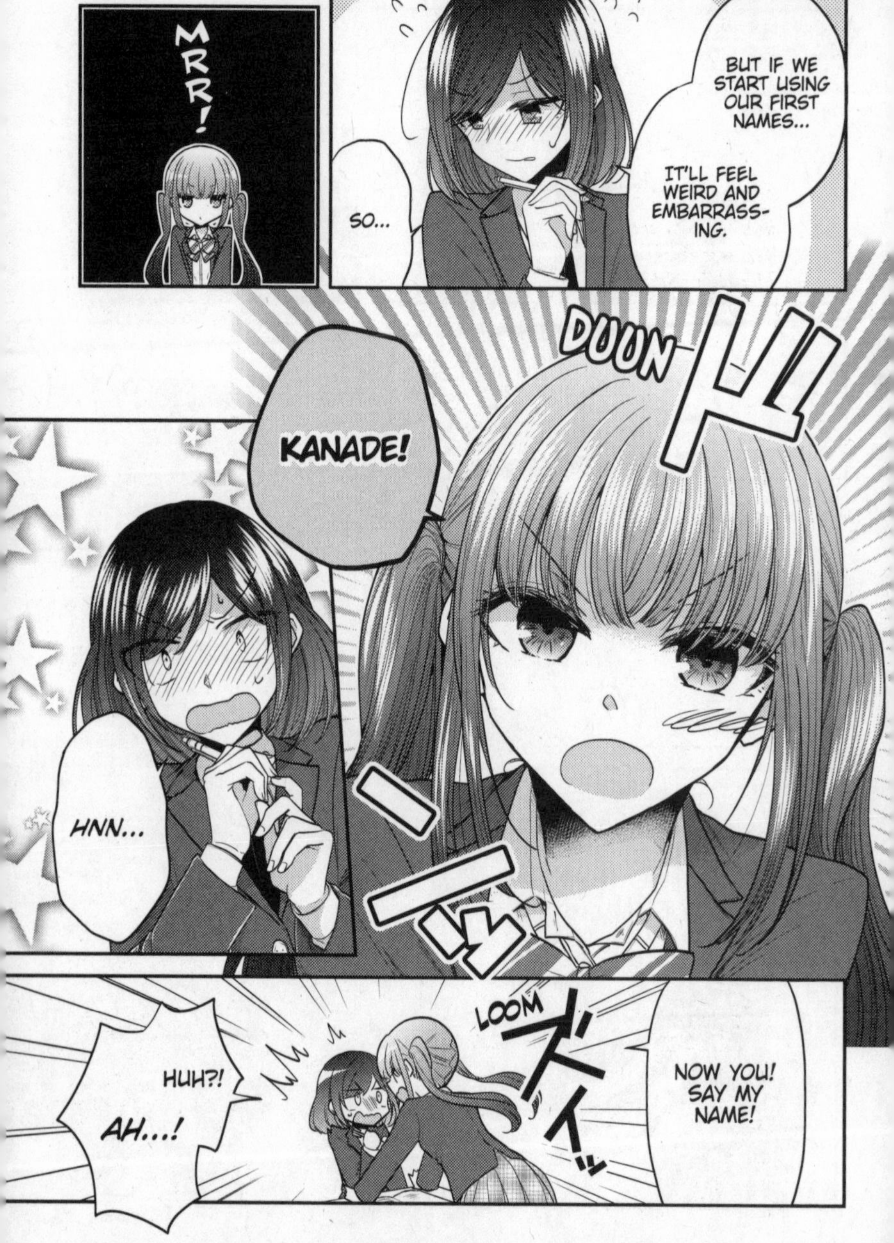
BUT IF WE START USING OUR FIRST NAMES...
IT'LL FEEL WEIRD AND EMBARRASS-ING.
SO...
MRR!
DUUN
KANADE!
HNN...
NOW YOU! SAY MY NAME!
LOOM
HUH?!
AH...!

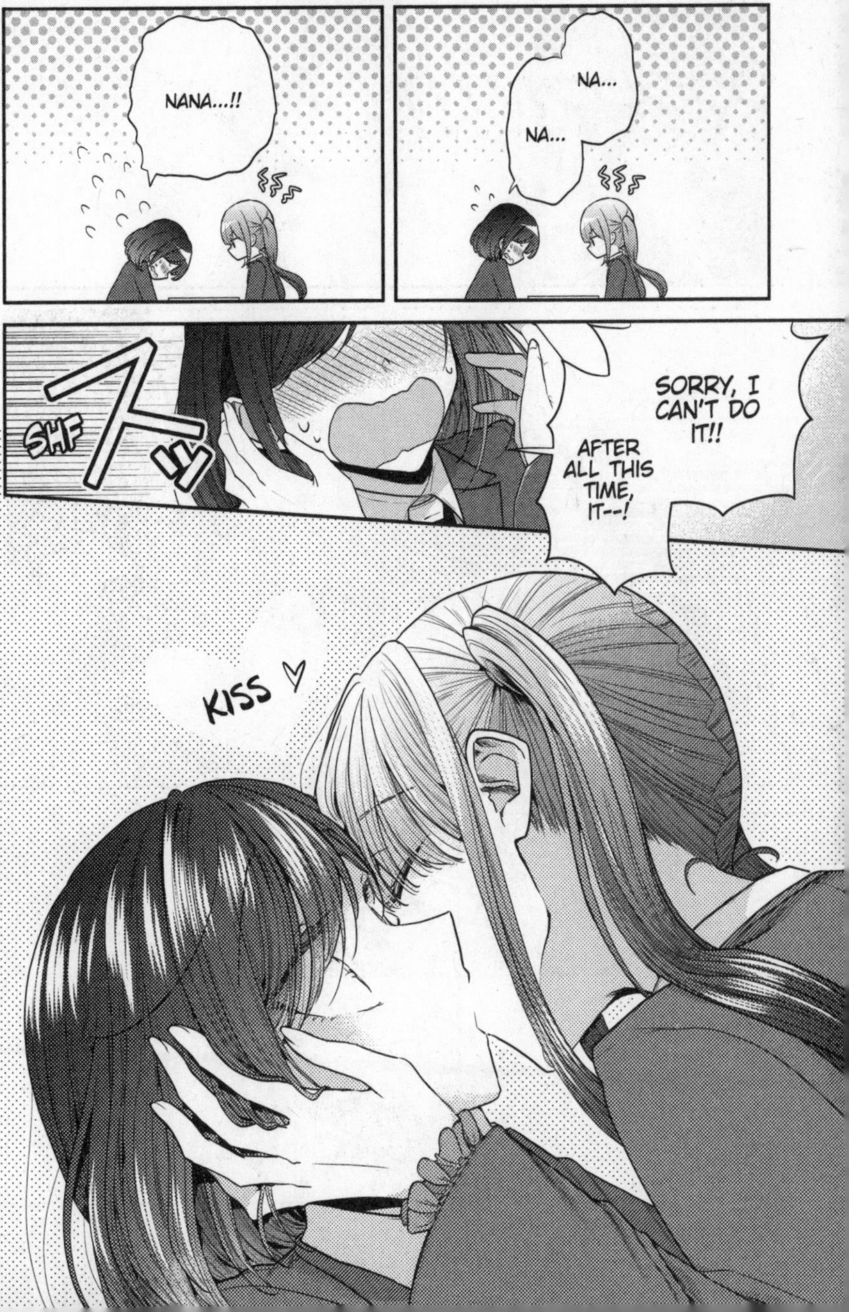
NA...
NA...
NANA...!!
SORRY, I CAN'T DO IT!!
AFTER ALL THIS TIME, IT--!
SHF
KISS ♥

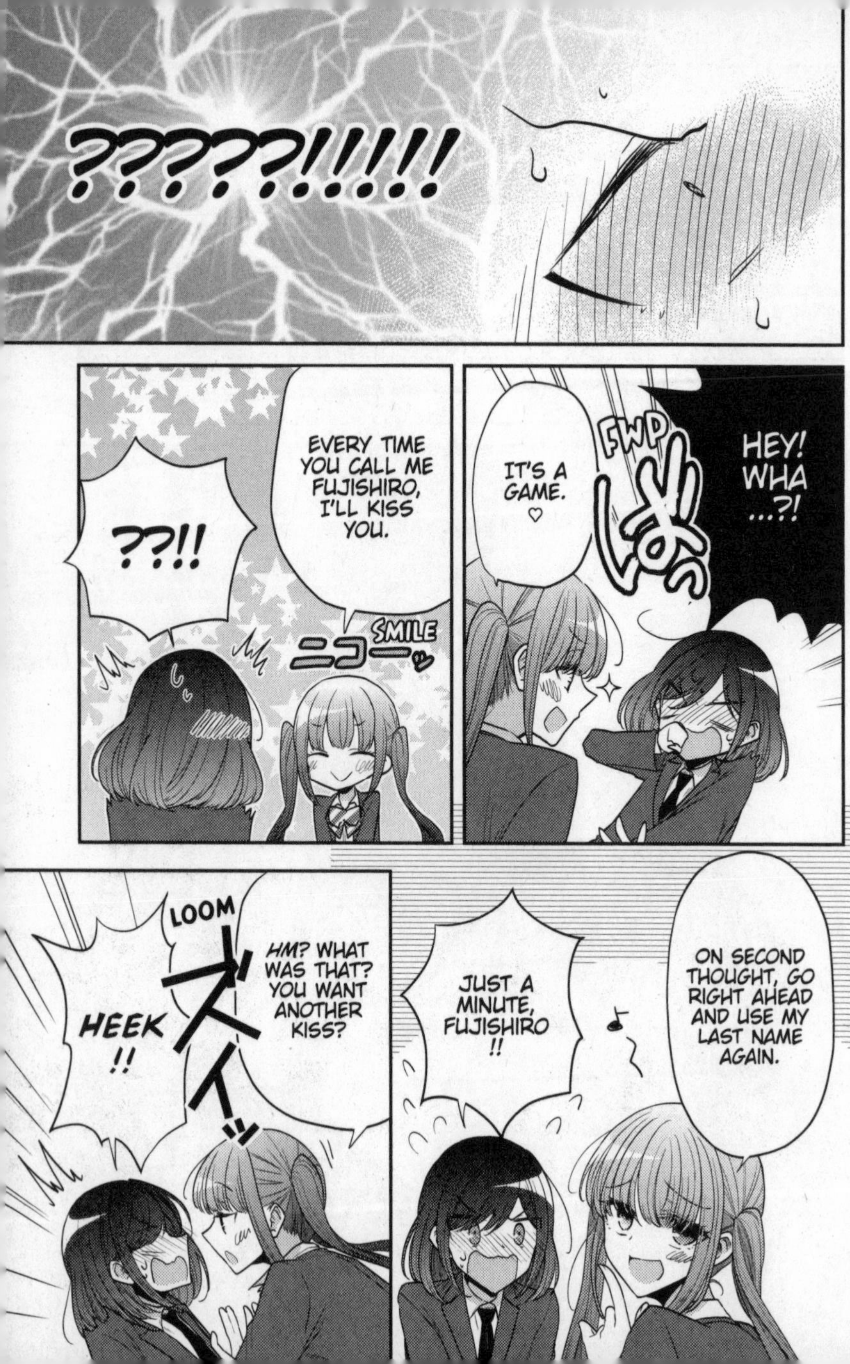
?????!!!!!!
HEY! WHA ...?!
FWP
IT'S A GAME. ♡
EVERY TIME YOU CALL ME FUJISHIRO, I'LL KISS YOU.
??!!
SMILE
ON SECOND THOUGHT, GO RIGHT AHEAD AND USE MY LAST NAME AGAIN.
JUST A MINUTE, FUJISHIRO !!
HM? WHAT WAS THAT? YOU WANT ANOTHER KISS?
LOOM
HEEK !!

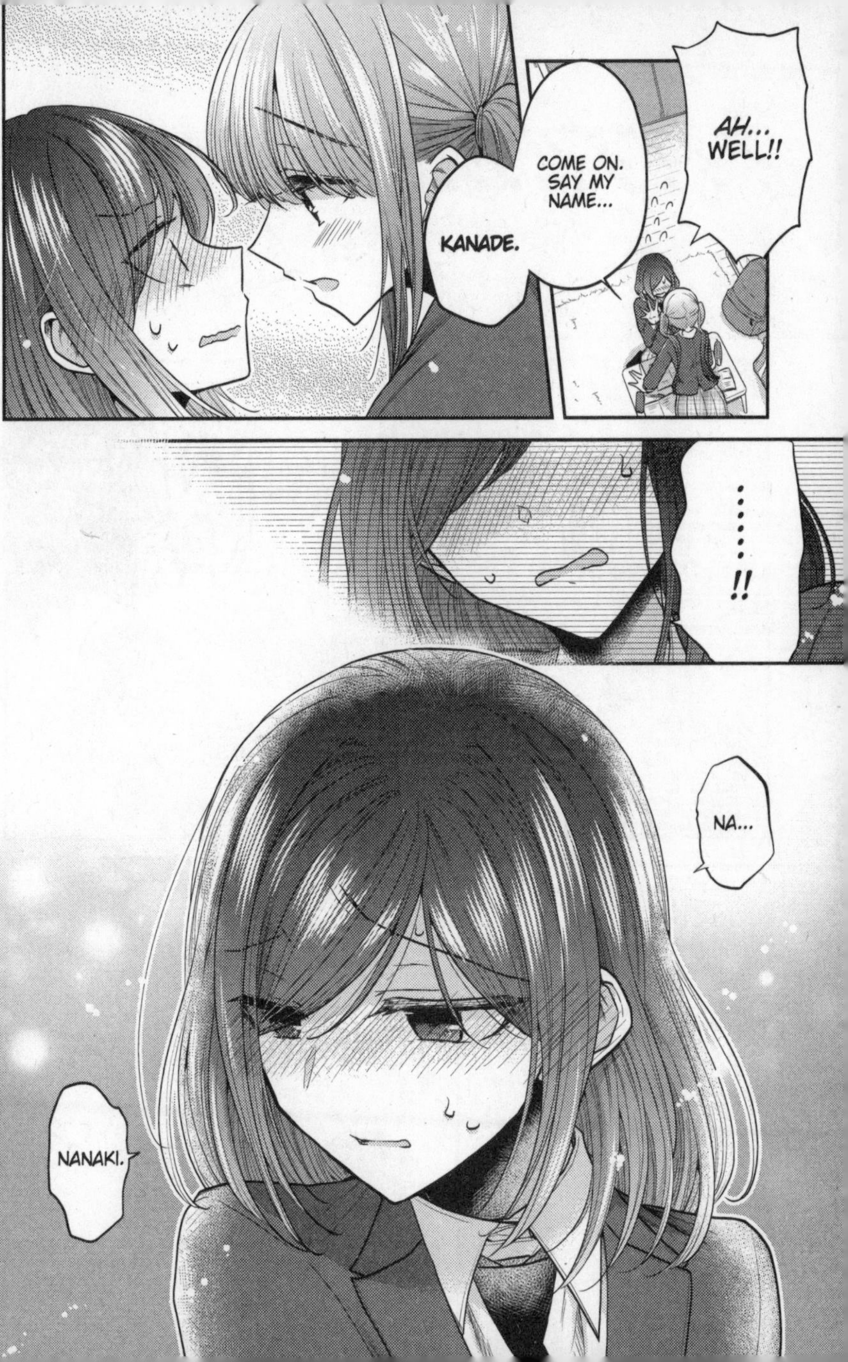
AH... WELL!!
COME ON. SAY MY NAME...
KANADE.
......!!
NA...
NANAKI.

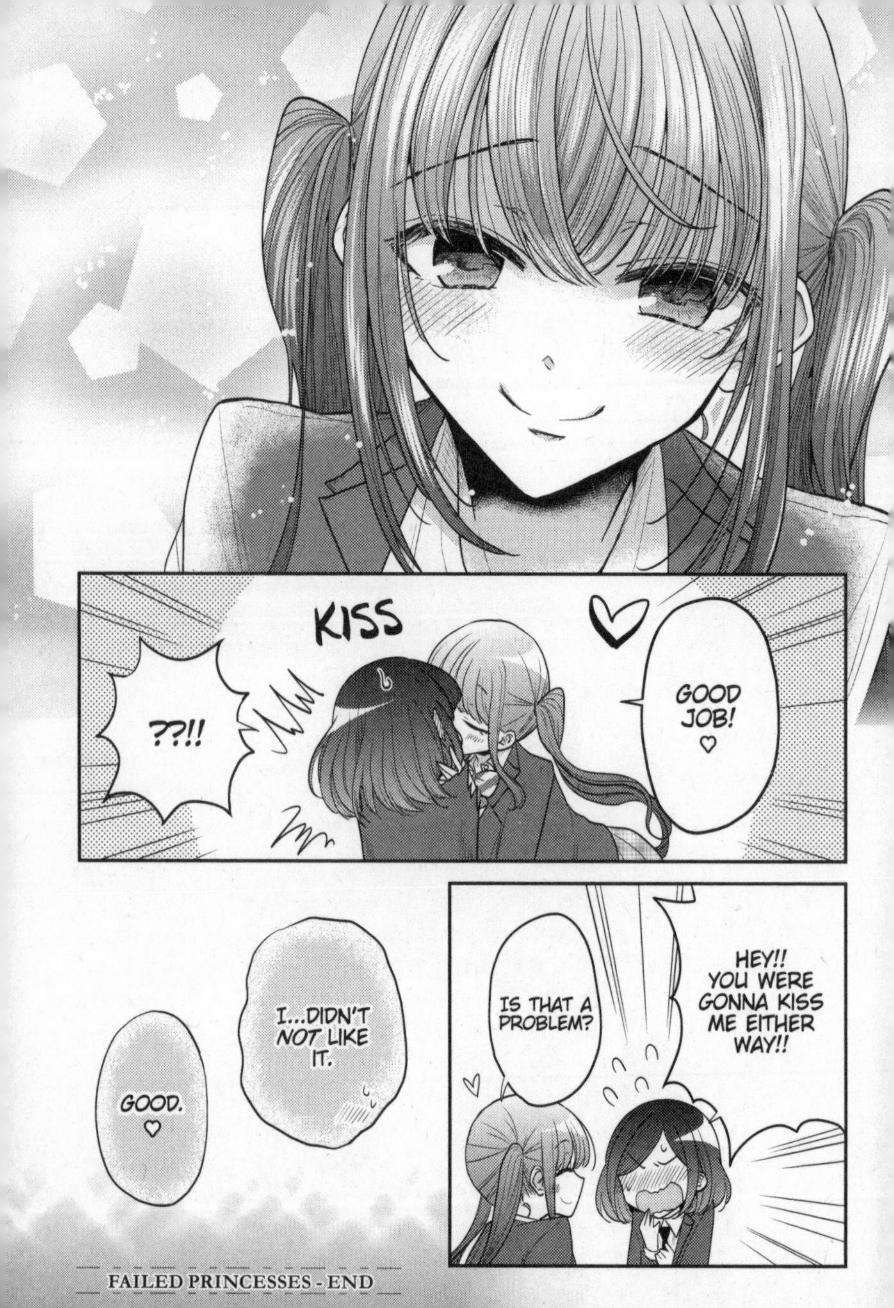
GOOD JOB! ♡
KISS
??!!
HEY!! YOU WERE GONNA KISS ME EITHER WAY!!
IS THAT A PROBLEM?
I...DIDN'T NOT LIKE IT.
GOOD. ♡

FAILED PRINCESSES - END

Failed Princesses

AFTERWORD

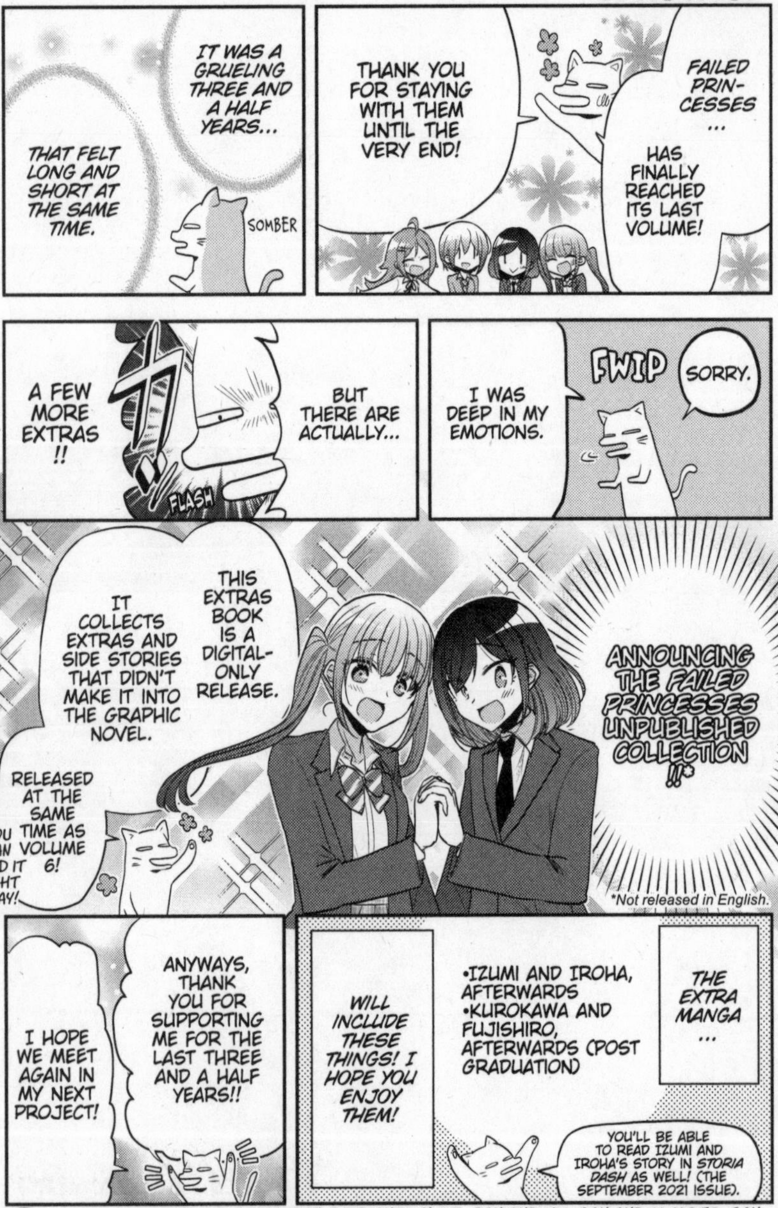
FAILED PRIN-CESSES ... HAS FINALLY REACHED ITS LAST VOLUME!
THANK YOU FOR STAYING WITH THEM UNTIL THE VERY END!
IT WAS A GRUELING THREE AND A HALF YEARS...
THAT FELT LONG AND SHORT AT THE SAME TIME.
SOMBER
FWIP
SORRY.
I WAS DEEP IN MY EMOTIONS.
BUT THERE ARE ACTUALLY...
A FEW MORE EXTRAS !!
FLASH
ANNOUNCING THE FAILED PRINCESSES UNPUBLISHED COLLECTION !!*
THIS EXTRAS BOOK IS A DIGITAL-ONLY RELEASE.
IT COLLECTS EXTRAS AND SIDE STORIES THAT DIDN'T MAKE IT INTO THE GRAPHIC NOVEL.
RELEASED AT THE SAME TIME AS VOLUME 6!
YOU CAN READ IT RIGHT AWAY!
*Not released in English.
THE EXTRA MANGA ...
•IZUMI AND IROHA, AFTERWARDS •KUROKAWA AND FUJISHIRO, AFTERWARDS (POST GRADUATION)
WILL INCLUDE THESE THINGS! I HOPE YOU ENJOY THEM!
YOU'LL BE ABLE TO READ IZUMI AND IROHA'S STORY IN STORIA DASH AS WELL! (THE SEPTEMBER 2021 ISSUE).
ANYWAYS, THANK YOU FOR SUPPORTING ME FOR THE LAST THREE AND A HALF YEARS!!
I HOPE WE MEET AGAIN IN MY NEXT PROJECT!

Special Thanks! EDITOR T-SAWA-SAN, DESIGNER K-ME-SAN AND N-I-SAN AND M-MOTO-SAN, WORK FRIEND AOI-SAN, DIALECT HELP ASAHI-SAN, YAWARA-SAN, AND EVERYONE WHO SUPPORTED ME. REALLY, THANK YOU VERY MUCH!!

Failed Princesses

[AFTERWARDS ~MIKI AND MAHO~] PLEASE ONLY READ AFTER FINISHING THIS VOLUME! ☆

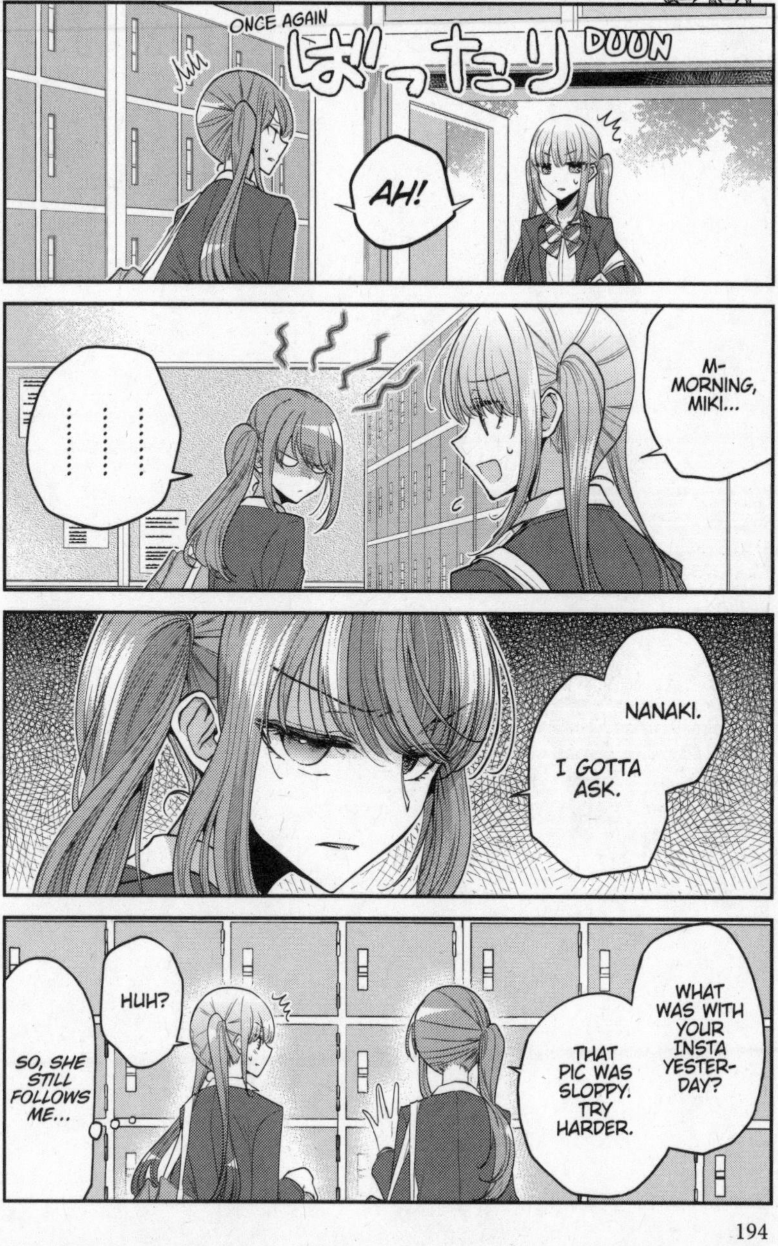
ONCE AGAIN
ぱったり
DUUN
AH!
M-MORNING, MIKI...
......
NANAKI.
I GOTTA ASK.
WHAT WAS WITH YOUR INSTA YESTER-DAY?
THAT PIC WAS SLOPPY. TRY HARDER.
HUH?
SO, SHE STILL FOLLOWS ME...

[AFTERWARDS ~MIKI AND MAHO~] PLEASE ONLY READ AFTER FINISHING THIS VOLUME! ☆

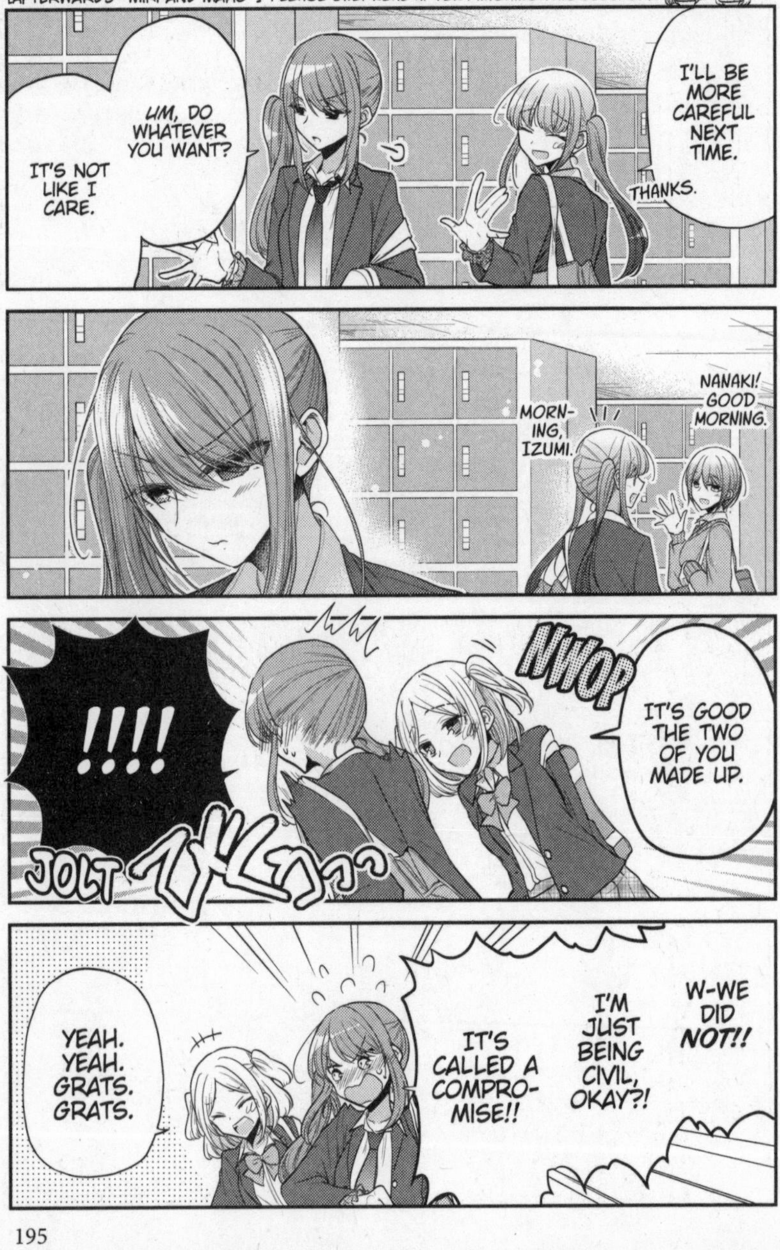

I'LL BE MORE CAREFUL NEXT TIME.
THANKS.
UM, DO WHATEVER YOU WANT?
IT'S NOT LIKE I CARE.
NANAKI! GOOD MORNING.
MORNING, IZUMI.
NWOP
IT'S GOOD THE TWO OF YOU MADE UP.
!!!!
JOLT
W-WE DID NOT!!
I'M JUST BEING CIVIL, OKAY?!
IT'S CALLED A COMPROMISE!!
YEAH. YEAH. GRATS. GRATS.

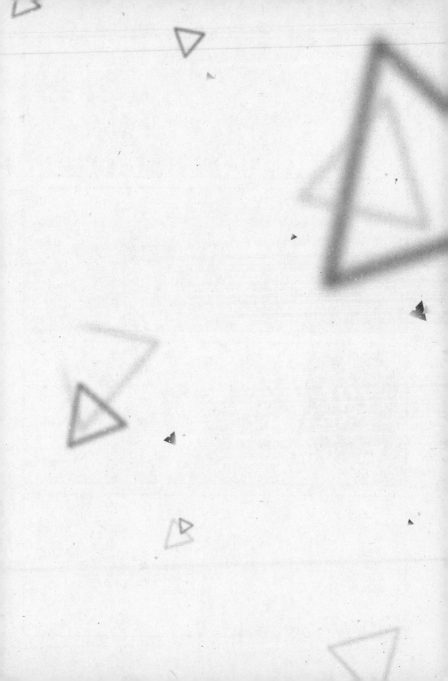

Failed Princesses

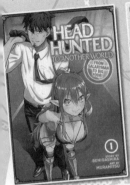
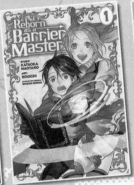
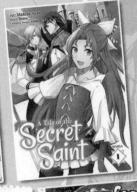
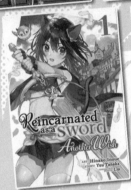
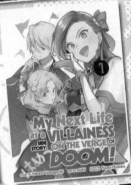
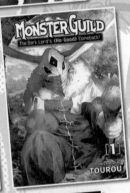
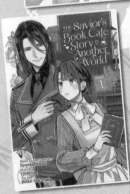
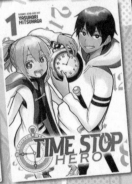
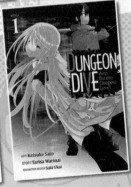

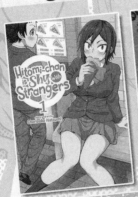
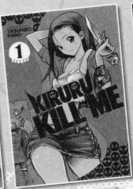
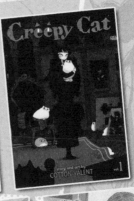
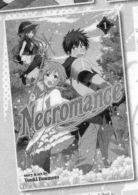
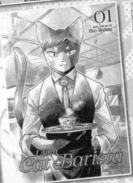
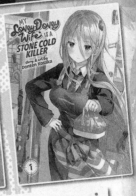
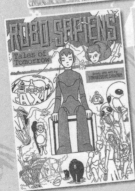
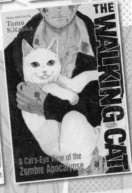
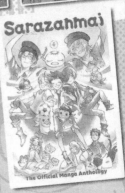

SEVEN SEAS ENTERTAINMENT PRESENTS

W9-CNR-209

Failed Princesses

VOLUME 6

story and art by AJIICHI

TRANSLATION
Angela Liu

ADAPTATION
Marykate Jasper

LETTERING AND RETOUCH
Rina Mapa

COVER DESIGN
Nicky Lim

PROOFREADING
Leighanna DeRouen

SENIOR EDITOR
Jenn Grunigen

PREPRESS TECHNICIAN
Jules Valera

PRINT MANAGER
Rhiannon Rasmussen-Silverstein

PRODUCTION DESIGNER
Christa Miesner

PRODUCTION MANAGER
Lissa Pattillo

EDITOR-IN-CHIEF
Julie Davis

ASSOCIATE PUBLISHER
Adam Arnold

PUBLISHER
Jason DeAngelis

DEKISOKONAI NO HIMEGIMI TACHI VOLUME 6
© 2021 AJIICHI / TAKESHOBO
Originally published in Japan in 2021 by TAKESHOBO Co. LTD., Tokyo.
English translation rights arranged with TAKESHOBO Co. LTD., Tokyo,
through TOHAN CORPORATION, Tokyo.

Seven Seas press and purchase enquiries can be sent to Marketing Manager
Lianne Sentar at press@gomanga.com. Information regarding the distribution
and purchase of digital editions is available from Digital Manager CK Russell
at digital@gomanga.com.

Seven Seas and the Seven Seas logo are trademarks of
Seven Seas Entertainment. All rights reserved.

ISBN: 978-1-63858-602-9

Printed in Canada

First Printing: November 2022

10 9 8 7 6 5 4 3 2 1

FOLLOW US ONLINE: *www.sevenseasentertainment.com*

READING DIRECTIONS

This book reads from *right to left*, Japanese style.
If this is your first time reading manga, you start
reading from the top right panel on each page and
take it from there. If you get lost, just follow the
numbered diagram here. It may seem backwards at
first, but you'll get the hang of it! Have fun!!

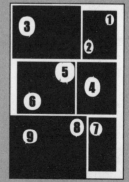